Intellectuals and the State in Twentieth-Century Mexico

Latin American Monographs, No. 65
Institute of Latin American Studies
The University of Texas at Austin

Intellectuals and the State in Twentieth-Century Mexico

By Roderic A. Camp

University of Texas Press, Austin

Library of Congress Cataloging in Publication Data

Camp, Roderic A.
  Intellectuals and the state in twentieth-century Mexico.

  (Latin American monographs; no. 65)
  Bibliography: p.
  Includes index.
  1. Elite (Social sciences)—Mexico. 2. Intellectuals—Mexico. 3. Mexico—Politics and government—20th century. I. Title. II. Series: Latin American monographs (University of Texas at Austin. Institute of Latin American Studies); no. 65.
  HN120.Z9E43   1985   305.5'52'0972   84-22050
  ISBN 0-292-73836-6
  ISBN 0-292-73839-0 (pbk.)

First Edition, 1985

Requests for permission to reproduce material from this work should be sent to:
  Permissions
  University of Texas Press
  P.O. Box 7819
  Austin, Texas 78713

To Emily

Contents

Tables

Acknowledgments

This work evolved naturally from my previous interests, beginning with the collective biography of Mexican political leaders, to their educational experiences, and, finally, their socialization. The catalyst for this book, however, was an NEH Summer Seminar in 1977, directed by the late Alvin Gouldner. Under his initial guidance, I explored the relevance of much theoretical literature by and about intellectuals. The Fulbright-Hays Program, the American Philosophical Society, and El Colegio de México aided my actual efforts to interview numerous intellectuals and public figures in Mexico. José Juan de Olloqui helped to arrange many of the interviews. The Central College Research Council and the University House Program of the University of Iowa supported various stages of research.

The manuscript benefited from several readings by colleagues. On individual chapters I owe thanks to Carl Solberg, Jean Meyer, Enrique Krauze, and Stanley Ross. To Daniel Levy, I owe a special thanks for his detailed criticisms of the entire work. Finally, I wish to thank Emily Ellen Camp for her numerous contributions to the birth of this book.

Intellectuals and the State in
Twentieth-Century Mexico

1. Introduction

Perhaps more than any group in Western culture during the twentieth century, intellectuals have shown an interest in writing about themselves that borders on narcissism. This self-indulgence has been especially obvious among North American intellectuals, who, because of our society's affluence, have the greatest opportunity for self-analysis and who can provide the audience that reads such appraisals. Yet, although literary and popular magazines occasionally overflow with essays about intellectuals, serious analyses do not abound. In fact, no scholarly study of North American intellectuals that covers the whole, or, for that matter, any great part, of this century exists.[1]

The intellectuals' self-interest, and their resulting essays, have benefits, most important, their insights into and speculations about the conditions of intellectual life. But, although better expressed and generally more insightful than most formal scholarship, their essays rarely go beyond the confines of a particular circle. They fail to compare themselves with intellectual groups elsewhere, and most seriously, they omit any empirical information in support of their interpretations. There has, however, been a recent tendency toward remedying these deficiencies, as the subject of the "New Class," of which intellectuals are a part, has become a popular topic for discussion.[2]

Not surprisingly, what is true of the state of our knowledge about North American intellectuals applies doubly to their counterparts in developing nations. This work will examine the multifaceted characteristics of intellectuals, their self-perceptions, their role in society, and their relationship to the state in Mexico since 1920. However, it will not consider the Mexican situation in isolation; rather, it will examine numerous hypotheses and characteristics of intellectual life elsewhere to determine their applicability to the Mexican scene and to that of developing nations as a whole. Further, this work will attempt to show the peculiarities of Mexican intellectual life as evolving from idiosyncratic cultural characteristics, special economic conditions, and the structure of postrevolutionary Mexican politics.

Mexico is an attractive subject for such a study. It is valuable in the first place because, as one of the few nations having undergone a major social revolution in the twentieth century, it provides much food for thought about the role intellectuals play in postrevolutionary societies, a theme of long-standing interest to the historian. Second, those who see a New Class executing an important role in government in industrialized societies may find interesting parallels in a country that has superimposed many of the characteristics of twentieth-century industrialization on a recalcitrant traditional culture. Furthermore, Third World development since World War II leaves little room for optimism, especially about political participation, and raises a question about the role intellectuals might play in governing their societies as well as in solving the plethora of problems that face them. Mexico provides valuable lessons to be used in these issues.

Although grave deficiencies in our knowledge about intellectuals exist, it is not enough to study them for that reason alone. Rather, the possibilities for developing some hypotheses and theoretical statements about intellectuals rely heavily on acquiring such information. In his examination of the North American intellectual, Charles Kadushin stated these needs rather clearly, arguing that

an adequate theory of intellectuals should contain an analysis of the general functions and roles of intellectuals in different types of societies, a description of the social types which play these roles and why they fit into them better than others, and an analysis of the recruitment process; these parts of the theory are, of course, much dependent on the definition of intellectual. A further component of a theory of intellectual life should include an analysis of the structure of intellectual life—the way it is organized, how it links into education systems, its relationship to political life, its economic basis and the degree to which it is "elitist" or "populist." Finally, and the very focal point of the debate on intellectuals: for example, the extent to which they represent a clerisy and are defenders of tradition or the extent to which they represent a major force of dissent and change.[3]

To fill in the gaps that these questions imply, I have dealt with a number of themes. One relationship that has always intrigued students of intellectual life is that between intellectuals and politicians. In Mexico, do the roles intellectuals and politicians play overlap? If they do, does Mexico then have a "power elite," at least as far as cultural and political elites are concerned? If so, what does this mean for public policy and, furthermore, for the politician's receptivity toward intellectuals' ideas?

A second broad theme important to intellectual life is how intellectuals are recruited; that is, how does an individual become an intellectual in Mexico, what channels does he follow, who are his mentors, what pool of leaders is he drawn from, and who has access to prestigious intellectuals? Historical circumstances indigenous to Mexico make this question even more interesting, since this study begins in 1920, the end of the more violent phase of the Mexican Revolution of 1910. To what extent are the intellectuals of the postrevolutionary period part of families prominent in the prerevolutionary period? The answer is important not only for knowing who Mexico's elite intellectuals are, but also for understanding the extent to which violent social upheaval had an impact on Mexican intellectual life. Furthermore, an examination of intellectual backgrounds would reveal the extent to which the Revolution opened up the cultural leadership to a new intellectual class, or a class different from those who sought political offices.[4]

In Mexico, because of the peculiarities of its political recruitment and socialization process, a knowledge of the position of the university, particularly the National University (UNAM) and the Colegio de México, is essential to understanding the structure of intellectual life and the interrelationship among intellectuals, professors, and politicians. The university is important in most cultures because it serves to certify and provide credentials for the majority of prestigious intellectuals. In Mexico, because employment opportunities are limited, as will be seen in later chapters, the National University's relationship with the state, and position as the employer of intellectuals, has implications for intellectual freedom. Furthermore, because the university education of elites is centralized, the degree to which intellectuals, professors, and politicians are socialized and educated in the same institution has important implications for their cohesiveness, ideological preferences, and even their career success in academic circles, government, or intellectual activities. In a comparative context, the extent to which overlap exists among intellectuals, professors, and politicians deserves careful examination. Is it unique to Mexico and other developing nations, or are such patterns also present in the industrialized nations?

Another broad issue to consider is the impact of economic conditions and social development on the characteristics of intellectual life. For example, are intellectuals more involved in government in Mexico than in the United States because of historical patterns and cultural differences in attitudes toward intellectuals, or do limited economic opportunities in the private sector make public sector careers a necessity? Similarly, to what extent does the level of literacy affect the publishing industry, the purchase of art, the appreciation of music, and the like, all of which determine the intellectual's livelihood? Does the level of social and economic development affect not only the occupational patterns of intellectuals, but their attitudes toward one another and their relationship to the state as well?

The condition of the media provides a microcosm of the larger economic situation of a society that affects intellectuals. Those who control the distribution and sale of films, newspapers, magazines, books, literary journals, and radio and television time have a marked influence on the ability of intellectuals to promote their views to political leaders and the masses alike. It is important to ascertain the extent to which government or the private sector dominates the mass media, and the influence of each in Mexico. Among the many issues the subject of mass media control raises is censorship, whether by the government, the private sector, or by intellectuals themselves. To what extent is there freedom of expression in Mexico, who limits it, and how does it compare with similar freedoms elsewhere? Moreover, how important are foreign influences on the media, either through financial control or as sources of information and ideas?

As we move deeper into the structure of intellectual life itself, one of the questions confronting the observer is the degree to which intellectuals are a cohesive, homogeneous body. For example, how divided are intellectuals on the issue of their political involvement? Do the majority of Mexican intellectuals wish to remain independent from political activity and government careers, or do they believe their responsibility is to take part in such activities? Perhaps intellectuals are divided on this issue and are forcing people to look to two sets of intellectual elites for leadership and ideological guidance. Of considerable importance to this series of questions is how intellectuals see themselves. How do they define their own role and evalute their prestige in Mexico? How does that assessment compare elsewhere? Definition is important. What type of intellectual is most common in Mexico? Do literary figures dominate? Why or why not? What about scientists? Why are they less prominent among Mexican intellectuals? Are artists, scientists, lawyers, and others omitted in equal degrees by all groups of intellectuals and political leaders in their perceptions of who is important? If so, why?

Like most groups, intellectuals are the products of certain institutions. Although they are formed in part by institutions such as universities, they also create their own institutions to enhance the prestige of their peers and to recognize those who have made significant contributions. These institutions usually take the form of professional organizations, semiestablishment intellectual societies such as the National College, and honorary societies. Furthermore, these institutions, or their creators, provide generous financial and psychological rewards to select individuals in the form of national prizes. It is therefore important to know who is active in these institutions and who is selected for such prizes. To what extent does the state select and support such individuals for recognition? Are there hidden requirements for membership? What rewards does this form of recognition provide to the recipient?

The ideology of intellectuals, as distinct from the intellectuals themselves, has been studied with much greater frequency in the Latin American context. For this reason, it will not be given significant attention in this work. However, certain aspects of ideological attitudes, most notably views of the state, will be examined. In this regard, we would want to know whether intellectuals think a particular philosophical bent has dominated their numbers since 1920. Also, as part of their self-evaluation and that of political leaders, one gauge of their possible influence is to determine whether the impact of intellectuals on the state has grown, declined, or remained the same.

In those cultures in which intellectuals have been studied, two geographical patterns in the structure of intellectual life emerge. The European model, represented clearly by France and England, is one of centralization of intellectual life in the political capital.[5] The U.S. model is one of decentralization of intellectual activities in many cities and suburbs. To what extent does Mexico follow either model? Is this a changing feature of Mexican intellectual life? What effect does it have on the other relationships just described? For example, the extent to which intellectual life is centralized has certain parallels with Mexican political life. Further, geographic centralization in a largely rural country may have a decided effect on the intellectual's awareness of society's problems, and on the ability to convey the existence of those problems to the masses.

Related to the effects of centralization is the ability of intellectuals to recognize new talent, to identify and cultivate those who will replace them as intellectual leaders. How aware are intellectuals themselves of the protégés waiting in the wings of provincial culture? Whom do elite intellectuals read? Whom do provincial intellectuals read? Is there a generation gap between the young and the old? If so, what are its implications? Such questions cannot be confined to formal means of communication; equally important are the informal, face-to-face channels, for which there are few records. Yet, in a society in which written information is often considered suspect, and in which important ideas are unshared, to whom and how often one talks provide a realistic measure of the exchange of ideas. Therefore, communications among intellectuals and between intellectuals and politicians are important.

Methodology

To provide the material from which to describe, analyze, and speculate about the Mexican intellectual, I have used two original bodies of information that complement traditional documentation from scholarly and nonscholarly literature. Because these information sources are somewhat unusual in the literature available on intellectuals, they deserve some comment here. The first is an original, computerized data bank of social background information and biographical and career data on some five hundred Mexican intellectuals and their relatives during the 1920 to 1980 period (I shall refer to it as the *MIBP* [*Mexican Intellectual Biography Project*]). To my knowledge, this is the first such *complete* data set ever compiled on a group of intellectuals in a single country that covers all intellectual disciplines over an extended period of time. Furthermore, it is the first empirical examination of the family background of intellectuals for several generations, and where possible, of other variables important to understanding intellectual activities.

Specifically, the data set contains fifty-four variables: date of birth; state of birth; region of birth; urban classification of birthplace; classification of birthplace as a capital or foreign city; place of residence as an adult; nationality of parents; intellectual background of parents and grandparents; intellectual background of children and grandchildren; number of generations having intellectuals in the family; the intellectual activities of sanguinary relatives or immediate in-laws; friendship with political leaders; kinship ties with political leaders; parents' socioeconomic status; prominence of parent or grandparent under the prerevolutionary or reactionary regimes; sex; type of primary and secondary education; level of education completed; location of preparatory education; location of university education; university class year; type of college degree; type of teaching experience; teaching experience abroad; training in professional field; location of advanced studies; extent of interdisciplinary education; receipt of fellowships; residence abroad; location of foreign travel; administrative position at the National University; presidency of major educational institution; career profession; intellectual discipline; ideological preference; membership in the intellectual elite; experience in prison or in exile; government career; responsibility for a government program; political party activity; elected political office; appointive political office; position in educational ministry; position in foreign relations ministry; membership in the National College; presidency of a cultural academy; membership in a cultural institute; position as publisher or editor; regular contribution to *Excélsior, El Universal, Novedades, El Nacional, Cuadernos Americanos, Siempre, Política, Revista de la Universidad, Historia Mexicana, Revista Mexicana de Sociología, El Trimestre Económico*; distribution and performance of works abroad; mentorship or group leadership; receipt of fellowship from the Center for Mexican Writers; service in the Revolution of 1910 or in a revolutionary government from 1910 to 1920; and service in the governments of Porfirio Díaz or Victoriano Huerta.

To select intellectuals for inclusion in this data bank, I combined a variety of approaches commonly used in the creation of elite data sets. In doing so, I have been influenced by the seminal work of Charles Kadushin on North American elite intellectuals of the 1960s and by Nelson Polsby's theoretical discussions of various approaches to studies of local elites. Kadushin essentially followed two different methods to determine his list of the North American intellectual elite. First, he examined the eight thousand or so persons who had written for leading intellectual journals from 1964 to 1968; he reduced the number to a more manageable size by considering only those individuals who appeared four or more times, or about 15 percent of all the contributors. Thus, he came up with a definition of a leading intellectual as simply any person who writes regularly for leading intellectual journals or has books reviewed there.

This is an effective methodology for some types of intellectual research, but it has certain limitations. In the first place, Kadushin automatically confines intellectual leaders to a group of individuals who use only intellectual journals as their primary means of communication. Since in my study I have not precluded the possibility that an artist, a musician, or a dramatist might use his own medium to convey intellectual ideas, I felt that such an approach would limit me to literary intellectuals. Second, Mexico, because of its own idiosyncrasies, created special problems in using borrowed methodologies: either they are impossible to use, or they are not entirely applicable. For example, intellectual magazines have not been long-lived in Mexico, and some of the more influential magazines, which leading intellectuals and politicians frequently read, are what we would label scholarly, academic journals. Furthermore, most Mexican intellectual magazines have never been indexed, so the use of Kadushin's methodology would require a complete survey of every issue published. Therefore, I tried to select a broader group of magazines, most of which have been published for many years and which represent a variety of disciplines. These magazines include such academic journals as *Historia Mexicana*, a Mexican equivalent of the *American Historical Review*, and such eclectic journals as *Cuadernos Americanos*, which publishes Latin American, North American, and Mexican writers who express themselves on a variety of literary and philosophical topics.

Kadushin's next step was to use his list of leading intellectuals, ascertained largely in a quantitative fashion, to provide a base for a smaller, selective list of the prominent intellectuals he wished to interview. In my own case, rather than allowing this larger list to determine my selection of leading intellectuals, I included an additional source. In 1978, I wrote to a selected group of prominent North American scholars, Mexican politicians, and Mexicans renowned in their respective disciplines (many of whom I suspected were leading intellectuals), and asked them to provide me with a list of intellectuals, regardless of field, whom they believed to have been most important in Mexican life after 1920. Armed with the responses of individuals knowledgeable about Mexican life, but from three different perspectives, I came up with a long list. Using this list as a basis, in 1978 and 1980 I interviewed prominent Mexican intellectuals and politicians. They in turn provided me with their own choices of Mexican intellectuals, just as Kadushin's interviewees provided him with additional names.

Kadushin found that there was considerable correlation between those who wrote most frequently for the leading U.S. intellectual journals and those his respondents named as important intellectuals; yet, although 8,000 individuals had originally written for such journals, his respondents provided only 232 different names. I found much the same to be true in my own interviewing. However, two qualifying conditions emerged. First, a certain number of younger intellectuals can be easily missed during a survey of well-established journals because their work is dispersed or available only in book form. For example, Carlos Monsiváis, one of Mexico's leading literary essayists, is practically unknown to North Americans specializing in Mexico, except in his own discipline. Further, to someone familiar with the intellectual scene since the 1920s, and with the individual accomplishments and contributions of Mexican intellectuals, it seems obvious that certain individuals who today are members of a select list of intellectuals will not be considered prominent a decade or two hence. Similarly, a problem that Kadushin did not have, since he focused his study on a five-year period, is how to give equal weight to those long dead. Obviously, certain historical giants in any culture stand out. In Mexico's case, young, middle-aged, and older respondents alike cast their votes repeatedly for figures like José Vasconcelos and Antonio Caso. But what about their important, if less-publicized, contemporaries? To some extent, North American scholarship has been influential in this regard, since much of the serious scholarship on Mexico's cultural history has been done by North Americans. Mexicans are influenced in their own historical appraisals by our research, and our decisions as to what and who are important.

To help assure the validity of the selection process, I read every leading critical work by Mexican and North American scholars I could locate that evaluated the contributions of poets, novelists, sculptors, musicians, journalists, scientists, physicians, philosophers during each decade since 1920. Those who repeatedly received recognition for the quality and breadth of their contributions were also added to my master list of Mexican intellectuals. Last, I examined the membership lists of Mexico's leading cultural academies and institutions, which admit members by invitation only, and especially their presidents, thus adding an element of the positional approach. Again, if these people were praised for their outstanding contributions, or appeared repeatedly on the list of intellectuals selected by the three groups mentioned earlier, I incorporated them into the final group as part of the data bank on Mexican intellectuals.

Within this large data bank (*MIBP*) of leading Mexican intellectuals, whose members have been determined by the level and frequency of their contributions, their institutional membership and leadership, the peer opinions of other intellectuals, their receipt of national prizes, the expert opinion of North American scholars, and the opinion of Mexican politicians, I have identified a Mexican *intellectual elite*, who were selected by scholars, politicians, and other intellectuals as *most influential*; that is, to be included in the elite intellectual group, a person had to receive a total of three votes, in any combination, from the three groups. This elite group may be seen in the same light as Kadushin's group, since its membership is affected by the age of the respondents and the date the survey was made. Although not as accurately representative of the sixty-year period from 1920 to 1980 as the larger group, it truly represents a group that has affected or is affecting the views of the respondents and is of value to this study for other reasons.

I have suggested that two sources of information for this study are unusual in the examination of intellectual life. The second of these is a series of oral interviews with and letters from intellectual and political leaders. Although several important studies, such as Kadushin's, have used interviews to complement their findings, none, to my knowledge, have sought the views of politicians and intellectuals alike. Thus, what I hope to reveal is what intellectuals believe about their relationship to the state and their role in Mexican society, and at the same time, to allow politicians to give their view of intellectuals and their influence on the state. I believe it is critical to have these views, since intellectuals' influence on the state is largely determined by their attitude toward and perception of each other. I further believe that politicians have provided certain insights into intellectual life not revealed in other studies.

A remaining source of information for this study, used only in the comparisons made between intellectuals and politicians, is the data bank referred to in the text as the *MPBP* (*Mexican Political Biography Project*). I began it in 1968, and it contains information, some of it in exactly the same format as the intellectual data set, on the careers, family ties, and social backgrounds of Mexico's prominent political leadership from 1935 through 1980. Although I have used it as a basis for three earlier studies, I have since expanded it in scope and size to include nearly fourteen hundred individuals about whom information is available for sixty-two variables. It is the most complete biographical data bank on Mexican leaders holding office during the last forty-five years. Additionally, the years of research devoted to creating this data bank have been helpful in the creation of the intellectual data bank, since a number of individuals qualify for inclusion in both data sets, and since many are related.

The criteria I used to select political leaders for the *MPBP* have been described in considerable detail in my *Mexican Political Biographies, 1935-1980* and *Mexico's Leaders: Their Education and Recruitment*. However, because I use this data bank for numerous comparisons with the intellectual subjects of this study, it deserves some comment for the reader unfamiliar with its use elsewhere. The individuals chosen for this biographical project were selected because (1) they held a political office of some national prestige, (2) they were thought to be influential by their living contemporaries, or (3) North American and Mexican scholars described their impact on the political system as substantial. Thus, as in the intellectual biographical project, I have used the positional and reputational approaches, common to much elite survey literature, to select those for inclusion. Essentially, public figures who were state governors, senators, repeating members of Congress, cabinet secretaries or subsecretaries, major decentralized agency directors or subdirectors, party leaders, or Supreme Court justices were automatically included in the *MPBP*. Moreover, leaders from the major labor, peasant, and professional unions were added to this original group.

However, I believed that the names offered by political leaders themselves would increase the value of a comprehensive list of influential national political leaders. Therefore, beginning in 1970, I began to correspond with and interview Mexican politicians whose names I originally obtained from my positional list, or who were later added as a result of suggestions from the correspondents themselves. Although I encountered few names not already on my positional list, a few individuals were added to the original list. Thus, I sometimes acquired the name of a political influential whose formal position would not have allowed him or her to be included.

Finally, in the compilation of the *MPBP*, I have perused several thousand articles and books on Mexican political life, and these, as a collective source of Mexican and North American expert opinion, have provided additional names and much of the biographical data. These sources have been especially useful in identifying opposition leaders of ephemeral political movements over the years. Since 1975, I have made a special effort to identify and acquire biographical information on such individuals. Also, I have introduced a caveat to these general criteria by including women and opposition party members whose formal political offices are not at the same level as the others included in the biography project.

The depth and breadth of the *MPBP* is such that it is not merely a sample of the individuals who meet these general criteria, but rather a nearly complete population. I have subdivided the larger biographical data bank into several categories to make the data more precise for comparative uses. This book uses two of these categories: the *Government Political Elite* and the *General Political Elite*. Tables citing the Government Political Elite refer only to figures who are part of the state apparatus, that is, persons who have served the Mexican government at the highest levels. Citations from the General Political Elite include all the cases in the Government Political Elite as well as opposition leaders and politicians, and women who have not reached the highest levels. Because the General Political Elite includes those who have had no direct role in managing the state, it provides a broader picture of Mexican political leadership.

Methodologically, I have assumed that I can examine the many questions raised in the Introduction by establishing who the Mexican intellectuals and politicians are, and by analzying detailed collective biographies of their career patterns and family backgrounds. Interviews with selected representatives of each group and a careful examination of numerous analytical, descriptive, and autobiographical accounts by and about intellectuals supplement the analysis. The reader will find nothing ideological about my approach, and, although much literature in this field takes on a class analysis, I do not approach it from such an angle. On the other hand, these interpretations are not ignored when they are apropos of the Mexican scene.

Essentially, this study focuses on the structural relationship between the intellectual life and the state, and the two groups that are primarily responsible for that relationship: intellectuals and politicians. It sharpens this focus by analyzing five broad assumptions. First, long-standing characteristics of Mexican society and its political culture have primarily determined the dominant patterns governing the relationship between the Mexican intellectual and politicians, and even a major social revolution did not effect significant structural changes in that relationship. Second, a basis for any relationship between intellectuals and the state, in Mexico or elsewhere, relies heavily on how each perceives the definition of an intellectual. There has been far too little emphasis in the study of intellectual life on the intellectual's own perception of who he is and the role he should play, and there is no information whatsoever on the politician's perception of these same issues. Third, for most of this century the relationship between the intellectual and the politician has been stable, but its future is less predictable now because a younger crop of intellectuals is pursuing a new self-definition, following a North American model, that is foreign to the tradition of state-intellectual relationships in Mexico. Fourth, intellectuals and politicians share many similarities in their recruitment patterns and career experiences, but important differences, accompanied by structural economic changes, are working toward their further separation. And finally, the ambience Mexican intellectual groups create is as detrimental to objective discussion and freedom of expression as is the larger environment the state establishes.

By describing certain aspects of my methodology and the special data sources, I do not want to give the reader a false impression that what will ensue in the following chapters is a purely empirical and quantitative analysis of Mexican intellectuals. On the contrary, the reader will instead find a humanistic approach using, when possible and where appropriate, quantifiable findings to buttress interpretations I or others have made on the basis of traditional documentary research. Traditional sources, I believe, provide the overwhelming evidence for my speculations about intellectual life in Mexico. I created and used the biographical data banks in this study because I found the study of intellectuals to be devoid of empirical evidence.

Ultimately the purpose of this book will not have been realized if the reader learns something about only Mexican intellectuals. I am concerned that some of what we learn from Mexico be applied to many developing nations and to an understanding of intellectuals in general. This does not mean that the Mexican case will be entirely applicable elsewhere, as the next chapter will make clear the special attributes of its political culture. Instead, I hope that this book, written in a speculative vein, will open up much more discussion about the role intellectuals might play in their respective societies and further our efforts at theorizing about intellectuals in general.

2. Politics, the State, and Intellectuals

An examination of the structure of intellectual life must include the political system. The Introduction implies that the relationship between the state and the intellectual has a significant bearing on many intellectual issues. Whether the issue is censorship, education, career opportunities, or political activism, only an incomplete understanding of the intellectual can be obtained if the political system is excluded. This is not the place for an extensive study of all aspects of the Mexican political system, but certain features characteristic of Mexico's political culture, the structure of the political leadership, and the way in which decisions are reached are especially relevant to intellectual activities.

The Mexican Model

Mexico's political system is unique among developing nations, and its uniqueness prevents easy categorization. The revisionism that characterizes all social science can be found in the studies of Mexico's political system during the last decade. Recent analyses have moved away from appraising it as a semidemocratic, modified one-party system, to seeing it as a semiauthoritarian regime.[1] To some extent, changing theories about the Mexican political system are the product of North American and Mexican scholars' efforts to fit the Mexican experience into one of a number of North American models. Not to do so ensures automatic criticism by other scholars, but the results of this difficult exercise are often artificial and superficial. Daniel Cosío Villegas, a leading intellectual and historian, questioned the efforts of North American scholars to explain the Mexican political process through such models.[2] Moreover, a North American political scientist and student of the Mexican scene has agreed that "much jargon of the social sciences seems to become a verbal mold into which empirical reflections about political life must be fitted."[3]

Rather than join these purely academic controversies, since this work's purpose is not a definitive analysis of the political system, let us characterize the Mexican political process by what we know about it, rather than place it in someone else's general categories. And more important, let us see what our examination of intellectuals can tell us about Mexico's political system, instead of what labeling the system can tell us about intellectuals. Structurally, Mexico's political system has certain formal similarities to that of the United States: it is a republic and a federal system with three branches of government. In practice, however, the two have little in common. Essentially, Mexico's governing class developed a political structure controlled by a small but circulating elite whose power derives from its control over the executive branch, primarily the federal bureaucracy and government-controlled decentralized agencies. Since the mid-1970s, a number of scholars, through separate studies of different aspects of the political system, have reached the conclusion that, although the Mexican state is authoritarian, "one can also appreciate its remarkable flexibility, a result of the generous limits on the scope of its activity within which quite sophisticated political games can unfold."[4]

It is this same flexibility that makes it so difficult for observers of the Mexican political scene to categorize it. Mexico's political leadership is committed to a pragmatic philosophy rather than to a rigid ideology or legal norms, and it is this pragmatism that determines the state's flexible behavior. Among the generations of political leaders who have developed the theory and practice of Mexican politics, thereby constructing a political culture that molds younger disciples, the only firm commitment since 1920 seems to have been to a universal concern for peaceful change and the continuation of a system effecting evolutionary development.[5]

The practice of Mexican politics has created a political culture that governs, to a great extent, the behavior of each succeeding group in the governing elite, since they, like their predecessors, are socialized to the norms of behavior present at the time of their initial recruitment into the political system. These norms of behavior have recently come under scrutiny by scholars, and more important, by the political-intellectual architects of Mexico's regimes.

Since the mid-1960s, when the Mexican economic miracle began to fall noticeably short of an equitable distribution of wealth and population pressures began to accentuate problems in land tenure, education, nutrition, housing, cultural integration, and other areas, critics inside and outside of the Mexican regime began to wonder whether the authoritarian pragmatism determining the rules of the political game was any longer sufficient to cope with these problems. A general disaffection with the government, and with the belief that the state could continue to cope with problems as it had done in the past, exploded with the events of 1968. The Mexican government found itself using brutally repressive measures against a demonstration of university students, largely the children of the middle classes, who upheld the regime and provided its leadership.

Government insiders during this same period failed to institute reforms that would increase internal democracy within the official party, but succeeding administrations have encouraged a liberalization of political structures by expanding opposition in the electoral arena. This attempt to increase political participation came about with the leadership's realization that, between 1961 and 1976, the percentage of registered voters who abstained rose from 32 to 39.[6] Furthermore, in 1976, Mexico devalued the peso, causing considerable economic harm to the middle classes while providing ammunition for less-authoritarian groups, led by government secretary Jesús Reyes Heroles, that called for increasingly liberal responses to Mexico's problems.[7]

It is too soon to be sure that the definitive impact of the government's reforms will be on the political process and on the long-term characteristics of the political culture. Most political observers seem to suggest, however, that the reforms have only been partially instituted, especially in the rural areas and in smaller communities dominated by more traditional party hacks. One of the reasons the Mexican government has found it difficult to carry out a liberalization policy is that most politicians believe that the decision of social groups to achieve democratization and independence by breaking away from the state is a definite rupture with the government and should be strongly combated. Even though it is allowing the strength of opposition political organizations to grow, the government is wary of the opposition's ability to form alliances with the masses, thus threatening the state's own hold over these segments of the population. On the other hand, it is also true that the leftist leadership in Mexico generally believes that only direct confrontation with the state will guarantee the independence of their group.[8]

In the 1970s the government switched tactics, from liberalizing the party from within, to liberalizing the party from without by using pressure from opposition groups.[9] In effect, the opposition parties, and the publicity they receive, force a wedge into the traditional bulwark of Mexican politics. Historically, one of the social groups that the government has controlled most successfully through the party and quasi-governmental organizations has been organized labor. Yet recently, more than any other group, organized labor has, through the umbrella organization of the Federation of Mexican Labor (CTM) within the official party, sought to prevent these government-sanctioned electoral reforms from reaching fruition. Because the majority of opposition parties are from the Left, labor leadership believes that these parties will try to organize the working class, thereby providing a direct threat to labor organizations and making labor the official party sector most likely to lose seats in the Chamber of Deputies.[10]

On the other hand, the government may be using the electoral reforms to exert greater control over the unions, which since 1970 have successfully bargained with the president for substantial wage increases in return for their support in times of political crisis. If labor has its way, and it seems to have been at least partially responsible for limiting the full implementation of electoral reforms in the administration of José López Portillo (1976-1982), the government runs the risk of foundering in the midst of other political crises because it has reneged on expectations produced among the politically active population. At the beginning of the de la Madrid administration, the moderates seem, once again, to have gained the upper hand. They have, however, unleashed other forces in the form of psychological expectations, which, in the case of intellectuals, change some traditional relationships.

A further implication of the recent political reforms likely to have an impact on intellectuals is the use of the Chamber of Deputies to co-opt local talent. Historically, the ruling groups in Mexico since the 1920s have attempted to draw local political opposition into the national fold, usually through the official party or through an appointment to the government bureaucracy. But as opposition to serving the government among certain educated groups and among intellectuals themselves increased in the 1960s, joining the government became an obvious sellout of their ideas and the organizations they represented. Instead, the government provided a more legitimate means of co-opting local talent by giving a limited number of seats to the leaders of opposition groups, who could then voice their criticisms in a national forum, under the watchful eyes of the federal government. By creating a form of "loyal opposition," the Mexican government has made it more difficult for opposition at the local level to get started and to grow into a troublesome organization.

Political Culture

The political culture of a society has implications for political and intellectual activity, since, to a large extent, his or her acquired values govern each participant's conduct in these two activities. What most strikes North Americans about Mexico's, and indeed Latin America's, political culture, is the nature of power. According to the most serious and provocative examination of the psychological and social implications of public power in the Latin cultures, social prestige is measured in terms of accumulated public influence, whereas in our society, achievement is measured in terms of accumulated wealth.[11] The acceptance of the assertion, carefully documented by Glen Dealy, that in Mexico the acquisition of public power is the primary goal of someone wishing to achieve social prestige, explains many interrelated characteristics about political behavior and about the role intellectuals play or would wish to play.

Far more than their North American counterparts, Mexican intellectuals have tried in word and deed, by definition and by role, to involve themselves in matters of the state. But in Mexico, the public person's "worldly success is directly correlated with his public power. And the test of public power is found in the extent of his friendships. Friendship, or *amicitia* as here used, does not pertain to sentiments of private congeniality but functions as a weapon of power. Personal relationships therefore must be cultivated, the circle of friendship extended. Playing the friendship game thus becomes a necessary way of life—as all-consuming as playing the money game within capitalistic cultures."[12]

Dealy provides a theoretical construct to support his notion that the acquisition of friends is the "currency of public power." By doing so, he has added a strong psychological dimension to the emphasis Mexicans place on the accumulation of friends in their public careers. In Mexico, and elsewhere in Latin America, the accumulation of friends has led to the importance of political groups. As I have argued elsewhere, Mexican politics is a series of interlocking pyramidal groups or *camarillas*, culminating in the president and his political clique.

The formulation of *camarillas* has many implications for the Mexican political process, among the most important of which is a reliance on friends to accomplish tasks inside and outside of politics. Thus, once an individual becomes a member of a political clique, his abilities are used to promote the career of the clique leader, and hence the individual's own career. Occasionally, he may use clique membership to accomplish some personal career goal, to obtain information, or to help a friend or relative outside of the immediate clique. Because clique identifications are not formal or permanent, the strength of a person's friendship with any single political influential is often hidden from view; therefore, individual politicians receive favors or are denied assistance because they have been closely identified with a politician or political clique.

A further effect of the *camarilla* system and the patron-client relationship it develops between the clique leader and follower is that it permits the Mexican politician to overcome ideological differences, thereby paving the way for internal compromises so uncharacteristic of Mexico in the first half of the nineteenth century. Larissa Lomnitz argues that the entire system benefits "from the existence of such contacts of an informal nature" because they serve to contain and eliminate sources of conflict at all levels, an extremely important key to stability in Mexican politics.[13]

Yet these multiple networks of friends can and do lead to dissension, though it is internalized. Because the entire Mexican political system, and especially the federal bureaucracy, is built on these group friendships, changes in the upward mobility of a public figure's career occur suddenly and often arbitrarily.[14] In spite of the personal bitterness sudden career changes produce among many individual politicians, it is not really the *camarilla* nor loyalty to any greater moral precept that keeps the Mexican political system together, but the understanding by nearly all public figures that, in order to rise phoenixlike from the ashes of a failed political career, they must bide their time and seek to broaden their friendships with new mentors who will assist their careers and counterbalance the influence of political enemies.

The fluidity of the *camarilla* system in Mexican politics opens it up to those intellectuals who have access to political *camarillas*. Intellectuals may use their skills to assist a politician in his political rise and to add prestige to his *camarilla*; on the other hand, intellectuals may demand political benefits for themselves. And although few intellectuals have been able to resist the temptation of public power, some have used their political contacts for different purposes. Furthermore, my analysis of the structure of intellectual life reveals that intellectuals, like politicians, form groups or cliques of which politicians with intellectual interests are members. Thus, many of the friendship networks overlap among politicians and intellectuals.

The *camarilla* is only one of the important features of the Mexican political system the desire to accumulate friends produces. Personalism is another, and it has several interesting implications for Mexican politics. The most well known of these, a widely discussed characteristic of the Mexican political system, is the loyalty of the masses and the governing classes to individual personalities, rather than to a political philosophy or party. As Edmundo González Llaca suggests, the personal characteristics of a leader are far more important to the typical Mexican than that leader's beliefs.[15] This is not to suggest that personalism and charismatic leadership are not found in other societies; rather, in Mexico these qualities are strongly emphasized.

The most important effect of the emphasis on individual personalities is the extent of power placed in the hands of Mexico's president. His political control stems from the fact that he wields the most political power and maintains the largest and most influential network of friends. The degree of personal adulation and loyalty extended to him increases his power and weakens that of others, thereby giving the president more room for maneuvering. For example, he easily sets the tone of his administration through his outward appearance. When President Luis Echeverría began to wear the tieless guayabera, along with a leather jacket, most of his collaborators, from cabinet ministers on down, quickly imitated him.

The importance of superior-subordinate relationships and the exaggerated loyalties they have engendered produce many side effects. Because friendships are so critical to political success, and because there is a constant tension and feeling of distrust, loyalty to individuals becomes highly valued. Friendship does not have its traditional meaning in Mexican society; rather, it is a pragmatic means to a concrete end.[16]

The Mexican political system, like all political cultures, has created a code of behavior as the result of this feeling of loyalty. One component of the code is an unwillingness to share information, since to do so benefits the careers of political competitors. This leads to considerable secrecy among Mexican politicians, whether they are discussing their own backgrounds or policy decisions. Octavio Paz describes government service in Mexico as "sort of a cult or sect, with the usual bureaucratic rituals and 'state secrets.' Public affairs are not discussed, they are whispered."[17]

But one of loyalty's effects on political behavior is carefully couched political conduct. The goal of the subordinate is to enhance the career of the superior, thereby enhancing his or her own chances for upward mobility. However, a misstep, for whatever reason, leads to "*congelación*," or in the parlance of Mexican politics, freezing someone. In his revealing study of the official party, David Schers describes the cause and effects of freezing.[18] The correct response to this penalty is silence, accepting the punishment stoically, in the hopes that you can redeem yourself in the eyes of your mentor. Mexicans call this punishment "being disciplined," and a willingness to accept disciplinary behavior from above signifies membership in the political club.[19]

Another characteristic of the political culture underscored by the Mexican's emphasis on loyalty is the politician's language. Evelyn Stevens describes how the form of conversation affects the quality of information transmitted: "In addition to softness of vocal tone, Mexicans employ circumlocution in what appears to be an attempt to put a cushion of words between themselves and their listeners."[20] Since the politician strives to avoid offense, which could reverberate negatively on his superior, he resorts to answering questions through circumlocution, vagueness, or even outright lying. Vicente Leñero, in *Los periodistas*, captured the style of the politician in several individual incidents, characterizing it thus: "When someone makes a direct observation or implies a direct response, the skillful politician feels an obligation—not to refuse your question—but to talk about historical precedent until neither the interrogator nor interrogatee remembers the question."[21] To the intellectual who seeks information with which to make critical judgments, a politician's circumlocution is frustrating.[22] Moreover, if overly polite forms of conversation are most acceptable among Mexicans, then to some extent the value independent intellectuals place on frankness blunts their influence on other groups, not because of what they have to say, but because of how they say it.

Political Structures

Some of the important features of Mexico's political culture, including the desire for public power, the acquisition of friends, and the subservience of honesty to loyalty, affect the processes of the political system, most important, those that involve recruitment, decision making, and presidential succession. In Mexico, as I argued earlier, a person's career depends largely on the ability to acquire influential friends and mentors. What is most astounding about this process is that it applies to all types of governmental structures, including the official party, the federal bureaucracy, and the decentralized agencies, and to all levels of government, including the state and local governments, and even the rural *ejido*.

The most important features of any recruitment pattern are who does the selecting, who is selected, and in what institutions the selection process takes place. Like their counterparts in the United States, successful Mexican politicians use a variety of channels to rise to the most influential posts in the political system. The most important channels have been the official party, the government unions, the judiciary, the Congress, the state and federal bureaucracies, and the military. Within these institutions, two career types have predominated: successful careers in the electoral sphere, achieved largely by combining positions in the party bureaucracy with a successive number of electoral posts, often culminating in the governorship of a state; and administrative careers, in which public figures who have never come directly in contact with the party or been nominated to hold electoral offices have risen to high ministerial posts.

In the years since the Revolution, most politicians have started their careers following the electoral pattern. From the 1930s to the 1960s, politicians often combined both patterns, alternating between elected posts and appointive offices in the federal bureaucracy. But in the last two decades, the career administrator has taken over Mexico's leadership. Today, the administrative pattern can be clearly seen in the careers of Mexico's recent presidents, and in those of their closest and most powerful collaborators.[23]

Further narrowing the successful career pattern in Mexico is the predominance of the National University in the recruitment process. The successful government official uses the National University as a place for identifying new talent and recruiting it to the fold. Furthermore, the university serves as the most important institution for the creation of political cliques among politically interested students, who then use these friendships to promote successful careers in the government bureaucracy. Thus, for generations, both professors and students have used other students as a base for developing the friendships necessary for acquiring political power in Mexico.[24]

That the National University is one of the most important places for acquiring such political friendships is significant for two reasons: first, it concentrates recruitment activity in one institution; and second, it centralizes recruitment in Mexico City. Thus, Mexico's political recruitment process encourages a level of homogeneity not to be found in the United States. The fact that the majority of successful politicians have lived in the same place during their adolescent years, have gone to school in the same environment, have had many of the same teachers, have read the same textbooks, have had many of the same friends, and have simultaneously begun their careers in the same agencies, leads to what C. Wright Mills called psychological affinities among the political leadership.[25]

As the process for political recruitment in Mexico becomes more centralized and homogeneous, it becomes closed. The pool of individuals from whom politicians are recruited narrows, and its members must have similar characteristics if they are to arrive at the top. The implication of this recruitment process for the intellectual is important because the intellectual's access to the politician is determined by the same characteristics helpful to the politician's career. Therefore, where the intellectual lives, where he is educated and with whom he has contact as a young person is important in establishing whether or not the intellectual and politician are speaking the same language, whether they listen to each other, and whether or not the intellectual will be used by the politician to further his government career and vice versa.

The characteristics of political culture and recruitment in Mexico directly affect the decision-making process, whether the concern is with policy or with personnel. In the case of policy decisions, the process is secretive, centralized, uninnovative, discontinuous, arbitrary, uncoordinated, and personalistic. Those individuals in the Mexican political system who are policymakers participate in some way in the allocation of governmental goods and services.[26] The blanket of secrecy traditionally surrounding the decision-making process in Mexico stems from the value politicians place on withholding information and from the competitiveness of their careers. One of the specific by-products of secrecy in policymaking is that competition among cabinet-level agencies often leads to the planning and execution of wasteful policies. Furthermore, because rivalries among various politicians exist within most agencies, departments in the same ministry are equally guilty of ignoring each other.[27] Thus, what appears to be a homogeneous team loyal to the president of Mexico is instead a group of individuals vying for power.

On the surface, one might expect considerable continuity in government policies because representatives of a single party have controlled the executive branch since the 1920s. Instead, the de-emphasis on ideological positions, and an emphasis on personal qualities, allow each president to set the tone for his respective administration. Because each of his collaborators attempts to please him rather than formulate policies built on previous decisions taken in his or her area of responsibility, little continuity in agency decisions exists from one administration to the next. An advantage of this lack of continuity is that a group, individual, or business that has been denied a favorable response in one administration may find itself welcomed during the next.[28] The discontinuity of decision making in Mexico affects intellectuals as much as any other group, in that their ability to influence policy as decision makers or as advisers is determined by who is president and who holds cabinet or subcabinet positions.

Another important characteristic of decision making in Mexico, similar to that found in the recruitment process, is the arbitrariness of individual decisions. According to one student of the Mexican bureaucracy, the president, contrary to popular belief, "delegates a great deal of authority to the Minister, so that in a real sense the Ministry is the personal empire of the man who leads it."[29] Thus, an individual minister can withhold funds for government projects from an individual, agency, or even a state.[30] Furthermore, because each collaborator understands the power the president, or an individual in high office holds, each attempts to manipulate the president or cabinet officer against someone so as to benefit his own career.[31]

Placing power in the hands of a few individuals centralizes decision making, although the degree of centralization has been exaggerated. The Mexican bureaucracy has over the years increased the number of agencies and positions having some influence over the allocation of resources. However, decision-making power is centralized in the sense that there are few institutionalized, legal channels used by the decision makers or those who seek to affect the outcome of their decisions. Mexicans seek out the top person in each agency for small as well as large matters. Guy Benveniste concluded that a minister "is under tremendous pressure, he may receive on the average 200 communications a day, official visits, telephone calls, delegations coming from the provinces, he must make speeches—he literally has no time to think."[32]

The centralization of power at various levels aggravates the need for personal contact. Personal friendships are as important to policymaking as they are to political recruitment.[33] Example after example in the memoirs of political officeholders illustrate the significance of such contacts, whether for obtaining funds for an individual project, for changing policy direction, or merely for personal gain.[34] Interestingly, some presidents have sought to limit the appeals of various people requesting funds by asking their own treasury secretaries to review, and if need be, veto presidential decisions.[35]

The importance of personal contacts to decision making in Mexico opens the door to varying degrees of influence from unseen or informal channels. Thus it is more likely that individuals will frequently use social ties to acquire political influence or to call on outsiders to provide them with sound advice and expert information. This is true in all political systems, but in Mexico the frequency of these contacts, and the extent to which they affect decisions, are greater than in many other political systems.

Intellectuals who wish to influence policy decisions in Mexico, if they have the social contacts, may find it unnecessary to hold high government office. Furthermore, more careful examination of individual government agencies may find that some lower-level positions play key roles in the policy process and that such positions might be filled by individuals whose careers may not be primarily political. Intellectuals use these informal channels of communication in the same way as do other Mexicans, but by doing so, they help to perpetuate a process that relies on informal, uncharted procedures shrouded in secrecy, a practice many politically active intellectuals have openly criticized throughout the twentieth century.

Last, the decision-making process in Mexico is not conducive to creative or innovative ideas. The person who makes waves, even when there are benefits, is more likely to risk his career and that of his superior, than to promote either or both. As many students of Mexico's political system suggest, the administrator or politician "is rewarded not for his innovativeness, initiative, or positive accomplishments in the making or implementing of public policy, but rather for his capacity to facilitate the functioning of the apparatus through the balancing of interests, the distribution of benefits, and the control of potentially disruptive or disequilibrating forces."[36]

My description of the recruitment and decision-making process in Mexico supports the contention that the acquisition of friends is the means those with political ambitions use to rise in the political system and to gain access to political decision-makers. For the intellectual who wishes to start a government career at the top, and who hopes to formally wield power at the highest levels in lieu of having informal influence as an adviser, is a path open? That is, by whom and how are individuals designated to hold top positions in the executive, legislative, and judicial branches of Mexican government?

Undoubtedly, in Mexico the federal bureaucracy is where most policy formulation and execution take place, and it is the structure through which most politicians rise. Intellectuals, if they have followed public careers, have likewise selected the bureaucracy in large numbers. As can be clearly seen from the data in table 1, the majority of Mexico's prominent intellectuals have held posts in the government (53 percent). The largest group, 46 percent, have worked for the federal bureaucracy. Although other forms of political activity are less common, it is still surprising that nearly a fourth of all intellectuals have been party activists and nearly a fifth have actually run for and held an elective post.

Because of their political proclivities and their involvement in public careers, it is important to describe, if only briefly, the likelihood of intellectuals receiving appointments to influential positions. The most important figure in the process of making personnel decisions in the Mexican political system is the president. His power is much greater than that of the U.S. president because he can and sometimes does intervene in

Table 1
Offices Held by Mexican Intellectuals
Who Have Pursued Public Careers
(*N*=178)

Career Choice	Type of Position (%)				
	Federal Bureaucracy[a]	Party Post[b]	Elective Post[c]	Education Ministry[d]	Foreign Service[e]
Public sector	46	23	17	36	25
No public career	54	77	83	64	75
Total	100[f]	100	100	100	100

Source: *MIBP.*

Notes: An individual is considered to have had a public career if he or she has held elective or appointive posts for five or more years or two or more positions for any length of time.

The *N* for this and all other tables involving more than one variable may vary, since responses with no information are excluded from the totals for each individual variable.

Unless otherwise noted, data for intellectuals in all tables refer to those considered prominent from 1920 to 1980.

[a]Defined as any position in the federal bureaucracy or a decentralized agency.

[b]Any position in any political party.

[c]Any position at the local, state, or national levels that is elective.

[d]Any position in the Secretariat of Public Education, excluding teaching and university administrative positions.

[e]Any position in the Secretariat of Foreign Relations, the Consular or the Foreign services.

[f]Percentage figures may not total 100, due to rounding.

the choice of an individual appointee or candidate for *any* elective, executive, or judicial post at the local, state, or national levels. Although it is important to recognize that the president can use his immense power to make many designations, it would be impossible for him actually to make most of them; moreover, in practice, he generally confines himself to those positions of greatest prestige, if not power.

The selection process in Mexico about which we have the most information is, interestingly, that for cabinet and subcabinet positions. In the majority of cases, the president personally knows the individual he wishes to appoint to a cabinet post. As one former cabinet member told an interviewer, "Personal relationships, friendships, and political ties greatly influence the selection of cabinets."[37] Yet, those relationships do not necessarily apply to the president himself. For example, Eduardo Suárez, a leading intellectual and student of political economy, was himself appointed to one of the most important cabinet posts, that of treasury secretary, in June 1935, on the basis of a recommendation by Emilio Portes Gil, a former president and collaborator of then-president Lázaro Cárdenas. Suárez did not personally know the president.[38] For a more recent example, I examined the public career of Agustín Yáñez to illustrate how one type of intellectual in public life achieved his positions. Yáñez's appointment

to a second high-level office was determined by his relation with the president, and not with his superior, the cabinet minister. Yáñez came to know López Mateos politically when the latter heard one of his addresses as governor of Jalisco. Like others before him, López Mateos was impressed with his speech-writing abilities, and asked Yáñez to revise his state of the union addresses from 1959 to 1962. Even after his appointment as subsecretary, his fundamental task was to write, research, and refine these speeches. Thus, once again, Yáñez's literary talents helped him achieve high office.[39]

Within the federal bureaucracy, regardless of level, there is flexibility in who makes the decision about appointees. Generally, the most important department heads are appointed by the cabinet secretaries themselves; the secretaries, in turn, delegate some appointive power to other individuals.[40] This delegation of power is important because it broadens the small pool of individuals from which selections are made, for reasons discussed earlier in this chapter. This means that the intellectual desiring to hold influential public positions who is a politician's student, professor, costudent, or associate in a professional organization, or a politician's colleague in some other bureaucratic position, increases his opportunities to do so.

In the electoral sphere, the president will frequently intervene to include a friend or political favorite as an official party candidate for senator or federal deputy. It is also evident that the president designates the majority leader in the Chamber of Deputies.[41] But not all of these candidates are presidential choices, since the secretary of government (*gobernación*), party leaders, labor leaders, and governors also are involved in making these appointments. Other than president, the most important electoral position is that of state governor, a position only rarely held by intellectuals since the 1930s.[42] Because so few intellectuals are likely to hold this post in Mexico, and because I have dealt with it elsewhere, a detailed discussion here of how they are chosen is unnecessary. However, insiders and scholars agree that the president designates gubernatorial candidates or exercises a veto over who is selected.[43]

The intellectual has stayed away from gubernatorial positions more than from any other influential position. The reasons are several. The majority of governors in Mexico make their careers in the federal government, but most are active within a sectoral organization or the party, and many have held other elective positions. These are the political activities in which intellectuals are least likely to have engaged. Furthermore, although newer generations of governors emulate more closely the background characteristics and careers of the successful federal administrator, they generally have more experience with the use of political skills directed toward large groups or the uneducated citizenry in general, situations intellectuals would probably find uncomfortable. Moreover, political careers are centered in the capital, and intellectuals, more clearly than politicians, have been unable or unwilling to leave the environs of Mexico City.

Nonstate Structures

The nature of political decision-making, the characteristics of political culture, and the features of political recruitment all suggest the limitations and benefits Mexican politics provides for intellectuals wishing to make their careers within the system, to influence policymaking, or to have access to those who do make influential decisions. In many other Latin American countries, the military and the church provide alternate career routes an intellectual might follow and alternative institutions through which political, social, and economic influence could be exerted. In Mexico, however, the liberal intellectuals of the nineteenth century, and the neoliberal and Marxist intellectuals of the twentieth century, were against the privileges that made clergy and officers separate castes. A principal tenet of the disparate philosophies of the 1910 Revolution was the removal of the church's influence on many aspects of Mexican life. Following the Revolution, the church's influence in Mexico slowly declined, as did the number of proclerical intellectuals or intellectual clergy. Only seven of Mexico's most prominent intellectuals since the 1920s have been members of the clergy (*MIBP*), although some intellectuals, like Antonio Caso, have represented a humanist, Christian view. Today, religious intellectuals exist in small numbers, but they are still unrecognized by the intellectual community and recent generations of political leaders.[44] The Mexican church, similar to the church in the rest of Latin America, is being stirred by new intellectual and ideological debates from within, but, even bolstered by recent growth and an improvement in economic resources, it has still not produced the active intellectual leadership found in many other Latin American countries.

The military during the nineteenth century provided a home for many of Mexico's leading politicians and intellectuals, but it suffered several severe disruptions during and after the 1910 Revolution. Intellectuals had little place in the revolutionary or postrevolutionary army, and as representatives of the educated class, they worked with the new generations of college-educated politicians after the 1920s to gradually eliminate the military's influence from Mexican political life. Not one of the 337 intellectuals in this study made the military a career (*MIBP*). The military in Mexico today is one of the most professional in the Third World in the sense that it has gradually removed itself from politics.[45] This is not to say that it plays no political role in Mexico, but only that the new, pragmatic technical officer corps, largely recruited from the lower-middle class, no longer has the social prestige nor the breadth of activities to attract intellectuals.[46] Unlike the church, which offers an environment where philosophy thrives, the military in Mexico has few ideologues to defend it or to campaign for an expanded or changed role.

If the church and the military are closed to the Mexican intellectuals as institutional channels through which they can exert an influence over society, there are two channels available to the intellectual who wishes to influence the state without closing ranks with it: opposition parties, and the private sector. From a structural angle, Mexico's opposition parties seem to offer little chance for intellectuals who wish to have political influence because, like the church, they lack prestige in the secular world of partisan politics. Second, and an explanation for their low prestige, opposition parties have not done well in Mexican politics since the establishment of the official party in 1929. Thus, they have never succeeded in winning at least 5 percent of the actual districts represented in the Chamber of Deputies, nor have they ever won a seat in the Senate.[47] As suggested earlier, these two elective positions have little or no influence on policymaking in the federal government. Through a position in a party, or even as a successful candidate of a party for the lower legislative body, the intellectual is not likely to have direct influence on the government. On the other hand, many intellectuals have participated in some form of electoral politics, have held party posts, and have been members or officers of short-lived opposition parties. If the political reforms were to encourage increased intellectual participation, opposition parties could become more important.

The most successful of these parties in Mexico has been the National Action party (PAN), which has fielded candidates in most national contests since the early 1950s. It was founded in 1939 by Manuel Gómez Morín, a leading intellectual figure. The PAN and, to a lesser extent, other opposition parties, do provide an alternative source of views, making it possible, as Evelyn P. Stevens suggests, "for the same message to be directed at high-level decision-makers in the government through four different channels: *viva voce* in the legislative chamber, and in print in the *Diario de Debates* (the congressional register), in the daily newspapers, and in the party organ."[48] Furthermore, the channels Stevens describes are taking on a new luster and significance as Presidents López Portillo and de la Madrid have allowed and encouraged the Chamber of Deputies to call cabinet and decentralized agency representatives to explain their policies and their deficiencies before the assembled members. Representatives of the opposition voice their own questions in this process. Moreover, the changes in the proportional representation law and the encouragement of other parties have produced an increase in opposition party representation in the chamber from 40 of 236 seats (17 percent) in the 1976-1979 legislature to 104 of 400 seats (26 percent) in the 1979-1982 session.

Intellectuals with a propensity for political activities have made opposition parties a useful vehicle for developing their reputations among government leaders. Many intellectuals who have joined the government for full-time careers have, however, been co-opted by the government because astute political leaders recognized their skills in persuasion, organization, and rhetoric as leaders of opposition groups. A survey of Mexico's elite intellectuals only reveals that David Alfaro Siqueiros and Diego Rivera served as members of the executive committee of the Communist party; that Narciso Bassols, Víctor Manuel Villaseñor, and Vicente Lombardo Toledano founded and were vice-presidents and president, respectively, of the Popular party (later the Popular Socialist party); that Antonio Díaz Soto y Gama established a political liberal club at the turn of the century and became famous for his speeches criticizing the government in the chamber during the 1920s, before it became government-controlled; that José Vasconcelos figured as the most notable opposition party candidate for president (in 1929) since the 1920s; that Alberto Vázquez del Mercado and Antonio Díaz Soto y Gama prominently supported the candidate opposed to the official party choice in the 1940 presidential election; and that Luis Villoro is well known for his activities in the Mexican Labor party.

It is fair to say that careers in opposition parties can lead to national recognition in the political arena and to government posts. But as a form of employment, or as a means of direct influence on policy, they are very limited in Mexico. This leaves the private sector as the only other alternative, yet, an examination of the professions in which intellectuals have made a living shows that 28 percent followed full-time careers in the government, 25 percent in education (nine-tenths of these were employed by public universities), 2 percent in the Catholic church, and another 2 percent in business (figures are from *MIBP*). The remainder were mostly self-employed professionals, or actually lived off of their creative and intellectual products. However, some, most important of whom were journalists, writers, publishers, and lawyers, worked for private enterprises, or contracted on a part-time basis to provide services to these organizations.

Mexican intellectuals have not been prominent entrepreneurs, nor have they served in positions in the private sector from which their influence might be directly felt by the federal government. The failure of intellectuals to assume positions of importance in the private sector is not surprising, since they are known universally for their avoidance of ties to this group. However, in Mexico the private sector is the only group that has offered, for some time, sufficient strength and independence from the government to make its influence on the state felt.[49] Since the 1920s, the private sector has, more often than not, found itself a ready ally of the state, adjusting its "pursuits in order not to provoke crises—problems, of course, but not crises."[50]

This underlying goal seems to have determined the relationship between business and the government well into the 1960s, when cracks in the long-standing alliance began to appear. The private sector's antagonism toward decisions taken by the state reached its apex in 1982, at the end of the López Portillo administration, and was highlighted by vociferous opposition of some groups to the government's nationalization of the banks in Mexico. The dissatisfaction with his administration, the general economic malaise it helped to introduce, did produce a distinct change in direction when Miguel de la Madrid, López Portillo's successor, took office. The dynamics of the political climate in recent years has led scholars to suggest that the private sector is considering the possibility of founding a new political party to represent its interests and that it is questioning past economic policies.[51] Whether or not business executives usually are in agreement with the state, and whether or not they can influence many decisions by trying to affect political decision-making, they make it more difficult for the government to maintain political equilibrium.[52]

It can be justifiably argued that the private sector, directly or indirectly, provides more channels for influencing government decision-making than do the military, the church, or even opposition parties. But except for the publishing and journalism industry, where intellectuals abound, the private sector has not sought out intellectual collaborators, nor have intellectuals looked for allies in the private sector. The reasons are many, but several of importance to the Mexican scene deserve comment. Most significant is that "family business, until about 1960, was the norm in Mexico since kinship provided the element of trust and loyalty an entrepreneur would look for in selecting his partners, associates, and administrators."[53] In other words, unless an intellectual was the child of entrepreneurs, or had been closely related, his access to a business career was most unlikely. In her research on business leaders in Mexico, about whom little is known, Larissa Lomnitz found that a business executive, like a politician, "requires a circle of persons, each of whom is connected to him through a relationship of trust."[54] Today, family-oriented businesses are in decline, and the entrepreneur, like the politician, must develop other means through which friends can be acquired. At present, there is insufficient information to suggest where such friendships are developed, but it is likely that educational institutions play such a role. However, the educational recruitment of business executives is more likely to take place at the Monterrey Institute of Technology, the Autonomous Technological Institute of Mexico, and the Ibero-American University, and not at the National Preparatory School or the National University.[55] Yet it is in the last two institutions, as we will see in chapter 8, that the intellectuals are overwhelmingly educated, more so than even the Mexican politicians.

Thus, we can surmise that, in addition to kinship ties that block intellectuals and business executives from forming friendship alliances, the location of their education has made social relationships between them less likely, particularly at an early age. This is not to say that leading entrepreneurs do not have many social friends among both intellectuals and politicians, but these friendships most often occur after they leave college. As family businesses become more rare, and as professional disciplines chosen by those with intellectual interests increase, we may see an influx of younger intellectuals among entrepreneurial positions.[56] But throughout the twentieth century, and for the present, the intellectual, in background and education, has had more in common with the politician than with the entrepreneur; this similarity may help to explain the degree to which intellectuals have found themselves employed in the public sector.

Conclusions

In the preceding pages, I have tried to analyze several features of Mexico's political culture and structure and the effect each might have on the role of intellectuals and their relationship to the state. As Mexico faces the end of this century, there are various reasons to suggest why intellectuals should or could play a useful role in Mexico's development.

When public debate on many issues breaks domestic unity, the opportunities for intellectual involvement increase accordingly. This is not to imply that many of the elements that restrict intellectual influence are disappearing overnight; rather, the milieu of Mexican politics in the 1980s is changing. The tone of this change can be seen in a small but significant number of recent cases of governors criticizing the federal government and deputies being outspoken, all of which makes the government itself more sensitive and less secure.[57]

The government's attitude toward the intellectual is also important. Mexican intellectuals believe their status is enhanced by a government seeking to honor or recruit them into public service. The two most recently completed administrations in Mexico, those of Echeverría and López Portillo, although having different political directions, both sought to incorporate the intellectual and to increase resources in areas of public spending beneficial to intellectual livelihoods. Therefore, it is not surprising that one intellectual could speak with optimism in saying that Mexico "is open to all kinds of possibilities for the intellectual. The intellectuals have the opportunity to go in any direction, the frontiers are present."[58]

As Mexico's political system evolves, and as the means of communication become widespread, the importance of oral and written communication skills have increased. Raymond Aron argues that "governments need experts in the art of speech."[59] Intellectuals, whose skills concentrate in the manipulation of symbols, are in greater demand in societies with rapidly expanding channels of communication. Furthermore, as the established political structure increasingly comes under attack, it requires ideological defenders as it adjusts to survive; this need makes ideology itself more important. As suggested earlier, Mexico finds itself in just such a political situation, and the state has sought out ideologists such as Jesús Reyes Heroles as reformers, or others from the outside to defend its reforms.[60]

Of course, the established political structures are not the only institutions in need of intellectual services. Intellectuals are also likely to provide the same skills to opposition parties and revolutionary movements.[61] The battle between the establishment and antiestablishment intellectuals focuses on ideology, and in turn, the dominance of ideological conflicts increases the demand for intellectual ideologists. Jeane Kirkpatrick aptly describes this circular phenomenon, one that increasingly applies to Mexico:

In any vital society, the initial attack on political authority (mounted by intellectuals) provokes a response and results in an intensified ideological struggle leading inexorably to the enhanced role of the new class. The greater the role of the new class in politics, the more ideological politics becomes; the more ideological politics becomes, the more important the new class becomes. Their critical skills are required to analyze the moral inadequacies of the existing society, their verbal skills to dramatize them. But other members of the new class are then needed to criticize the critics, to defend the symbols of legitimacy, to state the case for the values and beliefs embodied in the existing political culture and institutions.[62]

Mexican intellectuals are also likely to be important in the future because of the spillover impact of what Zbigniew Brzezinski calls the "technetronic society," that is, a society shaped culturally, socially, and economically by the impact of technology and electronics.[63] As the influence of technological developments makes decision making more complex, individuals possessing special skills and intellectual talents become more important. Increasingly, "knowledge becomes a tool of power, and the effective mobilization of talent an important way for acquiring power."[64] This does not mean that knowledge will replace the acquisition of friends as the key to power in Mexico, but that, in acquiring friends, the importance of their knowledge will and has already become more significant.[65]

A dynamic change supporting the increased emphasis of Mexico's leadership on knowledge and intellectual skills is the rapid expansion of what Fritz Machlup called "knowledge production." In the United States, production in knowledge fields is increasing at a rate about twice that of the rest of the economy.[66] Mexico, of course, is not keeping up with the United States, but in many areas, such as the communications media, publishing, and higher education, its expansion has been notable. Historically, the increase in literacy and a wide market for books correlates with the rise of the independent intellectual.[67] These increases are only recent in Mexico, where it has been estimated that only 6 percent of the population buys and reads books,[68] but they are persistent and visible. Furthermore, because

Mexican intellectuals are deeply involved in higher education, either as full-time administrators or career researchers and professors, they function in the capacity of certifying "other elites as technically competent."[69] Moreover, the impact of Mexican intellectuals-teachers on their politically inclined students is substantial.[70]

Mexican intellectuals are not likely to be important just because of their command of knowledge and the institutions spawning that knowledge, but because there is a growing gap between the technician and the generalist, and between the technician and the masses. The intellectual is a generalist by definition, but the modern Mexican intellectual, by acquiring a background in "newer disciplines" while retaining a breadth of interests, is able both to understand his or her specialty and to communicate to others the contents of that specialty. This ability allows the intellectual to serve as a bridge between the intelligentsia and the decision maker, and more important, between the educated citizen and the decision maker.[71]

Traditionally, the key function of intellectuals has been to provide or describe values for a society. Their importance socially and politically has stemmed from their potential for restructuring humanity's conception of itself and its society.[72] If the political leadership attempts to govern without the tacit support of at least a portion of the intellectual community, it will increasingly resort to the use of force.[73] Since Mexican political leadership in the last ten years has shown itself especially desirous of avoiding the use of force, intellectuals, for better or for worse, will be sought out by the administration.

Furthermore, signs of anti-intellectualism do not necessarily mean that intellectual influence politically and ideologically is on the decline. As Milton Gordon suggests, this attitude may be an "implicit admission that ideas *are* powerful preludes and instigators to action."[74] On the other hand, it is important to keep in mind that, if Mexican intellectuals decide to abandon their leadership role in society, they will leave its direction to the politician, who, according to Thomas Neill, is "not devoted professionally to the truth."[75] Thus, intellectuals are worth examining because their influence will be felt whether they are active or inactive in society and because of what they might contribute or take away.

3. The Mexican Intellectual

Nothing is more elusive in the examination of intellectual life than the definition of what an intellectual is. No two definitions are alike, and there is disagreement as to what really constitutes an intellectual in the twentieth century. It is necessary to clarify the concept of *intellectual* because the ambiguity surrounding the word is due more to a misunderstanding of other interpretations than to serious differences on most points. Furthermore, since part of my empirical evidence on the background and activities of intellectuals relies heavily on a survey of individual experiences, it is necessary to present the conceptualization I used to select the intellectual group in the data set described in the Introduction.

A Universal Conceptualization

The most agreed-upon meaning implied by the word *intellectual* is "a person with a high level of knowledge." As put simply by one sociologist a half century ago, intellectuals are "those who are vocationally concerned with things of the mind."[1] But, of course, a level of knowledge is not sufficient in itself as a definition, since it does not suggest the kind or source of that knowledge. For some students of cultural life, intellectuals, in addition to cultivating and formulating knowledge, must "have access to and advance a cultural fund of knowledge which does not derive solely from their direct personal experience."[2] In other words, as Robert Merton suggests, such individuals are exposed to and absorb the ideas of others, particularly other intellectuals. Further adding to this characterization, Alvin Gouldner suggests that the intellectual has acquired a specialized language as an accompaniment to that knowledge.[3] The intellectual, therefore, establishes a set of informal ground rules for acquiring knowledge and for expressing views and exchanging them with peers.

If we were to accept the definition of an intellectual as an individual with a certain level of knowledge and type of language not acquired solely from personal experience, our definition would include too many persons.

What separates the intellectual from the intelligentsia (a related but distinct concept) is the element of creativity. In the words of Gertrude Stein, a creator "is not in advance of his generation but he is the first of his contemporaries to be conscious of what is happening to his generation."[4] Thus, it is not necessarily discovering the new idea, concept, or process that describes the intellectual, but being able to recognize it when you see it and convey it to others.

Therefore, although a fund of knowledge is necessary to the intellectual, it is merely a vehicle he uses to recognize important ideas. The ability to recognize these ideas is determined by the *breadth* of the intellectual's knowledge, again, a quality separating the intelligentsia from the intellectual. The intellectual's breadth of knowledge gives him the necessary ability to spot new ideas in many disciplines. As one social scientist expressed this, "One might consider an intellectual a person who takes a wide range of abstract symbols and ideas seriously, and who does so in relation to a wide range of topics outside his immediate field of professional specialization."[5] Moreover, to function successfully as an intellectual, one has to be able to distinguish between what is a *general* idea and what is a particular piece of knowledge.[6] As Arthur Schlesinger suggests, "It is precisely the disinterested passion for great ideas, not the professional manipulation of small ones, which distinguishes the intellectual."[7]

The "disinterested passion" for great ideas that Schlesinger believes characterizes intellectuals is surely active some of the time. However, it often seems that intellectuals are rather passionately involved with their chosen ideas, perhaps because as a general condition they live, as Lewis Coser implies, for ideas, rather than off them.[8] Furthermore, the intellectual by nature searches for the truth, or at the very least, a truth. In fact, some scholars consider the pursuit or the propagation of truth as the functional definition of an intellectual.[9] This description does seem to ring true, since many examples can be given of the artist, scientist, or humanist who has discovered a new technique for conveying symbols to society, a new theory affecting people's relationship to the universe, or a new view of the role of the citizen vis à vis culture, and who is willing to persist and fight for the "truth" of his interpretations for many years. It would be fair to say that the "main work of intellectuals is fighting out the central arguments, and vying to be the ones who shape the spirit of their society."[10]

The intellectual's desire to command the direction of society is often translated into an intense feeling for certain chosen beliefs. Furthermore, as secular ideas have received greater attention in the twentieth century, and as political participation has increased, ideology itself has become a predominant influence in the political world and in intellectual life. The extent to which ideological currents have influenced the twentieth-century milieu has caused some observers of intellectual life to make ideology part of the definition of an intellectual. Lewis Feuer best expresses this view when he states that "no scientist or scholar is regarded as an intellectual unless he adheres to or seems to be searching for an ideology."[11] Feuer's flexibility in including the view that searching for an ideology is as important as actually achieving one is useful, since many intellectuals know more about who they are *not* than about who they *are*, in an ideological sense. Many never belong, no matter what their age, to any ideological camp. Those who do choose a definite ideological framework from which to expound their larger views of society are not likely to be intellectuals if they spend their time watching out for deviations from the given goals of their ideology. Rather, they are those who propose new goals.[12] In my view, an individual does not need to be an ideologist to qualify as an intellectual, and although most, especially those from humanistic and literary backgrounds, will be searching for a general philosophy, some, especially artists, unless their method of expressing artistic symbols can be described as an ideology, have little desire to search for an ideology.

A number of other important concepts emerge from the multitude of definitions put forth for intellectuals. One of the common popular conceptions, and indeed, a view shared by many intellectuals, is that they are confined to certain disciplines. Marcus Cunliffe conceived of the intellectual as an artist, poet, dramatist, novelist, and occasionally a composer, or at the very least a well-informed critic of one or more of the arts.[13] To his list, most intellectuals would also add other disciplines from the humanities and the social sciences. Whether Cunliffe's definition or a broader one that includes the humanities, fine arts, and some of the social sciences is used, there is little justification for excluding the scientist, lawyer, psychologist, or other individual solely on the basis of profession. It is true, however, that, in the view of both Mexican and North American elite intellectuals, literary types dominate their ranks. From the point of view of Mexican intellectuals, one of the reasons scientists often are excluded is that few political and cultural elites themselves come from scientific backgrounds or have been raised in an environment in which historically a high value has been placed on scientific endeavors.[14]

Later in this book, I shall conclude that certain disciplines in Mexico, and indeed universally, are more common than others among intellectuals. But the frequent presence of some disciplines and not of others should not automatically preclude there being "intellectual" disciplines. Thus, although humanistic and literary backgrounds abound, it is the aforementioned attributes that determine intellectual qualifications. In trying to explain why scientists might not be common to the North American intellectual elite, Charles Kadushin also suggests that the intellectual is an expert in dealing with high-quality general ideas on questions of values and esthetics and communicates judgments on these matters to a fairly general audience.[15]

The emphasis intellectuals give to a discussion of values and esthetics also suggests why they deal with abstract concepts, whether in reference to humanity, society, nature, art, or the cosmos.[16] Furthermore, the emphasis on values explains another characteristic of intellectuals: their role as interpreters of contemporary experiences as well as commentators on contemporary culture.[17]

Because intellectuals involve themselves with interpreting values, they have had to develop, by necessity, a language Alvin Gouldner appropriately labels "critical-reflexive discourse."[18] Gouldner argues that intellectuals universally agree that their positions be defended by rational arguments and that the status of the individual making the argument should have no bearing on the outcome. Intellectuals, if Gouldner is correct, not only accept such critical discourse as a given, but indeed, must become adept at it. Because their discourse involves values and esthetics, necessarily subjective topics, it is only natural that an enquiring mind must also be a critical one. As Coser suggests, "Intellectuals are gatekeepers of ideas and fountainheads of ideologies, but, unlike medieval churchmen or modern political propagandists and zealots, they tend at the same time to cultivate a critical attitude; they tend to scrutinize the received ideas and assumptions of their times and *milieu*. They are those who 'think otherwise,' the disturbers of intellectual peace."[19] Because intellectuals disturb the "intellectual peace" of their times, they are frequently seen as social critics, and more important, as antiestablishment or antiregime figures.

It seems fair to consider social criticism as part of the definition of an intellectual, if one is interested in those intellectuals who are largely concerned with obtaining a more humane and more rational social order.[20] This is a goal of most socially conscious intellectuals, but it is not a necessary prerequisite to becoming an intellectual, nor should creative and critical intellectuals be required to have a social goal in mind when they contribute to their particular discipline or activity. Social criticism has become so identified with the term "intellectual" that most people assume that an intellectual must favor those variously called "liberal," "avant garde," or "radical." Yet, conservatives are no less social critics than are liberals; rather, it is the direction of their criticism and their value premises that differ.

Equally important to understanding what an intellectual is, and central to the task of defining an intellectual, is the further premise, widely held, that intellectuals are alienated and antiestablishment. Although Marx seemed to imply in his references to intellectuals that they are instinctively engaged in a constant struggle with established institutions, including the state, such a struggle could be carried on within such institutions and in support of established institutions and against change.[21] Intellectuals by nature tend to be critical of the present because of what Lionel Trilling first described as a predisposition toward an adversary culture. He remarked that "any historian of the literature of the modern age will take virtually for granted the adversary intention, the actually subversive intention, that characterizes modern writing."[22] Again, words like *adversary* and *subversive* imply an opponent and a destructive intent, but they are not necessarily directed toward all institutional structures, or more specifically toward those in the public sector.

To these explanations of an intellectual can be added that of the most popular of revived theorists on intellectuals, Antonio Gramsci, who argued many years ago that intellectuals view themselves as autonomous from the ruling class.[23] Gramsci's point is important because he correctly suggests that this conceptualization *originates with intellectuals themselves*, not with students of intellectual life. Of the more than two dozen definitions of intellectuals I have encountered, not one includes independence from the state, although several definitions talk about the predisposition of the intellectual to work outside of the establishment and to be individualistic.

These definitions have many commonalities, but by themselves, each is incomplete. More often than not, because definitions are too narrow or too broad, social scientists, in their usual fashion, have tried to identify subgroups of intellectuals.[24] Most of these categorizations have sought to separate the political intellectual from the artistic intellectual, or the establishment intellectual from the antiestablishment intellectual.[25] Although such efforts are useful in analyzing the *role* of intellectuals, they are less helpful in defining "intellectual," since it can easily be seen that individuals perform many functions in a lifetime, or change emphases.

My analysis of these many definitions brings us back to the original question. How does one define an intellectual? In the Introduction, I discussed Charles Kadushin's methodological definition of an elite intellectual as simply a person "whom other elite intellectuals believe to be an elite intellectual,"[26] a phrase that Bruce-Briggs has modified for all intellectuals to "those who are recognized as such by other intellectuals."[27] This is an easy way out of the dilemma but is seriously deficient as a meaningful definition. If we do not know beforehand who an intellectual is, we are compelled to define such a group in order to ask members who they believe intellectuals to be.

But why are we really examining intellectuals? Surely not only to find out what intellectuals think about each other? Whom intellectuals consider important and whom they read are valuable and essential pieces in understanding the larger picture, but what they think may not be the most significant part of the picture. Briefly, if we expect intellectuals to play an important role in their society by influencing political leaders and professional people, then whom these latter groups consider to be important is of equal significance. The senator's senator, the baseball player's player, and the actor's actor are not necessarily the choice of the general, educated public, or some other professional group. This difference in choices has definitely been shown to be true in an earlier study I made of Mexican intellectual elites.[28]

It is incumbent on me to offer a definition of an intellectual with the foreknowledge that it will not be satisfactory to all readers. *An intellectual is an individual who creates, evaluates, analyzes, or presents transcendental symbols, values, ideas, and interpretations on a regular basis to a broad audience.* This definition does not see the intellectual as discipline-bound, but as an innovator in one or more disciplines who is comfortable in and communicates with others in different fields. Creativity is essential to this definition, for although the intellectual may be a critic, social or otherwise, his criticism must raise new, cosmopolitan perspectives and not merely be a catholic, scholarly exercise. Further, expressions of his cultural product to a broad audience guarantee that the intellectual will be known to other elites, and to the well educated.

A Mexican Intellectual's Definition

My definition of an intellectual is founded on the observations and experiences of a Western, Anglo-Saxon, democratic culture rather than on a Latin culture with an undemocratic tradition. Because Mexico falls into this latter category, it is important to examine how Mexicans define the term "intellectual," especially Mexican intellectuals and politicians, since the former's self-perception determines to some extent the role they play and who they read, and the latter's conceptualization affects who they listen to and recruit into government.

Many of Mexico's prominent intellectuals willingly commented on their views of the term "intellectual," although the complexity of the term naturally makes spontaneous definitions difficult. Two members of Mexico's intellectual group, from different eras and different backgrounds and viewed by others as elite intellectuals, provided two rather complete concepts. According to Ignacio Chávez, world-famous cardiologist, man of letters, and former president of the National University, an intellectual is someone having a broad "education, not necessarily formal, and the know-how to use his intellect to accomplish a goal."[29] On the other hand, an independent political essayist, Alejandro Gómez Arias, stated that, "in Mexico, we would understand an intellectual to be someone who handles ideas and disperses them to a broad audience, who has a cultural foundation more or less very broad, and who believes that his ideas should be taken into account."[30] These two definitions are compatible and seem to differ little from those offered by North American intellectuals and scholars, although Mexican intellectuals felt the term was used somewhat differently in Mexico than elsewhere. Among the many definitions the Mexican intellectuals gave, five common characteristics emerged: the use of intellect to live, the search for truth, the emphasis on the humanities, the creative bent, and the critical posture.

The idea that an intellectual is an intelligent human being who is dedicated to intellectual pursuits and who exercises his or her intelligence has been stated well by José Rogelio Alvarez, editor-in-chief of one of Mexico's most successful recent intellectual enterprises, *The Encyclopedia of Mexico*:

There are many confusions about what an intellectual is in Mexico. It occurs to me on first reflection that the character of an intellectual describes a person, who, when working, fundamentally utilizes his intelligence as the major focus of his work, whether it is in a profession or an occupation involving labor. This is important because many persons confuse the professional with the intellectual, and these are not the same.[31]

Thus, intellectuals from both cultures see their peers as performing intellectual labors. However, that alone is not sufficient to qualify a person for inclusion in this group in Mexican society.

For most Mexicans, it is not just what an intellectual does, but, similar to several North American observations, it is the attitude, the mental stance that qualifies someone for membership in the intellectual circle. Miguel Palacios Macedo, a political activist and influential figure with regard to economic legislation in the 1920s and 1930s, saw this element as a necessary ingredient: "An intellectual is in a privileged position. He is always looking for a way to resist lies. He is a person who might be considered a prophet, a person called upon to tell the truth, to examine what exists, and does not, in each country. It is an attitude."[32] Representing intellectuals from the plastic arts, Pedro Ramírez Vázquez, one of Mexico's most well-known architects, designer of the world-famous Museum of Anthropology and History, emphasized that the search for truth was better reflected in the esthetic quality or beauty of the intellectual product. To him, "beauty is the highest form of truth. If there is truth and honesty in the analysis of a problem, in the objectives for society, and in the use of materials, then the resulting product will also reflect beauty. For me, the space vehicles that have been built are an example of this kind of creation, and even though there was not a preoccupation with form, the result was a beautiful object."[33]

The element most common to the Mexican intellectual's definition of an intellectual is an emphasis on a humanistic background. For example, Luis Villoro, a politically active historian and member of the National College, thought that, "in Mexico, as far as the general means of communication are concerned, the term usually excludes scientists and refers to a man of letters, someone knowledgeable about the humanities, who can make a contribution to various disciplines or areas of study. If a specialist, even a scientist, goes beyond his own area and presents ideas or interpretations broad in scope, then he too would fall under this definition."[34]

Many Mexicans commenting on this humanistic background did not, like Villoro, automatically exclude scientists and others, but they repeatedly implied that it was natural in Mexico to do so. Furthermore, as the data in table 2 demonstrate, even elite intellectuals, when choosing their influential colleagues, largely omitted nonhumanistic individuals. According to the intellectuals who have provided these responses, not *one* scientist was thought to be sufficiently influential to be included among their choices. The literary and humanistic fields combined account for two-thirds of their choices. When North American experts and Mexican politicians are making the choices, other fields are better represented, especially fine arts and the sciences.

One provincial dramatist, reflecting on the reasons why Mexicans exclude certain groups, suggested that they stem from "the lack of ability of people talented in these disciplines to express themselves. The result is that many Mexicans spend a lot of time talking about fields they do not understand while pretending to understand them. They take the place of the experts while not really being experts."[35] For example, the late Daniel Cosío

Table 2
Intellectual Fields Represented among Mexican Intellectuals
(Percentage)

Group	Intellectual Field[a]					
	Literature	Fine Arts	Law	Humanities	Sciences	Social Sciences
Intellectuals selected by other Mexican intellectuals[b] (N=50)	34	4	10	32	0	20
All Mexican intellectuals[c] (N=320)	25	14	4	29	9	18

Notes: [a]For the purposes of this table, "literature" refers to poetry, essays, fiction, and drama; "fine arts" to architecture, plastic arts, and music; "law" to all fields of public law; "humanities" to history, philosophy, classics, archeology, religion, and education; "sciences" to physical and natural sciences, medicine, and mathematics; and "social sciences" to economics, political science, sociology, and anthropology.
[b]Those intellectuals selected by other Mexican intellectuals as having been most influential in Mexico from 1920 to 1980. See table 3 for those chosen and the respondents, and the Introduction for how they were chosen.
[c]These data are from the *MIBP*.

Villegas, one of Mexico's foremost historians, found himself, at the end of his life, writing popular political analyses on presidential succession and politics, a task no Mexican political scientist sought to undertake. Cosío Villegas himself thought that his effort, a commercial and popular success, was more important than the major historical work responsible for his international reputation.[36]

It is only natural to expect intellectuals to try their hand at other disciplines, since Mexicans too see the intellectual as someone with the broadest of interests.[37] Furthermore, the creative urge is a distinctive element in the intellectual's self-definition. The sculptor Angela Gurría saw the intellectual as "a person who is creative at his particular moment in life and interested in all that happens at that moment. Such a person cannot be an observer, but must be a participant in the use of his creative talents."[38] On the other hand, another Mexican sees the intellectual's creativity shifting from ideas to organizations. For him, "what is important today is that the intellectual is beginning to create something new—industrial enterprises to produce those products that use intellectual ideas. In a certain way, then, the intellectual is being a creator, not a creator of ideas as in the past, but a creator of cultural factories, something essential to the expansion and development of cultural life in Mexico."[39] The importance of contributing cultural factories can be seen in the career of historian Daniel Cosío Villegas, so admirably documented by his biographer, Enrique Krauze.[40]

Like their North American counterparts, Mexican intellectuals see a critical function as a necessary ingredient in their definition. Not surprisingly, because he himself has frequently played this role, Octavio Paz consistently refers to this intellectual characteristic in his writings and in interviews. For example, in *The Labyrinth of Solitude* he refers to the intellectual as the critical consciousness of the Mexican people, and in another instance, as one whose vital activity is critical thinking.[41] In 1978, in an interview with me, he reaffirmed this view:

Our conceptualization of what an intellectual is has changed over the centuries. Today, intellectuals are closely related to ideologies, criticism, and in recent years, they have become more and more political. Even artists, who often resent being involved in these issues, have become more political. Political opinions have replaced religion, and writers, such as García Lorca in Spain, who have been nonpolitical, have been equal victims of political repression and censorship.[42]

In the view of one Mexican intellectual, the inclusion of the word *critical* in the definition of his peers is what limits membership to a small number of individuals.[43] Therefore, this concept becomes decisive in the Mexican intellectual's interpretation of the term "intellectual." Again, we encounter an element of subjectivity when we try to measure or describe the presence of a critical function in the intellectual. One Mexican poet saw this critical ingredient as a psychic force, a mental attitude of sufficient magnitude to unsettle others. Like the stage presence of a great actor, the intellectual's ideas project a special quality. He argues that "at a conceptual level he is a person who by his very great stillness can cause or provoke enormous movements; that is, his pure ideas and unrest can provoke such movements. In the particular case of Mexico, it is very difficult for an intellectual to cause this type of physical movement outside of his own personal sphere."[44]

Each of the five concepts described earlier is common to the North American interpretations of an intellectual. The most striking feature of the Mexican intellectual's self-appraisal, as differing from that proposed by the North American, is his or her attitude toward the political activity or involvement of the intellectual. Interestingly, Mexican intellectuals made no reference to being independent of the state. One could argue that they may have automatically assumed this, but this does not appear to be the case. On the contrary, several individuals emphasized political activity as essential, and still others suggested that public involvement is necessary. Víctor Manuel Villaseñor, whose intellectual contributions have been in the political sphere and whose career has more often than not been in the public sector, argues that "it is critical to the definition of an intellectual that a person maintain a well-defined and clear point of view during his lifetime (not necessarily the same point of view), and have an influence on public life or politics."[45]

More concrete evidence of the intellectual's attitude toward public service can be seen in my survey of the career backgrounds of Mexican intellectuals from 1920 to the present. An incredible 28 percent made government service their full-time career. Those who were full-time professors or university administrators accounted for an additional 25 percent. Whereas over a fourth of the intellectuals chose public service for their life careers, more than half served the government in some capacity, if not for most of their lives (see table 1).[46]

Further confirmation of the phenomenon of intellectuals with public careers can be found in my examination of elite intellectuals. If we again look only at those intellectuals selected by other intellectuals as being most influential in Mexico, we find that, of the fifty individuals who are members of this elite (see table 3), twenty-three, or 46 percent, held a national political office of some sort. These figures indicate that, regardless of the criteria used to determine intellectual membership, the Mexican intellectual has long been active in the public sector, and furthermore, that intellectuals themselves are not averse to including the intellectual in government on a list of influential peers.

The Mexican intellectual is not the only person influenced by other intellectuals and worthy of defining them. It is more likely that the intellectual, if he is to have a significant influence on society, must affect the

Table 3
Mexico's Elite Intellectuals as Viewed by Other Intellectuals
(N=50)

Intellectuals Most Frequently Selected

* Octavio Paz (23)	José Gaos (4)
* Carlos Fuentes (14)	Agustín Yáñez (4)
* José Vasconcelos (14)	Juan Rulfo (3)
* Vicente Lombardo Toledano (13)	Carlos Pellicer (3)
* Daniel Cosío Villegas (11)	Edmundo O'Gorman (3)
* Narciso Bassols (10)	Mariano Azuela (3)
* Antonio Caso (10)	* Samuel Ramos (3)
* Manuel Gómez Morín (10)	* Alfonso Caso (3)
* Jesús Silva Herzog (7)	Víctor Urquidi (3)
* Jaime Torres Bodet (7)	Manuel Gamio (2)
Carlos Monsiváis (7)	* Antonio Carrillo Flores (2)
Gabriel Zaid (7)	* Jesús Reyes Heroles (2)
* Pablo González Casanova (6)	Silvio Zavala (2)
José Emilio Pacheco (6)	Luis Spota (2)
* Luis Cabrera (6)	Lucio Mendieta y Núñez (2)
* Diego Rivera (6)	Martín Luis Guzmán (2)
Víctor Flores Olea (6)	Enrique González Pedrero (2)
* Alfonso Reyes (5)	Luis González y González (2)
Luis Villoro (5)	Leopoldo Zea (2)
* Gastón García Cantú (5)	Gustavo Saínz (2)
José Luis Martínez (5)	Vicente Leñero (2)
Elena Poniatowska (4)	* José Clemente Orozco (2)
Jaime García Terrés (4)	Rodolfo Stavenhagen (2)
Héctor Aguilar Camín (4)	Enrique Krauze (2)
Fernando Benítez (4)	Carlos Pereyra (2)

Notes: Each respondent was asked to select up to fifteen prominent intellectuals. Forty-one Mexican intellectuals, artists, and academicians responded: Roberto L. Mantilla Molina, Ricardo Rivera Pérez, Raúl Cardiel Reyes, Lucio Mendieta y Núñez, Antonio Carrillo Flores, César Sepúlveda, Leopoldo Zea, José Emilio Pacheco, Miguel Palacios Macedo, Fernando Benítez, Pedro Ramírez Vásquez, José Alvarez, Jesús Reyes Heroles, Father Daniel Olmedo, Manuel Becerra Acosta, Edmundo O'Gorman, Gastón García Cantú, Martha Robles, Carlos Monsiváis, Ignacio Chávez, Octavio Paz, José Joaquín Blanco, Abel Quezada, Jaime García Terrés, Arturo Warman, Agustín Yáñez, Luis Villoro, Enrique Krauze, Alberto Vázquez del Mercado, Víctor Manuel Villaseñor, Jorge Espinosa de los Reyes, Jr., Enrique Espinosa, Angela Gurría, Ricardo Guerra, Salvador Elizondo, Paulina Lavista, Alejandro Gómez Arias, Enrique Florescano, Juan O'Gorman, and Cristina Barros de Stivalet.

Mexican intellectuals provided 126 names. The number of times an individual's name was mentioned appears in parentheses behind his or her name. Only those intellectuals receiving at least two votes appear in the table.

An asterisk next to an individual's name indicates that he also appears in table 4.

views of public figures. Therefore, it is important to understand the way in which Mexican public figures define intellectuals, since their interpretations, in part, determine whom they listen to and the role intellectuals play.

A Mexican Public Figure's Definition

An examination of the definitions that prominent public figures have provided suggests that there is a decidedly more activist tone to their conceptualization. They seem to emphasize four important qualities: a focus on ideas, a breadth of knowledge, the commitment to communicating their views, and a belief in the necessity of the intellectual's being active in public life. In contrast to the intellectual, they place less value on a humanistic preparation and on independence from public life. However, their concern with ideas has been well expressed by Antonio Armendáriz, a cultured public figure prominent in finance:

The fundamental preoccupation of the intellectual is with ideas. It is impossible to separate the function of teaching and studying from the intellectual because he does both. An intellectual can be a member of any profession, but it is not the technical knowledge he has to serve his profession; rather it is his constant devotion to thinking, to creating, to imagining new ideas that distinguishes him from his professional colleagues, activities from which he never rests.[47]

Mexicans who are active in public life, much like Octavio Paz and others, see the intellectual as a person of ideas. Moreover, there is a logical connection between the public figure's emphasis on ideas and his own concern with ideology. Since public figures themselves are likely to be ideologically committed, they see this commitment as important to the intellectual. Furthermore, their concern with practical issues and the problems of their society gives their stress on ideas a realistic tone. Mexican public figures see intellectuals as realists or people who express themselves "about the reality of their situation."[48]

The public figure in Mexico, although not seeing intellectuals as humanists per se, does see them as having a breadth of knowledge and interest beyond the bounds of individual disciplines. One former secretary of labor and senator saw the intellectual as a "person who deals not only with his personal achievements, but who in a sincere way goes beyond himself and forms broad views of the society he lives in."[49] Or, as a long-time ambassador suggested, an intellectual "is interested in all human affairs and their consequences, and is willing and able to take a stand on the issues he deems transcendental."[50]

The Mexican public figure's lack of emphasis on the intellectual's humanistic and literary experiences is strongly reflected in the intellectual fields of those persons they considered most important in intellectual life. A breakdown of the fields of the intellectuals they respect shows the following: literature, 8 percent; fine arts, 11 percent; law, 34 percent; humanities, 24 percent; science, 11 percent; social sciences, 13 percent.[51] Thus, literary and humanistic fields combined account for only 32 percent of the backgrounds of intellectuals chosen by public figures, in contrast to 66 percent of those selected by other intellectuals (table 2). Furthermore, unlike the choices made by intellectuals, elite intellectuals selected by public figures are well represented in the artistic and scientific fields. Most important, the choices of those in public life, whose own careers have generally begun in the practice of law, accentuated intellectuals with legal interests.

It would also be fair to say that public figures stress that intellectuals must communicate their ideas to others, most often through writing. In part, this emphasis stems from their view, reflecting their own personal commitment to public life, that Mexican intellectuals should not and cannot be ivory-tower figures lost unto themselves or their academic colleagues. Antonio Martínez Báez, secretary of industry and commerce in the 1940s, argued that, "fundamentally, an intellectual is a person in the field of letters who uses his academic formation to devote himself to the fruit of his mental work; that is to say, an intellectual needs to express the result of his thoughts, to communicate it, not just examine it."[52] But, unlike the North American or Mexican intellectual, who generally suggests that a broad audience is the target of this communication process, the public figure is concerned that only educated peers be the recipients of intellectual ideas.

But the majority of Mexican public figures go beyond this definition, arguing that the intellectual can and should be a public actor. Those Mexicans who have been most active in public life vigorously believe the two roles not only are interchangeable, but are one. They do not believe that all public figures are intellectuals, but rather that all intellectuals *should* be public figures. For example, Rosa Luz Alegría, the first woman appointed to a cabinet post in Mexico, argued that "the intellectual should be someone who has an obligation to society, he is a person who is representative of his time, and nothing is foreign to him. There are many intellectuals in name, but few in practice, using my definition."[53]

That public figures focus on a politically active role for the intellectual clearly reflects their choice of Mexicans who are most influential in intellectual life. A breakdown of the career backgrounds of elite intellectuals chosen by Mexican public figures as most influential since 1920 (table 4) reveals that, of the thirty-eight individuals, twenty-nine, or 76 percent, followed public careers, whereas only nine, or 24 percent, spent their lives in academic or independent professions. Thus, although Mexican intellectuals give considerable importance to intellectuals with public careers (table 3), in

Table 4
Mexico's Elite Intellectuals as Viewed by Mexico's Public Figures
(N=38)

Intellectuals Most Frequently Selected

* Vicente Lombardo Toledano (15)	David Alfaro Siqueiros (3)
* Manuel Gómez Morín (15)	Ignacio García Téllez (3)
* José Vasconcelos (15)	* Samuel Ramos (3)
* Narciso Bassols (11)	* Gastón García Cantú (2)
* Luis Cabrera (11)	* Pablo González Casanova (2)
* Daniel Cosío Villegas (10)	Víctor Manuel Villaseñor (2)
* Antonio Caso (6)	Nabor Carrillo Flores (2)
* Jesús Silva Herzog (7)	Isidro Fabela (2)
* Jaime Torres Bodet (7)	Enrique González Aparicio (2)
* Alfonso Caso (6)	Sotero Prieto (2)
Eduardo Suárez (6)	Manuel Sandoval Vallarta (2)
Antonio Díaz Soto y Gama (5)	Gabino Fraga (2)
* Alfonso Reyes (5)	Manuel Borja Soriano (2)
* Jesús Reyes Heroles (4)	* José Clemente Orozco (2)
Ignacio Chávez (4)	Rufino Tamayo (2)
* Octavio Paz (4)	Francisco Mújica (2)
Alberto Vázquez del Mercado (3)	* Antonio Carrillo Flores (2)
Miguel Othón de Mendizábal (3)	* Carlos Fuentes (2)
* Diego Rivera (3)	Mario de la Cueva (2)

Notes: Each respondent was asked to select up to fifteen intellectuals. Twenty-one political leaders responded to letters or personal interviews: Rosa Luz Alegría, Manuel Hinojosa Ortiz, José Juan de Olloqui, Leopoldo Solís, Luis de la Peña Porth, Andrés Serra Rojas, Fernando Zertuche Muñoz, Enrique Beltrán, Pedro Daniel Martínez, Sealtiel Alatriste, Antonio Armendáriz, Praxedis Balboa, Raúl Rangel Frías, Ricardo José Zevada, Mariano Azuela Rivera, Javier Gaxiola, José Angel Conchello, Alfonso Pulido Islas, Antonio Martínez Báez, and Gonzalo Robles.

Public figures provided ninety-nine names. The number of times an individual's name was mentioned appears in parentheses behind his name. Only those persons receiving a vote from two or more respondents were considered for inclusion in the table.

An asterisk by the name indicates that the person is also listed in table 3.

comparison with Mexican public figures, their emphasis is not nearly as obvious.

The differing images intellectuals and public figures have of elite intellectuals can be further underscored by examining the data in tables 3 and 4. If we look only at those elite intellectuals who are *excluded* from each group's list, the division becomes clear. Of the eighteen intellectuals on the public figures' list who did not appear on the list chosen by other intellectuals, an overwhelming percentage (72) followed careers in the public sector. If, on the other hand, we examine those intellectuals considered by Mexican intellectuals and academics to be part of an elite group, but excluded from the list chosen by public figures, we find the precise inverse relationship; that is, an overwhelming percentage (72) followed academic or independent careers.

Conclusions

What does this mean for intellectual life? As I surmised in an earlier article, Mexican intellectuals and political leaders, although sharing an appreciation for some of the same intellectual leaders, are also definitely being influenced by two distinct groups, as shown by the fact that eighteen, or nearly half, of the elite intellectuals thought to be important by Mexican public figures *did not even appear* on the list compiled from Mexican intellectuals' responses.[54] Furthermore, an even larger proportion of elite intellectuals (thirty, or 60 percent) appearing among the choices of Mexican intellectuals, did not appear on the list compiled from public figures' choices. Thus, each group really looks toward a different set of intellectual leaders. The significance of this is that

many intellectuals feel that they are not being listened to. They are correct. While politicians are not allergic to intellectuals as a group, many resent intellectuals who remain outside of public life. Therefore, politicians may be listening to one group of intellectuals, while intellectuals look to another group, those outside public life, as their own leaders. Thus, suspicion will grow between the two groups, and the gap between public policy and intellectual life may widen if politicians' and intellectuals' perceptions of each other cannot be reconciled and their relationship clarified.[55]

Furthermore, these findings demonstrate that their own professional orientations and career choices influence both intellectuals and public figures in their definition and their perceptions of elite intellectuals. They both are somewhat narrow-minded in whom they read or listen to, and by whom they choose to be influenced. Intellectuals in Mexico place a higher value on the independent intellectual, although career data for all intellectuals show them to have been in the minority among their peers in the twentieth century, especially among prominent cultural elites. Public figures, however, place a much stronger emphasis on elite intellectuals who, like themselves, have devoted their lives to a public career. That intellectuals are most impressed with literary and humanistic figures, whereas public figures give more credibility to the legal mind and to the scientist suggests an important division between the two. The politicians place value on being active and pragmatic, characteristics that have obvious implications. However, typical intellectuals in Mexico are excluding, almost automatically, entire fields of creative thought from their definitions and consideration.

As technology becomes more important, as it has in Mexico, traditional elite intellectuals must open their minds to the scientific thinker who can offer value judgments on the implications of applied technology. If humanistic intellectuals continue to divorce themselves from the ideas of their scientific colleagues, they will commit a fatal intellectual error and strengthen a division already found in the ranks of Mexican intellectuals. Although many of the issues that the policymaker in Mexico faces have moral and spiritual overtones, they also imply important choices in methods as well as goals. Breadth in today's intellectual means keeping himself or herself as well apprised of the pragmatic choices as of the ethical choices because the two are interrelated. To do this, intellectuals must read and exchange ideas with scientific and artistic colleagues, who approach issues from technological as well as esthetic perspectives.

Similarly, the public figure has to become more receptive to the critical ideas of Mexico's leading literary figures, especially the younger thinkers, many of whom have constructive suggestions to offer for Mexico's problems. If Mexico's political leadership continues to be influenced by one group of intellectuals, and intellectuals themselves seek leadership from another group, the influence intellectuals as a group can have on the policy arena in Mexico, and the number of possible alternatives from which political decision-makers might choose, will be reduced.

The differing views both groups have as to what an intellectual in Mexican society is also determine the role that individual plays and the influence he might exert on society. The next chapter examines briefly the historical role of the intellectual in Mexico and Latin America in the context of the universal perception of that role and the perceptions of Mexico's intellectual and political community, and why intellectuals may or may not be important to Mexico's future.

4. The Function of the Mexican Intellectual

The definition of an intellectual determines to some extent the role intellectuals play because it sets boundaries by which mentors, peers, and society in general socialize them. On the other hand, the role intellectuals play has affected their perception of themselves historically and helps to perpetuate a self-fulfilling pattern of behavior that coincides with their image of that role. Because the cause-and-effect relationship between definition and role is circular, little benefit can be obtained from pursuing it; rather, it is important only to recognize that a significant association exists between the definition of and the role actually played by the intellectual.

Many students of the intellectual have sought to identify meaningful causes for the intellectual's role. Actually, some of these causes are quite complex, and are probably overshadowed by a society's political structure and level of economic development. In general, intellectuals in an industrialized society can play roles different from those in a nonindustrialized society because of the variety of opportunities open to them. Furthermore, the degree of authoritarianism in a political structure, as measured by control over written and oral communication, art, music, and other symbolic forms, determines intellectual activities. These societal characteristics— essentially structural—modify universal perceptions about the roles intellectuals can or should play.[1] The controls over mass media, whether by the government or other groups, are so important to the role of the intellectual that I shall devote an entire chapter to them in Mexico.

Social Conditions and the Intellectual's Role

The influence the level of economic development has on intellectuals' activities is worth discussing here. The most significant social and economic determinants are level of education, literacy, distribution of income, and employment opportunities. In Europe an increase in the size of the reading public produced a corresponding increase in the demand for the goods intellectuals create. Furthermore, the growth of the middle class, especially of its control over politics, its demand for higher education, and the change in the social role of middle-class women, contributed to an environment favorable to an expansion in the number of intellectuals.[2]

Although Europe witnessed most of these changes in the eighteenth and nineteenth centuries, they did not take place in Mexico until after the 1910 Revolution. It is clear that after 1920 a new group of middle-class leaders, themselves well educated, emerged as Mexico's politicians.[3] Moreover, the middle class demanded and its leaders instituted wide-ranging programs in public education designed to expand literacy and to increase the numbers of college-educated technicians capable of managing the cultural, economic, and political organizations of society. Often, intellectuals-turned-politicians directed these programs, thus leaving Mexico with an educational legacy supportive of their own expanded role in society. But the process has been exceedingly slow, in part because resources were used elsewhere or devoted to *higher* education, and in part because population grew so rapidly.[4]

Deficiencies in education and literacy have a twofold effect on intellectual life. Most frequently mentioned is the impact these conditions have on the demand for intellectual goods, and, hence, on the employment opportunities for those who wish to use their intellectual skills on a full-time basis. Regardless of their field, most intellectuals write in order to communicate to a broad audience. Thus, as Fred Ellison suggests, "the high illiteracy rate, prohibitive costs of paper and equipment, ineffective distribution of books (especially to the interior), the low purchasing power of the populace, and inflation all contribute to the financial insecurity of the writer."[5] This financial insecurity has forced the intellectual into certain forms of employment. In fact, it could be argued that intellectuals in developing countries generally, and in Latin America particularly, have sought public careers because alternative economic opportunities were unavailable.

Underdevelopment also produces a subtler result, stemming from the intellectual's product. Whether intellectuals in Mexico must seek employment with the state or be self-employed or independent, their source of employment determines the characteristics of their product. Gabriel Zaid, an important Mexican poet and essayist unknown to most North Americans, argues that it is not the same thing to have the masses as your client as it is to work for a superior. He believes that the intellectual product of a dependent intellectual (one who works for an employer) is a distinct work for a special client, different from something produced by the independent intellectual.[6]

Economic conditions, control over the mass media, level of education and literacy, all influence the intellectual's role in society. The interaction among these variables also has an effect on intellectuals, since, like all individuals, they are products of their environment. Thus, the role of the intellectual can be swiftly altered, according to some observers, by the era in which he lives.[7] Even the pace of change from one time period to the next produces different intellectual functions, a quality identified by George Lichtheim: the reactions of Third World intellectuals "differ even more strikingly from those of their Western predecessors who grew up in a stabler environment with a slower tempo of change."[8] The rapid pace of development, often identified as a cause of societal frustration and frequently mirrored in the works of intellectuals, encourages intellectuals to experiment readily with a wide variety of political and economic theories of change and propels them to take antiestablishment positions. Sometimes intellectuals will exceed the level of frustration present in society as a whole, and their views, rather than reflecting those of the masses, will become interpretations of an isolated social group with few interclass ties.

The educational influence of Western culture in Mexico and Latin America, specifically that of North America and Western Europe, has not been carefully examined. Its influence on intellectual life in Mexico, although indirect, is substantial. Important among these influences is the degree to which the North American definition of an intellectual, and hence, its implication for the role intellectuals play, affects the educated Mexican's, and especially the intellectual's, own perception about that role. Mexican intellectuals are exposed in their domestic education, and in advanced studies abroad, to the works of leading North American scholars and intellectuals.[9] Furthermore, they frequently admit to being influenced by foreign authors and professionals in their respective fields.

In fact, it might be argued that one of the reasons scientists play a lesser role than other professionals in Mexican intellectual circles is that they often pattern themselves after their North American mentors. More than any other intellectual group, Mexican scientists have been educated, in Mexico or abroad, in the universal world of scientific culture dominated by North America.[10] If role modeling is important, then it is not surprising that scientific intellectuals, like their North American counterparts, have tended to remain outside of political activities. Although one cannot always predict the cause-effect relationship between the North American cultural values learned by these scientists and the roles they have followed, they are, by comparison, the least indigenous intellectual group in Mexico.[11]

Foreign Determinants of Intellectual Roles

Many nationalists and Marxists talk about "cultural imperialism," but few studies exist that examine its influence, whether on the masses or on a cultural elite. In Mexico, the obvious influences can be seen everywhere, but the more subtle, and perhaps more significant, effects have not been analyzed. The influence of cultural imperialism on intellectuals seems significant in Mexico because so much of the literature read there is produced in the United States. Foreign culture influences not so much the reader's opinions about the country from which that literature comes, as the theories and values the native culture applies to its problems, and the determining of its priorities.

Of the 332 intellectuals about whom I have travel information, exactly two-thirds have lived abroad for a year or more, making Mexican intellectuals of the twentieth century a well-traveled group. When intellectuals are broken down according to their ideological orientation (I have information on 221), we encounter little difference between the two most well-represented ideological groups, the neoliberals and Marxists, as far as their having lived abroad. Forty-eight percent of the neoliberals, compared with 41 percent (from data in the *MIBP*) of all intellectuals, have lived in the United States, whereas 36 percent of the Marxists have had this experience. Both neoliberals and Marxists were nearly comparable in terms of their living experiences in Europe. Therefore, the impressions neoliberal intellectuals have of the United States are formed more frequently from firsthand experience, whereas those of Mexican Marxists come from other sources. Although conclusions cannot be reached on the effects such travel has on the intellectual, differences in the residential experiences of the Marxist and non-Marxist do seem worth examining.

This foreign influence on the ideology of intellectuals and on their relationships is substantial. For example, because of the paucity of Mexican literature in a variety of disciplines, North American literature becomes an important substitute.[12] North Americans familiar with the Mexican scene read and review certain native intellectuals, help to publicize them, and indeed, certify them, in the eyes of both the Mexican and North American cultures. To be published in North America, to have a show in New York City, to perform a concert in Los Angeles, are measures of intellectual prestige. Prestige is like a snowball: it grows on a core of repeated recognition by others. But in those societies that are infants in developing a sense of national identity, international recognition carries more weight than national.

Preference for outside recognition is also due to the belief, not entirely unfounded, that merit plays a lesser role in the recognition given to Mexicans by their own prize committees, national institutions, and cultural academies than it does in recognition from foreign cultures. The belief that some personal connection or political motivation governs these awards in Mexico is widespread, whereas recognition from abroad is believed to be attained on the basis of merit.[13] Of course, cases exist of individuals with great artistic or political merit who become so closely associated with foreigners that they depreciate their image in Mexico. Such was the case of Rufino Tamayo, who, for years, sold his artistic works in New York galleries, but was not given the recognition he deserved in Mexico.[14] But, if we pass over those who have become overly identified with a foreign culture to the detriment of their own, we find that many intellectuals become more important in the eyes of the Mexican intellectual community *because* they are important in the eyes of the North American scholarly and intellectual community.

The influence of North American scholarship becomes self-perpetuating. North American authors and a new generation of Mexican intellectuals see certain individuals as more important than others, and as their views are reinforced by each other, the reputations of these individuals are built up on the scholarship of each new generation of scholars and intellectuals. Further, our higher education system is structured on the Ph.D. dissertation, and since the North American scholar most likely suggests the topic or individual to be examined by the graduate student, he can pass knowledge and prejudice on to a disciple. Thus, certain people can earn remarkable reputations among North American scholars, reputations not equally shared by other Mexican intellectual groups.

Moreover, because the North American scholarly community has more ties with the Mexican intellectual community than with Mexico's political leadership, their perceptions as to which intellectuals are important coincide more than they do with the views of politicians.[15] This is clearly illustrated in my examination of Mexico's intellectual elite, when the selections of elite intellectuals by other Mexican intellectuals and by Mexican politicians are compared with those made by a representative group of North American scholars. Of the forty-four individuals chosen as important intellectual figures in Mexico since 1920 by the North American scholarly community (table 5), thirty-one, or 70 percent, coincided with those selected by Mexican intellectuals, whereas only twenty, or 45 percent, of their choices could be found on the list provided by Mexican politicians.

It can be argued that one effect of the North American influence on Mexican intellectual life has been to help continue the division that exists between the two groups of intellectuals from separate intellectual fields and with different career orientations. This important North American influence can probably be found in other developing countries that lack a literate society, a well-established and diversified publishing industry, and broad educational opportunities. Further the North American scholar's outlook has an impact on the American foreign policy community's view of who is important and who should be listened to.[16] Embassy staffers use North American scholarship to identify who is considered important, and those whose views are translated into English have a wider audience among that community, so the North American scholarly and foreign policy communities definitely ignore certain groups of intellectuals.

The influence of education abroad on Mexico's intellectual community can be seen from the institutional perspective as well. Again, the

Table 5
Mexico's Elite Intellectuals as Viewed by North American Scholars
(N=44)

Intellectuals Most Frequently Selected

** José Vasconcelos (22)	* Lucio Mendieta y Núñez (4)
** Octavio Paz (20)	* Víctor Urquidi (4)
** Daniel Cosío Villegas (20)	** Jesús Reyes Heroles (3)
** Carlos Fuentes (18)	* Carlos Monsiváis (3)
** Samuel Ramos (15)	Rodolfo Usigli (3)
** Vicente Lombardo Toledano (13)	Gonzalo Aguirre Beltrán (3)
** Jaime Torres Bodet (13)	* Edmundo O'Gorman (3)
** Alfonso Reyes (13)	** José Clemente Orozco (3)
** Pablo González Casanova (12)	Andrés Molina Enríquez (3)
** Jesús Silva Herzog (11)	Julio Scherer García (3)
** Antonio Caso (10)	* Antonio Díaz Soto y Gama (3)
* Martín Luis Guzmán (9)	Ignacio Bernal (2)
* Agustín Yáñez (8)	Miguel León Portilla (2)
** Narciso Bassols (6)	Edmundo Flores (2)
* Manuel Gamio (6)	Ramón Beteta (2)
* Mariano Azuela (6)	Agustín Basave Fernández del Valle (2)
** Diego Rivera (5)	* Silvio Zavala (2)
* David Alfaro Siqueiros (5)	Moisés Sáenz (2)
** Alfonso Caso (5)	José C. Valadez (2)
** Manuel Gómez Morín (4)	* Juan Rulfo (2)
** Luis Cabrera (4)	* Rodolfo Stavenhagen (2)
* José Gaos (4)	* Luis Spota (2)

Notes: Each selected up to fifteen intellectuals. Twenty-four North American scholars responded to a questionnaire: Marvin Alisky, Rodney D. Anderson, David Charles Bailey, Lyle C. Brown, John S. Brushwood, Harold E. Davis, Gabriella De Beer, Susan Eckstein, Felicity Trueblood, William P. Glade, Charles A. Hale, John P. Harrison, Harold E. Hinds, Kenneth F. Johnson, Donald Mabry, Michael C. Meyer, Robert A. Monson, Martin C. Needler, Susan K. Purcell, William D. Raat, Patrick Romanell, Stanley Ross, Henry Schmidt, and Evelyn P. Stevens.

The North American respondents provided ninety-six names. Only those persons receiving a vote from two or more respondents were considered for inclusion in the table. The number of times an individual's name was mentioned appears in parentheses behind his name.

A single asterisk indicates that the intellectual's name also appears among those individuals thought to be important by other Mexican intellectuals (table 3) or by public figures (table 4). Two asterisks indicate that the person's name appears in both tables. No asterisk means, of course, that only North American scholars considered the person important.

methodological processes of a foreign culture can be decisive. For example, most Mexicans believe that the two most prestigious publicly funded institutions in Mexico, the Colegio de México and the National Autonomous University, clearly represent two educational models. The Colegio de México is patterned structurally after the elite North American graduate school, in that it uses a full-time faculty almost exclusively and provides virtually every student with sufficient aid to study full time.[17] Its ideological orientation is objective, scholarly, and, except for the fact that its publications are in Spanish, it mirrors the latest methodologies North Americans employ. Furthermore, it emphasizes the social sciences and history, not literature and the other humanities. As described by one of its graduates and professors,

el Colegio opened intellectual territories in the academic field by creating a new kind of social researcher unknown, until then, in our countries: the professional intellectual. Since then, El Colegio de México has had a fundamental influence in our cultural scenery: one of moderation, of avoidance of ideological nonsense (one of our main sicknesses), of scholarly outlook, method, theories and styles. In short: a new intellectual *ethos*.[18]

Daniel Cosío Villegas, an intellectual who studied in the United States and who involved himself professionally with North American scholarship, created and founded it. To some critical Mexican politicians, Cosío Villegas turned El Colegio de México into El Colegio de Texas.[19]

In contrast, the National Autonomous University, or as it is more commonly known, the National University, has followed a different course. It uses a predominance of part-time professors, a characteristic typical of Latin American public universities; it is often the subject of violent strikes and battles between contending ideological and political factions; and many of its textbooks are Marxist in tone and orientation, to the exclusion of other views.[20] Structurally, the National University is patterned after the European model, historically native to Latin America and Mexico. Ideologically, it is being heavily influenced by philosophical assumptions and methodologies equally foreign to its traditions and needs, but they are less likely to be from the United States, except in certain schools.

Again, the implication of the orientations found in these two influential institutions of higher education is that foreign intellectual approaches have determined the methodology of their intellectual process and, in the case of El Colegio, the very structure of the educational system. By borrowing intellectual approaches and educational systems, Mexico, like so many other developing countries, has failed to stimulate innovation and to some extent, self-confidence among its scholars and intellectuals. This phenomenon has been described well by Cinna Lomnitz, an internationally recognized seismologist, who argues that self-reliance is the key to creative, innovative scientific research in Mexico. He believes that Mexican scientists have permitted themselves to depend too heavily on their U.S. colleagues for the development of scientific programs and projects used in Mexico. He describes in glowing terms the self-confidence and savings in resources that came from developing, on their own, a computer software project to coordinate earthquake studies in Mexico during the 1970s.[21] Lomnitz's argument, however, also applies to the nonscientific disciplines, which have relied heavily on North American or European methodologies and processes as well.

Many of the features of North American cultural influence contribute to the low self-esteem intellectuals have. In the North American culture, according to Melvin Seeman, many "intellectuals adopt, without serious efforts to build a reasoned self-portrait, an essentially negative, minority view of themselves to find, in addition, some plausible ground for believing that this failure in self-conception is not independent of role performance."[22] Intellectuals in the United States are ready to accept stereotypical views of themselves without evidence that they are true. And, although it has been suggested that economic conditions greatly influence the role they play, according to one author, "The prestige or esteem accorded to the intellectual by his public, his psychic income, may often be more important to him than the economic return."[23] Two common illustrations of these statements come to mind. Intellectuals who believe, for example, that they should be arm-chair philosophers and who further believe that society has defined this as their task, may be less likely to venture out in search of a pragmatic role and to encourage peers to do the same. Once they believe themselves to be little valued by society, they are not likely to venture into the policy arena as leaders of other social groups. Instead, they will confine themselves to addressing peers and those with similar ideas from the new class.

Cultural Determinants of Intellectual Roles

The extent to which the North American intellectual's own view has been carried to Mexico is difficult, if not impossible, to measure. Historically, there are many reasons why the Mexican intellectual should have greater self-confidence and should be willing to engage pragmatically in political affairs. In the first place, although the Mexican media may be underdeveloped compared with that found in the United States or in Western Europe, the "outstanding characteristics of Latin American culture are the persistent esteem for humanistic education, the high regard for poetry and poets, and the comparatively widespread interest in reading literary criticism in newspapers."[24] Not only has a background in the humanities and literary skills been appreciated by the public, but intellectual qualifications, rather than being hidden, as is likely in the United States, are embellished,

publicized, and even fabricated by Mexican and Latin American politi- (
cians.[25]

In contrast to the North American culture, which has grudgingly supplied greater economic support for the intellectual, Latin American culture has provided a more enviable situation. Yet, in Mexico's past there seems to be a fluctuation between historical periods favorable to and strongly against the intellectual playing an important role in society. Despite the collaboration of an occasional intellectual of first-rate stature, such as Justo Sierra, the regime of Porfirio Díaz, which dominated the last two decades of the nineteenth century and the first decade of the twentieth was, as John Rutherford states, fundamentally anti-intellectual, a government run by an elite of hard-headed, businesslike technocrats.[26] During the 1920s and 1930s, after the Mexican Revolution, intellectual contributions to society in music, art, education, finance, and law enjoyed a renaissance never before experienced in Mexico. But as Mexico consolidated its political system and incorporated the new revolutionary values into law and into the educational system intellectuals were no longer sought after, because a highly educated intelligentsia of lawyer-politicians replaced them.

This pattern persists, modified only by the fact that newer disciplines have found more representatives, and a technocracy of economists, engineers, architects, lawyers, and accountants, often with advanced degrees and studies abroad and with careers in the bureaucracy, has replaced more politically active and ideologically committed intellectual predecessors. Since 1940, the state has alternately wooed and ignored the intellectual. In this hot and cold relationship, some intellectuals have sought, sometimes successfully, to make careers in the government, but others never tried, or if they did, failed.[27] Simultaneously, although economic opportunities to support intellectual activities have expanded in Mexico, few intellectuals can actually support themselves exclusively from such activities. Thus, if Glen Dealy's explanation that social prestige, gained most commonly through political power rather than control over economic resources, is most sought after in Latin cultures like Mexico, the intellectual begins to find himself in limbo.[28]

The intellectuals' role is both ambiguous and frustrating, since they live in a society that is psychologically and traditionally supportive of an important role while it simultaneously denies them access to economic rewards and ignores them politically. It is impossible to determine which of these failures most frustrates them, but interview after interview definitely suggest their disgust with the unavailability of economic rewards and imply at least indirectly that they may be adopting the North American intellectual's concern. Their envy of the North American market for intellectual goods and the greater independence it brings also seems to be part of a growing universal intellectual culture having certain commonalities across societal boundaries. These commonalities are determined by countries like the United States, which, through media, education, books, and the marketplace, form the tastes of the urban Mexican intelligentsia with the education, interest, and money to buy the art, listen to the music, attend the films, and read the books intellectuals produce.

The Role of the Mexican Intellectual

The intellectual's role in Mexico is affected by certain strucutral peculiarities of the political and economic system, but generally, the role of the intellectual in most societies has been seen as that of a creator of values. As one student suggested, "The intellectual is supposed to be able to ask the right questions, search for the correct answers, arrive at sound solutions to complex problems. In a healthy society it is the intellectual who determines the values that the rest of society accepts."[29] Again, however, certain societal characteristics determine what type of role the intellectual can and does play as a formulator of values. In the Soviet Union, for example, intellectuals have been described as those who refuse to accept the dominant Bolshevik conception of the creativity of the masses.[30] This view of the Soviet intellectual has certain parallels with the Mexican situation.

It might be said that, since the 1940s, the Mexican intellectual has consistently refused to accept the government's version of the revolutionary ideology, believing it to be misguided or, more often, misinterpreted. However, it would be unfair to conclude that the Mexican intellectual determines the values that the rest of the society accepts, because large numbers of the population do not come in contact with intellectual products, and elementary education is the only exposure to Mexican culture another sizeable group receives. Since that education is a collection of values the postrevolutionary governments have fashioned to their own liking, rather than to the intellectuals' liking, it cannot be said that intellectuals determine their values, or indeed, understand these groups.[31]

This is not to say that the Mexican intellectual does not influence other Mexicans. However, in Mexico and other developing societies, his potential audience is smaller than that found in Europe or the United States, or even in societies like Cuba, China, and the Soviet Union, where the intellectual has for the most part become a mouthpiece for the values of the state, and thus has a large captive audience. Among the small professional class in Mexico, intellectuals have definitely influenced a generation of Mexicans to examine themselves and their culture, a result of the typical array of intellectual activities in the teens and 1920s.[32]

Some scholars believe, moreover, that, whether intellectuals do or do not influence their society, in many developing countries, they are concerned with ideas to a greater extent than are intellectuals in the United States.[33]

One reason for this belief is that professional people in developing countries like Mexico are probably less specialized, more broadly educated, and thus more interested in ideas outside their particular vocation. Furthermore, it has also been suggested that the pace of change, the number of countries newly independent, the declining influence of religion, and worldwide political instability have all led to a greater interest in secular ideologies and political and economic theories. Compatible with the rise in interest in secular ideologies, and perhaps a product of it, is the fact that today, ideology has become the primary concern of the intellectual.[34]

Some scholars believe that the intellectual's primary role is to serve as an ideologue, although intellectuals are not the only ones concerned with this function in Latin America.[35] The role of the intellectual as an ideologist has become more pronounced in this century. One of the qualities found among intellectual ideologists in developing countries is their emphasis on economic development. To some scholars, the intellectual has become "the ideologist of economic development" and is competing with others for leadership in his society.[36] John Friedmann has concluded that the "near-universality of the ideology of economic development is itself evidence of the creative role of ideas in historical evolution" and evidence also that the community of "modern intellectuals is becoming international."[37]

The emphasis on economic development and on the issues it raises among intellectuals in Mexico and elsewhere in Latin America may explain why certain fields, such as the fine arts and science, are not frequently found among backgrounds of leading intellectuals. Overtly, intellectuals with scientific and artistic interests would be the least interested in or capable of expressing views directly concerned with economic development, even though it is likely that the scientist will become indispensable as technological solutions to development become more widespread and necessary. Moreover, Mexican art, like art elsewhere, has moved away from the expression of social messages, toward abstract, symbolic images. Literary types and those with social-science backgrounds are on the increase because the latter are well trained in the methodology and the ideology of economic development and the former are sensitive to the psychological and social issues development raises and have the best skills available to express their interpretations.

The data in table 6 indicate how clear these trends are in Mexico. In the first place, three intellectual fields have been relatively unchanged among leading intellectuals born during the core years 1880 to 1929: the sciences, the fine arts, and archeology and anthropology. It is recognized universally that the sciences have become increasingly important, and Mexico is no exception to this trend; but among younger intellectuals science has not increased in importance. The fine arts demonstrate a remarkable consistency, except among those intellectuals born between 1900 and 1909, the

Table 6

Intellectual Fields of Mexican Intellectuals, by Birth Year

(N=329)

Year of Birth	Percentage in								
	Humanities	Social Sciences	Archeology Anthropology	Sciences	Literature	Fine Arts	Law	Medicine	Total
Pre-1880	38	13	0	5	28	5	8	5	102
1880-1889	40	8	6	8	10	15	4	8	99
1890-1899	23	16	5	5	21	15	10	7	102
1900-1909	22	11	5	2	34	23	2	3	102
1910-1919	26	21	4	6	26	15	2	0	100
1920-1929	14	27	7	5	32	14	2	0	101
1930-	13	13	13	4	48	9	0	0	100
Column average	25	16	5	5	27	15	4	4	100
	(N=83)	(N=51)	(N=17)	(N=16)	(N=88)	(N=48)	(N=14)	(N=12)	(N=329)

Note: Data are from the *MIBP*, 1920 to 1980.

generation most influenced by the new developments in Mexican art beginning in the late teens and especially during the 1920s. Many artists from this generation were taught by the masters.

These data also illustrate that two traditional fields, law and medicine, appear to be disappearing altogether as endeavors for the intellectual. The days of the renaissance physician, someone like Ignacio Chávez, a man who combined his medical activities with intellectual pursuits, are over. Medicine has now become a profession exclusively for the intelligentsia, not the intellectual. The same is true of law. The explanation for this change, allowing for the fact that law has never been very important to intellectuals in Mexico, is that the Revolution created a legal vacuum in which legal, social, and economic change were intertwined, thus making it necessary for the intellectual jurist in the 1920s to include important philosophical questions in the analysis and creation of law.

The most noticeable change in intellectual backgrounds has occurred among those intellectuals who have sought to influence Mexico through the humanities, literature, and the social sciences. The level of intellectuals engaged in the social sciences has reached 25 percent in the present generation (born since 1920), essentially double the percentage in earlier generations. The humanities, on the other hand, have begun a gradual decline, from about 40 percent of the intellectual backgrounds of those born before the turn of the century, to about half that during the revolutionary period, followed by an even smaller percentage in the last four decades. Literary figures, on the other hand, well represented among the oldest generation, and less well-represented among the next generation (1880-1899), now make up over 30 percent of Mexico's present intellectual generation.

The contemporary intellectual's role has become identified with political activism because of ideological commitments. Initially, during the twentieth century, Latin American intellectuals concerned themselves with persuading their governments and the middle and upper classes that development was a necessary objective.[38] Once those societies became committed to the idea of development, the manner in which it was to be accomplished and for whom became the most important issues. The current focus on goals has occurred because Mexico and Latin America face a deteriorating situation economically and politically in the process of development. In the words of one Latin American, this led intellectuals to search for radical solutions.[39] The search led in turn to a confrontation between two competing groups of intellectuals, the first focusing on the liberal tradition, which implies that the world changed through an evolutionary process, and the second invoking a Marxist tradition in which structural change can transform the present.[40]

The division into liberal and Marxist camps has made modern revolutionary politics more ideological in nature, thus reinforcing the role of the intellectual ideologue.[41] Since ideological reference points are so important in the arguments over economic development, intellectual groups have sought to borrow Western and non-Western values as justifications for their respective theories.[42] To obtain support for their theories of economic development, many Mexican and Latin American intellectuals have become politically involved, competing with the professional politician and with economic leaders. But once involved in competition for support of their views, the pragmatism of the political arena subjects them to the same criticism directed toward politicians, that they deviate from the original statement of ideas that launched their role as leaders.[43] However, in acting out the role of political activist, intellectual ideologues are more restricted than competitors because their commitment to the values of their ideology is usually stronger. The resulting rigidity leads to personal and political weaknesses in the public arena. It is this rigid commitment to a set of values that discourages compromise—an ingredient missing in most Latin American societies—and that probably explains the vehemence with which intellectuals attack other intellectuals who they believe have abandoned their intellectual cause.[44]

Another side effect of the ideological role intellectuals play is that they are less likely to be identified with a social group. Politically, intellectuals are not committed to an alliance with any social class, nor with the intelligentsia. However, agreement is far from universal on this point, and the evidence suggests that, if intellectuals themselves cannot agree on which values and goals are most important, it is unlikely that they will find a social class or stratum with which they also can agree. Since intellectuals have their own interests and goals, as both Walzer and Gouldner have suggested, they are likely to experiment with different group alliances.[45] In industrialized societies, this view of the nonaligned intellectual seems well supported.

In Mexico, where class allegiances are sharper and distinguished by other characteristics attractive or repellent to intellectual influence, it seems probable that intellectuals will associate themselves, if they are not revolutionary ideologues, with the middle class. This is their only viable audience. Almost no cases exist of the intellectual trying to organize or associate with the peasants, though some may have sought to represent their interests intellectually and others have conducted social experiments involving the Mexican peasant.[46] More has been accomplished between the intellectual and the laboring class, probably because of the historical precedent set by precursor movements before the 1910 Revolution.[47] In recent years, as organized labor has expanded in scope and in skill, politically active intellectuals have become more interested in the possibilities of an intellectual-led political labor movement.[48] This is true only for the capital, however.

In Latin America, the role of the intellectual as social critic has been seen as even more important than as interpreter of values, as ideologue, or as representative of any group or class. This is also true in non-Western developing countries, where the politically active intellectual tends to be a social revolutionary critical of the status quo.[49] In the United States, Charles Kadushin sees the function of the intellectual as submitting society and its ideas to basic criticism.[50] Yet, few North American intellectuals are social revolutionaries. The reason may be found in Kadushin's conclusion that, although 60 percent of U.S. intellectuals thought their role was to be critical of society, only half of those thought that their criticism implied making policy suggestions.[51] North American intellectuals believe that they play the role of critic, but their criticism is not necessarily directed toward the government in the form of a mandate for change; rather, it is directed toward society itself, which, if it becomes persuaded by the values implicit in the intellectual criticism, can mandate its own change. Perhaps the democratic structure of U.S. society creates a different critical task for the intellectual.

As their role evolved in the United States, intellectuals did not find it necessary to serve in government or indeed to have direct access to government leaders, since, if they could persuade the public, or at least those who participated politically, their views would influence society. Their role evolved as interpreters of the goals and ideas of certain groups, whose demands they then redirected toward society as a whole. In Mexico, however, intellectuals have always aimed their demands toward a social and political elite, those who govern society not by a mandate from the masses, but by manipulating the system for their own benefit. Thus, the role of intellectuals has been to persuade the members of the governing class directly that their views are important, and failing to do this, to become part of the political elite themselves, since they often are already members of important social groups.

To be a social critic in Mexico and Latin America, therefore, is not the same as in the United States. The audience affects the role. In Mexico, the intellectual has been a social critic only sporadically.[52] Historically, Mexican intellectuals have fluctuated between participating in the government and remaining outside of it. When they remain outside, their role as social critic increases; when they are members of the government, it decreases. Furthermore, whether inside or outside of government, the extent to which they can or do act as social critics is determined by the state's receptivity to their ideas.

When intellectuals are not successful as social critics or, more often, would like to see themselves more successful as social critics, they join the state or battle for control in the political arena. This is an unlikely decision in the United States; in Mexico and in Latin America, it is exceedingly common. As I pointed out earlier, the majority of Mexico's intellectuals have served government in an important capacity. Thus, as one Latin

American writer noted, it is not the participation of intellectuals in public life that is noteworthy, but the extent of that participation.[53] It is worth noting why Mexicans, unlike their North American counterparts, have played this role. Historically, the Latin American had some experience with local self-government but almost none on a national level. Thus, after independence came in the early 1800s, all individuals with higher education were desperately needed to govern their societies. Furthermore, the Catholic church, which had a religious monopoly in Latin America prior to independence, was formally associated with the state, thereby incorporating the allegiance of the well-educated clerics and clergy-teachers, at that time the profession of many intellectuals. Moreover, most of the regurgitated Enlightenment ideas presented in support of Latin America's independence came from generations of professionals educated at a small number of native universities.[54] Therefore, beginning with independence, intellectuals had a decisive and important role in the Latin American political scene.

In Mexico, however, according to one historian, intellectuals have held power only on three occasions: during the 1850s, in a period known as the Reform, when liberals imposed their sway after years of anarchy and civil war; during the late 1860s and early 1870s, when a foreign monarchy was replaced by the restoration of a liberal republic; and indirectly, in the early 1920s, when José Vasconcelos exerted considerable influence through his leadership in the Ministry of Education under President Alvaro Obregón.[55] However, intellectuals in other eras exerted considerable influence in certain policy areas, if not putting their imprint on the whole face of a government. What is most important about the Mexican intellectuals' role in relation to public life is that they believe it is natural for them to be involved politically, and they have followed several avenues in pursuit of that role.

The role that Mexican intellectuals play is often different from that in which their North American colleagues engage. A number of reasons have been discussed to explain why these roles should differ and their implications for their respective societies, but within the Mexican context, it would be revealing and worthwhile to describe the views Mexican intellectuals and politicians have concerning the intellectual's role, since it is these two groups that largely determine the continuation of the present pattern and the intellectuals' impact.

A View from Intellectuals and Politicians

When Mexican intellectuals in this century talk about the role they play, they are quick to distinguish the time period under discussion and the difference between the role they *should* play versus the role they *actually* play. Their feelings about the role they should play are difficult to measure in a precise fashion, but the general impression I received (from interviewing numerous intellectuals) is that they are frustrated with their lack of opportunities and would like to see themselves have greater influence in Mexico.

Interestingly, even though many roles are possible, and Mexican intellectuals identified many of those discussed earlier in this chapter, they essentially see themselves in two ways: as creators or thinkers, or as pragmatists or doers. For many intellectuals, the first of these roles is of primary importance because Mexico requires an independent source of ideas, criticism, and alternatives useful to its development. The intellectual as a creator of ideas has a significant beginning in the period after 1920, when an ideological vacuum existed. The intellectuals were called on to reorient the Mexican people to a future opened up by the Mexican Revolution. This experience has been well described by historian Enrique Florescano:

In the recent past they played an important role in the consciousness raising of the Mexican people, and this role has been undervalued in the past. The growth of nationalism in Mexico after the Revolution was encouraged by Mexican intellectuals. The generations of the 1920s and 1930s were the creators of what we today are benefiting from in an intellectual sense. This occurred in many areas such as art, music, literature, in which a great consciousness and integration of works took place. The most relevant work of these intellectuals was to recuperate the historical roots and integrate them with the new ideas in social and political fields that appeared after the revolution.[56]

Mexican intellectuals also believe that an independent view and objective judgment are essential to their role. Octavio Paz has persistently advocated the need for the Mexican intellectual to create values. Today, he believes that the intellectual's responsibility in performing this task is even more crucial than it was earlier in this century. For him, "Mexican intellectuals are more ideological today than before. I think that an intellectual magazine like *Vuelta* has to fight two things: the state, or power without ideas; and ideological orthodoxy, having little widespread power. The sectarian influences are particularly strong in some of our universities."[57] Perhaps Paz is more sensitive to this task because he himself has suffered on many occasions from the abuses encouraged by ideological orthodoxy and an insensitive state.

In analyzing their role as critics, Mexican intellectuals have been critical of analysis devoid of practical options. Even representatives of the moderate Left, such as Pablo González Casanova, sociologist and former rector of the National University, called on leftist intellectuals, whether in parties or universities, to reduce the level of criticism providing no alternatives, and instead to "provide concrete alternatives for obtaining power and winning political battles."[58] There is also agreement among Mexican intellectuals that a variety of possibilities must be discussed and made available to a wide audience. As one provincial playwright reasoned, "I think the intellectual should create a feeling of inquisitiveness, unrest, in the area he knows best. He needs to publicly air the disadvantages and advantages of alternative choices in his field. This freedom of expression is essential to the development of Mexico."[59]

Mexican intellectuals divide, and not always clearly, not on their belief that intellectuals should mold the values of Mexican society, that they should identify weakneses and strengths, and that they should provide independent judgments of these shortcomings, but on where and how they can best achieve this role. In his earlier writings, Octavio Paz wondered aloud about where Mexican intellectuals should fulfill their primary task:

In Mexico, the intellectual's mission is political action. The Mexican intelligentsia has not only served its country, it has also defended it, honestly and effectively. But in so doing, has it not ceased to be an intelligentsia? That is, has it not renounced its proper role as the critical conscience of its people?[60]

Paz himself resolved this dilemma by leaving the state, resigning his diplomatic post after the 1968 student massacre. He now is a model of the Mexican intellectual outside of government serving as a critical consciousness of the people. Obviously, Paz's diplomatic career (he is a career foreign service officer and may return at any time) is evidence that he at one time believed the intellectual in Mexico could be intellectually independent while serving the state. Why have intellectuals like Paz changed their minds?

Octavio Paz used his resignation to protest symbolically the government's policy toward the students and its use of violent repression, though he was the only intellectual in the administration of President Gustavo Díaz Ordaz to do so.[61] This reason for his resignation is well known, and it served as a signal to younger, active intellectuals. However, a lesser-known reason may have been his frustration with his inability to alter the government's policies on students. He indicated in an interview with me that, prior to the student massacre, he received a circular from then-secretary of foreign relations Antonio Carrillo Flores, asking Paz, as his government's representative to India, to offer any insights and suggestions he might have about the increasingly difficult confrontations between student groups and the Mexican government. Paz was happy that the government was so concerned with the complexities raised by the student-government relationships and that it would request advice from its ambassadors. He responded in considerable detail, discussing the background of the problem, the attitude of the students toward the government, and the measures the government could take to respond nonviolently and effectively to responsible student demands. He forwarded this multipage document to the secretary of foreign relations. Shortly thereafter, he received a communication from Carrillo Flores indicating that he was greatly impressed by Paz's observations on this question and had passed his memorandum directly on to President Díaz Ordaz.[62]

The importance of this little-known anecdote is twofold: first, it reveals that the Mexican government does attempt, at least on occasion, to ascertain the views of intellectuals on issues about which they have an informed opinion; and second, it demonstrates that the Mexican president definitely received some alternative suggestions for defusing the student problem, but that he chose, for whatever reason, to follow a different direction and ignored the suggestions of one of Mexico's most prominent thinkers. With the advantage of hindsight, it can be easily concluded that Díaz Ordaz made a serious miscalculation, and that the student massacre went beyond the deaths of many young people and innocent bystanders to have an impact on the views of the subsequent relations between the state, the middle class, the students, the intellectuals, and the foreign scholarly and intellectual community.

Whether intellectuals see their role as public servants frustrated by the system, or see the intellectual as a failed politician, most intellectuals do serve the Mexican government. Many, as has been suggested, do so not out of a commitment to public service but out of necessity, like the generation of politicians who grew up during the early decades of the twentieth century. Still, whether necessity or service propels the intellectual into government, many intellectuals believe that serving the state is their *primary* role in Mexico, or at the very least, one of several acceptable choices.

The views of Mexican intellectuals toward their own role in society, whether they are describing the role they believe they have played, or whether advocating the role they should play, reflect a definite division on the question of whether or not the intellectual should serve the government. The majority of established intellectuals, who are part of an older generation, appear to agree with Fernando Benítez's statement that "sometimes the intellectuals feel obligated to fill public offices and I believe when they are authentic intellectuals, they carry out this function in an exemplary manner. The intellectuals are those who have helped Mexico advance. This country needs that type of intellectual to direct it, and this is what makes the presence of intellectuals so necessary."[63]

I found earlier that the perceptions of intellectuals and public figures as to what an intellectual is differ on several important points. When we examine politicians' views of intellectuals in Mexico and contrast them with those of the intellectuals themselves, we find that politicians too are open to the idea that the intellectual can play a dual role in Mexico, rather than function exclusively as a government servant. No public figure, however, expressed the belief that the intellectual should not or could not serve the state and thereby relinquish his credentials as an intellectual.

Mexican politicians tend to feel that the intellectual should be involved in public life; they distinguish two ways in which the intellectual can function in the public sector. Jesús Puente Leyva, a leading economist, public administrator, and former head of the delegation of official party deputies to Congress from the state of Nuevo León, sees the task of the intellectual in

Mexico in a light similar to that of C. Wright Mills:

There are intellectuals and intellectual artisans. I think that a true intellectual, regardless of his interests or activities, is inspired by ideology and by certain changes in the political and social environment. The intellectual artisans are really technocrats, who are more closely tied to practice or pragmatic activities than to ideas. The intellectual doesn't normally make decisions, but suggests and plans alternative approaches. Today, I believe all intellectuals, with very few exceptions, come from universities or centers of higher learning. The record in Mexico demonstrates that intellectuals have been more concerned with political life or associated with political ideologies while the technicians have been involved in the administrative life of the country.[64]

Puente Leyva's technicians are what I have called "intelligentsia," and therefore should not be considered "intellectuals." But his other type of intellectual, the adviser, is equally important, and he believes that this type of intellectual needs to "play a more active role, not just in the rationalizing of ideas or policies already suggested, but in creating and stimulating these ideas."[65] Again, the career experience of the individual reflects his perception of the tasks the intellectual should perform, whether that individual is an intellectual or a politician.

Public figures, like Mexican intellectuals, believe intellectuals use ideological skills to support the governing class. As a former cabinet officer suggested, "The intellectual in Mexico plays an important role in political life and supplies the class in power with many of the ideological formulas for the realization of proposals of the class that exercises that power, including both technical instrument and juridical methods. I think their role is not as important as the intellectuals themselves would like it to be, but they do have a role in correcting and improving errors made by the governing class."[66] Although no public figure stated that Mexican intellectuals are the allies of a specific social class, several did see them as aloof from the masses, a phenomenon best described by Manuel Hinojosa Ortiz, a former senator and assistant secretary of agriculture, who believes intellectuals "form small groups or 'capillas' that are disassociated from the popular masses; who, as a result, do not know who intellectuals are. There is a reciprocal ignorance; neither the people influence the intellectuals, nor the intellectuals the people."[67]

The tasks Mexican public figures attribute to intellectuals are more narrowly focused than those that intellectuals see for themselves. Politicians tend to see intellectuals as carrying out ideological tasks that generally bring them into the political arena. In Mexico, however, political involvement more often than not means becoming part of the established political structure, since the Mexican system, although permitting opposition, has never allowed a viable opposition party to gain control of the legislative or executive branch. Thus, if the structure of the Mexican political system were different, more intellectuals might follow the route of providing leadership to opposition political parties, instead of becoming part of the government. Antonio Carrillo Flores, who believes intellectuals should contribute their services to public life, also argues for the necessity of expanding alternative ways in which the intellectual can participate politically:

In Mexico I have always thought that we lacked the equivalent of the Republican party of the United States or the Conservative party of Great Britain. The problem is that few people who remain outside of PRI can achieve important government positions. The Supreme Court has been the institution with the most exceptions, such as Alberto Vázquez del Mercado and Gabino Fraga. We need a viable alternative that can also provide opportunities for intellectuals.[68]

Conclusions

The views Mexican intellectuals and public figures offer of the role intellectuals play suggest several important implications for understanding the structure of intellectual life in Mexico. In the first place, an examination of the universal perceptions of the intellectual's role reveals a somewhat wider range of functions than found in Mexico. More important, it seems clear from the Mexican case, and from studies of developing nations in general, that an important cause of the differences in roles from one culture to the next can be simply explained by differences in the level of economic and social development, especially the level of literacy and education. Furthermore, the structure of the political system, the role of the government in economic life, and the degree of political participation also restrict the channels available to the intellectual. The economic, social, and political structures are important determinants of intellectual roles, and the cultural psychology present in the society, in terms of priorities in career goals and personal achievements, affects intellectual behavior as well.

The definitions intellectuals and public figures provide for the intellectual also influence their interpretations of the intellectual's tasks. Tradition and experience often determine the degree to which the intellectual plays a certain role, such as a public servant, in Mexico. The level of the intellectual's involvement in public life has fluctuated from one decade to the next in the context of a consistently important public role not found in cultures like the United States'. The functions political and intellectual groups believe intellectuals should have also seem to be determined to a great extent by personal experience, especially whether or not an individual has followed a career within the government or outside of it. However, the experience of older intellectuals is far more homogeneous than that of younger intellectuals, who for the first time have access to a greater number of opportunities, primarily in higher education and outside of the public sector. Older intellectuals like Ignacio Chávez, who did not hold public office, still saw themselves as working for the government and for the Mexican people through their activities.

The most important change revealed by this analysis of the intellectual's role in Mexico is the one that took place in the mid-1960s, markedly after 1968, in the intellectual's attitude toward government service. For the first time in the twentieth century, intellectuals not only had different economic choices available to them, but they were actually considering the philosophical implications of serving the state and carrying on their task as the critical conscience of the people. The question of whether the two are mutually exclusive became an issue of primary importance in the 1970s. Octavio Paz has been the important figure in this controversy, but he is in a unique financial position as one of Mexico's leading intellectual figures, a position not shared by many other, younger intellectuals. Whether this newly developed division among intellectuals as to their role will grow remains to be seen. At a time when Mexico's political and economic systems are under great strain, intellectuals not only are maintaining their historical ideological diversity, but have further separated themselves from the state.

It is likely that this division will grow, since younger intellectuals pattern themselves on the behavior of their mentors. If a large number of mentors remain outside of public life, their disciples are likely to do so, too. Moreover, the increasing influence, in particular intellectual influence, of North American culture only encourages Mexican intellectuals to divide into two camps, since the North American intellectual experience is clearly outside of public life. The impact the changes in role playing will have on Mexico is difficult to estimate, but their influence will surely be felt. For example, if intellectuals who leave public life, or decide not to involve themselves in it, join the political arena as members of opposition parties, they will expand the pool of individuals skilled in the manipulation of words and symbols from which opposition groups can recruit leaders. If, on the other hand, they choose to join the ranks of the independent and politically unmotivated, their influence will be exerted in a different direction.

If the Mexican intellectual community continues to separate into two camps, it is likely that the ideological divisions among Mexico's educated population will increase, and the government will find it increasingly difficult to obtain a consensus. The reasons for this are twofold. As tables 2, 3, and 4 make clear, both intellectuals and politicians choose to be more influenced by intellectuals whose careers coincide with their own perceptions of the role they believe the intellectual plays. If intellectuals increasingly listen to and follow the lead of an independent camp of colleagues, and public figures listen to and are influenced by the intellectual active in public service, then their suspicions of each other will grow and probably their views of what issues are most important and the solutions for resolving them will differ.

5. Family Background and Education

The backgrounds and careers of the intellectuals affect the structure of intellectual leadership and its relationship to the state. In Mexico, where social class is well defined, where economic and political power is concentrated in the capital, where education is an urban phenomenon, a person's background and place of residence determine not only the likelihood that he or she will be allowed to develop intellectual skills, but, equally important, whether the established intellectual community will recognize those skills. Furthermore, since I am suggesting that Mexican intellectuals might offer viable alternatives to policies put forth by the political leadership, the extent to which they are representative of the population at large and their proximity to politicians are determinants, to some extent, of their philosophical outlook and their ability to influence public figures. Many background and educational variables are important in establishing the recruitment patterns of Mexican intellectuals and the degree to which political and intellectual leadership overlap.

Consequences of Birthplace

The distribution of community, state, and region where Mexican intellectuals are born and where they later reside differs markedly from the distribution of the general population. An examination of the state of birth of Mexican intellectuals reveals that, of the 331 individuals about whom I have birthplace information, over two-thirds were born in just six of the thirty-two entities in Mexico, or abroad. The birthplaces of Mexican intellectuals in order of their importance were Federal District, 33 percent; Jalisco, 10 percent; foreign, 8 percent; Michoacán, 5 percent; Veracruz, 5 percent; and the states of México and Puebla, 4 percent each (figures are from the *MIBP*). Depending on the census period one looks at, the figures for these states, excluding the Federal District, are not substantially different from the figures for the general population. However, the figure for the Federal District is significantly disproportionate to that of the general population (table 7). At the time when most intellectuals in my sample were born (1900-1909), Mexico City accounted for approximately 5 percent of the Mexican population, whereas 15 percent of the intellectuals born during those years were born there. Even in 1950, when 14 percent of the population resided in the capital, it was strikingly overrepresented among the birthplaces of intellectuals.

The overrepresentation of the capital among the birthplaces of Mexican intellectuals is not surprising, and previous studies show that a disproportionate number of the political elite also come from this location. What is surprising, however, is that, in comparison with political leaders (table 7), with regard to place of birth, intellectuals are much less representative of

Table 7
Regional Origins of Mexican Intellectuals, Politicians, and General Population

Region of Birth[a]	Percentage of			
	Intellectuals[b] (N=331)	Intellectual Elite[b] (N=54)	Political Leaders[c] (N=1,315)	General Population[d]
Federal District	33	35	15	5
East Central	11	11	15	22
West	15	9	15	16
North	8	11	16	11
South	3	6	10	14
Gulf	8	6	13	12
West Central	13	15	14	21
Foreign	8	7	1	—[e]
Total	99	100	99	101

Notes: [a]Regional divisions are as follows: *Federal District; East Central*, Hidalgo, Puebla, Querétaro, San Luis Potosí, Tlaxcala, Zacatecas; *West*, Aguascalientes, Baja California del Sur, Colima, Durango, Jalisco, Nayarit, Sinaloa; *North*, Baja California del Norte, Chihuahua, Coahuila, Nuevo León, Sonora, Tamaulipas; *South*, Chiapas, Guerrero, Oaxaca; *Gulf*, Campeche, Quintana Roo, Tabasco, Veracruz, Yucatán; *West Central*, Guanajuato, México, Michoacán, Morelos.
[b]Data from the *MIBP*, 1920 to 1980. This group was selected by scholars, politicians, and other intellectuals as most influential.
[c]Data from the *MPBP* for the Government Political Elite, 1935-1980.
[d]The 1910 census data are used to give an approximation of the residence of all Mexicans during a period closest to the date of birth of the largest number of intellectuals and political leaders in my two data sets.
[e]Not included in data.

the general population. Certain states and regions have been significantly underrepresented in the birthplaces of intellectuals, most notably the South. Furthermore, there are substantial differences in the patterns of intellectuals' versus politicians' birthplaces.

Most important among these differences is the disparity in the number of persons born in the North. Intellectuals from that region are woefully underrepresented (only 8 percent of all intellectuals), whereas the North accounted for 16 percent of the birthplaces of politicians. That the North has consistently increased its proportion of the general population since the 1920s, reaching 15 percent of the total by 1950, exaggerates this regional underrepresentation among intellectuals. A historical explanation may account for this difference. The Mexican Revolution of 1910 changed political-recruitment patterns, shifting them from the traditional regions of the East and West Central to the North,[1] as the "Sonoran Dynasty," men from the northern states of Coahuila, Nuevo León, Sonora, and Chihuahua, dominated revolutionary and postrevolutionary leadership. Since we know that the home state of the president influenced somewhat political-recruitment patterns in later administrations, it is not unreasonable to expect many political figures to come from the same states as their superiors.[2]

The foreign birthplaces of intellectuals and politicians offer another striking difference. Very few political leaders in Mexico have been born abroad. The simple explanation is that few politicians are the children of foreign parents, or of Mexican parents who have traveled widely and lived abroad. The exception to this, accounting for nearly all of the fourteen public figures born outside of Mexico, were children of career diplomats. For example, María Téllez Benoit, subsecretary of foreign affairs in the López Portillo administration, was the daughter of an important politician who became the chargé d'affaires in Washington, D.C., her birthplace.[3] Furthermore, being foreign born, except as a child of Mexican parents, prevents an individual from holding most public offices in Mexico.[4]

Of course, intellectuals with foreign birthplaces also come from parents in the diplomatic corps, especially since those from intellectually predisposed families often find a source of employment in the Consular or Foreign Service. In reality, although the parents of several Mexican intellectuals have been in the Foreign Service, most were not born abroad. An excellent example is Carlos Fuentes, whose father was a career officer.[5] More often, the intellectual, unlike the politician, is an immigrant, born in another country because his or her parents were foreigners. For example, the four individuals with foreign birthplaces from the intellectual elite sample (table 7) illustrate this pattern: Rodolfo Stavenhagen, born in Frankfurt, Germany, was the son of a businessman who fled to Mexico in 1939 from the Nazis; Elena Poniatowska, a journalist, was born in Paris of a French father of Polish origin who married a Mexican; Luis Villoro, a historian, born in Barcelona, grew up the child of a wealthy Creole mother from San Luis Potosí and a Spanish father, a physician; and José Gaos, noted philosopher and native of Gijón, Spain, typifies the intellectual refugee fleeing Fascist Spain during the civil war.

The number of foreign birthplaces among Mexican intellectuals not only distinguishes them from the typical political leader, but also makes them a less homogeneous group than politicians. If we examine the nationality of the parents of Mexican intellectuals, classifying them as non-Mexican if at least one parent was a foreigner, we find that at least 15 percent of Mexico's intellectuals have a non-Mexican parent or parents, and that, not surprisingly, over half of these are from Spain (*MIBP*). The foreign nationality of their parents is a characteristic even more exaggerated among the intellectual elite, where 19 percent came from mixed nationalities. Again, although some politicians such as Carlos Hank González, director of the Federal District Department from 1976 to 1982, have foreign backgrounds, they are exceptional.

These figures for intellectuals are important because studies of intellectual thought in Latin America and elsewhere frequently attribute the influx of new ideas to foreigners. Not surprisingly, ten (or 19 percent) of Mexico's leading intellectual elite figures since the 1920s came from such backgrounds.[6] Furthermore, the influence of the Spanish exiles in cultural activities such as higher education and publishing in Mexico has been well documented.[7] Not only do foreign-born intellectuals serve as channels for new and sometimes revolutionary ideas, but their foreign experience and their familiarity with a culture other than their own probably give them a cosmopolitan flavor that influences their outlook and that of their colleagues. This is supported by the fact that, although only 11 percent of Mexico's leading intellectuals were known to have Marxist philosophies, 36 percent of those intellectuals receiving their preparatory education abroad held such views (*MIBP*).

Finally, the birthplace date in table 7 suggest that the entire western region, containing the important city of Guadalajara, has been equally well represented among the intellectual and political leadership. The state of Jalisco, however, of which Guadalajara is the capital, has not fared particularly well among the political leadership since the 1930s, although it has produced more than its share of intellectuals. Perhaps one of the explanations for this discrepancy is that, historically, Jalisco was a center of Catholic influence, and in the twentieth century it became the site of a bitter conflict, known as the Cristero War, between the church and the state. Its Catholicism and political conservatism are pronounced, in contrast to Mexico City, and its environment is conducive to producing intellectual leaders who represent this current of ideological thought. A successful political leader in Mexico would have to avoid this conservatism, since it contradicts the revolutionary rhetoric and ideology necessary to the successful careers of most political leaders.[8]

The most striking characteristic of the birthplaces of Mexican intellectuals is the number from Mexico City. The reasons Mexico City is so well represented are many. Most important is that Mexico City, like many capitals of Latin America and other developing countries, has dominated the political, cultural, and industrial life of the country since independence. Because Mexico City has been the center of political power and the source of economic growth, it has perpetuated itself as the central city. Socially, it acts as a magnet to mobile elements of the population, especially the middle class. A microcosm of this situation exists in most provinces in Mexico, with the capital usually serving as the social and economic center of influence.

The result of this capital-city dominance is that intellectuals, in terms of their birthplaces, are even more unrepresentative and elitist than the data in table 7 suggest. Of the 331 intellectuals about whom I have information, 241, or 73 percent, were born in capital cities (of the intellectual elite, 40, or 74 percent). Yet, when we examine the data Peter Smith provides for political leaders from 1900 to 1970, we find that only 41 percent of his sample were born in capital cities.[9] Intellectuals overwhelmingly come from urban communities, capitals or otherwise, much more so than politicians. The fact that 86 percent of the intellectuals in my sample came from urban backgrounds (compared to 63 percent of the politicians) is especially extraordinary, since my sample of intellectuals is older (45 percent born before 1900) than my sample of politicians (29 percent born before 1900). Not only are politicians more representative of individual states and regions, but within those regions, they are more likely to come from smaller towns and villages than are intellectuals.

Consequences of Residence

As place of birth has many consequences for intellectuals, so does place of residence. One of the reasons intellectuals come from a narrow spectrum of the Mexican population is that they are children of professional people who have lived, for generations, in urban settings. These relatives, some of whom lived in the early nineteenth century, have either lived in Mexico City or a state capital. Only 3 percent of these relatives lived in nonurban communities. Thus, whether one discusses elite intellectuals, intellectuals, or intellectuals' relatives, an overwhelming urban bias in their place of residence can be found (*MIBP*).

The fact that over 90 percent of Mexico's elite intellectuals since 1920 have made the capital their adult home has serious consequences for intellectual life and for the relationship between intellectuals and politicians. The most important implication is the centralization of intellectual life in the capital. Mexican intellectuals are only continuing a tradition already present throughout Latin America in the 1800s. E. Bradford Burns, in an interesting observation about nineteenth-century historians, concluded that, with rare exceptions, they "resided in the capitals, partly because of the educational and cultural advantages but also, significantly, because most of them were connected at one time or another, in one way or another with the governments."[10] Burns suggests, therefore, that the location of the government, as a major employer of the educated elite, even in the colonial period, determines the location of its prospective employees, whether intellectuals or intelligentsia.

The concentration of intellectuals living in the capital distinguishes Mexicans from their North American counterparts. Although the stereotypical view is to expect New York to produce and serve as the residence for most intellectuals, Kadushin found that, during the 1960s, only 51 percent of the North American intellectual elite resided in the New York City-area (defined as within a fifty-mile radius of the Empire State Building), even though one-third of that group had actually grown up there.[11] Thus, although Mexico City and New York are somewhat comparable in the large proportion each city contributes to its respective country's intellectual leadership, Mexico City gives birth to and draws many more intellectuals to its fold as adults.

The capital, because it becomes the home of an overwhelming number of Mexican intellectuals, takes on other qualities that only help to perpetuate its importance. The first of these, but with practical consequences, is psychological: "Residents of Mexico City take for granted that their capital provides cultural leadership in setting styles and developing trends. They regard the provinces as culturally backward and provincials have apparently accepted that assessment."[12]

According to Coser, the homogenous focus in many disciplines stems from the centralization of intellectuals in a capital city. He describes Paris, but if Mexico City is substituted, his analysis is still apt: "The fact that most significant intellectuals, be they literary or artistic, academic or political, are thrown together in a few major centers of the city, helps to give cohesion to a cultural milieu that is amazingly homogeneous even though it may be differentiated by ideological, philosophical or political cleavages and by functional diversity."[13] A latent benefit of this physical proximity is that intellectuals shorten their lines of communication and increase the speed of transmitting their ideas.[14] However, in Mexico, this latter effect is somewhat complicated by the interaction of competing groups, which do not necessarily exchange their ideas in an open arena.

The economic, institutional, and structural support given to the intellectual in Mexico City hardly exists in other urban centers, even in the important cities like Guadalajara. Although Guadalajara is the second-largest city in Mexico, most of its leading intellectuals or cultural figures believe it devoid of any cultural support for intellectual activities. An example is the publishing field. Local newspapers, which have provided careers and supplemental income to many Mexican intellectuals, do not give much coverage to cultural activities. In a survey of *El Occidental*, one of Guadalajara's leading papers, the number of articles devoted to cultural affairs, broadly defined, is markedly less than can be found in *Excélsior*, one of Mexico City's leading dailies. Whereas *Excélsior* generally devotes about 10 percent of its weekday coverage to such subjects, *El Occidental* averages less than 1 percent.[15]

Cultural magazines at the regional level are in even worse shape, although exceptions can be found. As we shall see, even on the national level they tend to be short-lived and economically insolvent, but this is more pronounced regionally. In the words of Manuel Rodríguez Lapuente, editor of the official cultural magazine of the University of Guadalajara, "Today, there are none. Look, I am the editor of the university newspaper—it only comes out irregularly. Cultural magazines do not exist here, we are very poor in such publications."[16] Publishers are even more scarce. The only way to get something published, according to one provincial dramatist, is to have it published in Mexico City, and that would be possible only if it seemed to be of some national importance.[17] Other institutions, whether they be galleries for the artist, or theater companies for the works of the dramatist, are nonexistent or inferior in number and quality.[18]

The general lack of a supportive cultural environment in the provinces, brought on by the concentration of intellectuals in Mexico City, has a psychological effect on the provincial intellectual. In the first place, most of Mexico's intellectuals, or at least members of the cultural elite, do not believe that any intellectuals actually exist in Guadalajara, or, if they do, only in minute numbers. For example, Guillermo García Oropeza, speaking frankly about this, stated, "I am typical of the pattern [of the intellectual who goes to Mexico City] that suggests that Mexico City is everything. If you do not live in Mexico you don't exist. Until I went to Mexico City, I did not have a chance of publishing anything."[19]

Furthermore, the centralization of intellectual life affects the quality of information provincial leaders receive. Many of the cultural leaders from the provinces believe that on most issues the orientation of the intellectuals in the capital is the same as that of those living in the provinces. But this belief may be due to the fact that nearly all of their information comes from Mexico City, or from abroad, rather than from local sources. Repeatedly, provincial intellectuals, like national intellectual figures, mention the same names, and many of the same journals and newspapers, both foreign and domestic, as having been important in the development of their ideas.

In the realm of intellectual ideas, differences do exist between the provinces and the capital. Because established intellectuals are concentrated in Mexico City, they are familiar with each other, but tend to ignore talented individuals who reside in other regions. An excellent illustration occurred in a 1980 interview between Carlos Landeros, a Mexican journalist who has covered the cultural scene for at least the last two decades, and Elena Garro, well-known playwright and novelist. In the interview, Garro began telling Landeros about an outstanding Guadalajara poet, Ernesto Flores, but Landeros openly admitted that he had never heard of him.[21]

One of the complaints Mexicans and Latin Americans have directed toward their intellectual communities is their readiness to accept foreign ideas and methodologies that have little applicability to local problems and issues. Mexico City, for example, is the most cosmopolitan of cities. Foreign styles, food, dress, goods, and, most important, ideas are common in the capital. One prominent sociologist recently expressed this concern to the North American scholarly community:

We must develop our own theoretical models to interpret correctly and coherently the problems of our society. This does not imply chauvinism and it does not deny the universality of science. It recognizes that many of the sociological schools and theories that fed our intellectual development were conceived under different concrete historical and cultural conditions.[22]

In achieving this goal of developing solutions from within, it might well be the provincial intellectual community that can best provide some indigenous insights, since it is less contaminated by external influences, both good and bad, than is Mexico City.[23] Some Mexican intellectuals and scholars, in recognition of this need, have made concrete moves to refocus attention on the provinces. One of the intellectual leaders of this movement is historian Luis González, who, in addition to his superb scholarship on local history, helped to create and at present directs the Colegio de Michoacán, in Zamora, a regional version of the prestigious Colegio de México. The establishment of these and other institutions supportive of the products intellectuals create and produce provides some of the necessary incentive to persuade residents of Mexico City to leave.

As suggested earlier, background variables affect the intellectual's relationship to political leaders in many ways. With regard to residence, there is a striking concentration of former and would-be politicians in Mexico City. The same is true of the leading intelligentsia. Once an individual goes to Mexico City and is educated there, he rarely leaves it, at least permanently.[24] The close physical proximity of intellectuals to politicians increases the likelihood that they will move in the same social circles. This same pattern occurs in London and Paris; in the former "it is quite common to find writers, journalists, Oxford dons and Members of Parliament mingling at cocktail parties or similar occasions, and as these men continuously 'rub against each other,' they develop a set of common assumptions transcending institutional affiliations and functional divisions."[25]

Social contacts lead to the friendships necessary to successful political and intellectual careers. For the intellectual with a natural interest in public service, the chances that he or she will be asked to serve increases with the number of social contacts among public figures. Yet, according to one Mexican intellectual, "the main problem with Mexican intellectuals in this century—and perhaps even before—has been their lack of distance from political power, that is, from government."[26] I shall analyze the validity of this assertion further in later chapters, but even if only partially true, it suggests that one explanation for why Mexican intellectuals have served in government, more so than their North American counterparts, is that they reside in the capital, along with most of Mexico's leading political figures.

Consequences of Social Background

Intellectuals are born in urban areas and subsequently reside in Mexico City in part because of the socioeconomic status of their parents. The status of their parents not only is important in determining where intellectuals are born, but has a decided effect on their environment as children, their access to certain schools and higher education, and ultimately, their social and political friendships. There has been much scholarship in recent years on socioeconomic background variables and their implication for political leadership. Most notable among the relationships examined has been that between the social background of the politician and his or her decisions on government policies. Surveying this literature, Nelson Polsby has concluded that knowledge of a person's socioeconomic background is insufficient for predicting policy positions.[27] There are so many variables, other than class background, that intervene in the formation of a person's ideas and in his ability to implement them as policies, that it is impossible to measure such a relationship. Yet, this does not make social class background unimportant, for, as Peter H. Smith suggests in his study of Mexican political leaders, "people from an identifiable social class, for instance, are conditioned by that common experience, and they are inclined to share a set of common assumptions."[28]

Mexican intellectuals and scholars agree with Smith that class background is important to an intellectual's attitudes and interests. Even Mexican politicians themselves consider it to have been significant.[29] However, most of the literature has focused on what a person accomplishes in relation to those beliefs, rather than on the beliefs themselves. In the first place, intellectuals have a freedom of movement not found among those pursuing political careers. Simply put, the structure of political life in Mexico, which requires every important political leader to subordinate his own views to those of the immediate superior or the president, does not allow for an accurate measure of actual attitudes. Furthermore, even in less authoritarian political systems, compromise is a feature that masks strongly held views. Intellectuals, however, can express their beliefs much more freely than politicians, beliefs that reflect the entirety of their socialization experiences, including those found in their home environment. Of course, the importance of family background on intellectual attitudes varies from one individual to another, but its "true" effects are more easily seen than among politicians.

The class background of parents of Mexican intellectuals is extraordinarily clear. An overwhelming number of intellectuals come from middle and upper socioeconomic backgrounds. Whether one considers the elite intellectual or important intellectuals in general, the figures are the same: over 94 percent come from the middle or upper class (*MIBP*). On the other hand, of those about whom I have information on class background (203), only 6 percent come from working-class backgrounds.

These figures are important for several reasons. Students of intellectual life believe that a common social background, in combination with close physical proximity, contributes to a sense of cohesion in the intellectual community.[30] Historically, the class background of intellectuals with revolutionary political tendencies has been shown to be influential. Theda Skocpol concluded that, "in France, Russia, and China alike, the relevant political leadership precipitated out of the ranks of relatively highly educated groups oriented to state activities or employment. And the leaders arose especially from among those who were somewhat marginal to the established dominant classes and governing elites under the Old Regime."[31] Aron puts the argument in a more contemporary context by suggesting that, as the children of lower classes who pass through the university increase in number, they are more likely to favor radical social change than are their middle- and upper-class peers, thus undermining the political and social establishments.[32] This might be true, since there is evidence in Mexico to suggest that students from lower socioeconomic backgrounds have more radical views.[33]

Two processes, however, work to moderate such influences. First, the young person from a working-class background needs to find immediate employment; thus, he or she often adjusts personal views to correspond to those of the prospective employer, whether in the public or private sector. Second, like politicians from the lower classes, intellectuals from a similar background tend to be overwhelmed by the established intellectual environment, rather than attempting to change it.[34] The pressures on intellectuals from these backgrounds to conform is far greater, since they have been a tiny minority, whereas for many years, a substantial group of Mexico's political leaders came from working-class backgrounds. Some evidence exists to show, however, that prior to the Mexican Revolution of 1910 the class backgrounds of intellectuals determined their ideological views, since upper-class elite intellectuals favored moderate, liberal, democratic reforms, whereas the transitional middle groups had a more radical view[35] and wanted to form alliances with other groups, such as peasants and workers.

The representation of middle- and upper-class backgrounds among Mexican intellectuals is more overwhelming than it is among intellectuals in the United States. Kadushin found that only 10 percent of the fathers of elite North American intellectuals in the 1960s were from blue-collar occupations, but that 40 percent of the fathers of younger elite intellectuals were manual workers.[36] In Mexico, that pattern has not occurred, since all eighteen intellectuals born after 1930 about whom I have information have come from middle- or upper-class parents. Even the middle-aged generation, that is, those born between 1910 and 1930, is definitely in this same category, since sixty-two of sixty-five, or 95 percent of that group, have similar backgrounds (*MIBP*). The implication is clear. As the educational system in the United States has expanded, and even though the professional classes have grown rapidly, those skills and credentials necessary to an intellectual career have been made accessible to more children of blue-collar workers. In contrast, in Mexico, where the middle class is much smaller and the working class much larger, the expansion of the educational system has done little to help the child of working-class parents join Mexico's intellectual leadership; if anything, that leadership is becoming more middle class and homogeneous.[37]

Interviews and correspondence with Mexican intellectuals document their belief that family background influences their attitudes and values. Several examples are worth detailing. Arturo Warman, a prominent anthropologist who has devoted much of his effort to examining the plight of the Mexican *campesino*, had this to say about his family and his intellectual interests:

Beginning in my youth, I had to work constantly and the family had to make up the difference between the expenditures and the real income we had coming in to maintain our standard of living. Because I had to work, I came to know the *campo* [rural area] in Mexico—it is amazing, but I have worked for twenty-four years, since all my academic studies were done in combination with employment.[38]

Warman's direct interest in peasant problems, unusual for a Mexican intellectual, is the result, according to his own account, of his parents' economic situation and his having to work.

The case of a young female intellectual, Martha Robles, is equally revealing, for she strongly believes her philosophical attitudes are in direct response to certain conditions she disliked about her upbringing and parents' background. Robles's mother, like her own mother, was a strong personality, talented in business, who married at seventeen, but refused to conform to the traditional expectations of marriage for a Mexican woman. Robles's father, a successful lawyer who disliked his profession and who dabbled in the classics, was active in politics. He served as a federal deputy for PAN and was the first PAN candidate for governor of Jalisco (he opposed Agustín Yáñez in a bitter campaign). Robles calls her grandfather's impact on her intellectual formation decisive. Her strong attitudes about the liberation of women stem, she believes, from the very traditional attitudes of her father and grandfather toward female roles in a family with seventy-two grandchildren, of which she is the only female with a college education, and from a grandmother and rebellious mother who were independent, but lonely because of that independence.[39]

Robles's description of her family, even in the paraphrased excerpts recorded here, suggests another characteristic common to the backgrounds of many prominent intellectuals in Mexico: the presence of intellectual interests among relatives, or relatives who themselves were intellectuals. Over and over again, in interviews with or biographies about intellectuals, some type of intellectual or intellectually related activity, however marginal, appears in the background of a close relative.[40] These biographical data can by no means be considered complete, but I have been able to document with historical sources the family backgrounds of many Mexican intellectuals. Nearly one-third of Mexico's leading intellectuals are themselves related to other, older intellectuals. Amazingly, 9 percent were third-generation intellectuals, and 4 percent were known to have four or more generations of intellectuals in their family tree. Intellectual elites followed the same pattern in Mexico (*MIBP*).

The presence of intellectual antecedents does not guarantee that a young person will become an intellectual or be recognized for intellectual achievements. Yet, considering the exclusiveness of my definition, the presence of intellectual antecedents is rather striking. When we narrow the definition of generation kinship ties to just parents or grandparents, we find that one of every four prominent intellectuals in Mexico since 1920 is the son, daughter, or grandchild of intellectuals (*MIBP*). One point of interest, however, is that the intellectual elite is less exclusive in this regard (only one of seven) than is the general group of intellectuals. Thus, family ties have not been as important as other qualities in achieving outstanding recognition among elite intellectuals.

Nevertheless, two types of intellectual family with intellectual antecedents are present in Mexico: those extending back to the nineteenth century and well before the Mexican Revolution; and those actually produced by the social upheaval of the Revolution. Among the most well-known of the former type is that of Justo Sierra, prominent nineteenth-century intellectual, statesman, and educator. This family is important because it illustrates the continuity of intellectual interests and talents within a single family over generations spanning many years of anarchy, chaos, and social upheaval, and because it illustrates the breadth of political ties characteristic of a single family. What is important to understand from the description of this family is that the first-generation member, Justo Sierra O'Reilly (1814-1861), was the illegitimate son of a priest, and therefore without social status, who took his mother's name. He rose to prominence after receiving an excellent education from seminary fathers and a law degree. His brother Santiago Sierra O'Reilly became a priest and a notable figure in the caste wars of Yucatán. Justo founded several newspapers and enhanced his career by marrying the daughter of Santiago Méndez, the governor of Yucatán. They had several children, among them Santiago Sierra Méndez (1850-1880), a novelist, journalist, poet, and newspaper publisher who died tragically in a duel with Irineo Paz (Octavio Paz's grandfather) at age thirty over an article he wrote. His son and grandson also were writers. Santiago's brother, Justo Sierra Méndez (1848-1912), is the most prominent member of the family. He held many public posts during the regime of Porfirio Díaz, including justice of the Supreme Court, federal deputy, and secretary of public education. Actively involved in numerous intellectual endeavors, he founded newspapers and wrote regularly for Mexico City dailies. His reputation was such that, despite his services to the Porfiriato, President Madero appointed him as ambassador to Spain in 1912, his last public post.

During the twentieth century, his son Manuel J. Sierra held several important posts in the Secretariat of the Treasury, including that of *oficial mayor*, and he wrote many articles and books. Manuel's wife's father, Joaquín de Casasús, a prominent lawyer, professor, and founder of the National School of Business, was related to other nineteenth-century oligarchic families. De Casasús's father-in-law, Ignacio Altamirano, was a leading nineteenth-century intellectual and educator. Justo Sierra's grandchildren, Javier and Manuel Barros Sierra, distinguished themselves in public life, and Javier, who was the secretary of public works and rector of the National University, was an outstanding mathematician. His son Javier is following in his father's and great-grandfather's footsteps, having served as director of the Institute of Fine Arts.[41]

The Sierra Méndez family illustrates how a self-made intellectual family of the early nineteenth century, after marrying into other notable families, has continued to have family members prominent in intellectual life after 1920 (three of its descendants are in my sample of intellectuals). But the Mexican Revolution of 1910, like the independence of Mexico in the 1820s, gave birth to a new generation of families, often part of an emerging middle class, who would provide the social leadership of Mexico's postrevolutionary political and cultural leaders. An excellent example of this type is Mariano Azuela's family. Azuela, best-known for his colorful and realistic novels of the Mexican Revolution, was the son of a small but successful rancher in the provincial town of Lagos de Moreno, Jalisco, where he grew up in the 1870s and 1880s. As a medical student, he began to write a column for the Guadalajara newspaper, and he completed his first book in 1907. During this period, he used his friendship with Governor José López Portillo y Rojas, grandfather of President López Portillo, to help opponents of the Díaz regime. He practiced medicine from 1899 to 1911, and then became political chief of Lagos under President Madero. In 1915 Azuela served Francisco Villa's forces as a physician and went into exile in El Paso, Texas, in October of that year. He moved to Mexico City in 1916, where he practiced medicine for most of his life. He had ten children, among them Mariano Jr., a noted lawyer, expert on writs, and Supreme Court justice; and Salvador, prominent student leader, supporter of José Vasconcelos's presidential campaign in 1929, dean of the School of Philosophy and Letters at the National University, author, and for many years president of the Seminar of Mexican Culture. A third generation is now represented in intellectual life with the literary contributions of Arturo Azuela, who writes for the review at the National University.[42]

The overall findings about family ties are important, especially when one remembers that Mexico underwent a major social revolution during the lifetimes of two-thirds of the intellectual sample. Certain intellectual families continued to be well represented in the various generations spanning this century because the leadership of the Mexican revolutionary governments did not, according to some scholars, produce radical social change.[43] The revolutionary programs have been described in this way: "Despite the far-reaching reforms of the 1930s, these social programs were carried out with a minimum of bloodshed, virtually no exiles, and little in the way of total ruination of the landed families, reduced though they were in material resources. Moderate forces remained sufficiently powerful through all the stages of the Revolution to prevent the extremists from fully implementing their programs or ideologies."[44] The moderates referred to were not only political leaders, but often the children of the antirevolutionary elite, who became the intellectuals and the intelligentsia of the postrevolutionary era.[45] In fact, of the 319 intellectuals about whom I have information, 22, or 7 percent, were the children or grandchildren of individuals who held prominent positions under Porfirio Díaz or the reactionary regime of Victoriano Huerta (*MIBP*).

This does not mean that the children and grandchildren of antirevolutionary families were themselves antirevolutionary, since concrete examples exist to show otherwise. For example, Víctor Manuel Villaseñor, whose father was an inspector for the Díaz government and who served as a federal deputy from 1900 to 1913, was strongly supportive of the Revolution, having been influenced by Salvador Alvarado and Luis Cabrera in the 1920s, both leading figures in the revolutionary movement.[46] On the other hand, intellectual moderates from similar family backgrounds are common, of which no better representative can be found than Alfonso Reyes, distinguished man of letters, who never advocated an extremist ideology, and who was noted for his independent, but mild, positions on such issues.[47] He was the son of Bernardo Reyes, a key political and military figure during the regime of Porfirio Díaz, who opposed the Revolution and was imprisoned by President Madero in 1912 as a counterrevolutionary leader. Bernardo Reyes was killed the following year while leading a successful rebellion against the government.

The continuity of intellectual families over several generations has not come just from those with a grandfather or father prominent in the Díaz or Huerta regimes. In fact, many intellectuals in the twentieth century who have come from intellectual families are the children or grandchildren of important figures who supported Benito Juárez and the nineteenth-century liberal tenets institutionalized in the Constitution of 1857.[48] Many of these families left their grandchildren with dual heritages, one favoring the status quo, the other, the restoration of the Republic as it had existed in the late 1860s and early 1870s. For example, Narciso Bassols, a leading intellectual during the 1930s and 1940s, was the great-nephew of Sebastián Lerdo de Tejada, whose sister married Bassols's grandfather, a notable Catalán guitarist who emigrated to Mexico. Bassols's maternal grandfather established a religious press in Puebla, where he authored several works. The impact of Bassols's family has led his biographer to conclude that his philosophy was a heritage of the radicalism of Lerdo and the Catholicism of his grandparents.[49]

The importance of middle- and upper-class backgrounds and the intellectual occupations of most of the parents of Mexican intellectuals in twentieth century is that intellectual leadership is somewhat hereditary. Almost no intellectuals who come from lower socioeconomic backgrounds reach a recognized position in the intellectual community. Whereas their parents are often first-generation members of the middle class, this is almost never true of the intellectual himself. In the Soviet Union, which underwent a revolution at about the same time, but with greater social and political consequences, similar conditions have emerged. According to one author, at least two-thirds of the intelligentsia are members by birth, and a "closer analysis reveals that the Soviet intelligentsia, which plays a leading role in the society and provides its ruling elite, has in fact become largely hereditary."[50]

Mexican intellectuals, like their parents and grandparents, are passing on their intellectual proclivities to some of their children. Of the 317 persons about whom I have information, 38, or 12 percent, had children or grandchildren who were intellectuals (*MIBP*). If we broaden kinship ties beyond those of children and grandchildren, and look both horizontally and vertically in terms of generations, the extent of kinship ties can be seen. Intellectuals within the same family appear to be fairly common in Mexico, since at least 30 percent of the intellectuals have brothers or sisters, wives or husbands, sisters- or brothers-in-law, aunts or uncles, nephews or nieces, or multiple combinations of these who are also intellectuals (*MIBP*). In a society like Mexico, where family ties help to establish social prestige, kinship takes on an added importance. As C. Wright Mills suggests, prestige is like wealth and power: it tends to be cumulative. The more of it you have, the more you can get.[51] Thus, the prestige of one's family increases opportunities for an intellectual or political career, or both.

The importance of social ties is not confined to other intellectuals related to one's family, even though these ties may be fairly common. Equally important are the social and kinship ties intellectuals have with Mexican politicians. Among Mexican intellectuals prominent in the twentieth century, 78 of the 305 individuals about whom I have information were or are related to members of Mexico's political leadership.[52] Among Mexico's elite intellectuals, that figure is even higher, since exactly a third of them were related to prominent public figures (*MIBP*). These findings are important because they demonstrate that there is a sizeable overlap among the families that supply Mexico's political and intellectual leadership. This suggests further evidence of a power elite among cultural and political leaders since the Mexican Revolution. Moreover, it would be fair to assume that anyone having relatives among the political leadership could easily move within their social circles, and furthermore, have easier access to still other politicians who could broaden their social contrasts.

Socially, Mexican intellectuals are closely tied to the political establishment. Of the 324 intellectuals about whom I have information, 242, or 75 percent, were friends of Mexican politicians. In the case of Mexico's elite intellectuals, 86 percent maintained friendships with politicians (*MIBP*). That most intellectuals are well acquainted with political leaders is both a cause and a result of their involvement in public life. Any intellectual who has served in public office is likely to emerge from that experience with more political friends. On the other hand, friendship with a politician increases the opportunities of obtaining such a post. Furthermore, for the intellectual who does not wish to be involved directly in public service, informal channels for influencing policymaking are available through personal ties.

Consequences of Education

In Mexico, where access to education is still not widespread, and was even less so during the 1930s and 1940s, a person's state of birth, the size of the native community, and, of course, the socioeconomic background of parents, often determine the desire to attend school, and more important, the ability to do so. The educational patterns of Mexican politicians clearly demonstrate this relationship.[53] In the case of intellectuals, this relationship does not merit testing, because the overwhelming number of intellectuals are from urban birthplaces, middle- and upper middle-class backgrounds, and have reached higher levels of education (table 8).

The differences in educational attainments between the intellectual and the politician are striking, again remembering that the politicians in my population are younger. Only 6 intellectuals, or 2 percent of the total, did not go beyond the level of normal school in their education, whereas 20 percent of all politicians had only a normal school education. Of the intellectuals who did not complete a university degree, the majority completed preparatory school in a course of studies following an academic track in preparation for the university. Most of the intellectuals who did not go on for further formal education were in the arts or in journalism and found academic credentials unnecessary to a successful career. In general in Mexico, the myth that the intellectual is self-educated, whether a poet, painter, musician, or writer, is just that, a myth. If we look at the intellectual's professional field and we classify intellectuals according to whether they self-trained in their respective professions or received formal training, we find that 89 percent (294 of 329) obtained formal instruction (figures are from the *MIBP*).

In Mexico's educational system, once students complete primary and secondary school, they continue, if they are going to pursue an academic

Table 8
Education of Mexican Intellectuals and Politicians

Highest Level Completed	Percentage of		
	Intellectuals[a] (N=325)	Politicians[b] (N=1,311)	Intellectual Elite[a] (N=53)
Primary	0.3	7	2
Secondary	1.0	7	0
Normal	1.0	6	0
Preparatory	18.0	5	15
University	38.0	54	42
Postprofessional	10.0	5	9
MA	4.0	3	4
PhD	18.0	7	21
LLD	4.0	0[d]	2
MD or DDS	7.0	7	6
Total	101.0	101	101

Notes: [a]Data from the *MIBP*, 1920 to 1980.
[b]Data from the *MPBP* for the Government Political Elite, 1935 to 1980.
[c]Data for LLDs received by politicians were combined with PhDs. Most of these degrees were LLDs, not PhDs.

program, in a preparatory school program. Many of Mexico's intellectual leaders did not have secondary education because, until the 1920s, young people went directly from primary school into an extended preparatory curriculum.[54] Their preparatory education is important for several reasons. First, nearly one of five intellectuals received *only* a preparatory education (table 8). Therefore, knowledge about the preparatory school they attended indicates which institutions are important in the certification processes of intellectuals. Second, the preparatory education of political leaders in the Federal District determined the likelihood of their continuing their education in Mexico City.[55] Third, the education of intellectuals in certain institutions increases the prospect of their having contact with future and present political leaders who are students and professors, especially if they do not progress beyond the preparatory level.

Mexican intellectuals, like their political counterparts, have been overwhelmingly educated at a single preparatory institution, the National Preparatory School in Mexico City (table 9). Again, when one considers the Mexican population living in Mexico City during the years of this study and the proportion of intellectuals born in Mexico City, the number is surprising. One out of two intellectuals received their education at this one institution. Precisely the same proportion of all political leaders with a preparatory education attended this school. Thus, the chances of an intellectual attending the National Preparatory School making friends with a budding politician were substantial, especially if their preparatory education occurred before the 1950s, when increasing enrollments forced preparatory education to be decentralized among various branches in Mexico City.

Furthermore, the regional preparatory schools attended by political leaders were generally those most frequently attended by intellectuals, most notably the University of Michoacán or its predecessor, the Colegio de San Nicolás de Hidalgo, and the Universities of Puebla and México. The Universities of Veracruz and Oaxaca did not fare nearly as well among intellectuals as among politicians. The most likely explanation for this disparity is that neither of those two states was as well represented among intellectuals' birthplaces as among politicians', and since parents tend to send their children to the regional institution closest to home if they cannot afford to send their children to Mexico City, birthplace indirectly determines the location of preparatory education for many children.

Two further important differences distinguish the intellectual from the politician with regard to preparatory education. Most important, a sizeable proportion of Mexico's intellectuals have received their education in an environment not frequented by the politician: in private schools, seminaries, and foreign academies (table 9). More than one out of every four

Table 9
Preparatory Schools Attended by Mexican Intellectuals and Politicians

Institution	Percentage of	
	Intellectuals[a] (N=202)	Politicians[b] (N=592)
National Preparatory School (Mexico City)	48	48
University of Michoacán or Colegio de San Nicolás de Hidalgo (Morelia)	3	5
University of Guadalajara (Guadalajara)	4	5
University of Puebla (Puebla)	2	3
University of State of Mexico or Scientific and Literary Institute of Mexico (Toluca)	2	2
University of Veracruz (Jalapa)	1	3
University of Oaxaca or Institute of Arts and Sciences (Oaxaca)	1	4
Foreign	15	1
Seminary	8	2
Private colegios	5	3
All others	9	25
Total	98	101

Notes: [a]Data from *MIBP*, 1920-1980
[b]Data from *MPBP* for the Government Political Elite, 1935-1980

intellectuals attended one of these institutions, whereas only 7 percent of Mexico's political leadership did so. These figures suggest that, unless they were related, or made social contacts through some other channel, a fifth of Mexico's intellectuals, *during the time* they did go to preparatory school, were unlikely to meet any future politicians.

Illustrative of this effect is the relationship between preparatory school location and friendships with political leaders. Although 74 percent of Mexico's intellectuals had such friendships, 89 percent of the National Preparatory School graduates and 88 percent of the state preparatory school graduates (the institutions most commonly attended by politicians) had such friendships. In contrast, only 57 percent of the intellectuals who were graduates of seminaries and private schools subsequently had such friendships. If we carry this relationship further and look at the preparatory school intellectuals with government careers attended, we find that, whereas slightly over half of all intellectuals had government careers, 69 percent of the graduates from the National Preparatory School and the state preparatory institutions followed such careers; only 32 percent of those who attended private and religious schools ended up in similar positions (figures from the *MIBP*).

Of the three types of preparatory institution—public, private, and foreign—foreign preparatory schools is the largest category (15 percent) not attended by politicians. Most intellectuals educated abroad were of foreign nationality, or were artists, dramatists, or musicians who could not obtain a quality education in their field of interest in Mexico. Nearly all of those receiving their preparatory education abroad attended schools in Spain, other parts of Latin America, France, or, in some cases, England or the United States. Furthermore, those few native Mexicans who left Mexico for their preparatory education were generally members of the generation born prior to 1900, when educational specialties at this level were less developed.

The preparatory education of intellectuals also differs from that of politicians because of the number who have attended seminaries and private schools. Until the 1920s, most of the children of wealthy families attended private schools, especially at the primary and secondary levels, whereas most of the children of working and middle-class families attended public schools.[56] Although a number of older politicians also attended seminaries, especially for their secondary education (a fact some would like to hide because of the antichurch rhetoric common to Mexican public life), their attendance was exceptional, and not as common as for the intellectual.[57]

The higher socioeconomic status of intellectuals, their urban places of birth, and the social and political attitudes of their parents have all contributed to the differences in the type of preparatory education for a sizeable number of intellectuals and politicians. The same elements that contributed to a higher number of intellectuals than politicians actually reaching the preparatory level are responsible for the higher numbers who have received university and postgraduate educations.

The location of university education of intellectuals has the same importance as that of preparatory education. But, since 80 percent of Mexico's leading intellectuals have both a preparatory and a university education and since many may have attended a preparatory school not attended by the political leadership, the location of professional studies takes on added importance. The institution itself is also important because of the differences in educational ambience certain public and private institutions in Mexico provide, environments affecting the attitudes and beliefs of intellectuals and politicians.[58]

The pattern of universities attended by Mexico's intellectuals has very definite biases, in many ways similar to the pattern of its political leaders (table 10). The most striking characteristic of the location of universities attended by intellectuals is the substantial number who have attended the National University, even when the figures for intellectuals who did not attend a university are included. If we consider only intellectuals who have attended college, we find that two-thirds went to UNAM. These figures (table 10) not only illustrate the past importance of the National University in the educational experiences of Mexico's intellectuals, but demonstrate once again the importance of that institution in the education of two of Mexico's leadership groups. Furthermore, the overwhelming number of intellectuals who have attended a single institution only enhances the homogeneity of their already similar residential and socioeconomic backgrounds. Because an equally disproportionate number of political leaders have attended this institution, chances for social contact and for recruitment into political groups remain strong.

Many variables affect the relationship of Mexican intellectuals with the state. Among the most important of these is the location of the intellectual's

Table 10
Universities Attended by Mexican Intellectuals and Politicians

Institution	Percentage of		
	Intellectuals[a] (N=327)	Intellectual Elite[a] (N=52)	Politicians[b] (N=1,309)
UNAM	59	71	45.000
University of Michoacán or Colegio de San Nicolás de Hidalgo	2	2	1.000
University of Guadalajara	2	4	2.000
San Carlos Academy (National School of Fine Arts)	5	4	0.000
National Conservatory of Music	2	0	0.001
Various U.S.	2	2	2.000
European or other Latin American	9	4	21.000
Did not attend	13	4	28.000
All others	7	10	22.000
Total	101	101	101.000

Notes: [a]Data from *MIBP*, 1920-1980
[b]Data from *MPBP* for Government Political Elite, 1935-1980

education. Since the intellectual and the politician in the twentieth century have chosen to be educated at the same institution, the possibilities for a tie to be established between the two groups occurs at a very young age. Furthermore, as I suggested in chapter 2, since friendship is such a critical element to the political culture and to a successful political career, anything that brings the politician and the intellectual in close proximity only furthers the probability of their establishing bonds of trust at a young age, even before they have embarked on a definite career. Moreover, as I shall illustrate in chapter 7, mentor-disciple relationships, crucial to the recruitment and careers of politicians and intellectuals, occur at the university.

Intellectuals who did not attend the National University are distributed among several other types of institutions. The two most important provincial institutions for university-educated intellectuals are the Universities of Guadalajara and Michoacán. These two institutions frequently show up among the provincial schools attended by politicians, also. However, intellectuals again diverge from the educational pattern of politicians in the numbers who have been educated abroad. One out of every ten intellectuals in Mexico receives his or her university education from a foreign institution, usually in Europe, although some also graduate from U.S. and Latin American schools.

The other apparent difference in the pattern of universities attended by intellectuals and politicians is the number of intellectuals who have attended the San Carlos Academy or its successor, the National School of Fine Arts, or the National Conservatory of Music, both in Mexico City. These two institutions, of course, are the most prestigious that could be chosen by students wishing to pursue a career in the arts or music. Thus, these choices in and of themselves are not surprising. However, because of the proportion of intellectuals who have attended the School of Fine Arts, it is an institution deserving further study. These two institutions are also important because they do not appear in the university backgrounds of Mexican politicians. Intellectuals attending these two institutions were not as likely to make the social contacts with future politicians necessary to careers in the government. Other than the fact that music and art inherently tend to be subjects less inclined toward political statements, the lack of student companions interested in public life in these two schools may explain why artists and musicians have been least successful among all intellectuals in rising to high political office.[59]

The educational data in table 10 include only locations where individuals completed work toward their first degree. However, if we examine those intellectuals who received some type of advanced academic training abroad or in Mexico, we find that 45 percent of all intellectuals did experience some form of graduate education, and the majority abroad (*MIBP*). Furthermore, the greatest number of intellectuals receiving graduate education in any one country study in the United States. Actually, more intellectuals (37 percent of those with advanced education) have received it in the United States than in Mexico. Because one out of every three Mexican intellectuals has done graduate work abroad, they are exposed directly to the educational methodologies and ideologies of foreigners. Furthermore, although I do not have comparable data for politicians, and although many politicians, especially younger ones, are increasingly receiving advanced education abroad, this educational experience has been much more universal to intellectuals.

One cannot attribute specific ideological orientations to these foreign educational experiences, but the literature Mexicans are exposed to, the subjects in their disciplines in vogue, and the focus of the particular discipline are affected. Moreover, such influences do not just creep into the creative product; they also appear in teaching, something many intellectuals do. Therefore, whatever influences they receive from this experience are passed on to succeeding generations, including their intellectual disciples.

Both the location and the level of advanced education of intellectuals are important to understanding the homogeneity of their background, their possibilities for political careers, and their similarities to public figures. But equally important to their educational backgrounds, and to their future careers, is the type of professional degree intellectuals with college educations obtain. When the degree fields of Mexican intellectuals are divided into the twelve most frequently chosen disciplines, several interesting patterns emerge (table 11).

Intellectuals have chosen law overwhelmingly over any other type of degree. The study of law is important to the future career of the intellectual in two ways. First, as the data in table 11 make clear, law degrees have been even more important to the political leader than to the intellectual, and both groups have primarily attended the National Law School at UNAM. Thus, the opportunities for interchange between the two groups are heightened by their discipline and the location of their education. Furthermore, since a law degree provides skills traditionally useful to political careers in many cultures, including Mexico and the United States, it would be more natural for a person to seek government service with a law degree than with, say, a degree in art.

One of the important differences between Mexican and North American intellectuals is the involvement of the Mexican in public careers. Although I have already discussed certain structural explanations, an additional reason emerges from data on the college educations of Mexican intellectuals. Because many have been educated in law, even if they do not practice it as a full-time profession, they can follow government careers and maintain the contacts necessary to those careers. It can be argued that the educational

Table 11
College Degrees Earned by Mexican Intellectuals and Politicians

Type of Degree	Percentage of		
	Intellectuals[a] (N=261)	Intellectual Elite[a] (N=45)	Politicians[b] (N=968)
Law	39.0	58.0	56.0
Economics	3.0	2.0	7.0
CPA	1.0	2.0	1.0
Medical or dental	10.0	7.0	10.0
Science	4.0	0.0	—[c]
Engineering	6.0	2.0	10.0
Agricultural engineering	1.0	0.0	3.0
Arts & letters	25.0	27.0	13.0[c]
Music	2.0	0.0	—[c]
Plastic arts and architecture	9.0	2.0	1.0
Business administration	0.4	0.0	—[c]
Political science	0.4	0.0	—[c]
Total	101.0	100.0	101.0

Notes: [a]Data from the *MIBP*, 1920-1980.
[b]Data from the *MPBP* for the Government Political Elite, 1935-1980.
[c]The figures for political leaders under arts and letters include all other types of degrees received by politicians, including plastic arts, music, political science, business administration, and sciences. The actual number of degrees in music, plastic arts, political science, and the sciences is minuscule. Most of the degree holders in this category actually received their education in arts and letters, with a smaller number in business administration.

structure itself, because it long encouraged degrees in law among the college-educated population, has acted to funnel intellectuals into public life, a characteristic foreign to the North American intellectual scene. In fact, among North America's intellectual elite in the 1960s, none were lawyers.[60]

Law degrees have been important in the university educations of many Mexican intellectuals, but so have degrees in arts and letters, held by a fourth of all intellectuals. Because of the interdisciplinary orientation of my definition of an intellectual, we could expect such degrees to be plentiful among Mexican intellectuals, as well as among intellectuals in general. But what is surprising about this figure in Mexico is that it runs counter to those degrees encouraged and made available by the educational system.

Clarence Haring has explained why degrees in arts and letters are rare:

The university there is a grouping of professional faculties—Law and Political Science, Medicine, Engineering, Natural Sciences, Agronomy, Commerce, and Economic Sciences—aiming solely at professional competence, and lacking the "cultural" objectives of the undergraduate college associated with university instruction in the United States and England.[61]

A further significance of the high number of liberal arts degrees among intellectuals is that they attend schools not attended by many political leaders. Indeed, it may well be liberal-arts graduates who compose the group of intellectuals who are recognized by other intellectuals but not by public figures. Thus, the educational system plays an important role in separating some intellectuals from the politicians at a young age, even as it is bringing others together.

One of the reasons most politicians do not follow a liberal-arts curriculum may be their socioeconomic background. The choice of a traditional profession is much more likely when an individual has few or no family resources to sustain or initiate a career. The typical politician, before deciding on a public career, realizes that a professional degree is the only key to economic security. Although the politician is increasingly from a middle-class background, in the early decades this was not true. The gradual change in the background of political leaders, away from working-class parents toward middle-class parents, may also account for the decreasing emphasis on law, and an increasing emphasis on some of the newer professional degrees in the social sciences.

Two conditions in Mexico's education system do work to lessen the separation of liberal arts majors from majors in specific professions at Mexican institutions. In the first place, many of these individuals were in the same program at the National Preparatory School, thus making contact before they attended a professional school. Using Jaime Torres Bodet and Samuel Ramos as examples, we encounter a multitude of lifelong friendships with political figures, which developed from their respective educations at the National Preparatory School and the Colegio de San Nicolás de Hidalgo (University of Michoacán) in Morelia. Second, contrary to the stereotype of the Mexican politician as parochially educated, many, although taking a professional career, have also taken courses in philosophy, literature, and esthetics and, perhaps equally important, have directed or participated in the intellectual reviews common to numerous student groups at the preparatory schools and the National University.

Another college degree that distinguishes the intellectual from the politician and the intelligentsia is that in the plastic arts. Although a small number of the politicians in my sample earned a degree in architecture, none obtained one in the plastic arts. Earlier, in my examination of the degree-granting institutions, I indicated that most were earned at the National School of Fine Arts, its antecedent, the San Carlos Academy, or abroad. Again, the importance of the large number of intellectuals who earn these degrees is that this group has fewer ties to the established political structure than do other intellectuals, and their aloofness from government political leaders may stem from their early separation in the educational system.

A further implication may be drawn from the data in table 11: virtually all Mexican intellectuals are absent from the educational field likely to attract many future entrepreneurs, business administration. Although intellectuals do make contact with business leaders through social relationships, family ties, and their careers, these ties are less likely to occur at a young age, because of an emphasis on different educational disciplines. Different degrees not only separate the intellectual and the business executive socially, but perhaps help to explain why intellectuals do not align themselves ideologically with entrepreneurial groups in the same way they do with political allies in the state.

Conclusions

The background information examined in this chapter, and the comparisons that are drawn with politicians and, in some cases, with intellectuals elsewhere, do not fully explain the uniqueness of Mexican intellectuals, nor their differences from the political leadership. I have discussed educational patterns and their relationship to family background, residence, and place of birth to suggest that there are some structural characteristics in Mexican society—and even some givens, through chance or fate, over which the individual intellectual has no control—that make the pursuit of an intellectual career possible and improve the intellectual's chances for contact with political leaders. Thus, for example, if all other background and career variables were similar, the intellectual who attended the National Preparatory School and the National University would be more likely to have the opportunity to follow a public career, and indeed, to *choose* to follow one, if only part time. On the other hand, the intellectual who did not choose these institutions, or who had them chosen by parents, would not be inclined toward a career in the federal bureaucracy, nor have as many opportunities to make this route feasible.

Although many informal characteristics and choices are involved in the career patterns, personal relationships, and ideologies of individual intellectuals, certain background conditions and structural patterns have channeled them into or away from certain situations. It is clear from the comparative data that intellectuals differ from political counterparts in that they are much more urban, from a middle- or upper-class environment, and more likely to have a foreign-born parent. Over time, as these patterns have changed, the politician, at least in the case of the first two variables, has become more like the intellectual. In the past, however, all three of these variables helped to explain the differences between these two important groups. Furthermore, family background suggests that the Mexican Revolution produced fewer changes for the intellectual than for political leaders. The continuity of intellectual families before, during, and after the Revolution requires further examination and a rethinking of our speculations about the consequences of social upheaval on intellectual leadership in the postrevolutionary era. Moreover, close family relationships between the intellectual and political communities help to explain why, historically, there has been little division between the Mexican intellectual and the politician and may suggest one reason why political stability became a byword of the Mexican system after 1929.

The conditions that led to many intellectuals and politicians having shared experiences and, consequently, some shared values, are now being changed by newer patterns in education. Today, more intellectuals are being educated abroad, in different schools from those traditionally attended by intellectuals and politicians and, most important, they are pursuing different degrees. It is clear from the evidence presented in this chapter that the choice of a college program does have considerable consequences for how intellectuals define their role in Mexican society, especially their relationship to the state. The direction of these changes is equally clear: as more intellectuals choose the humanities, more also define their responsibilities as being outside the state.

The birthplace, residence, family background, and education of the Mexican intellectual have many significant implications for understanding the structure of intellectual life and differ in many ways from the experience of intellectuals in other cultures. Furthermore, the figures shed light on why the role of the North American intellectual is in many ways so different from that of the Mexican intellectual. Last, an analysis of these data, and speculations as to the cause and results of certain patterns, have important implications for understanding the possibilities for the existence of a power elite in Mexico. In the following chapter, the career experiences and the fields of Mexico's important intellectuals will be examined for what they can tell us about their recruitment and future direction.

6. Career Patterns

In the preceding chapter, a number of significant patterns stemming from family background, place of birth, location and level and type of education for the intellectual were identified. To some extent, all of these influence the career choices Mexican intellectuals make. This chapter will examine the types of careers Mexican intellectuals follow, the implications of their choices for the structure of intellectual life, and the subsequent effects on the state's recruitment of intellectuals. Individual professions help to determine the likelihood that an individual will play an intellectual role. As implied earlier, the role of intellectuals in any society is defined, to some extent, by their own perceptions of intellectuals and their role. Charles Kadushin has suggested with great insight the importance of analyzing the relationship between occupation and the intellectual's role:

Though we often speak of the elite intellectual as if he were a person, the intellectual is a social role, for nobody is wholly an intellectual. Some persons spend most of their time playing this role, some spend less time, and some are not at all in the running. One should not debate whether atomic scientists are just as much intellectuals as are literary critics. Rather, one must consider why, under varying conditions, persons who play certain occupational roles also play the role of intellectual.[1]

Mexican intellectuals, like their counterparts elsewhere in the world, have followed a variety of occupations, either subordinate to or dominating their intellectual activities. As Kadushin correctly argues, very few intellectuals engage in actions qualifying them for this label on a full-time basis, nor do they necessarily occupy themselves with intellectual pursuits at a constant level over long periods.

Occupations: Uncommon Choices

An examination of the occupations of Mexican intellectuals reveals a fairly narrow range, mostly professional. The most obvious conclusions from the data in the *MIBP* are that certain occupations have traditionally attracted intellectual types, or perhaps that certain occupations tend to produce intellectual types. Among Mexican intellectuals, the most frequent full-time careers, accounting for 86 percent of all intellectuals, have been government officials, 28 percent; college professors, 17 percent; journalists, 10 percent; self-employed writers, 9 percent; artists and architects, 8 percent; educators (administrators), 7 percent; and lawyers, 7 percent. Few Mexican intellectuals emerge from those occupations tied to business, religion, medicine, engineering, economics, labor relations, filmmaking, music (all 2 percent or less), or the military (none).

There are universal reasons for this, but other explanations are embedded in the peculiarities of the Mexican scene. The exclusion altogether of the military was something of a surprise, given the fact that in the nineteenth century many intellectuals were not averse to combining intellectual roles with careers as officers. After the Mexican Revolution, the military was no longer a popular career choice among middle- and upper-class children, since it was inundated by many working-class people who were self-made revolutionaries. Although the officer corps has gradually become middle class, they are the sons of the postrevolutionary middle-class and are often related to other members of the officer corps.[2] Furthermore, Mexico, unlike most other Latin American countries, has succeeded in separating the military from politics, subordinating it to civilian political leadership. Thus, its role is formal and essentially professional, with little place for creative and critical intellectual minds. Most of the officer corps has come in recent years from the national military academies, schools that do not share the ambience of cultural and overt political activities found at the National Preparatory School and the National University.[3]

Many intellectuals have made their careers in Mexican politics, but the vast majority have done so within the federal bureaucracy and not within party or electoral politics, the realm through which labor leaders reach the top. The only Mexican intellectual in my sample who was engaged in labor politics is Vicente Lombardo Toledano, who combined his union leadership with political and intellectual interests. But Lombardo Toledano was also exceptional in that he came from a wealthy family, whereas most of the leading labor organizers, at least until the 1960s, came from lower socioeconomic backgrounds, having themselves been blue-collar workers.[4] Since few Mexican intellectuals fit this pattern, it is not surprising that Carl Sandburgs and Eric Hoffers are uncommon to the Mexican scene.

Perhaps the most surprising omission among professions chosen by Mexican intellectuals are careers in acting and film directing. The reason is twofold. Most intellectuals and cultural leaders do not believe the film industry is a serious, influential enterprise in Mexico. As one important newspaper editor, Manuel Becerra Acosta, suggested, "The film industry in previous years was one that represented nostalgia for the past. Now it has become an industry of imitation, and when it does try to deal with social realities, they do not make use of our own realities. I think the reason for this may be commercial."[5] The failure to use reality in Mexican cinema, according to one filmmaker, has not always been the case. Salomón Laiter believed that, in the era of "El Indio" Fernández and Julio Bracho, filmmaking "was more important than our literature, and on a par with our painting. That is, it was an art intimately connected to reality, aware of its resources, and very able to express what was then interesting."[6]

Although not as poorly represented as the film industry among Mexican intellectuals, music has not fared very well. In fact, it was a surprise to find no musicians among Mexico's intellectual elite, even though Carlos Chávez received a vote or two from his peers for inclusion in this group. Again, this has something to do with the ongoing self-definition of a Mexican intellectual. Many intellectuals do not recognize the intellectual contributions music can make, because they believe that the medium itself is not conducive to intellectual communication. Furthermore, though Mexican music developed a strong sense of nationalism, even in orchestral compositions by Chávez and Silvestre Revueltas, during the 1930s, it has been largely imitative of European trends.[7] Some Mexican musicians themselves consider their music to be elitist, directed toward the middle class, and without social and political significance.[8]

The other reason intellectual musicians are uncommon is that they tend to follow an atypical pattern during their early years, especially since it is difficult for them to obtain training equal to their ability. For example, one of Mexico's leading composers during the early part of the twentieth century was Manuel Ponce, the son of a well-to-do accountant who had once suffered domestic exile for serving Maximilian. Like many musicians of his age, Ponce first learned piano from a family member, and then, after studying privately, applied his musical skills as an organist in the Catholic church. After briefly attending the National Conservatory of Music in Mexico City, Ponce went to Germany in his late teens to study. Throughout the first two decades of this century, he spent much of his time living abroad, in Germany, Cuba, France, and the United States.[9] Even though Ponce is considered the father of the Mexican school of music, his socialization experiences differed from those of other intellectuals of his generation.

Few Mexican intellectuals have worked in business (2 percent) or been clergy (2 percent). In chapter 2, I suggested some of the reasons neither of these fields offer opportunities to the typical intellectual, although both may expand as career choices for intellectuals in the future. In the case of the church, it is worth mentioning several additional explanations, one being religious beliefs themselves. Although I did not have sufficient information to categorize intellectuals by their religious beliefs, Marsal's study of Mexican political essayists between 1955 and 1969 shows that only 5 percent were practicing Catholics, whereas 76 percent were nonbelievers and 10 percent practiced no religion.[10] Among the intellectuals, nonreligious people may not be as extensive. However, the presence of antireligious values at an early age would eliminate careers in the clergy as a choice for intellectuals. Furthermore, when other intellectuals strongly hold antireligious views, church intellectuals are isolated. Second, the role of the church itself in Mexico may inhibit the possibilities for intellectual contributions from within the institution. As Father Daniel Olmedo, a leading church historian, suggests, "Mexican intellectuals in the clergy are trapped by the pastoral problems that we have, and my impression is that the level of work being done is not equal to that carried out in earlier periods."[11]

The most obviously neglected careers among intellectuals are in the sciences and medicine (2 percent), even though some of these are subsumed under the field of education. The fact that only one individual among the intellectual elite was either a physician or an engineer, both scientific professions, indirectly suggests that the sciences as an intellectual field were not particularly well-represented among Mexican intellectuals as a whole (table 6). Only 5 and 4 percent of Mexico's intellectuals were engaged in scientific and medical research and writing, respectively, and even fewer made their living, except through teaching, in the practice of these professions.

Science has not been an appealing profession to the budding intellectual. In general, few college-educated people in Latin America follow careers in science.[12] Talcott Parsons provides a general comment on why this is so, an explanation applicable to the Latin American and Mexican scene:

A serious problem was posed, however, when the empirical sciences began to grow in relative significance: the experimental method necessitated technological operations, and the gentleman was not permitted, except for the use of arms, to "work with his hands. . . ." There has been a certain tendency to consider the scientist as not quite a "nice person," his calling as one not suitable for a gentleman.[13]

Medicine has fared best among the sciences because "one of the few manual techniques that appeals to Latin Americans is surgical skill, for it is greatly esteemed, gives high personal prestige, and social and economic rewards."[14] It is also a traditional discipline available to those who have sought higher education, even during the colonial period.

The Mexican attitude toward scientists and scientific research is changing. Some intellectuals attribute this to the influence of North American ideas on the educational curriculum. Others believe a universal trend toward greater emphasis on scientific research as a solution to the world's problems is having an effect in Mexico, too. Although most people assume the general public is not interested in science in Mexico, the National Council of Science and Technology began publishing *Ciencia y Desarrollo* in 1971, with a circulation of several thousand. By 1980, this slick, well-illustrated magazine reached an audience of fifty-five thousand, much larger than for most intellectual journals.[15]

A second, more abstract, reason why intellectuals do not follow scientific careers, and why scientific interests are not prominent among recognized Mexican intellectuals, is the philosophical difference between the scientist and the humanist, or what C. P. Snow described as the two cultures, represented by literary types versus the physical scientists.[16] In the field of politics, the traditional, liberal-arts educated Mexican, often trained in law, is confronting the technician, well educated in the social sciences, especially economics. So far this increased specialization has not led to unbridgeable fissures between the two groups. Many observers argue, however, that the humanistic intellectual finds it difficult to communicate with the scientist and worries that the scientist subordinates human values to technological ends.[17]

Mexican humanistic and literary intellectuals do not believe science should be automatically excluded from intellectual life, but they definitely seem to be on a different wavelength as far as considering Mexican scientists as intellectuals or as having made intellectual contributions. In spite of the fact that the most prestigious government-sponsored intellectual academy, the National College, has always had many scientists (in recent years, they are even more numerous), Mexico's intellectual establishment does not name scientific intellectuals to its list of prominent figures since 1920. Political leaders, however, do not share this bias.[18]

This same pattern seems to have occurred in the United States, where Kadushin found only one scientist, a biologist, among the 172 elite intellectuals in his sample. He suggests that the reason North Americans omitted scientists from their choices is that as a group scientists tend to be "diffident about communicating their non-expert personal values and feelings to general audiences. When they do make policy or value pronouncements, these tend to be one-shot affairs in the mass media."[19] Thus, one could argue that the style of communication determines peer perception of the role that individual plays and, particularly, whether or not an individual qualifies as an intellectual.

Additionally, scientists have often specialized to such an extent that they restrict their communications to other scientists. One Mexican anthropologist suggested that scientists have not had a major impact on intellectual life because of their specialization, and that this tendency is likely to continue because science is becoming more rather than less specialized. He further suggested that Mexican scientists have become "more associated with foreign influences than with expanding their own influence here."[20] Again, this suggests a similarity with musicians, who also have been strongly tied to foreign influences in methodology and content. This influence has been even stronger among scientists, and continues to be important.

In several recent studies of small groups of scientists, Larissa Lomnitz found that nearly all had "spent varying amounts of time in Europe and in the United States, where they have often published their more important work. On returning to Mexico many suffered a culture shock in reverse, often with severe and lasting consequences."[21] Because of a lack of support for scientific research at Mexican universities, the drop-out rate among senior scientists is alarming.[22] Another disadvantage to the intellectual in choosing this career is that the scientific intellectual produces few intellectual disciples because intellectual types are not attracted to science, and because senior people in their forties and fifties leave it. One can point to many successful physicians who owe their training to Ignacio Chávez, but he did not have *intellectual* disciples.

Occupations: Frequent Choices

If we now turn to the professions chosen most frequently by intellectuals, several important implications are worth examining. Of course, the most frequent choice is a government career. The reasons intellectuals have sought government employment have been alluded to in a variety of contexts in the preceding chapters, and it would be redundant to summarize them again. But the second-largest group of intellectuals were full-time professors, and in reality, they should be combined with educators, since this latter group, generally holding administrative posts, also are long-time professors or researchers or both.

Education is a niche in which intellectuals can be found universally. Among North American intellectuals, approximately 40 percent are college professors.[23] In Juan Marsal's earlier study of Mexican essayists, 72 percent were professors or academic researchers.[24] Furthermore, Kadushin found that, among older North American intellectuals, who would have operated in an economic environment and marketplace for intellectual goods more nearly approximating that found in Mexico today, the number of academicians was higher: 60 percent of those over the age of fifty had followed careers in higher education.[25]

Mexican intellectuals have followed academic careers in large numbers for several reasons. Historically, education in Latin America and Mexico has carried with it a high level of social prestige. Thus, most professional people who have been highly successful have tried to teach, at least part time.[26] Furthermore, intellectuals have always seen academia as a refuge from forms of political censorship elsewhere in society. Intellectuals have also believed that working for the university, even though it is funded from federal monies, is a "clean" occupation, independent of government control. There have been some cases in which academic freedom has been abused, and individual department publications have adhered to ideological orthodoxies, but since 1920 the National University has generally maintained a remarkably open environment for teachers of all ideological persuasions. However, fewer intellectuals in Mexico than in the United States have made teaching and administration full-time careers because Mexican universities, until very recently, have been unable to hire more than a few full-time professors, and most individuals could not survive on the small salaries. Although 24 percent of Mexico's intellectuals have followed academic careers on a full-time basis, what is remarkable is how many have taught part time during most of their active professional years.

Mexican intellectuals have been deeply involved in Mexican higher education: 82 percent of all intellectuals have taught, and 75 percent have taught in Mexican universities (table 12). Institutions of higher education, more than the government itself, have attracted the intellectual: only 53 percent of Mexico's intellectuals have held two or more positions in government or served for five or more years in a government post (*MIBP*). Perhaps what is notable about Mexican intellectuals is not the difference in the numbers who have worked in the government and those who have taught, but that the majority has combined both activities sometime during their careers. Among Mexico's intellectual elite, the figures for both activities is even higher: 72 percent have held public posts and 85 percent have taught at the university level.

The institutions at which Mexican intellectuals have taught are important for many reasons. In the first place, the limited number of private universities in Mexico channels teaching into publicly supported institutions. This is clearly revealed by the data in table 12, which show that only 3 percent of the intellectuals have taught exclusively at private or foreign universities. Few intellectuals are drawn to private universities because the nonsectarian, liberal-arts institution in the North American tradition is a rarity. Those private institutions that do exist are either strongly attached to the interests of the private sector, such as the Autonomous University of Guadalajara and the Higher Institute of Technological Studies in Monterrey, or they have religious affiliations, such as the Ibero-American University in Mexico City. Even more important is the fact that most intellectuals live in Mexico City and therefore must teach at institutions located in that city, of which the most important are public.

The most striking feature of the teaching patterns of Mexican intellectuals is that they teach at a very small number of institutions. Fifty-nine percent of all Mexican intellectuals have taught at the National University, or the National University and some other institution, including the National Preparatory School and the Colegio de México. If we examine figures for *just* those intellectuals who have taught, we find that 73 percent, or nearly three-quarters of all teaching intellectuals have taught at a single university.

Table 12
Teaching Activities of Mexican Intellectuals and Politicians

Location of Teaching Experience	Percentage of		
	Intellectuals[a] (N=331)	Intellectual Elite[a] (N=55)	Politicians[b] (N=1,315)
Never taught	18	15	55.0
UNAM or UNAM and elsewhere	40	42	21.0
National Preparatory School	2	0	1.0
National Preparatory and UNAM	13	16	1.0
Primary or secondary	5	0	5.0
School of Fine Arts, Theater, or Plastic Arts	4	2	—
National Conservatory of Music	1	0	—
Colegio de México	2	4	—
Colegio de México and UNAM	6	13	—
State university only	5	4	14.0[c]
Private or foreign university only	3	6	0.3
Total	99	102	97.3

Notes: [a]Data are from the *MIBP* for the years 1920 to 1980.
[b]Data are from the *MPBP* for the Government Political Elite, 1935-1980. Twenty, or 1.5 percent of the political leaders taught at the National Polytechnic School only, an institution not used in coding our intellectual data set.
[c]This category for politicians included all other publicly supported institutions, most of which, however, were regional universities.

When the concentration of intellectuals who have taught at the National University is compared with politicians who have followed teaching careers, we find both similarities and differences. Mexican politicians have also taught in large numbers, but, predictably, not nearly as many as their intellectual counterparts. Again, it is not significant that fewer politicians than intellectuals have taught at all—a difference that would be expected— but it is significant that both groups have taught in sizeable numbers, and more important, have often taught at the same institutions. If we examine only those political leaders who have taught, we find that 52 percent gave classes at the National University. The location is important because, as I have demonstrated elsewhere, the National University is the major institutional locus for political recruitment in Mexico, and teachers play a significant role in this process, either as recruiters themselves, if they follow public careers, or as recruits, if their coprofessors or students elect to follow public careers.

The comparative figures in table 12 also demonstrate several other important findings about teaching careers. Second in importance to the National University as an employer for teaching intellectuals has been the National Preparatory School. Nineteen percent of all intellectuals who have taught have taught at that institution, versus 6 percent of all teaching politicians. The National Preparatory School, like the National University, is important to both groups because of its location in Mexico City and because most of the intellectuals and politicians who have taught there are alumni. Intellectuals have taught there in much larger numbers than politicians because the interdisciplinary atmosphere is inherently attractive to the intellectual mind and because writers without professional degrees, especially journalists, have been able to teach there but not at the National University.

The increasing importance of the Colegio de México in the teaching careers of Mexican intellectuals, and therefore its importance as an institutional locus for Mexican intellectual life, is also revealed by the figures in this table. The fact that 10 percent of Mexico's teaching intellectuals were employed there does not truly reflect this institution's growing influence as an intellectual employer. In the first place, the Colegio de México was founded after half of my intellectual sample had terminated their careers. Second, it has concentrated on certain disciplines to the exclusion of others, and only recently has it begun to emphasize some of the humanistic disciplines so popular among intellectuals. Last, the number of professors and students at the Colegio during its lifetime is minute compared to the number at the National University. Thus, proportionately it is quite possible that the Colegio de México has obtained a larger share than the National University of the intellectuals who have taught. Although some politicians in recent years have begun to teach at this school, they have not been very well-represented until the Miguel de la Madrid administration.[27]

The figures for the Colegio de México are interesting because, as I suggested in an earlier chapter, its orientation and methodology are rather different from the National University's. This suggests the possibility of two patterns developing in Mexico. In the first place, as increasing numbers of intellectuals teach at the Colegio, it may become the focus of a separate intellectual group whose posture and attitudes differ substantially from those of intellectuals teaching at the National University. At present there is a tendency toward this, and in the minds of intellectuals some competition between the two institutions exists. This pattern is moderated, however, by the fact that the majority of individuals who have taught at the Colegio have also taught at the National University. Second, if intellectuals increasingly spend their time at the Colegio, and there is no corresponding increase among political leaders teaching at this institution, the traditional overlap among intellectuals and politicians at the National University will decline in importance. Because the Colegio's has not been a highly politicized environment, even excepting the labor problems in 1980, and because it has not been shown to be a place where political recruitment takes place, it is not likely that large numbers of politicians would or could teach there. Therefore, any increases among Colegio intellectuals would probably have a corresponding effect in promoting intellectual careers independent of the state.

The centralized teaching experience of Mexican intellectuals also implies that, although a steady minority of politicians continue to reside for short times in the provinces and to recruit provincials into public life through their educational experiences, intellectuals rarely use these opportunities, thereby condemning the provincial intellectual to permanent obscurity unless he or she takes the initiative, and is financially able, to come to Mexico City. In this way, a profession supportive of intellectual life—teaching in higher education—reinforces the elitist background of intellectuals from middle- and upper-class families, with urban birthplaces and residences in the capital, without bringing in new blood, that is, Mexicans who do not fit this pattern.

Because of the importance of full-time careers in higher education, whether in teaching or in administration, it is worth analyzing, if only briefly, those positions in higher education over which intellectuals have some control. For example, if we examine the national schools directed by intellectuals we find several patterns conforming closely to their career choices and their intellectual interests. Of the eighty-four individuals, or over a fourth of all intellectuals, who have directed the most prestigious professional schools and institutes in Mexico, their efforts have concentrated in two institutions, the National School of Law and the National School of Philosophy and Letters. A fourth of the intellectuals who have held administrative posts have held them at these two institutions because their educations have been in the fields of law or arts and letters and because the majority of them received their education in these fields from these two schools.

It is equally important to note that the deanship of the National School of Law is a prestigious position among Mexican lawyers, and a position of considerable political importance and prestige among lawyers with political ambitions. Thus it should be stressed that Mexican intellectuals have been very much involved in directing the curriculum and the specific professional school from which most politicians have graduated. If one believes that the socialization influences of a college education are important—and there is evidence to suggest that they are—it is significant to understand that politicians are being formed by Mexican intellectuals.[28]

If we look at those professors whom politicians themselves considered to have been most important during their years at the National Preparatory School and the National University, we find that a large number of them are among Mexico's leading intellectuals. For example, of the twenty-four individuals who politicians thought were their most influential teachers at the National Preparatory School from 1911 to 1950, fourteen, or nearly 60 percent, were among Mexico's leading intellectuals, among them Antonio and Alfonso Caso, Julio Jiménez Rueda, Vicente Lombardo Toledano, Samuel Ramos, Alfonso Reyes, and Agustín Yáñez.[29] If we examine a similar list for the National School of Law, we find that, among the thirty-four notable professors selected by politicians, twenty-two were prominent intellectuals, including Narciso Bassols, Ramón Beteta, Antonio Carrillo Flores, Manuel Gómez Morín, Luis Recaséns Siches, and Alberto Vázquez del Mercado.[30] These names suggest that many of Mexico's politicians have been the students of Mexico's leading intellectuals, and that there has been a substantial overlap between prominent educators and intellectuals in Mexico. Thus it is difficult to separate the cultural leadership from Mexico's political leadership.

Intellectuals have also sought the leadership of Mexico's most prestigious universities, especially those in Mexico City. According to their geographic, residential, and educational biases, they have dominated the presidencies of two institutions: the National University and the Colegio de México. In fact, of the thirty-five intellectuals to have held such positions, eighteen, or half, have been rector of the National University (*MIBP*). Since rectors are very influential in the selection of professional-school deans, it is not surprising that many of Mexico's intellectuals have served as deans under intellectual presidents.

Since its founding in 1939, the Colegio de México has been clearly dominated by the intellectuals in my sample. But the data also show that Mexican intellectuals have not been widely tied to the state university system as administrators. Although intellectuals could have headed numerous regional universities, most permanently left their provinces for Mexico City. The implication once again is that nationally prominent intellectuals have little to do with regional institutions, as either teachers or administrators.

Government careers, followed by employment in higher education, have been most popular among Mexican intellectuals, but the data also show that many intellectuals are surviving primarily as writers, whether as journalists or free-lancers, or as editors and publishers. Nearly a fourth of Mexico's intellectuals (23 percent) make their living directly from the written media. Not unexpectedly, this is also true of North American intellectuals, since 40 percent make their living as editors or staff members of leading journals and newspapers, and an additional 15 percent are free-lancers.[31] The higher figures among Kadushin's sample of North Americans is to be expected, first because he selected them on the basis of writings, and not on any other medium, and second, because the level of economic development in the United States would permit larger numbers of intellectuals to make a living in this manner.

A small but persistent minority of intellectuals can make a living from their writings, although nearly all have supported themselves with secondary occupations. Even for many of Mexico's most prestigious intellectuals, accomplishing this feat will never be possible. For example, a historian like Daniel Cosío Villegas, in his last years was supported by income from his membership in the elite National College, a pension from his years with the Bank of Mexico, and his salary from the Colegio de México. It was only five years before his death, when his four popular paperbacks on the Mexican political system sold enough copies to earn him at least 500,000 pesos in royalties, that he could live on his writing. In contrast, his *Essays and Notes*, which he sold from 1966 to 1969, sold only 150 copies.[32] Yet, that even a small number can achieve self-sufficiency allows them a certain independence of action, thus molding the career channel of the independent intellectual (to be discussed later).

More important, that nearly a fourth of Mexico's intellectuals make their living with words indicates why literature has become an increasingly important field among contemporary intellectuals. As the data in table 6 clearly show, literature is not only the single most important intellectual field intellectuals follow, increasing in importance as the humanities began to decline, but it has grown as an intellectual profession. In a society where literacy is still limited to only two-thirds of the population, the increasing influence of literary activities and professional careers that depend on the written word raises the question of why writers dominate the Mexican intellectual world. One explanation is that many intellectuals themselves believe, as Carmen Castañeda has suggested, that the definition of an intellectual at the very least should include the quality of "literary productivity, not in the sense that a person must write literature, but that he express his work in words."[33]

A second reason literary people are beginning to dominate intellectual professions and interests is that they, more than any other group of intellectuals, have tried to create forms of employment for their peers and themselves. In other words, the literary intellectual has begun to see the value of entrepreneurial interests. Kadushin was impressed with the degree to which North American intellectuals were involved in similar activities and suspected that a "high degree of entrepreneurship characterizes the life of the intellectual elite of most advanced societies."[34] John Brushwood has noted this phenomenon in the career of Gustavo Sainz, a well-known novelist, when he stated that Sainz's "influence among writers is enormous—not necessarily in the usual sense of literary influence, but with regard to enhancing the status of the writer in Mexico. In a variety of contexts—editorial, pedagogical, administrative—he has promoted literature."[35]

Some figures on the editorial and publishing activities of all Mexican intellectuals point up the importance of the entrepreneurial role among writers, or intellectuals who communicate primarily through written form (*MIBP*). Nearly a third of all Mexican intellectuals have been editors of one or more newspapers or journals, and 14 percent have been publishers. Thus, nearly half of Mexico's intellectuals are known to have been involved in an activity directly related to promoting the writings of other individuals and providing them with financial assistance and prestige.[36] Although many artists have served as mentors to the younger generations, there are few if any artists in Mexico who have opened galleries to distribute the works of their peers or younger artists, or who have published books with others' work in them. Many have been entrepreneurs, but only in promoting their own works.

A special reason why literary figures and humanists in general have played an important role in Mexican intellectual life is the relationship of these two fields of activity to politics. As one author suggests, it has been traditional in Latin America to expect the writer to be a political figure, or at least to emphasize political and social criticism in his or her writing, because rigid censorship and repression have prevented such information from being communicated in any other fashion.[37] In particular, the novel is an important medium for social and political polemics in Latin America.[38]

After writers, the profession next in importance among intellectuals is that of practicing artists and architects. In several cases, such as that of Juan O'Gorman, an individual has simultaneously engaged in two professions in the plastic arts, as an architect and a painter. Surprisingly, most of the individuals in this category have followed careers in the arts, not in architecture. Although the minority were architects, their profession differs in one important respect from the plastic arts—in the ability to make public life a career. Architecture, because of its practical applications, has of course been a profession followed by several successful politicians.

Among Mexican intellectuals, one of the most well-known architects, winner of the National Prize in the Arts in 1973, is Pedro Ramírez Vázquez, who held a cabinet post in the López Portillo administration. Ramírez Vázquez followed the typical educational pattern of Mexican intellectuals, graduating from the National Preparatory School and the National University. His choice of a public career was influenced by many factors. In the first place, his brothers, both law graduates, became prominent figures in the administration of Miguel Alemán, just after Ramírez Vázquez graduated from college. Their constant discussion of political ideas influenced his values considerably. Second, among his mentors was professor José Luis Cuevas, one of the first urbanists in Mexico, who advised Ramírez Vázquez that "an urbanist who was not in public life was a person who studied urbanism as only a hobby."[39] His early career was assisted largely through government contracts, from the Secretariat of Labor, the School of Medicine at the National University, and numerous projects for the Secretariat of Public Education, especially under the leadership of poet Jaime Torres Bodet, another intellectual who followed a career in public life. Although a number of intellectuals-architects have not been as successful as Ramírez Vázquez in their creative and political pursuits, his relationship to the government typifies the careers of many of his peers.

Government support has often been critical to intellectuals in the plastic arts. For artists in the immediate postrevolutionary period, José Vasconcelos's efforts to stimulate indigenous art aided the muralist generation and, indirectly, its disciples. Furthermore, not only has the government supported individual artists at various times in their careers, but their work has gained wide publicity as a result of government contracts. The differences between architects, and sculptors and painters is that the former have very often followed successful careers in public life, whereas the latter almost never follow such careers. This is not to suggest that Mexican artists have not been politically motivated, or have not been active in politics, but, as I suggested earlier, those with political interests have concentrated their efforts in opposition groups, especially in the small Mexican Communist party in the 1920s.[40]

The more important question to be raised about the presence of artistic careers among intellectuals, however, is why art has declined in influence among younger intellectuals, and why it is not better represented as an intellectual activity. This is an especially important question, given the prominence of art in Mexican intellectual life immediately following the Revolution. Alistair Hennessy argues, for example, that, "whatever other original features the Mexican Revolution may have, it is difficult to deny that it produced the most dynamic revolutionary art of the twentieth century.[41] The muralist movement, of course, was the center of this revolutionary art, and one student claims it achieved a degree of success in the 1930s never before experienced by any artistic movement in the Western Hemisphere.[42] Furthermore, Hennessy suggests that the painters, not the literary intellectuals, were the self-assertive leaders of Mexican culture during this period.[43]

The Mexican mural movement died out, and Mexican art as a whole took a backseat to the literary intellectuals for a variety of important reasons. One point of view among Mexican intellectuals is that the mural movement and the feelings it created in painting "were fired up by the Revolution, but then painting became an old lady, a prostitute, and began to die out."[44] Abel Quezada suggests why this was so: "Muralism was an official art that was devoted to representing things Mexican. Ultimately, it fell into a form of demagoguery. Some artists are exploiters of Mexican reality—these are artists who paint from the point of view of certain styles, which contain nothing relating to reality."[45] Too many of the muralists became dominated by an ideology, and as ideologists first and artists second, their artistic creativity suffered. To the art historians examining this period, what started out as a dynamic, creative movement in Mexican art and culture became a stagnant movement stifling other forms of artistic expression in the 1940s and 1950s.[46]

Art, like the revolutionary governments themselves, became conservative in the 1950s and has never recovered its leadership of Mexican cultural trends and in the realm of intellectual ideas. Accompanying this conservative trend has been a movement away from government patronage of the arts to a greater dependence on private patrons.[47] By the 1960s, Mexico's artistic community had firmly divided into two artistic directions: the formerly quasi-official, revolutionary school of muralists; and the unrepresentational, international movement, led by Rufino Tamayo, of abstract painters. Tamayo himself said, "I am an international painter—not nationalistic at all."[48]

Some artists believe that the social value of Mexican art lies in the part it plays in a broader trend in the plastic arts: a movement away from a collective to an individualistic concept of how the work should be undertaken. This more historical interpretation has relevance to the Mexican scene because there *was* a common enthusiasm and overlapping of ideas that gave the Mexican mural movement its cohesion.[49] This idea has been eloquently expressed by Juan O'Gorman:

Art in the Middle Ages was sort of an ally of the church and the faith of the people. Art had a special place in this era and was related to people through their faith and religion. But today, the masses have no relation to art because it is not at the service of faith or religion. Humanism had a much higher value then than it does today, and the technology then available was used in the service of religious faith. Even after the Renaissance this phenomenon continued, although not in the form of religion, but rather it became a cultural and state concept. In the romantic era, religion was further depreciated but art was still a reflection of the masses. Victor Hugo is a good example of this in the nineteenth century—he was popular because he understood and wrote about the exploited classes; that is, he was the conscience of the French people during his own age in opposing the oppressive forms of power and defending the interests of the masses. Today, there is specialization within the arts. In the past, artists worked together, and the works formed an integral whole because they had the same religion, faith, ideology. Work has become individualized, not collective.[50]

And yet, this same collectivity of goals, in conjunction with an alliance with the Mexican state, led, after an initial burst of creative leadership, to the eventual demise of indigenous Mexican art and its leadership of Mexican culture in general. For whatever reason, artistic careers, although still important to Mexican intellectual life, are not pursued by leading young intellectuals.

Career Choices and Public Service

Regardless of the profession intellectuals follow, their choices do have an important effect on their relationship to the Mexican state. Before the Revolution, when intellectuals were dependent on the state for employment, most of Mexico's educated population held government positions, and those with ideas opposed to government policies found it increasingly difficult to advance within the system.[51] This frustration among a group of intellectuals eventually led to revolutionary activities. Thus, the ease with which an intellectual's profession makes him employable by the state, in lieu of the availability of other occupations, can make him more or less likely to criticize the state. In the case of artists, who since the 1950s have remained outside of the state in Mexico, many were sympathetic to the Revolution itself. Today, however, although they might find it easier to criticize the state, their medium and their skills do not make this an easy task. Since many intellectuals, and very definitely politicians, believe that an intellectual must express social and political values, it is only logical that artists find it more difficult to be accepted and treated as intellectuals in Mexico. This is clearly why the only artists who appear among the list of elite Mexican intellectuals are muralists: Orozco, Rivera, and Siqueiros. All were politically active and all three part of a much older generation.

Once the intellectual pursues a particular career, he also increases or decreases the likelihood of becoming involved in public life (table 13). The likelihood of a public career may be due to friendships developed or missed at a professional school few politicians attend, or it may be supplemented by the omission or addition of social relationships developed during professional activities. Furthermore, compatibility might be a factor in determining whether or not certain types of intellectuals choose to become involved in public life, even if compatibility is confined to ideological beliefs. Earlier I suggested that attendance at certain schools produces intellectual graduates who are more or less likely to have certain philosophical beliefs. Individuals who are Marxists are much less likely than people holding any other ideological beliefs to pursue public careers (only 37 percent) (*MIBP*).

Ideological beliefs are important in determining an intellectual's participation in government, and certain beliefs can be found among larger numbers of intellectuals in one profession than in another. For example,

Table 13

College Degrees, Professional Careers, and Government Service among Mexican Intellectuals, 1920-1980

Career	Type of Degree															
	None		Law, Economics, CPA		Medicine		Sciences		Engineering		Arts & Letters		Art, Music, Architecture		Total	
	No.	%	No.	%	No.	%	No.	%	No.	%	No.	%	No.	%	No.	% of Subtotal
Public[a]	27	42	80	73	18	69	2	20	9	47	25	39	13	45	174	54
No public career	38	58	30	27	8	31	8	80	10	53	41	61	16	55	151	46
Subtotal	65	100	110	100	26	100	10	100	19	100	66	100	29	100	325	100

Table 13 (continued)

Career	Lawyer		Educator		Business		Writer		Musician		Artist or Architect		Physician		Journalist		Publisher		Total	
	No.	%	No.	%	No.	%	No.	%	No.	%	No.	%	No.	%	No.	%	No.	%	No.	% of Sub-total
Public[a]	14	61	29	36	1	14	7	24	3	43	7	25	7	88	14	40	2	20	84	37
No public career	9	39	52	64	6	86	22	76	4	57	21	75	1	13	21	60	8	80	144	63
Subtotal	23	100	81	100	7	100	29	100	7	100	28	100	8	101	35	100	10	100	228	100

Notes: [a] As in table 1, an individual is considered to have had a public career if he or she held elective or appointive posts for five or more years or two or more positions for any length of time.

[b] Professions exclude government careers (ninety-two individuals), clergy (seven individuals), none of whom held public posts), engineers (three individuals who did not hold public posts), and three intellectuals who were an economist, labor leader, and actor (only the labor leader held public office), or a total sample of 333 intellectuals.

intellectual Marxists actually were found among five professions: public officials, educators and professors, writers and poets, artists, and journalists.[52] Those professions unrepresented among Marxist intellectuals included lawyers, physicians, musicians, engineers, economists, public accountants, and business executives.

Finally, one additional explanation to account for certain intellectual professions being well represented among those following public careers is the change in attitude among younger intellectuals. As I argued earlier, younger intellectuals are choosing more and more to remain outside of public life. The majority of intellectuals born before 1910 served the Mexican state. Beginning with the generation born after 1910, and especially after 1920, many Mexican intellectuals have chosen not to serve the state (data from the *MIBP*).[53] Their decision to remain outside the state suggests not only a changing pattern, but, as they choose professions different from those older intellectuals choose, their career choices will help to reinforce the parting of the ways between the intellectual serving the state and the intellectual remaining outside the state. For example, three-quarters of the intellectuals who were lawyers in my sample were born before 1900. On the other hand, nearly two-thirds of the intellectuals who were full-time professors or researchers were born after 1900. In this way, as the career choices of younger intellectuals are predominant, the structure of Mexican intellectual life itself will be changed.

In a sense, many of these educational and career patterns are responses to the level of Mexico's economic development. For example, thirty years ago, a Mexican writer could not make a living entirely from writing, something that Edward Shils, in his excellent study of Indian intellectuals in the 1950s, found to be equally true.[54] But today, in both India and Mexico, many intellectuals are writers exclusively. It can be argued, therefore, that the level of economic development determines not only the structure of intellectual life, but also who actually plays intellectual roles.

Other Experiences

Two other experiences are equally important to the Mexican intellectual's career, orientation, and attitude toward the government. In a society like Mexico, where the government has the power to exile an individual without due legal process, the intellectual, among others, is subject to an arbitrary fate unsettling to his livelihood and family stability. This can color intellectuals' attitudes toward the state in two ways: they may become cautious and distant, or they may develop a stronger commitment to politics. Surprisingly, 19 percent of Mexico's intellectuals prominent since 1920 are known to have been forced into exile or imprisoned for political reasons by a government, either Mexico's or Spain's (*MIBP*).

One reason for the high number of exiles and prisoners is the rapid changes in governments and leadership groups from 1911 to 1929, during and immediately following the Mexican Revolution. Another reason is the influx of Spanish exiles who achieved leadership positions in Mexico's intellectual circles after 1936. Despite these two situations, data also suggest that many of Mexico's intellectuals, whether native or foreign born, have been willing to suffer the consequences of expressing views contrary to those of the government in power. Compared with most Latin American countries, Mexico's record of keeping intellectuals at home, and not languishing in prison, is very good.

Because Mexico underwent a major social revolution during the period covered by this study, and because many of Mexico's leading intellectuals after 1920 were old enough to have participated in the Revolution, it is worth examining their experiences with revolutionary and reactionary regimes. From the data in the *MIBP*, of the ninety-nine intellectuals who were old enough, nineteen served in the prerevolutionary regime of Porfirio Díaz or in the reactionary government of Victoriano Huerta. Although they represent only 6 percent of the leading intellectuals after 1920, what is important is that their having served these governments did not exclude them from being recognized for intellectual accomplishments in the postrevolutionary period. These figures suggest that intellectual abilities, if they are first-rate, can overcome serious political errors, even in a period of Mexico's history during which an official revolutionary rhetoric dominated public or primary education.

The data also demonstrate that many of the intellectuals were directly involved in the Revolution, or served revolutionary governments. In fact, of the 101 individuals who might have participated in these events or governments, nearly half did so. This figure is important because it documents the fact that Mexico's leading intellectuals in this century were not armchair philosophers in times of social upheaval. Many actually fought in the Revolution. For example, David Alfaro Siqueiros, one of Mexico's foremost muralists, while a student at the National School of Fine Arts participated in a strike to revise the antiquated teaching methods there and in a student conspiracy against Victoriano Huerta. Moving from student activism to political activities, he joined Venustiano Carranza's army in 1914, serving as an officer before becoming military attaché in Paris in 1917.[55]

Large numbers of intellectuals joined the revolutionary governments at a time when their future, and that of the government's was not assured. Furthermore, although comparable data are not available, intellectuals as a group, compared with other groups in Mexican society, appear to have been very well represented in revolutionary activities. The heavy participation of intellectuals from these generations in such affairs has the approval of their younger peers. Equally important, it suggests that their active involvement in revolutionary governments aided Mexican intellectuals and their disciples, both in the pursuit of their own careers and with regard to the budding careers of other, as yet undistinguished, intellectuals.

Conclusions

All of the educational choices, career patterns, and experiences discussed here provide insights into why certain professions dominate Mexican intellectual life, and why certain intellectuals are more likely to follow public careers. Conclusions about these patterns also imply their importance for intellectual recruitment, that is, how an individual joins the ranks of leading Mexican intellectuals. But if we look beyond the specific experiences of, the degree qualifications of, and the individual professions Mexican intellectuals follow, we find certain career prototypes emerging: the *governmental career*, lifetime or late-blooming; the *quasi-governmental career*, in a publicly funded institution or supported by government contract; and the *nongovernmental career*, of a person either independently wealthy, self-employed in the private sector, or employed by a private firm.

A brief examination of the experiences of intellectuals who typify these prototypes reveals many characteristics about intellectual careers in Mexico and about the structure of intellectual life itself. Intellectuals who have followed government careers are essentially of two types: those who have made public service a lifetime commitment, beginning with their graduation from college; and those who, inadvertently and later in life, found themselves following successful public careers because of their intellectual reputations.

An outstanding example of an intellectual who devoted his entire life to public service is Antonio Carrillo Flores. Upon his graduation in 1929, he became a minor official in the Secretariat of the Treasury. But in 1930, his former professor, José Aguilar y Maya, appointed him as a federal agent to the Attorney General's Office, and in 1931, he was promoted to a position as head of the Legal Department. From that point on, Carrillo Flores held a succession of government positions until 1980, when he was appointed ambassador to the Soviet Union. Other leading intellectuals who typify this pattern include Jesús Reyes Heroles, Jesús Silva Herzog, Eduardo Suárez, and Ramón Beteta. These intellectuals have during all or much of their careers so subsumed their intellectual pursuits to their political activities that they almost seem to lose their identity as intellectuals. Indeed, this is the very reason why some intellectuals in Mexico would not consider them peers.

The majority of Mexican intellectuals who follow successful public careers and make government service a lifetime commitment usually begin while they are students, or as recent graduates. However, a less common prototype is the intellectual who mixes private and educational activities with public service but, although serving in government posts, many of them prestigious or influential, does not become politically involved to the extent of establishing a political clique to promote his career or those of friends. Illustrative of this pattern is the career of Agustín Yáñez, who, unlike many of his peers, was atypical because of his working-class background, his attendance at parochial schools in Guadalajara, and the beginnings of his intellectual and professional endeavors in that provincial capital. In the 1930s he moved to Mexico City, where he taught at several institutions, including the National Preparatory School. During these years Yáñez established his literary reputation as one of Mexico's foremost novelists. He became in 1952 the PRI candidate for governor of Jalisco, his home state, because President Adolfo Ruiz Cortines sought to use Yáñez's prestige and intellectual reputation and his quality as a political outsider to solve state political problems. For essentially the same reasons, including his oratorical and writing skills, Yáñez held cabinet-level posts in the two following administrations.[56]

A second group of Mexican intellectuals is indirectly intertwined with the state. These are the individuals who hold quasi-governmental positions, or positions in institutions or organizations legally independent of the government, but supported largely by state funds. The most prominent set of institutions in this netherworld between the private and public sectors are public universities. Intellectuals have always been drawn to universities. And, in the twentieth century, Mexican intellectuals wanting to serve their society have often ended up in publicly funded agencies or educational institutions because the private sector offered few alternatives in the realm of education and medical research. I shall analyze the relationship between the university and the state in chapter 8, but for now suffice it to say that it is complex, and that political influences of many sorts bear on this relationship, whether at the state or national levels.

Ignacio Chávez is a good example of someone who has followed the quasi-government pattern and, in a sense, has never formally held a "government" post. Although Chávez earned a living as the heart specialist of many of Mexico's prominent social and political figures, his first employment was as rector of the University of Michoacán in 1920, the university he graduated from in that year. From an extraordinary beginning, Chávez moved to Mexico City, where he later became dean of the National School of Medicine (in 1933), director of the General Hospital in Mexico City (a public institution) in 1936, and then founder and director of the National Institute of Cardiology in 1944. Finally, he served as rector of the National University from 1961 to 1966, returning to the Institute of Cardiology in 1970.[57] In reality, other than his own medical practice,

Chávez never directed an institution supported by private funds.

Other intellectuals who, unlike Chávez, had litttle administrative ability or inclination toward administrative posts, found themselves working for the government through temporary contractual arrangements. This situation was especially true in the 1930s and 1940s for many of Mexico's leading artists, musicians, and dramatists. The government, particularly the Secretariat of Public Education and subsidiary institutes or agencies, led by intellectuals like José Vasconcelos, Narciso Bassols, Jaime Torres Bodet, and Agustín Yáñez, provided the means for supporting intellectual colleagues in a variety of occupations. Vasconcelos, as the first postrevolutionary minister of education, is responsible for starting this trend toward government support of intellectual activities. Thus, the Mexican state, unlike the government in the United States, has provided an important source of income for the majority of Mexico's intellectuals in the plastic arts as well as for intellectuals in other disciplines, whether they are musicians directing the National Symphony Orchestra, or historians at the National Archive or the National Institute of Anthropology and History. Again, these positions take on added importance in Mexico because there are so few positions with equal compensation and prestige available in the private sector.

Intellectuals who do not typically fit the first two career prototypes, which capture the vast majority, end up with careers in the private sector. A small number of this group are independently wealthy, and although many of them teach at public institutions or occasionally hold public office, they are primarily involved in these activities for other than financial reasons. Most of the individuals in this group, however, are engaged in practicing their professions. For example, Alejandro Gómez Arias, who has written for *Siempre* during the last two decades, and who at one time was an editor for *Política*, has practiced law, and among his clients have been some of Mexico's leading intellectuals.

Other than the independent professions such as law, medicine, and accounting, the majority of intellectuals who work in the private sector but are not self-employed have been journalists. Carlos González Peña, for example, who was a founding member of the Atheneum of Youth and author of many novels, wrote for most of Mexico's leading newspapers and directed several important supplements and publications. Still other intellectuals have been business executives, or have worked for large private firms outside of the publishing world. The historian Atanasio Saravia Aragón, president of the Mexican Academy of History from 1941 to 1957, began earning a living as a bank teller, then moved from one managerial position to another in the National Bank of Mexico until he became president of the board in this important private firm. And, of course, a small number of Mexico's intellectuals followed professions in the priesthood, such as Angel María Garibay Kintana, missionary and expert on Nahuatl culture, who directed the compilation of the *Diccionario Porrúa*.

The career patterns of Mexican intellectuals are important in determining their contact with those in the public sector, and to some extent, their attitudes toward the state itself. Furthermore, as we shall see in the following chapter, intellectuals following certain types of career patterns are more likely to be recruited into intellectual circles. How intellectuals are recognized and become members of leading intellectual circles, and the subsequent impact of their recruitment on the structure of intellectual life and its relationship to the state, will be analyzed in the following chapter.

7. Intellectual Mentors and Circles

The fascination of writers and academicians with political life has produced many scholarly and impressionistic treatments of recruitment. The process by which young intellectual prospects are recognized and incorporated into the cultural leadership of a society has rarely been studied, however, and most available written observations are impressionistic. With some imagination, though, we can borrow appropriate models from the political world and apply them to the world of intellectuals. An understanding of the recruitment process of Mexican intellectuals is important in shedding light on the possibility of reaching a recognized position in the intellectual community, in understanding the contributions this process makes to separating or unifying the intellectual and the politician, in identifying institutions and individuals important in promoting the careers of others, and in establishing unity among leading intellectuals.

Comparative research on recruitment through various political channels suggests several means by which young people and adults are normally recruited into public life. In general, the structure of the political system has determined these channels.[1] For example, the more open the system, the greater the number of possible channels, and the greater the tendency for the individual to achieve success on his own, because of prior ability or recognition in a field other than politics. However, because the intellectual world lacks comparable organizations, such as political parties, whose purpose is to recruit a prospective member, the channels intellectuals regularly follow are narrower and smaller in number than those available to politicians.

The Intellectual Mentor

Universally, intellectuals follow two broad recruitment paths: a rise under the guidance and protection of a mentor, and a rise because of ability. The autobiographies of American intellectuals imply that older intellectuals sponsor young intellectuals.[2] This mentor-disciple relationship has also been found in England, whose cultural structure is more centralized and thus has more in common with Mexico's. Coser concluded that "beginners in British intellectual life must know someone in authority if they are to make their way."[3]

Who are these mentors and how do they meet young intellectuals? In the United States, the prestigious journals and the cliques that surround them, intellectual groups or circles, and especially editors, have the power to make or break an intellectual's reputation. Interviews with North American intellectuals have confirmed this belief, particularly the view that journals control the status of the literary intellectual.[4] A similar pattern exists in Mexico. Henry Schmidt, describing intellectual recruitment during the decade from 1910 to 1920, specifically that of Samuel Ramos, has this to say:

Intellectual life was focused in the Atheneum, which stimulated the exchange of ideas and fostered creative aspirations under the sponsorship of a patron, usually a prominent teacher, a military man, or a leading politician, while a small magazine often was produced as an outlet for local talent.

It was in such a tradition and in such a magazine, *Flor de Loto*, that Ramos entered the intellectual world.[5]

Mexican intellectual recruitment, dominated, like political life, by mentors or patrons, falls into a category labeled "sponsored" recruitment.[6] The Mexican intellectual, however, unlike North American counterparts, is not as commonly found by the journal or an editor; rather, the basis for the initial friendship, even prior to the Mexican Revolution, often is that of teacher and student, as Schmidt suggests. Studies of North American intellectual life make no mention of the university or preparatory school as the key to intellectual sponsorship. Undoubtedly, there are cases of this, and in earlier eras, when Ivy League schools dominated many aspects of political, social, and intellectual leadership, the North American university played a more important role.[7] In the last half century, however, this pattern has not been true in the United States.

The importance of universities as a locus for Mexican intellectual recruitment is similar to their importance in England. Coser concluded that "the integrated character of the British intellectual community is also apparent when one turns attention to the process of recruitment to intellectual positions. Here too common background and close communication networks are crucial. Most English writers and literary critics start their careers as Oxbridge undergraduates."[8] Mexican intellectuals themselves believe that the student-teacher alliance has been a common form of the mentor-disciple relationship in Mexico. Yet, they also believe that this pattern, so common to the intellectuals dominating the twentieth century, is changing because of the size of Mexico City, because of an increase in student enrollments and the number of universities, and because of the growing complexity of the intellectual environment itself.[9]

The mentor-disciple bond, common to intellectuals from many cultures, has found an attractive niche in Latin America for other, special reasons. For example, Bernardo Houssay, in discussing the careers of eminent Latin American scientists, believes favoritism is widespread in academia. According to his analysis,

It is often the man who is submissive and obedient, who never argues or does the work which his superior assigns, or has influential friends or relatives, who gets ahead, while the most capable, hard-working, and original is left behind, unless he is too outstanding to be ignored. We have often seen eminent specialists, the best in their field, fail to win a post which was given to some local candidate with more friends and more years of routine teaching.[10]

In Mexico this situation is made worse by the fact that aspiring scientists, like intellectuals in all disciplines, have few options, and since competing scientific institutions are very few, the "possibilities of changing tutors are correspondingly limited."[11] As one Mexican intellectual from the plastic arts suggested, "Persons are more important than institutions in helping young architects, . . . young people are attracted to individuals, not institutions, . . . institutions work better at informing, rather than forming young people."[12]

Academic studies may exaggerate the importance of conforming to the views of an influential mentor as a means to the top in Mexico and in the rest of Latin America, but elsewhere these same patterns are prevalent. Coser argues, for example, that the establishment quickly absorbs intellectual rebels in England, and that it is they, rather than the establishment, who change.[13] Moreover, because we normally think of intellectuals as free spirits, we sometimes mistakenly assume that, when working for an industry or organization devoted to the dissemination of knowledge or "truth," they will be free to express conflicting views. A study of the *Washington Post*, one of America's most prestigious papers, concluded, "The *Post* is no different from any large institution or business, where the people who agree with and conform to the wishes of their higher-ups, who have the same set of values, will find that this is helpful in their own career climb."[14] However, Mexico and the United States differ in that many newspapers of equal prestige exist in North America, and the able journalist can find equally challenging and remunerative employment elsewhere, whereas in Mexico, choices would be limited.

Additionally, the mentor-disciple system places considerable power in the hands of a few individuals. For those intellectuals who express their views through the written media, the power of the editor or publisher is tremendous. Furthermore, the established intellectual, whether he edits a journal or not, has to be informed about who the potential newcomers are. Yet, members of the North American intellectual elite are largely ignorant of newcomers.[15]

Older intellectuals in Mexico show a similar ignorance of younger figures, and in a recent interview, Juan José Arreola, a leading literary figure, publicly stated, "Where are the young authors—I do not see them?"[16] Although Arreola was lamenting the scarcity of new talent, his perception might well have been unfounded, for many young Mexican writers are easily hidden from view.

In societies in which sponsorship dominates recruitment, disruptions in the social structure can easily change the patterns. Even in the United States, younger intellectuals during the 1960s rejected the existing journals, circles, and groups.[17] In Mexico one would expect recruitment patterns to have changed substantially after the Mexican Revolution. Interestingly, however, the recruiters changed from the Porfirista intellectual groups to a younger generation, many of them disciples of the older group brought to the forefront of cultural life by the postrevolutionary governments; the recruitment *patterns* remained unchanged.

The importance of the National Preparatory School and the National University as recruitment institutions, and the importance of professors as recruiters, were not altered by the Mexican Revolution. Because Mexico City continued to grow and to dominate educational and intellectual activities, the young people from the provinces were drawn into its fold. Institutions able to compete with the National University did not emerge in the 1920s and 1930s; furthermore, as the self-made military figure and the working-class politician disappeared from the scene in the 1940s and 1950s, alternate mentors became fewer in number. College-educated mentors, who were also teachers, regardless of their public or academic careers, took over as intellectual mentors. The expansion of university education and the development of other knowledge industries beginning in the 1970s is destroying the dominance over recruitment of the traditional institutions and the professor.

The University and Recruitment

The persistence of the university as a recruiting locale and of the professor as the mentor to most successful intellectuals deserves further comment. One explanation of their importance to Mexico is that most intellectuals have attended the National University, many of them have taught there, and the majority have pursued academic or government careers. For those pursuing academic careers, graduation from the National University and an attachment to a professor-mentor is almost a necessity for success within that university. Richard King has concluded that, at the state-university level, "recruitment from among an institution's own graduates (and promotion from within) seems very much to be the rule, a finding that squares with the analysis of the source of professional training of professors."[18]

At the National University, promotion and recruitment practices have only recently begun to be studied. Larissa Lomnitz, who teaches there, describes the typical professor: "The profesor personally directs their [the students'] thesis, helps them to obtain scholarships and uses them as assistants. Most of the research personnel in the University, and many outstanding professional people as well, have absorbed such informal apprenticeship periods under a staff member, who may eventually have recommended them for an academic position."[19] In fact, Lomnitz's description of the internal structure of UNAM is similar to the series of hierarchical, overlapping groups that I have used to characterize Mexico's political system.[20]

Lomnitz's careful examination of the mentor-disciple relationship among scientists is revealing of how such patterns occur, and equally important, of the serious implications they have for intellectual cooperation and the acquisition of knowledge. Instructors recruit young scientists, usually when they are juniors or seniors. Once their professors accept them as assistants, they become members of what Lomnitz labeled a "scientific family," a group belonging to a senior researcher or tutor. These "families" often extend back through at least three generations of student-professor relationships. Such relationships, she found, were openly paternalistic. "Your tutor is like a second father to you. He leads you by the hand every step of the way. If you disobey that will be the end of you."[21]

The consequence of the mentor-disciple relationship and the existence of scientific families is a decided lack of cooperation among Mexican scientists. Lomnitz found that "the exceptional cases of collaboration between principal investigators were among descendants of the same scientific lineage, i.e., scientistis who had formerly worked under the same tutor. There was not a single case of collaboration between members of the two major power groups in the institute."[22] "Deep reaching differences in language, method, levels of abstraction and approach to research problems" stemming from those educated in the tradition of European science and those receptive to the North American school, further exacerbate divisions,[23] again reflecting the structural impact of external cultural influences on a society's internal intellectual community.

Undoubtedly, the shortage of facilities for scientific research and the unwillingness to share scientific knowledge make possible the characteristics Lomnitz found. In other disciplines, though, especially those most popular among intellectuals, the closed, unstimulating environment she describes is not generally found. This can be illustrated in philosophy, specifically in the career of one of Mexico's leading intellectuals and teachers in this century, Antonio Caso, a man with numerous disciples. Although he established many friendships with his contemporaries, such as José Vasconcelos, in the Atheneum of Mexico, it was in his classroom that he formed several generations of students. Dozens of intellectuals have attributed to Caso a direct influence on their philosophy and personal formation as his students, and prominent political figures, from the same generation, have ranked him as equally important.[24]

Except for a brief period during which Caso held several administrative posts at the National Preparatory School and the National University, and a year as a traveling ambassador, he devoted his entire career to full-time teaching. He was not involved in editing or publishing intellectual reviews; therefore, unlike many of Mexico's younger intellectuals, he did not attract disciples or peers through the written medium. Furthermore, Caso himself was independently oriented, had no tendency for establishing groups, and never used his considerable influence over younger minds to perpetuate his influence or philosophy within the School of Philosophy and Letters at the National University or in the intellectual world in general. In fact, his disciples were from many academic disciplines and formed diverse intellectual circles as they matured.

Many of the characteristics of intellectual recruitment can be found among individuals looking toward careers in the public sector. Again, it is the National University that serves as a focus for the mentor-disciple pattern. Mexican public figures want to teach at the National University in part so they can identify prospective talent. As Charles N. Myers suggests, "It is for the purpose of recruiting and grooming these students, rather than for the money involved, that many of the high-level government *técnicos* are willing to teach at the National University and other institutions in the Federal District."[25] Furthermore, individual government agencies advertise part-time employment and summer jobs for students as a further means of attracting capable young people to public service.[26] Students who have decided, prior to entering college, that they are committed to a public career purposely choose to attend the National University, knowing in advance that this is where political contacts essential to a successful career are made.[27]

Many intellectuals, as I suggested earlier, have followed public careers. In doing so, their friendships at the university and the National Preparatory School have served them doubly. Illustrative of this pattern are the early years of poet Jaime Torres Bodet, who attended the National Preparatory School and graduated at the age of fifteen in 1917. Like most members of his generation, he chose to follow a career in law, enrolling in the National School of Law the following year. But unlike most of his student friends, he abandoned the study of law after two years. After publishing his first book, at sixteen, he formed a group known as the "New Atheneum of Youth," which included Luis Garrido, poet Enrique González Rojo, poet José Gorostiza, and others. By 1920 his precocious talent caught the eye of José Vasconcelos, who appointed him secretary of the National Preparatory

School while he was still in his teens. One year later he became private secretary to Vasconcelos when the latter served as rector of the National University.

In 1922, he cofounded *La Falange*, drawing together many of his friends from the National Preparatory School, including poets Carlos Pellicer, Bernardo Ortiz de Montellano, and Xavier Villaurrutia. In 1927, Villaurrutia, with dramatist Salvador Novo, began publishing *Ulises*, which not only gathered the group from *La Falange* and Torres Bodet's group from the "New Atheneum of Youth" but recruited additional collaborators, including poet Roberto Owen. In 1928, *Contemporáneos*, the most famous of a succession of literary reviews, was established. It brought together most of the people who had been accumulated gradually from one literary enterprise to the next, and many of whom had been together at the National Preparatory School.[28] These literary and intellectual ties led Jaime Torres Bodet to a highly successful career in the field of foreign affairs and education, and the diplomatic and educational careers of his peers were often intertwined in his own.

The other path Mexican intellectuals follow is what might be described as recruitment by ability. Individuals who follow this path, instead of relying on a mentor to provide recognition in intellectual circles, have reached certain positions in the cultural world, or gained recognition from their peers on the basis of their intellectual contributions. As Luis Villoro suggested, obtaining a national prize is one means by which a provincial intellectual, young and unknown, can quickly become recognized, because such an award will attract the attention and interest of various intellectual circles.[29]

Intellectuals who are recognized by their peers on the basis of ability can also achieve public posts in the same manner. It is clear, for example, that Agustín Yáñez reached top levels in Mexican public life because of his literary reputation, and that three successive presidents believed that his reputation and integrity embellished their administration.[30] According to his closest collaborators, unlike the typical public figure in Mexico, Yáñez was never part of a political group, nor did he himself organize a *camarilla* to promote the careers of his colleagues.[31] The intellectual who achieves recognition from the intellectual community or the politician without benefit of a mentor is, however, the exception.

The Journal and Recruitment

Many intellectuals, like Mexican politicians, find their mentors outside the university. But whereas the politician may have found a patron in the ranks of the PRI, in the labor or peasant organizations, in the military, or in the bureaucracy itself, the intellectual is more likely to find a contact through the small magazine or journal. The editor is especially important in bringing together protégés and intellectuals who do not teach. For example, José Vasconcelos's protégés were attracted to him in his capacity as a university administrator (like Jaime Torres Bodet, who functioned briefly as his private secretary when Vasconcelos served as rector of the National University); in his campaign as a presidential candidate in 1929 (as was the case of novelist Mauricio Magdaleno); and as the founder of the journal *Antorcha*, on which Samuel Ramos, Pedro de Alba, and Daniel Cosío Villegas worked.[32]

Editors and journals have been equally important in the careers of younger intellectuals like Octavio Paz, who, during his long years of poetic and literary activities, has been associated with various intellectual circles surrounding individual journals. In the 1970s, after leaving the cultural supplement of *Excélsior*, he founded *Vuelta*, whose regular contributors include poet Gabriel Zaid, historian Enrique Krauze, and novelist Salvador Elizondo.

Journals have long played a significant role in the recruitment and certification process of intellectuals. In North America, intellectuals are divided into a number of circles or small groups loosely related to journals. Kadushin has described their interrelationship this way:

Elite American intellectual life consists of a loosely allied and interpenetrating trinity: the prestigious intellectuals, the prestigious journals, and the leading circles. Leading intellectuals write for the leading journals and the combination of journals and intellectuals produces the leading circles. Each acts to bolster the other. A journal is important because people who are already important write for it; a person becomes important because he writes for an important journal; and the social network assures that only important people write for important journals.[33]

The Role of Intellectual Circles

Traditionally, intellectual journalists are seen as vehicles for the dissemination of ideas to larger educated groups. Furthermore, they provide a link among various intellectual groups. Kadushin found that the U.S. journals most admired for their influence were most hated for their cliquishness; they behaved like king-making institutions, "rather than as flexible salons encouraging the exchange of ideas."[34] Mexican intellectuals and public figures uniformly connect the major intellectual journals with the control of specific intellectual groups. One Mexican suggested the following representative description:

There are some good papers and excellent magazines here, but each one tends to be controllled by some group or interest. All of these, such as *Excélsior*, or the publications of the Colegio de México and the Fondo de Cultura Económica, are publications of elite groups. It is very difficult for a person who writes to publish in them if they do not belong to the group in control of that publication. For example,

Siempre has what we call a Mafia, which has included Fernando Benítez, José Luis Cuevas, Carlos Monsiváis, and others. These group divisions exist because most intellectuals are receptive to ideas paralleling their own preferences. Here we call these groups *cenáculos*. Actually there are very few independent intellectuals in Mexico, or intellectuals who have not formed groups.[35]

The extent to which such domination over intellectual journals exists is difficult to measure. If both younger and established intellectuals believe it exists, they will not submit articles to many other journals, nor will they tend to associate with prominent members of other groups. Yet there are cases in which individuals representing different groups write for the same journal. One of the most successful journals in this respect is Jesús Silva Herzog's *Cuadernos Americanos*, established in. 1942. An examination of the magazine's leading contributors between 1942 and 1971, as measured by the number of articles contributed, reveals two important characteristics. First, Silva Herzog, although himself a believer in many Marxist tenets, has included many non-Marxist contributors and, in fact, contributors from a variety of ideological positions and disciplines are represented. The second important feature of *Cuadernos Americanos* is the extent to which foreign scholars, especially other Latin Americans, are represented. At least twenty-six (the figure is probably higher), or a third, of its leading writers, were foreigners, and several were North Americans.[36]

An examination of one of Mexico's leading historical reviews, *Historia Mexicana*, from 1951 to 1971, reveals that historians, foreign and native, attached to various groups or independent, have also been well represented among the contributors, although Marxist historians not particularly so.[37] *Historia Mexicana* is, of course, a more intellectually focused journal in that its subject matter is confined to history, and therefore the breadth of disciplines would not be expected.

Cuadernos Americanos and *Historia Mexicana* are exceptions to the general rule of narrow representation within Mexican intellectual reviews because they have achieved an objectivity of purpose partly sustained by successful and long lives. Their longevity has given them a sense of balance. Literary and politically oriented reviews, however, are not generally characterized by balanced objectivity. Yet even among influential contemporary reviews or supplements, when Mexicans are pressured, they can find cases of intellectuals who write in publications controlled by a variety of groups. For example, Carlos Pereyra, a regular contributor to *Nexos*, a publication directed by Enrique Florescano, a historian who has many collaborators drawn from the Institute of Anthropology and History, also writes for the *Siempre* and *Proceso* supplements. Similarly, Huberto Batiz, a writer for the supplement to *Uno Más Uno*, allegedly controlled by the *Nexos* group, is an independent who directs literary studies at the National University.[38]

If intellectual groups that control reviews do exist in Mexico, and, according to intellectuals, they do, then what is their importance to intellectual life? One view holds that groups with established reputations are able to obtain financial backing for their work and their reviews. According to one young novelist, "Today, the well-established intellectuals are monopolizing the market. The young ones are not being represented. We have to ally ourselves with someone if we want access. There are no well-known authors who are helping young ones make it. It is too competitive, too few readers for too many writers."[39] Thus intellectuals clearly perceive the necessity of attaching themselves to an intellectual mentor so that their works will be published in the Mexico City journals and be examined by prominent publishers. In the eyes of intellectuals, especially younger ones, attachment to a circle is often essential to career success.

A second view explaining the expansion of groups and their connection to journals has been suggested by poet Jaime García Terrés, himself a former editor of _La Universidad_, the cultural review of the National University. For García Terrés, the size of many journals, and the increased staff functions, require a sizeable collaborative effort from fellow intellectuals, who are compensated largely by having their names on the masthead or having their contributions published.[40]

Intellectual circles in other societies have certain characteristics different from those found in Mexico. Irving Howe describes the American intellectual in New York City as essentially a loner in relationships with other intellectuals and in the practice of his work, unlike the European intellectual, who engages in a steady exchange of ideas and preliminary discussions with peers.[41] Although work habits are difficult to ascertain, this constant exchange on an intellectual level does not seem prevalent in Mexico, either. On the other hand, the kind of fraternity or social contact found among literary groups in Paris and London does seem common to the Mexican intellectual, at least in the 1920s and 1930s.[42] This type of relationship is psychologically important. As Coser suggests, "Intellectuals need an audience, a circle of people to whom they can address themselves and who can bestow recognition; and they need regular contact with their fellow intellectuals."[43]

Another characteristic that emerges from Kadushin's examination of North American intellectual circles is their de-emphasis on formal leadership and their indirect ties between various members.[44] Although these characteristics appear to be true of comparable Mexican groups, the Mexicans seem more inclined to identify a titular head, if not formally, at least informally. Thus, when responding to the question of whether groups exist, or whether intellectual journals are dominated by individual groups, intellectuals in Mexico are likely to identify a single leader, such as Octavio Paz and his group, or Carlos Monsiváis and his group.

The dominance of a single figure within a group is particularly Mexican, for a similar phenomenon exists among political groups, or *camarillas*. Because intellectuals are freer in their associations, and because ideological considerations bring about changes in their personal affiliations, their groups tend to be less durable than those found in politics. Although political groups are equally dynamic, a small core tends to last many years if the leading individual or core member can sustain a series of influential positions over a long period.

Intellectual circles generally come and go, partly because they center on a journal; only as long as the journal appears is there a logic for the group's existence. Shifra Goldman, for example, described the evolution of the New Image painters in Mexico, a group led by Francisco Icaza, Arnold Belkin, and José Luis Cuevas in the late 1950s to promote innovative art forms and a philosophy of art. To express their ideas, they published a magazine entitled *Nueva Presencia* in 1962, which terminated in 1964, after five issues. According to Goldman,

It is hard to pinpoint an exact date or reason for *Nueva Presencia's* demise. It was caused by a combination of petty jealousies, misunderstandings, and tensions about money, as one artist or another accused the galleries of favoritism or of not handling money matters equitably. There was envy of the leading positions of Icaza and Belkin, who were constantly in the press as spokesmen for the group; at the same time the members of the group tended to leave organizational activities in their hands.[45]

Similar reasons can be found for the demise of literary groups, which have lived a tenuous existence over the years.

In Mexico, geography is an important influence in the creation of modern intellectual circles, since residence in Mexico City is a key to the social contact necessary for establishing such circles. Moreover, although the increasing size of Mexico City would seem naturally to discourage the influence of geographical concentration by decentralizing groups *within* the metropolitan area, this apparently has not taken place. A familiarity with cultural circles in Mexico suggests that, in a city of many millions, intellectuals, and indeed, other sets of leaders, frequent the same haunts, especially restaurants. No intellectual or politician can be interviewed in such locales without greeting several other equally prominent peers. As a respondent humorously suggested, because intellectuals go to only a small number of establishments, one of Mexico's cultural leaders could not have an affair in Mexico City without quickly being found out.

One of the important consequences of the geographic concentration of intellectuals in Mexico City and their disproportionately middle- and upper-class backgrounds, is that Mexican intellectuals associate and exchange their views with individuals from similar backgrounds. Class background is so homogeneous among Mexican intellectuals that their interchange with each other is an effective socializing agent predetermined, to some extent, by a similarity in educational and career experiences. This natural socializing tendency is reinforced by certain groups' dominance over journals. Many intellectuals believe that "there is no real contact between magazines and the reality of the Mexican situation, which would oblige the intellectual to discuss many other views. The intellectual review in Mexico has become a closed universe with intellectuals discussing their views and those of other intellectuals."[46]

Another characteristic of the intellectual group in Mexico is its tendency to be inbred. As Lomnitz has suggested, Mexican scientists have shown this trait over several generations. Inbreeding is probably more typical of intellectual scientists, or musicians, because they operate in a narrow environment and among fewer peers. The Mexican literary world has expanded, even though Selden Rodman could describe it in the 1950s as cliquish, intimate, and inbred.[47] Still, among certain literary circles, groups pass on their influence from one generation to another, although their influence may be purely intellectual, rather than social. For example, Jaime Torres Bodet, who at one time included José Gorostiza and Salvador Novo among his circle, was the disciple, but not the student, of poets Enrique González Martínez and Luis Urbina.[48] Of course, intellectuals who teach are more able to influence succeeding generations of intellectuals than are their peers who do not teach.[49]

The most important consequence of intellectual circles in Mexico is the detrimental effect they have on intellectual communication. Historically, one can find examples of the divisions among intellectual groups during the Porfiriato, and even, despite the image of a monolithic structure, among political groups.[50] In the postrevolutionary period, however, Mexico has evolved a series of unwritten rules that have institutionalized the behavior of various political groups and that make stability the key principle of the regime. On the other hand, in the intellectual world there is no overriding incentive for cooperation.

One of the individual consequences of the fluidity in Mexican intellectual groups is that loyalty is often short-lived, resulting in much personal bitterness between individual intellectuals. For example, José Joaquín Blanco in his insightful biography of Vasconcelos notes that his intellectual friends "abandoned him and passed, like Alfonso Reyes, to the enemy side; only [Carlos] Pellicer and [Julio] Torri remained faithful. Diego Rivera insulted him—of all places—in a mural at the Secretariat of Education."[51] Such disloyalty leads to personal vendettas, and again, Vasconcelos provides a classic example. Alberto J. Pani, who was his favorite in the early years when he directed the Popular University, became the hated "Pansi" in Vasconcelos's autobiography.[52]

Personal animosities discourage intellectual cooperation and promote factionalization. Larissa Lomnitz has hypothesized that weak peer cooperation among Mexican scientists arises from the emphasis on vertical cooperation engendered by the disciple-mentor relationship and, I should add, by a group system dominated by a single figure.[53] A little-known and little-understood consequence of this isolation among scientists is the heavy dependence on ideas from abroad and a tendency toward overspecialization.[54] These observations about scientists have logical implications for other disciplines, particularly the social sciences. In a recent paper discussing North American scholarship's misuse of inappropriate foreign methods to study the Mexican scene, Robert Peterson provides an example of a prominent Mexican political scientist making the same mistake.[55]

That intellectuals find it difficult to remain in intellectual circles over long periods, or to organize themselves effectively may be the result of strong personalistic tendencies.[56] When pressed on the subject of group cohesion, intellectuals universally replied that it was difficult to break into one group once you were identified with another. Just as intellectuals may censor themselves out of fear of anticipated censorship by the government, so they may not attempt to express their views outside their own groups, because they have already concluded that such an attempt would be futile.

Intellectuals also admitted that some groups, which on the surface give the appearance of being unified, are, in reality, quite diverse, individualistic, and nonconformist.[57] Their diversity has led one intellectual, José Joaquín Blanco, to suggest that some groups, like those Octavio Paz and Carlos Monsiváis, are interchangeable. He argues that often individuals from both groups can be found at the same social gatherings, and that many of the alleged disagreements are based on rumor rather than substance.[58] Another intellectual asserts that the novelist José Emilio Pacheco, who has worked with both Paz and Monsiváis, and who attributes his own intellectual influences to both men, straddles the two factions.[59]

Many intellectuals see the diversity within the intellectual groups as a product of a changing environment. The relationship between mentor and disciple as a basis for the group was, according to one public figure, "closer and richer in the earlier years. The smallness of these groups, and the closer relationships between mentor and disciple, stemmed from more intimate contacts between students and professors. Now more openness exists in the formation of these relationships, but the closeness is lacking."[60] To a Mexican poet, not only is size today detrimental to the structure of the traditional intellectual circle, but so is the behavior of intellectuals themselves. For him, the lack of discipline among politically active, younger intellectuals, expressed by their focus on instant inspiration or spontaneous anger rather than on disciplined work, explains the tenuousness of these groups and their relationships to one another.[61]

One long-standing feature of the intellectual circle in Mexico is the overlap between intellectual and political groups. The concentration of future intellectuals and political leaders in Mexico City, and at the National University, has served as an important bridge between the two groups, cementing friendships that often last a lifetime. One of the bonds helping to bring these two circles together stems from fictive and sanguinal kinship ties, whose influence was demonstrated in chapter 5. Kinship ties are important in the creation of intellectual circles, as illustrated by Antonio Caso's choice of brother-in-law Vicente Lombardo Toledano as director of the National Preparatory School and his ties with Pedro Henríquez Ureña, another brother-in-law.[62]

The interrelationship between intellectuals and politicians is enhanced by their similar experiences at the university. The 1940s' student generation, which came to dominate both political and cultural circles in the 1970s and 1980s, followed these earlier patterns. For example, during his student years in the 1940s, poet Fedro Guillén was a close personal friend of poet Wilberto Cantón and of Luis Echeverría, and among their circle of friends were Rodolfo Echeverría, brother of the future president, Arsenio Farell, future director of the Federal Electric Commission, and Emilio Uranga, leading philosopher of the 1950s era. Fedro Guillén was further tied to the older, established generations by his father's close friendship with José Vasconcelos. As young students, Wilberto Cantón, Luis Echeverría, and José López Portillo traveled together to Chile under the sponsorship of Chile's consul in Mexico, Pablo Neruda.[63]

The difference between political *camarillas* and intellectual groups is that among political cliques loyalty must be stronger for the individual to survive. A break with a political mentor requires attachment to another mentor if a young politician is to succeed in the political milieu. In intellectual life, however, after initial sponsorship by a mentor, a capable intellectual can leave his sponsor and pursue a successful career unattached to anyone, or, if the situation permits, establish his own intellectual group. Independence is much more frequent among intellectuals because by nature they tend to be autonomous, and once they have received recognition, they can find outlets for their works in a variety of sources. Thus, if they choose, intellectuals can survive outside the boundaries of a circle, whereas politicians, because there are no alternative avenues, cannot.

The Independent Intellectual

Although Mexican intellectual life is dominated by intellectual circles and by mentor-disciple relationships, the phenomenon of the independent intellectual is alive and well. Many of these intellectuals, however, are not talking with the people with whom other leading intellectuals are talking.

The isolated intellectual in Mexico falls into two categories, those isolated by age, and those by choice. Although the two are often interrelated, intellectuals with a predilection for being loners seem to increase their isolation as they grow older. For example, although José Vasconcelos was a leader or member of several important intellectual circles in the first two decades of this century and was a mentor to a generation of leading intellectual figures, by the 1950s he had lost contact with the significant intellectual figures of the time. When Selden Rodman interviewed Vasconcelos during this era, he asked him to identify intellectuals who analyzed the masses in their works. When Vasconcelos suggested that contemporary writers knew nothing about the masses, Rodman persisted: "How about Juan Rulfo and Montes de Oca?" Vasconcelos's reply: "Never heard of them."[64]

Twenty-five years later, in my interviews with notable intellectual figures, I found similar examples of older intellectuals who were unfamiliar with new intellectuals. Lucio Mendieta y Núñez, when volunteering the names of contemporary influential intellectuals, gave the names of members of the older generation, most of whom were politicians.[65] Agustín Yáñez, who demonstrated a vague familiarity with younger writers, although admitting he did not know them personally, indicated to me that since 1970 he had confined himself to his personal work and was unwilling to provide examples of influential younger writers for fear of omitting some.[66]

Not only does this mean that older intellectuals are isolated from younger intellectuals and that communication between these two groups is limited, but it also implies that younger intellectuals are rarely able to seek out older intellectuals as sponsors. Furthermore, the lack of communication between generations promotes misinformation and rumor among all intellectuals. For example, Kadushin found that most North American intellectuals were not influenced by the radical *New York Review* and did not agree with radical politics, but because such views appeared in print, they assumed other intellectuals were influenced.[67] Thus, when communication does not cross generational boundaries, intellectuals have a distorted view of themselves and the influences on their peers.

Among prominent Mexican intellectuals, however, there are numerous examples of those who have purposely followed independent paths. Edmundo O'Gorman, who could be classified in this category, explains why: "I have never formed a group. I have always been very independent. I think it is really a personal matter, a personal preference of one individual or another. I think it is the case in Mexico that many do form such groups and that they are often isolated from one another. The very formation of a group assumes a certain attempt to be somewhat exclusive because you are demonstrating that you wish to be different."[68]

Intellectual loners, as they might be called, are probably not well represented among leading intellectuals because they have fewer formal disciples to remember them and their contributions. Yet, in spite of this problem, many cases of intellectual loners, like O'Gorman, exist among leading Mexican intellectuals. Among novelists, a typical illustration is Juan Rulfo, who had no mentor and has no formal disciples.[69] For some intellectual disciplines, intellectual loners are at a real disadvantage because it is nearly impossible for them to constitute a school or a community. As Larissa Lomnitz argues, in the world of science "new scientific models or approaches arise because they are accepted and promoted by schools of thought, not individuals."[70] Similar arguments might well be made for the arts, music, and literature.

Nevertheless, independent Mexican intellectuals have served as models for other intellectuals, even if the potential impact of their creative contribution is lessened by their lack of peers and formal disciples. For example, Carlos Fuentes, who seems to have had no Mexican mentors, repeatedly admits Octavio Paz's influence on *Where the Air Is Clear*.[71] Similarly, the popular novelist Luis Spota has been influenced by Rulfo.[72] Indirect intellectual influences are no surprise, but it is important to remember that the presence of intellectual circles, the reliance on mentor-disciple relationships, and the value of groups in promoting new interpretations or schools of thought, do not preclude possible influence for the work of the individual intellectual.

My previous examination of intellectual circles, to which most Mexican intellectuals belong, suggests numerous consequences of the relationship among Mexican intellectuals, and between intellectuals and politicians. The overlap between political and intellectual groups, common to Mexico, does not exist in the United States. Furthermore, the connection between the U.S. intellectual and the scholarly community is, at best, tenuous and intermittent.[73] In Mexico, however, as I have argued in previous chapters, political leaders and intellectuals have strong ties, which in the past have been emphasized by their education at the National University, and more recently, at the Colegio de México, and by the establishment of intellectual circles that included young people with intellectual and political ambitions. A brief examination of some of the better-known groups since the 1920s reveals some important characteristics passed on from one generation to the next in Mexico.

Some Important Intellectual Groups

Chronologically, the purview of this book is from 1920 to the present, but the establishment of the Atheneum of Mexico in 1910 became a reference point for a succeeding series of groups. Among the founding members of the group were Antonio Caso, its first president, Alfonso Reyes, and José

Vasconcelos. According to one student of this intellectual circle, its members were searching for an "authentic expression of its culture, to try to see that America formed part of Western culture and as a consequence, its independence and personality were not against this culture, but formed within it."[74] This fundamental thesis has been passed down to the present generation through Samuel Ramos, Octavio Paz and Leopoldo Zea.[75]

But because this movement coincided with the upheavals associated with the Mexican Revolution, it is often presented as one in which there was unity among the intellectual collaborators. Such was not the case within this intellectual circle, nor within any succeeding circles.[76] Furthermore, like most intellectual trends, the philosophical postures taken by its members were never unified or sharply delineated from trends dominating intellectual life at the time. Although most remembered as a vehicle by which younger intellectuals could break the ties with the positivism of the Díaz era, the break was never complete or decisive among the Atheneum's members.[77]

What this group did accomplish was to prepare Mexico's youth for the difficult road it was to follow, to broaden its outlook on cultural issues, to expand its range of ideas, and to provide for institutions such as the Popular University to assist in the rehabilitation of the country.[78] Furthermore, the expanded membership of this intellectual circle was very much involved in public life: some, like Vasconcelos, in the creation of institutions and programs having a major social influence, and others, like Alfonso Cravioto, in careers in the Foreign Service or elective office. For both groups, there was little distinction between public service and intellectual independence; the two were intertwined, as if the nation demanded their contributions. The responsibility of the intellectual to serve the state, and therefore the nation, was instilled in a younger generation, members of the Generation of 1915, who committed much of their careers to public service, and whose influence and attitude discrepancies have been carefully analyzed by Enrique Krauze.[79]

The best-known intellectual group in the 1920s, following the violent phase of the Mexican Revolution, is that of the aforementioned Contemporáneos. Although described both as an ideological orientation and as an intellectual group, it reacted to some of the developing trends in the 1900s that dominated other contemporary groups. Among its philosophical tenets was an opposition to narrow forms of nationalism, the promotion of intellectual alternatives in the arts, drama, and literature, and the defense of liberty of expression.[80]

Its members, like the older Atheneum and 1915 generations, found mentors and supporters in the government bureaucracy. Patronized by Genaro Estrada, historian and diplomat, then subsecretary of foreign relations, group members Jaime Torres Bodet, José Gorostiza, and Roberto Owen found diplomatic positions. Others were employed through the intervention of Salvador Novo, in the Ministry of Education. In the opinion of Carlos Monsiváis, although they were not formally associated with the smaller circle of poets and authors, Carlos Chávez in music and Rufino Tamayo in art gave substance to the Contemporáneos' philosophy in their own disciplines, and therefore were intellectual collaborators.[81] One of the commonalities of the Contemporáneos with succeeding intellectual groups, their common acquaintances at the National Preparatory School and the National University, was the basis for their relationship.

During the 1930s, existing intellectual circles in Mexico were over-shadowed by the influx of a loosely defined but extremely influential group of Spanish refugees. Although the Spaniards, like other foreigners, were limited in their eligibility for administrative posts in the government bureaucracy, they filled many important posts in academia, particularly at the National University and the Colegio de México, the latter founded to use their talents. As the only author to study their influence in any depth concluded, since the 1940s, "it has been virtually impossible to attend the university, particularly the Faculty of Humanities, without encountering either a Spanish professor or a Mexican trained by a Spanish professor."[82]

Perhaps more important is the Spanish contribution to the supporting institutional structures essential to the expansion of intellectual life, their publishing houses, which today are among the most respected and successful in Mexico. According to José Rogelio Alvarez, editor of the *Encyclopedia of Mexico*, the Spanish exiles were primarily responsible for the revival of editorial production, changing and developing art criticism, the teaching of philosophy, the restructuring of the social sciences, and the expanded publication of translated works. For Alvarez and his generation, the Spaniards "opened up a worldwide influence in Mexico. The windows of this country were opened up for us to see out and for ideas to enter."[83]

In the 1940s, however, several Spaniards did help to form a more typical intellectual circle, a group that became known as the Hiperión. Its members included Emilio Uranga, Leopoldo Zea, Jorge Portilla, Ricardo Guerra, Luis Villoro, Eduardo García Máynez, Víctor Urquidi, and José Gaos. They and others affiliated with the movement wrote for the supplement to *El Universal* and *Novedades* and for the philosophical review published by the National University.[84] According to Hiperión's members,

It had a dual purpose: on one hand it was an attempt to bring philosophy into some kind of relation with the national culture, to use philosophical interpretations to explain and discuss our culture. Also, we wanted to make philosophy more related to the realities of Mexican life. Second, we wanted to fight against a tendency of philosophical dabblers, that is, to make the use and study of philosophy in Mexico more rigorous."[85]

Philosophy's focus on the Mexican identity, that is, trying to find out what it meant to be Mexican, was boosted by Mexico's isolation from Europe during World War II, which forced Mexicans to turn inward and analyze their own problems.[86] Structurally this group was loosely tied together, and unlike most intellectual groups in Mexico, it had no titular leadership. Its intellectual impact in philosophy and literature, however, was substantial.

In the following decade, two circles of intellectuals are remembered for their influence on Mexican culture. The first was a group of writers who dominated the supplement to the daily newspaper *Novedades*. "México en la Cultura" was established in 1949, and its directors were Pablo González Casanova, sociologist and later rector of the National University, Jaime García Terrés, poet and later director of the Fondo de Cultura Económica, and Fernando Benítez, a prolific author and journalist. During its twelve years, from 1949 to 1961, it published political and literary essays on national and international culture, and supported many causes.[87] When Fernando Benítez was removed as director in 1961 because of the leftist orientation of the supplement, the entire staff resigned, thus bringing to an end one of the longest-lived associations in recent Mexican cultural history. Again, although a loose association, this cultural supplement became the vehicle through which its adherents advocated a series of intellectual themes.

The second group important to the 1950s, but short-lived in comparison to the "México en la Cultura" group, was that of *El Espectador*. Like its predecessor, *El Espectador*, established in 1959, became the focal point of a group, but it was essentially a political review, not literary or philosophical. Its members, sympathetic to the Left, strongly urged the creation of a new Left that was undogmatic, cultured, and informed. Among its collaborators were Víctor Flores Olea, Enrique González Pedrero, Carlos Fuentes, Jaime García Terrés, Francisco López Cámara, and Luis Villoro, all of whom provided some continuity between the new group and its predecessors.[88] One of the characteristics of intellectual circles in Mexico is their dynamic quality, the fluidity of movement from one group to another over time. Thus, intellectual circles take on new members and lose old members, a feature important to the expansion of social and intellectual contacts among various intellectuals of different persuasions, disciplines, and generations. To intellectuals who grew up during this era, the appeal of *El Espectador*, which produced only six issues, was its critical posture.[89]

Following the demise of *El Espectador*, in 1961 a new group of intellectuals, again sympathetic to the Left, founded the journal *Política*, which lasted through 1967. Among its staff and collaborators were the economist Alonso Aguilar, Fernando Benítez, Fernando Carmona, José de la Colina, Carlos Fuentes, Vicente Lombardo Toledano, Salvador Novo, Emilio Uranga, Víctor Rico Galán, Víctor Flores Olea, Alejandro Gómez

Arias, Enrique González Pedrero, David Alfaro Siqueiros, and Angel Bassols Batalla.[90] In 1964, an important group of intellectuals abandoned the journal. The reasons are disputed, but one explanation is that *Política* had become overly critical of differing intellectual beliefs and inquisitorial in tone.[91] Although the group supporting the establishment of *Política* tried to promote objective discussion with the hope of unifying the Mexican Left, it became apparent by 1964 that this goal would not be achieved.[92]

The differences of opinion that led to the division of the *Política* group and eventually to its demise not only characterize the intellectual Left in Mexico, but reflect a deeper issue in Mexican cultural life: the natural tendency toward factionalization. The membership of this group again illustrates the movement of some intellectuals from one circle to another over time and suggests in some ways that intellectual fraternization, even though it does not lead to unity among Mexican intellectuals, is more widespread than it seems on the surface. Furthermore, intellectuals who pursue political careers were present in intellectual circles in the 1960s, as was true in the 1920s, but their presence was not common, nor have they been able, unlike their predecessors, to reach cabinet rank, where the possibility of influencing policy exists. The *Política* group did commit itself directly to political issues, not only in writings, but through moral support for the establishment of the National Liberation Movement in 1961.[93]

Since the 1970s two groups have dominated the intellectual scene. The first is led by Mexico's renowned poet Octavio Paz, who affiliated with many important intellectual circles and journals in earlier decades. In 1971, Paz recruited a number of writers to contribute to *Plural*, a cultural supplement to *Excélsior*. Among the many prominent intellectuals writing for *Plural* during this period were Daniel Cosío Villegas, Carlos Fuentes, Gabriel Zaid, Rafael Segovia, Gastón García Cantú, Víctor Flores Olea, and Luis Villoro. According to Paz, they tried to treat issues that had not received much public discussion in Mexico, including the contemporary political situation.[94] Stanley Ross, however, suggests that *Plural* eventually evolved into an almost exclusively literary magazine.[95]

In 1976, when Julio Scherer García was removed as editor of *Excélsior*, Paz and most of his collaborators resigned. Paz re-formed the elements of the *Plural* group as *Vuelta* the following year, with the expressed purpose of continuing "the liberal critical tradition of Daniel Cosío Villegas" and of trying to deal with "twentieth-century intellectual issues being widely discussed in Europe and the United States."[96] *Vuelta* continues to be published, and in addition to its editorial board, which includes Salvador Elizondo, José de la Colina, Enrique Krauze, Tomás Segovia, and Gabriel Zaid, its contributors have included Enrique González Pedrero, former editor of *Política* and PRI leader; Julieta Campos, writer and wife of González Pedrero; Jorge Ibargüengoitia, a novelist; and Larissa Lomnitz, anthropologist and wife of Cinna Lomnitz, member of the advisory board of *Nexos*.

Competing with *Vuelta* for leadership of the Mexican intellectual community is *Nexos*. The intellectual circle surrounding this journal is associated with the Department of Historical Investigations, located in the Chapultepec Castle, under the direction of historian Enrique Florescano. Among its editors and contributors are Héctor Aguilar Camín, historian; Guillermo Bonfil, anthropologist and former government official; Lorenzo Meyer, historian from the Colegio de México; Carlos Pereyra, essayist; José Luis Reyna, political scientist from the Colegio de México; Luis Villoro, historian and member of the National College; José Joaquín Blanco; Cinna Lomnitz, seismologist from the National University; and Pedro González Casanova, sociologist, member of the editorial board of *Cuadernos Americanos*, and formerly part of Lucio Mendieta y Núñez's group. Many members of this circle are identified with Carlos Monsiváis, also a member of the advisory board, who has a small group inside *Uno Más Uno*, the intellectuals' newspaper, and *Siempre*, an older magazine with moderate leftist leanings.[97]

Conclusions

The composition of these and other intellectual circles and editorial boards reveals the important role groups play in Mexican intellectual life. In the first place, Mexican intellectual circles, even now, do not exclude people with important political careers. By including political intellectuals among their membership, intellectual circles serve to continue and promote the interchange between the intellectual and the politician, even if that relationship seems to be on the decline. As journals and circles become more important in the recruitment and certification of Mexican intellectuals, replacing the university as the primary source of recruitment, they provide a structural component that widens the gradual separation among intellectuals following public careers, intellectuals independent of the state, and intellectuals and politicians in general.

Some journals and groups continue to rely on contacts made at the university, examples of which can be found on the board for *Nexos*, where relationships often extend back to the Colegio de México. Generally, however, there is a movement away from these contacts, at least among intellectuals in literature and other humanistic disciplines. Furthermore, many cases do exist of independent intellectuals who, like Alberto Vázquez del Mercado, burned themselves out early in their careers because they were too uncompromising, and who, although respected, are often forgotten and have a lesser influence on the intellectual community.

The universities are declining as a source of intellectual mentorship and contact because of the increasing diversity and size of institutions of higher education. Moreover, as prominent Mexican intellectuals find sources of employment outside academia, they are more likely to attract disciples through other means. The growth in economic opportunities for intellectuals outside the state allows them greater independence and encourages them to pursue careers outside the government. As the following chapters demonstrate, the specific career choice of an intellectual mentor, the political events of 1968, and the posture of a generation of intellectual leaders toward public service all affect the long-term relationship between intellectuals and politicians.

It can be argued, therefore, that membership in intellectual groups increases the visibility of intellectuals and their influence, whether through the promotion of their work or through the efforts of younger generations of disciples. As the university declines in influence, and as more intellectuals choose to follow paths independent of the state, Mexico's intellectual life will take on more characteristics of that found in the United States, the most important of which is the separation between political and intellectual leaders.

8. Cultural Academies and Institutions

A variety of cultural organizations that certify intellectuals, provide them with a livelihood, increase their prestige, and promote their careers are integral to the intellectual community in all modern societies. The availability of these institutions, their financial strength and independence, and their source of income all influence the structure of intellectual life and the relationship between intellectuals and the state. Furthermore, their location and accessibility determine the avenues that many younger intellectuals will follow, and the unity of the several generations of intellectuals who converge on society at any given time.

Studies of other societies reveal several discernible categories of cultural organizations that function to certify and promote the careers of individual intellectuals. Among the most important in Mexico are cultural academies, such as the National College or the Seminar of Mexican Culture; professional organizations, such as the National Academy of Medicine; foundations, such as the Center for Mexican Writers; and universities, most notably the National University and the Colegio de México. These organizations are extremely important to those intellectuals Edward Shils labels "institutionalized," that is, those who are formally involved with such institutions as active members or administrators. On the other hand, intellectuals independent of these institutions are also influenced by cultural enterprises that distribute intellectual goods, such as publishers, bookstores, libraries, journals, and newspapers.[1] As will be seen in this chapter, these institutions, whether they certify the intellectual or distribute his goods, exercise control by their selection or exclusion of certain intellectuals.

The Importance of Mexican Cultural Institutions

Most Mexican intellectuals believe that supportive cultural institutions, governmental and nongovernmental, are sorely lacking in their society. Their complaint is likely to be repeated universally among intellectuals, but nonintellectuals in Mexico agree in this assessment. When Mexicans were asked to identify cultural institutions important since 1920, their responses were limited to the National University, the Colegio de México, the Seminar of Mexican Culture, the National College, and occasionally, a more specialized academy such as the Mexican Academy of Language or the Mexican Academy of History.

One of the explanations intellectuals themselves offer for why cultural institutions are lacking in Mexico is their own failure to recognize this need and to take the initiative in establishing institutional support for their activities. Enrique Krauze argues that the typical Mexican intellectual does not place a sufficiently high value on his independence, either from the state or from other groups, to perceive the importance of such institutions.[2]

Philosophically, another difficulty may be that "many intellectuals . . . do not see the relationship between practical work and intellectual work—they want to leave the former to other individuals."[3] In his biographical work on Daniel Cosío Villegas, Krauze has stressed the importance of Cosío Villegas's role in the creation of cultural institutions, whether the Colegio de México, the Fondo de Cultura Económica, or journals such as *Foro Internacional, El Trimestre Económico,* or *Historia Mexicana.*[4] As José Rogelio Alvarez argues, Cosío Villegas is unique because not only was he an intellectual himself, but "he started projects and directed institutions that helped intellectual activity. His influence was due far more to his actions than to his ideas."[5]

The general failure of intellectuals to take the initiative in establishing cultural enterprises in the 1930s and 1940s may have consequences for the future. As Jaime García Terrés suggests, today there are individuals who recognize this failure, but "it has become very expensive to create a new cultural industry. In Cosío Villegas's era, although he was very aggressive in his efforts, the time was appropriate for the creation of these enterprises, since so few existed, and he was able to get help from private individuals and the state."[6] One consequence of the small number of cultural institutions and organizations in Mexico is the continued importance of only a few cultural organizations in the certification process and, moreover, of their centralization in Mexico City. On the other hand, a decision by someone in the private sector to fund and establish a new foundation would have a strong possibility for success because competition is limited, and intellectuals are always in search of independent funding for their projects.

Other factors, including general literacy rates, and more important, the availability of books to the general public, may explain the limited availability of cultural institutions. In 1980 only three hundred permanent libraries were operating in Mexico, and, according to Javier Barros Valero, at that time director general of publications and libraries of the Secretariat of Public Education, compared with other nations, proportionately, Mexico has a "dramatic scarcity of books, libraries, bookstores, and readers."[7]

Because libraries act to disseminate knowledge and to stimulate reading, thereby affecting the demand for the consumption of books, they are a key variable that leads to the expansion of knowledge production and intellectual activity. Prior to 1940, with only two exceptions in Argentina, there were no fully established schools for training librarians in Latin America.[8] In Mexico in 1980, only twenty-five individuals yearly were trained in archive or library management.

Pragmatically what is most important about some cultural institutions is the direct support they provide to intellectuals as simple employers and boosters of intellectual prestige. The employment function of the National University and the Colegio de México is obvious from the figures given in table 12 and will be discussed further in this chapter. What is less well-known is that several of the cultural academies, primarily the National College, provide a pension for prominent intellectuals.[9] Although the numbers benefiting from such monetary subsidies are small, the prestige of being one of the few beneficiaries increases accordingly. Conversely, intellectuals lend their prestige to these cultural institutions by accepting membership when proffered.

In his examination of contemporary Spain, Julián Marías found very few intellectuals "who refuse to participate in these institutions, and many of the most valuable and personally independent intellectuals appear to be associated with them and actually project their prestige through institutions which are not really in their hands and which do not fulfill their criteria."[10] Thus, the system of cultural institutions feeds on itself: state- or privately funded organizations financially support intellectuals and intellectuals permit their own prestige to improve the image of the beneficiary institution, thereby increasing the institution's ability to continue fostering the intellectual's influence in the intellectual community.

The extent of the intellectual's role in Mexico's cultural academies is illustrated by the evidence in the *MIBP*. An examination of the most exclusive cultural academies, where membership is by invitation only and for life, demonstrates that nearly two-thirds of my sample of intellectuals are known to have been members. Furthermore, membership in one prestigious institution often leads to membership in another. Thus, of the 332 intellectuals about whom I had membership information, 90 belonged to two or more of these organizations. Comparative data that include the intellectual elite are also quite revealing, since, surprisingly, although an equally large proportion of this group has belonged to such organizations, more have belonged to only one. The extent to which intellectuals have led these organizations is also illustrated by the fact that a fifth of them have been academy presidents.

One of the important structural influences on the orientation of cultural institutions and the relationship between the state and the intellectual is the unavailability of privately funded institutions. There are numerous Mexican academies that are supported by their membership, but there are few major cultural, privately funded foundations that directly benefit intellectuals. Whereas the North American intellectual elite, because it was frequently in charge of substantial budgets, was to some extent tied to the established financial and organizational structure of the private sector, in Mexico this apparently is not the case.[11]

The reasons for Mexico's failure to develop private foundations and intellectual attachment to such groups are several. Enrique Krauze suggests that historically the private sector was "uncultured, conservative, pro-clerical, and anti-intellectual. The consequence of this is that almost all cultural assistance in Mexico came from the government with the good and bad consequences that it implied."[12] The church-state conflict in Mexico eliminated the church as an important and competing force in subsidizing intellectual activities. But as the church becomes modernized, and there is plenty of evidence to suggest diverse ideological tendencies within the Mexican church, it may increasingly favor reforms, and thereby provide support for research that examines new social avenues.[13]

A second explanation offered for the failure of the private sector to intermesh with the intellectual community is the belief among intellectuals themselves that private foundations in Mexico "are less independent than those supported by the government. We [Mexicans] do not yet have sufficient accumulation of capital to make independent financing of institutions available. A first step has begun to take place—through the formation of collective galleries."[14]

One important exception to the general lack of private cultural foundations that support intellectual activities in Mexico directly is the Center of Mexican Writers. Originally founded in 1950 by North American author Margaret Shedd with funds from the Rockefeller Foundation, it was attached to Mexico City College in Mexico City, and later to the Mexico-North American Institute of Cultural Relations. In 1958, however, it became independent, and it received its last Rockefeller Foundation funds in 1965. The center was intended to support the efforts of young Mexican writers between the ages of twenty and forty with fellowships. As of 1975, more than 151 fellows had received support, including such writers as Juan Rulfo, who wrote *Pedro Páramo* as a fellow, Carlos Fuentes, Rubén Bonifaz Nuño, Emilio Carballido, Rosario Castellanos, and Juan José Arreola.[15] The original board of directors included Francisco Monterde (who replaced Shedd as director in 1963), Alfonso Reyes, Ramón Beteta, Julio Jiménez Rueda, Efrén C. del Pozo, Arturo Arnáiz y Freg, all important intellectuals themselves; Eduardo Villaseñor, cofounder of the Fondo de Cultura Económica, and a patron of many of Cosío Villegas's projects, and Plácido García Reynoso from the government financial sector;

and Carlos Prieto, a financier and long a patron of many cultural journals and projects.[16] In the 1970s, Juan Rulfo devoted most of his time to guiding the fortunes of this institution.

The general lack of private-sector support for intellectuals is by no means a phenomenon confined to Mexico. The only other developing country analyzed from this perspective is India, and the author of that study concluded that patronage from nongovernmental bodies was rare.[17] The failure of the private sector to compete with the government does raise several questions about intellectual life in Mexico and elsewhere in the developing world. One question raised indirectly by the information about the Center of Mexican Writers is the extent of foreign influence in the promotion of cultural activities. For example, at the recommendation of the American Chamber of Commerce in Mexico, Nelson Rockefeller arranged a grant for the establishment of a North American library, the Benjamin Franklin Library, in 1942, and two years later, also through the efforts of the American Chamber of Commerce, the Mexican-North American Cultural Institute was founded. Both of these institutions encourage the transmission of North American attitudes and values through the literature they provide.[18] Although the educational benefits of the library and institute, and, since 1965, the support of intellectuals from the independent Center of Mexican Writers, are undeniable, such foreign support may inhibit domestic private development of similar institutions.

A constantly reappearing but subtle theme underlying the complaints of Mexican intellectuals about the inadequacy of such institutions, the inefficiency of cultural enterprises, and their failure to organize, is a natural tendency to compare themselves unfavorably with their northern neighbor. Such comparisons may do far more damage than good, and instead of motivating change they increase cynicism about the inadequacies of Mexican efforts. In justifying the creation of the *Encyclopedia of Mexico*, José Rogelio Alvarez attempted to cope with some of these tensions:

The *Encyclopedia of Mexico* itself is an attempt to provide a depository for Mexican ideas and knowledge, rather than serving as a universal encyclopedia, and is a reaction to the loss of the Mexican current I described earlier. There has always been an identity crisis in this country, whether revolving around the personality, ideology, economy—today we again are in a crisis of identity. The young people have become like young people everywhere—they have lost their Mexican identity.[19]

Another consequence of government domination of cultural institutions is their centralization in Mexico City. One of the possibilities for decentralization is exemplified in the establishment in 1979 of the Colegio de Michoacán, in Zamora. Its first president, Luis González y González, a prominent historian and member of the National College, has himself been a leader among Mexican historians in focusing attention on local and provincial history. The purpose of this new institution is to emulate the Colegio de México on the local level by promoting provincial cultural activities and using their contributions.[20] If this effort is successful, Mexico could conceivably explore, as a cultural complement to educational decentralization, a program similar to that of the Division of Public Programs of the National Endowment for the Humanities in the United States. This division provides funds at the state level for numerous cultural activities, thereby keeping the programs themselves, the funding agency, and most important, the decision making, local.

The Academies

Given the centralization of cultural institutions in Mexico City, and the influence of the government in Mexico's most prestigious organizations, it is well worth exploring their establishment, membership, and activities to determine the extent of involvement of leading Mexican intellectuals and the type of intellectual who participates. Without doubt, the most prestigious of existing Mexican cultural academies is the National College (see table 14). The college was established in 1943 under the auspices of the Secretariat of Public Education. Its governing statutes made clear the desire to represent all currents of thought philosophically, both artistic and scientific, but strictly excluding all interests motivated by active politics.[21] President Manuel Avila Camacho nominated its original members, although their names were given to the president by then secretary of public education Octavio Véjar Vázquez, who delegated the actual selection to Alejandro Gómez Arias, his private secretary.[22]

The overall purpose of the National College, then as now, is to serve as a vehicle for the dissemination of its members' knowledge through regularly sponsored conferences or shows open to the public. It also publishes the members' work. In 1943, during its first year, the college held 153 conferences with an average attendance of some fourteen hundred persons.[23] The original members were Mariano Azuela, Alfonso Caso, Antonio Caso, Carlos Chávez, Ezequiel Chávez, Ignacio Chávez, Enrique González Martínez, Isaac Ochoterena, Ezequiel Ordóñez, José Clemente Orozco, Alfonso Reyes, Diego Rivera, Manuel Sandoval Vallarta, Manuel Uribe Troncoso, and José Vasconcelos. Of these fifteen, three were from the fine arts, five from the sciences, three were literary figures, three were from the humanities, and only one was in the social sciences. Thus the college, under government auspices, gave much more representation to the arts, and especially to the sciences, than have intellectuals themselves. Of the original fifteen members, seven are considered by the intellectual community to have been members of the intellectual elite.

Not only was the distribution among the disciplines well balanced, but,

Table 14
Careers of Members of the National College, 1943-1976

Name	Membership in Elite	Intellectual Field	Public Career:[a] Level (Agency)	Academic Career:[b] Level
Mariano Azuela	x	L	low	none
Alfonso Caso	x	SS	high (SEP)	high
Antonio Caso	x	H	low	high
Carlos Chávez		FA	middle (SEP)	low
Ezequiel A. Chávez		H	high (SEP)	high
Ignacio Chávez	x	S	low	high
Enrique González Martínez		L	high (SEP)	low
Isaac Ochoterena		S	none	middle
Ezequiel Ordóñez		S	none	low
José Clemente Orozco	x	FA	none	none
Alfonso Reyes	x	L	low	high
Diego Rivera	x	FA	none	none
Manuel Sandoval Vallarta		S	high (SEP)	high
Manuel Uribe Troncoso		S	none	low
José Vasconcelos	x	H	high (SEP)	high
Ignacio González Guzmán		S	none	high
Manuel Toussaint		FA	middle (SEP)	high
Silvio Zavala	x	SS	middle (SEP)	high
Arturo Rosenblueth (1947)		S	none	low
Antonio Castro Leal (1948)		L	middle (RREE)	high
Jesús Silva Herzog (1948)	x	SS	high (SEP)	high
Gerardo Murillo (1950-1951)		FA	middle (SEP)	none
Daniel Cosío Villegas (1951)	x	SS	low	high

Table 14 (continued)

Name	Membership in Elite	Intellectual Field	Public Career:[a] Level (Agency)	Academic Career:[b] Level
Samuel Ramos (1952)	x	H	high (SEP)	high
Agustín Yáñez (1952)	x	L	high (SEP)	low
Jaime Torres Bodet (1953)	x	L	high (RREE)	low
Guillermo Haro (1953)		S	middle	low
Manuel Martínez Báez (1955)		S	high	high
Eduardo García Máynez (1957)		H	none	high
José Adem (1960)		S	none	middle
José Villagrán García (1960)		FA	low	high
Victor L. Urquidi (1960-1968)	x	SS	low	high
Antonio Gómez Robledo (1960)		L	middle (RREE)	low
Octavio Paz (1966)	x	L	middle (RREE)	none
Miguel León Portilla (1971)		H	none	middle
Ignacio Bernal (1972)		SS	middle (SEP)	low
Rubén Bonifaz Nuño (1972)		L	none	middle
Antonio Carrillo Flores (1972)	x	L	high (RREE)	high
Ramón de la Fuente (1972)		S	none	middle
Alfonso García Robles (1972)		H	high (RREE)	none
Marcos Moshinsky (1972)		S	none	middle
Jesús Romo Armería (1972)		S	none	middle
Emilio Rosenblueth (1972)		S	none	middle
Fernando Salmerón (1972)		H	high (SEP)	high
Ramón Xirau (1973)		L	none	middle
Julián Adem (1973)		S	none	middle
Carlos Casas Campillo (1974)		S	none	middle
Héctor Fix Zamudio (1974)		H	low	middle

Name	Field		Public service[a]	Academic[b]
Jesús Kumate (1974)	S		none	low
Jaime García Terrés (1975)	L	x	middle (RREE)	middle
Bernardo Sepúlveda (1975)	S		middle	middle
Leopoldo Solís (1976)	SS		high	low

Key: L=literature; SS=social sciences; H=humanities; FA=fine arts; S=sciences or medicine; SEP=Secretariat of Public Education; RREE=Secretariat of Foreign Relations.

Notes: [a]Level of public service is defined as low = any employee of the federal bureaucracy below department head; middle = any position in the federal bureaucracy from department head up, but not higher than *oficial mayor*; high = *oficial mayor* through cabinet secretary.

[b]Level of academic service is defined as low = professor at full or part time; middle = director of seminar or department; high = dean of a professional school, director of research institute, secretary general, or rector.

Year in parentheses after a member's name is the year he was invited to join.

equally important, intellectuals with long attachments to the state were not chosen exclusively. In fact, of the fifteen, five (three of them scientists and two of them painters) had never held public office, and three more (Antonio Caso, Ignacio Chávez, and Alfonso Reyes) had held only low-level positions in the government. The intellectuals chosen to represent the college were balanced fairly evenly between those with public careers and those without, a balance comparable to the proportion found among intellectuals as a whole. When we examine their academic careers, the interrelationship between the National University (as the leading educational and cultural institution) and the National College (as the leading academy) becomes clear: except for the painters Diego Rivera and José Clemente Orozco, and the novelist Mariano Azuela, all of the members taught at the National University, five were president of that institution, and a sixth, Alfonso Reyes, was president of the Colegio de México.

The National College, to represent a larger number of intellectuals, doubled its size to thirty members in 1972. Since the original fifteen were designated, each succeeding member has been selected by a committee from the college. In making their selections after 1947, when the first of the original group died and left a position vacant, the National College has followed very definite discipline biases. Of the thirty-seven individuals ushered into the National College from 1947 to 1976, 19 percent were in literature, 35 percent were in the sciences, 16 percent were in the social sciences, 5 percent were in law, 16 percent were in humanities, and 8 percent were in the fine arts. In contrast, among all leading intellectuals, 25 percent have been in literature, only 9 percent in the sciences, 18 percent in the social sciences, 4 percent in law, 29 percent in the humanities, and 14 percent in the fine arts (table 2). The National College has overrepresented the sciences to the substantial underrepresentation of the humanities, fine arts, and, to a lesser degree, literature.

Methodologically, the reason for this discrepancy is that many of the scientific members of the National College are not, according to my criteria, or in the opinion of their peers, intellectuals. A further explanation, significant to an understanding of the role of the National College, is that nearly all of the scientists listed in table 14 are nonpolitical, and most of the post-1947 group are better described as experts, or members of the intelligentsia, whose works are read by their scientific peers, and not by the well-educated lay person or by intellectuals. This finding indirectly supports the contention that the National College, the most prestigious cultural academy in Mexico, has a decidedly establishment flavor, in the sense that most of its members are not outspoken critics of the government, or of contemporary social and economic problems in Mexico. This trend is further illustrated by the fact that, since 1952, the social-science field has been represented by only three members: the only economist and critic of the government, Víctor Urquidi, for many years president of the Colegio de México, is one of two members to have resigned his lifetime appointment (in 1968); the other two social scientists are Ignacio Bernal, who works in precolonial archeology and anthropology, and Leopoldo Solís, who has held high posts in the Bank of Mexico.

Other indicators of the serene and respected careers of National College members can be seen in their relatively few antiestablishment activities. Only four of the fifty-two members have been exiled by the Mexican government at some point in their lives, and two have been imprisoned for their political beliefs. These figures are somewhat lower than those for intellectuals in general (*MIBP*). Ideologically, the college is dominated by neoliberals, but in proportions larger than in the general population of leading intellectuals. Whereas only two Marxists (4 percent) can be found among the members listed on table 14 (Diego Rivera and Jesús Silva Herzog, neither of whom could be considered really orthodox), 16 percent of the general intellectual population is Marxist (*MIBP*). Another significant variable is the age of the college's members. No one younger than forty has ever been invited to join, and most were invited in their late fifties and early sixties. Because the typical member is older than the average age of leading intellectuals, he represents a more mature generation of Mexicans.

A further characteristic of interest in the background of the National College member is his involvement in public affairs. Of the members about whom I have information, only three have held elective office. On the other hand, over half of the members have held appointive positions in the federal bureaucracy, a figure similar to that for intellectuals in general. Of those holding government positions, fifteen did so in the Secretariat of Foreign Relations,[24] and an equal number in Public Education. These two federal agencies capture the lion's share of intellectuals who follow careers in public life, or who dabble briefly with public office. Although the government-career person is well represented among the National College members, this pattern may change gradually as the number of scientists continues to increase and of literary figures and humanists decreases. Not only younger literary figures have chosen not to follow government careers, but most scientists have confined their careers to academia. Symbolically, therefore, the government supports an intellectual institution whose younger prototype is more typically the independent intellectual, and thus it adds to changing the traditional pattern.

Although the National College is not inbred with family members who dominate generation after generation (only three sets have sanguinal relationships: Alfonso and Antonio Caso [brothers], Julián and José Adem [brothers], and Arturo and Emilio Rosenblueth [father and son]), it is useful to determine the extent to which its incoming recruits are the disciples and students of established members, and whether the mentor serves as a model for the budding career of the disciple. The mentors included in the *MIBP* were not meant to be exclusive, since intellectuals at various points in their careers come under the influence of different individuals. However, where known, an attempt has been made to identify a decisive personal influence, generally one occurring very early in an intellectual's life. Although I have complete information on only about two-thirds of the mentors of the members of the National College, of the thirty-four about whom I have information, fourteen were themselves disciples of older members of the college.

One would expect that leading intellectuals would produce leading disciples in the next generation, and that therefore those disciples would have more chance to be named members of the National College if the mentors were members. But the fact that nearly *half* of all members from 1943 to 1976 were disciples of other members suggests the importance of a mentor and, indirectly, the strong influence mentors exercise on succeeding generations and on membership in cultural academies.

Even more striking is the influence of a mentor as a model after which intellectual disciples pattern their own careers. Of the twenty members who followed public careers about whom I have information on their mentors, eighteen, or 90 percent, had mentors who also served the state. Of those eleven who did not choose to serve the state, nine, or 82 percent, had mentors who did the same. These figures suggest that intellectuals' self-definition, their role, and the career that they should follow are strongly influenced by their mentors. If the mentors of the younger intellectual generations, and those mentors forthcoming, are themselves primarily outside of public life, then we can expect the number of prominent intellectuals who have not served the state to increase.

Second in importance to the National College as an interdisciplinary cultural academy is the Seminar of Mexican Culture, which, like the college, was created by Secretary of Public Education Octavio Véjar Vázquez. Initially larger than the college, its constitution permits twenty-five members, who were selected in 1942. Its disciplinary orientation is quite different from that of the National College. Of the original twenty-two members, fifteen, or 68 percent, were from the fine arts, that is, the plastic arts, music, and architecture (table 15). Only three represented the humanities, and one the sciences; three were from literature, and not even a token representative came from the social sciences. Later members did give better representation to the humanities and literature, but the sciences are not well represented and the social sciences have never been represented.

This academy also differs from the National College in that seven members admitted from 1942 to 1970 have been women, thus providing them with a fairly decent representation, especially since four of the original

Table 15
Members of Seminar of Mexican Culture, 1942-1970

Name	Intellectual Field	Member of National College	Mentor(s)[a]
Fanny Anitúa	FA		María Aispuru de Lille
Mariano Azuela	L	x	None
Carlos Bracho	FA		Mateo Hernández
Julián Carrillo[b]	FA		Flavio Carlos
Luis Castillo Ledón	H		NI
Esperanza Cruz	FA		NI
Francisco Díaz de León	FA		Saturnino Hernán, *José Vasconcelos*[c]
Aurelio Fuentes	FA		NI
Mathilde Gómez	H		NI
Frida Kahlo[b]	FA		*Diego Rivera*
Enrique González Martínez	L	x	
Arnulfo Domínguez Bello	FA		NI
Gregorio López y Fuentes	L		NI
Gabriel Méndez Plancarte	H		NI
Manuel M. Ponce	FA		Cipriano Avila, Martín Krause
Luis Ortiz Monasterio	FA		NI
Máximino Martínez	S		NI
Antonio M. Ruiz	FA		NI
Angel Zárraga	FA		Julio Ruelas
Fernando Soler	FA		Domingo Soler
Alfredo Gómez de la Vega	FA		Fernando Díaz de Mendoza
José Luis Cuevas	FA		NI
Vito Alessio Robles (1943)	H		NI

Table 15 (continued)

Name	Intellectual Field	Member of National College	Mentor(s)[a]
Miguel Bernal Jiménez (1943)	FA		Ignacio Mier y Arriaga
Amalia González Caballero[b] (1944)	L		Luis Castillo Ledón
Antonio Castro Leal (1945)	L	x	*José Vasconcelos*
Carlos González Peña (1945)	L		Irineo Paz
Francisco Orozco Muñoz (1945)	H		NI
Pedro Daniel Martínez (1947)	S		Manuel López Aguado, *Antonio Caso*
Guillermina Llach (1947)	H		NI
Jesús Reyes Ruiz (1947)	L		NI
Wigberto Jiménez Moreno (1947)	H		NI
Juan D. Tercero (1948)	FA		NI
Agustín Yáñez (1948)	L	x	*Manuel Sandoval Vallarta, Luis Castillo Ledón*
Carlos Graef Fernández (1949)	S		*Manuel Sandoval Vallarta*
Manuel Martínez Báez (1949)	S	x	Gustavo Baz, Manuel Martínez Solórzano
Dionisia Zamora (1950)			NI
Eduardo García Máynez (1950)	H	x	*Antonio Caso*
Rodolfo Usigli (1951)	L		NI
Salvador Azuela (1951)	H		*Antonio Caso, José Vasconcelos*
Enrique del Moral (1957)	FA		José Gaos, Carlos Obregón Santacilia
Mauricio Magdaleno (1957)	L		*José Vasconcelos*, Narciso Bassols
Salvador Aceves Parra (1958)	S		*Ignacio Chávez*, Salvador Zubirán
Francisco Monterde (1963)	L		Luis González Obregón
Antonio Acevedo Escobedo (1964)	L		Pedro de Alba, Carlos Noriega Hope
Jorge González Camarena (1965)	FA		Mateo Herrera, Francisco Díaz de León
Pablo Castellanos (1967)			NI

José Rojas Garcidueñas (1969)	H	NI
Ernesto de la Torre Villar (1969)	H	NI

Key: FA=fine arts; L=literature; H=humanities; S=science and medicine; NI=no information.

Notes: [a]The mentors listed in this table are not meant to suggest that other individuals did not serve in this capacity, but only that these individuals were known to have such an influence; where possible they were selected because their influence occurred earlier in the disciple's career.

[b]Julián Carrillo is the father of Antonio Carrillo Flores, who is a member of the National College. Amalia González Caballero was the wife of historian Luis Castillo Ledón, a founding member of the Seminar of Mexican Culture. Frida Kahlo was the wife of Diego Rivera. A year in parentheses is the year member invited to join.

[c]An italicized name indicates National College membership.

members were women. Equally interesting is the finding that the two most important academies are not dominated by the same figures. Only six Seminar of Mexican Culture members have been invited to join the National College: Mariano Azuela, Enrique González Martínez, Antonio Castro Leal, Agustín Yáñez, Manuel Martínez Báez, and Eduardo García Máynez, and all became members of the National College after joining the Seminar of Mexican Culture.[25]

The data in table 15 also suggest that National College members have been important in producing disciples who themselves have appeared in the membership of the Seminar of Mexican Culture, but that influence has not been overwhelming. Of the twenty-five members about whom I have information, only ten were the disciples of leading intellectuals who themselves were members of the National College. However, an examination of the mentors does reveal that several persons have been particularly influential with younger generations, especially José Vasconcelos and Antonio Caso. Furthermore, the list suggests considerable diversity among the mentors, and even non-Mexicans like José Gaos have had an influence.

In addition to the two national cultural academies, a number of cultural institutions with a particular disciplinary focus exist in Mexico. Many were established during the nineteenth century, whereas others, like the two preceding academies, are of recent origin. For example, the most important of these among the arts is the Academy of Arts, founded in December 1966, under the direction of Agustín Yáñez, then secretary of public education, and José Luis Martínez, director of the National Institute of Fine Arts. Originally, the academy's members included only artists, art historians, and art critics, but later membership was expanded to include people in architecture, sculpture, drawing, and music.[26] The Academy of Arts maintains a very even balance among these disciplines. Of the twenty-nine members named since its establishment, only two, José Villagrán García and Carlos Chávez, have been members of the National College.

In the humanities, perhaps the most prestigious of the academies is the Mexican Academy of History, established in 1919. Over the years, the academy's leadership has sought financial support for its activities and its journal from financial institutions such as the National Bank of Mexico or La Tabacalera Mexicana, S.A., and from such influential leaders of the private sector as Carlos Prieto, Agustín Legorreta, and Pablo Macedo.[27] Of the more than forty members inducted between 1919 and 1970, only three, Manuel Toussaint, Alfonso Caso, and Silvio Zavala, were members of the National College. Thus it is apparent that the discipline-oriented academies allow many others outside of the two national academies to be represented and to have access to the prestige that membership in a cultural institution provides.[28]

National Prizes

Intellectuals have been recognized by and have benefited from the prestige granted to them by cultural academies, publicly or privately financed. In 1945 the government began directing its efforts toward promoting or indirectly influencing intellectual recognition through national prizes. Such prizes are one of the means by which an intellectual's career can receive a substantial boost. Originally, the support was more in the way of prestige than money, since each prize was only 20,000 pesos, or 1,600 dollars. However, in 1965, each prize was increased to 100,000 pesos, or 8,000 dollars.[29]

An examination of the prize winners between 1945 and 1976 suggests several important characteristics about the recipients (table 16). Most important is that recipients of these awards are mature people at the prime of their career or past their productivity peak; their average age at the time of the award is sixty-two. Thus, the national prizes given by the government are for long years in an activity and, with a few exceptions, confined to scientists in their forties; they cannot be seen as promoting a promising intellectual's career.

The national prizes therefore, do not bolster, on the basis of merit, the independent career channel of very many intellectuals. On the other hand, although each prize is awarded with government funds, the selection committee has not exclusively favored intellectuals or intelligentsia who have followed public careers, either full- or part-time, since only twenty-eight, or 39 percent, have been employed in the federal bureaucracy, a figure smaller than that found among intellectuals in general. Furthermore, the establishment intellectual academies have received mixed representation. Not surprisingly, National College members have been well represented among the ranks of national prize winners, with twenty-seven recipients, or 38 percent of the awards. However, the Seminar of Mexican Culture, representative of a different and broader group of intellectuals, has accounted for very few recipients, only 11 percent. Last, not a single woman has received a national prize.

The backgrounds of the 1980 prize winners, Leopoldo Zea in history, José Luis Martínez in literature, Carlos Orozco Romero in art, and Guillermo Soberón in science, are representative of historical trends. There have been accusations of political motivations determining the choices of the award committee, and undoubtedly, personal preferences, and not always merit, influence the outcome on occasion, but there is no way to ascertain the extent to which these accusations are true.[30] What can be safely conclued is that, although critics of the government have been represented among the recipients, for example, Daniel Cosío Villegas, David Alfaro Siqueiros, and Jesús Silva Herzog, on the whole, those with

Table 16
National Prizewinners in Arts, Sciences, and Letters, 1947-1976

Name and Date of Award	National College Member	Seminar of Mexican Culture	Public Career	Age at Award
Alfonso Reyes (1945)	x		yes	56
José Clemente Orozco (1946)	x		no	63
Manuel M. Ponce (1947)		x	no	61
Maximiliano Ruiz Castañeda (1948)			yes	48
Mariano Azuela (1949)	x	x	yes	66
Diego Rivera (1950)	x		no	64
Candelario Huizar (1951)			no	67
Nabor Carrillo Flores (1957)			no	46
Carlos Chávez (1958)	x		yes	59
Gerardo Murillo (1958)	x		yes	83
Martín Luis Guzmán (1958)			yes	71
Manuel Sandoval Vallarta (1959)	x		yes	60
Alfonso Caso (1960)	x		yes	64
Ignacio Chávez (1961)	x		no	64
Jesús Silva Herzog (1962)	x		yes	70
Guillermo Haro (1963)	x		no	50
Ignacio González Guzmán (1964)	x		no	68
Rufino Tamayo (1964)			no	65
Blas Galindo (1964)			no	54
Carlos Pellicer (1964)			yes	65
Angel María Garibay K. (1965)			no	73
Arturo Rosenblueth (1966)	x		no	66
David Alfaro Siqueiros (1966)			no	70
Jaime Torres Bodet (1966)	x		yes	64
José Adem (1967)	x		no	46
Roberto Montenegro (1967)			no	82
Luis Ortiz Monasterio (1967)		x	yes	61
Salvador Novo (1967)			yes	63
Marcos Moshinsky (1968)	x		no	47
Salvador Zubirán (1968)			yes	70
José Villagrán García (1968)	x		yes	67
José Gorostiza (1968)			yes	67
Ignacio Bernal (1969)	x		yes	59
Fernando Alba (1969)			NI	NI
Francisco Díaz de León (1969)		x	no	72
Silvio Zavala (1969)	x		yes	60
Justino Fernández (1969)			no	59
Carlos Graef Fernández (1970)		x	no	59
Jorge González Camarena (1970)		x	no	62
Juan Rulfo (1970)			yes	52

Table 16 (continued)

Name and Date of Award	National College Member	Seminar of Mexican Culture	Public Career	Age at Award
Jesús Romo Armería (1971)	x		no	49
Daniel Cosío Villegas (1971)	x		yes	73
Gabriel Figueroa (1971)			no	64
Isaac Costero (1972)			NI	NI
Antonio González Ochoa (1972)			NI	NI
Luis Sánchez Medal (1972)			no	53
Juan O'Gorman (1972)			no	67
Rodolfo Usigli (1972)		x	yes	67
Carlos Casas Campillo (1973)	x		no	57
Pedro Ramírez Vázquez (1973)			yes	54
Agustín Yáñez (1973)	x	x	yes	69
Ruy Pérez Tamayo (1974)			no	50
Emilio Rosenblueth (1974)	x		yes	48
José Chávez Morado (1974)			no	65
Rubén Bonifaz Nuño (1974)	x		no	51
Edmundo O'Gorman (1974)			yes	68
Joaquín Cravioto (1975)			no	52
Guillermo Massieu (1975)			no	55
Arcadio Poveda (1975)			no	45
Manuel Alvarez Bravo (1975)			no	73
Francisco Monterde (1975)		x	yes	81
Antonio Gómez Robledo (1976)	x		yes	68
Efraín Huerta (1976)			no	62
Rodolfo Halffter (1976)			no	76
Luis Barragán (1976)			no	74
Julio Prieto (1976)			no	64
Eduardo García Máynez (1976)	x	x	no	68
Samuel Gitler (1976)			no	43
Julián Adem (1976)	x		no	52
Ismael Herrera Revilla (1976)			no	45
Wenceslao López Martín del Campo (1976)			NI	NI
Reynaldo Pérez Rayón (1976)			yes	48

Note: NI = no information.

strong political views, and with views highly critical of the state, have not been chosen often. It is also true that small groups of intellectuals, regardless of discipline, have never had exclusive control over the prize winners, and that many types of intellectuals, both independents and institutionally affiliated, have been recipients.

The Universities

The most important cultural institutions influencing Mexican intellectual life are the universities, especially the public universities, and primarily the National University and the Colegio de México. Universities generally are important in any intellectual community because they are leaders in research and develop new trends in most disciplines; they act as an important bridge between the generalists and the specialists; they socialize educated groups in society, including intellectuals; they produce the consumers and creators of intellectual goods; and they are an important source of mentor-disciple relationships.

Mexican universities act as initial gatekeepers to the intellectual community, since 80 percent of the leading Mexican intellectuals are college educated in a society in which only a tiny percentage (2 percent) of the general population has reached that level. Because higher education is limited to so few Mexicans, having a college degree, as Hugh Smythe suggests, invariably seems "to bring about relatively high-prestige employment," whether in cultural affairs, business, or politics.[31] Today's intellectual in Mexico or the United States is unlikely to reach national status without a college education, so it is important to determine which institutions ultimately certify an individual for intellectual status.

Universities do not play this role for North American intellectuals. The size and proliferation of universities in the United States has doomed them not to serve as certifiers of the intellectual elite, and they have not spawned networks of American intellectuals.[32]

In Mexico, the university has been much more important in the certification process and in the creation of intellectual networks. The Mexican university functions more significantly in this capacity because the universities, until very recently, have been few in number, because intellectuals, as I demonstrated earlier, have received their educations and taught in a limited number of institutions, and because Mexican universities have been important in the creation of intellectual circles. Although Norman Birnbaum has argued that universities are part of the system of power in Western societies because of their ability to give or withhold the degrees valued so highly in those cultures, the plurality of the North American educational system prevents that power from being narrowly held or inaccessible.[33] However, there is more truth to Birnbaum's assertion with regard to societies in which education is restricted to an upper socioeconomic group, as in the case of Mexico, and in which universities are deeply involved in the political system, especially the recruitment process.

Universities are universally recognized for their role as knowledge producers. In Mexico, *public* universities dominate higher education. Each state has a public university, and Mexico City is the site of three important public institutions: the National University, the National Polytechnic Institute, and the Metropolitan University.[34] Mexico City, however, attracts a disproportionate number of college students, just as it attracts a disproportionate number of intellectuals. Postgraduate education is even more concentrated there than are professional-degree programs. As of 1980, 50 percent of the institutions offering postgraduate degrees were located in the Federal District and Nuevo León, yet 90 percent of the students enrolled in postgraduate programs were in Mexico City, even though, of the 511 programs available in Mexico, only 291 were in Mexico City (163 were in Jalisco, Nuevo León, Veracruz and Puebla, and 57 were elsewhere).[35]

To the state, the advantage of the educated specialist is a de-emphasis on antagonistic ideologial orientations and a willingness to work for the state or the private sector.[36] In many developing countries, such as India, few intellectuals have been willing to make full-time careers in academia; rather, because the state itself had larger libraries, greater prestige, better salaries, qualified personnel with whom to discuss one's ideas, and research facilities, they were attracted to government careers.[37] In Mexico, however, the state has used its resources to build up the universities and to make them more attractive to intellectuals. In this way, although the state has used the university as a recruitment channel for intellectuals and politicians, it has helped to establish an independent cultural institution attractive to many intellectuals, thus avoiding a vicious cycle found in other developing societies that perpetuates inferior universities.

The broadest role played by the university in the cultural milieu is its socializing function, both for the educated citizen and the individual intellectual. As Seymour Martin Lipset and David Riesman suggest, not only does the university transmit existing culture, and those beliefs that help to legitimize the political system in a society, but, by "serving to certify other elites as technically competent through their control of formal education and helping to produce the ideational and cultural resources that the various collectivities need, the culture-producing centers have been gaining in their ability to exercise great influence over the other elites, whether in government, the churches, business establishments or the mass media."[38]

Recognizing the importance of the university in the socialization process of Mexico's future leaders, both the government and the intellectual community have sought to control or maintain the content and autonomy of the curriculum. Historically, most Latin American countries have accepted the proposition that "the political ideologies of a society should be developed in a university."[39] Moreover, academies have been found to be "intensely ideological" in their thinking.[40] The fundamental question, however, is whether ideologies should all be freely represented or whether the state should promote one orientation. This issue developed into a national debate in Mexico in 1933, with Vicente Lombardo Toledano and others arguing for the teaching of only Marxist ideology in the university and educational institutions. Antonio Caso strongly opposed this as a flagrant violation of academic freedom.

The preservation of academic freedom in the university is a universal strength and a significant element in the relationship between the intellectual community and the state. Studies of North American and British faculty indicate that university professors lean more to the Left than to the Right in their social and political interpretations.[41] Furthermore, Ladd and Lipset found that, although university faculty and students held similar views, and that 46 percent were liberal or to the Left whereas only 28 percent were moderately or strongly conservative, the general public held reverse views; that is, 42 percent were moderately or strongly conservative whereas only 20 percent were liberal or to the Left.[42]

It is clear that the university serves to liberalize students, and that faculty encourage views that question widely accepted attitudes and traditions in society as a whole. Furthermore, among academics, it is not parents' political views that determine their ideological leanings, but rather their experiences as students that push them to the Left of society in general. According to Ladd and Lipset, these students "chose the liberal arts, and especially the social sciences, in a proportion far in excess of their peers who were not similarly liberalized."[43] The result of this pattern is that "selective recruitment of more left to liberal persons into the social sciences contributes significantly to the (relatively) highly liberal position of these fields in the array of academic disciplines."[44]

Because certain disciplines encourage and therefore attract students and faculty with more liberal views, disciplines are important to the ideological position of the individual intellectual, including his stance toward the state. As Gouldner suggests, "It is more non-technical or 'useless' parts of the university which support rebel ideas."[45] Juan Marsal has demonstrated that the Mexican university produces leftists by finding a relationship between the leftist ideologies of leading essayists and a university education. Furthermore, he found that the essayists who themselves taught were more likely to be leftists than those who did not teach.[46]

Historically, however, Mexican social science, most likely to breed intellectual minds with views different from those in power or from society in general, has been very underdeveloped, and only recently have these fields begun to take hold in the universities. As one social scientist has suggested, the growth of Mexican universities "indirectly made it possible for intellectual criticism to be more serious and critical, and increased critical evaluations of Mexican development models."[47] The continued expansion of the social sciences, generously financed by public funds, is likely to encourage increased criticism of government policies, and furthermore, to contribute to the increasing number of intellectuals who remain outside the state's apparatus.

The educational system is also critical to intellectual life in that it usually socializes the intelligentsia and the future intellectual in certain universal values. Most important among these values is the concept that all questions in the scholarly process are to be dealt with according to some type of impersonal criteria.[48] And yet, in the Mexican context, although these values are being taught, other personalistic values are also present. The conflict between the Latin culture Glen Dealy has so aptly characterized and the North American cultural values is visible in the university environment, where a paradoxical situation exists in which the guiding methodological constructs are objective and the personal values are not. Thus the university ambience, when it emulates the North American scholarly model, creates an ambivalent and foreign atmosphere for the socialization of the intelligentsia and the future intellectual. It can be surmised that both groups, when they are not incorporated into the state, are critical of their own society and the structural components of their system because they unconsciously or consciously compare it with ideal models learned through university education.

The socializing function of the university raises a pertinent question concerning who has access to the universities and which groups are in control of their resources. Because of the influence it has on society, one view argues, the national university provides an "additional channel of communication and power" in Latin America.[49] This is why Mexican intellectuals and the state have been concerned at various periods with the content of the curriculum. Originally, in the immediate postrevolutionary era, the conflict over the university stemmed from differences in definition of purpose. Vasconcelos hoped to make the university a force for changing society, a place in which "students would become aware of and involved in the struggle for a more just society," and not just a training ground for skilled technicians.[50] In particular, progovernment groups wanted to use the curriculum to combat the upper-class social values and the opponents of the Revolution then present at the university.[51]

Today the university remains a crucible of political ideologies, but is it a conservative or a liberalizing influence? The answer to this question, because of many complex properties, is difficult to assess. Several facts, however, shed some light. First, despite a rapidly expanding public education system, including the university, Mexico today still has an elite system in which very few students (3 percent in 1969, in 1980 estimated at 6 percent) who originally registered in primary school reach the university.[52] Second, most of the students who graduate are the children of middle-class or upper-class parents. Third, it is likely, on the basis of my data about the professors at the National Preparatory School and the National University, that most college educators themselves are from the middle class, similar findings to those of Ladd and Lipset for U.S. professors.[53] Fourth, although the Mexican public education system has expanded, according to Barkin public expenditures on education (as a proportion of gross domestic product [GDP]) are still among the lowest in the world, and most resources are "channeled to the higher levels where access is more tightly controlled."[54]

In England, which has long had a socially elitist educational system, the expansion of universities and the increase of professional groups have benefited "the different social classes in almost exactly the same proportions; but this has meant, if anything, an increase in the absolute grip which the higher classes have on the system in general and on the more prestigious universities in particular."[55] In fact, in Europe the increase in universities has not changed the proportion of working-class families represented, and most of the increase has come from the rise in the number of female students. The number of male students from blue-collar families has declined or stagnated. I would argue that Mexico is following this same pattern, and that, except for a period immediately following the Revolution and into the 1930s, the upper and middle classes have accounted disproportionately for most of the college graduates and educators. These groups use the university as a key to their economic and social survival.[56]

The control of the Mexican public university by the middle class does not mean that the ideologies represented there are conservative; rather, it suggests that, administratively, the direction of the university overall is likely to be moderate. Although it protects radical intellectual ideas and the authors of those ideas, the university does have informal boundaries among its people beyond which, out of self-interest, they are not likely to go. The difficulty is that the major universities have begun a self-selection process, in which ideological considerations increasingly determine the discipline students follow, or their choice of a university itself. Thus, the student who leans toward an education in the social sciences, and who professes Marxist beliefs, is likely to choose the National University, whereas a similar student with more moderate views and outstanding qualifications will try to attend the Colegio de México, or a private institution. On the other hand, if the student is already in the National University and is shopping for a department, the ideologically moderate student will find it difficult to follow a career in many of the social sciences, because the Marxist flavor of the curriculum will be too strong. He will therefore choose a different discipline more compatible to his ideological views.[57]

Additionally, the older college graduates, who control the university administration, and especially intellectuals themselves, are likely to act as a conservatizing influence on the definition of the university's role. Although many radicals want to see access to the university expanded, most Mexican intellectuals, and indeed the politicians who control the purse strings of the public universities, are concerned about a decline in the quality of students. T. S. Eliot suggested that the intellectual "is very much concerned with the maintenance of *quality* and with the constant reminder of what is easily overlooked: that is, if we had to choose, it would be better that a few people should be educated well, than that everyone should be educated moderately well."[58]

Although the underlying rationale expressed here would rarely be stated publicly by an intellectual or politician, privately most intellectuals I interviewed agreed with this philosophy and, indeed, complained constantly about the mediocrity of recent college graduates. As one intellectual suggested, "In Guadalajara, Monterrey, Mexico City, everywhere, the level of university education has declined tremendously. The size of the student body has really contributed to this decline as well as to the decline in the quality of the professor."[59] A further implication of this trend is not only that the intellectual tends to favor quality over quantity, and therefore a more elitist educational system, but also that the expansion in higher education, rather than promoting a larger audience for sophisticated cultural works, is, through an inferior preparation, actually proportionately reducing the audience.

Finally, in Latin cultures the university plays a role different from that usually found in North America—as a locus for establishing social contacts crucial to successful public and intellectual careers. As I argued previously, such relationships are important to student and professor, or to disciple and mentor. Glen Dealy offers a clear assessment of this function:

For example, formal education institutions do not exist to convey technical knowledge that will be economically useful, as in capitalistic cultures, but to provide a place where young men may begin to sort out and establish hierarchies of power. They prepare the youth for a lifetime of such activity. Barzini describes the process in Italy whereby "many boys acquire their wisdom in school: they learn how to get ahead smoothly, how to defeat rivals while retaining their friendship." That takes skill.[60]

The presence of these groups in Mexico has been definitely established. I discussed the importance of these relationships for intellectuals in chapter 7; here, I wish only to reiterate that, among the various cultural institutions, the university is the one most important to the intellectual in establishing ties with mentors, peers, and disciples, and friendships with political leaders that consequently affect the intellectual's career and attitude toward the state. No other Mexican cultural institution plays such an influential role.

The National University

Throughout the discussion of intellectual education and cultural institutions, I have implied that the National University is overwhelmingly the leading organization in Mexico. It was established in 1910 by reuniting the National Preparatory School and the professional schools of law, medicine, engineering, fine arts (architecture), and graduate studies. It has been historically important, following several roles played by universities generally, for "creating new options for social mobility, channelling social and political criticism into acceptable formats, and constructing the ideological foundation and the political culture of the Mexican national ethos."[61]

The National University's socializing role for the intellectual is obvious, since the majority receive their educations there. As Henry Schmidt suggests, because the curricula of both the National Preparatory School and the National University stress national consciousness, its tenets among the intellectuals have been reinforced.[62] Mexican politicians from the early postrevolutionary generations received the same influence from these two schools.[63] Lomnitz argues that in recent decades the National University has turned its focus to "a new allegiance to the state through the creation of a political culture which stresses—in the case of Mexico—the art of political infighting (conflict and negotiation) as skills to be utilized toward the preservation of the system."[64] The degree to which politically active and future intellectuals incorporate these beliefs into their personal value system is difficult to measure, but interviews Arthur Liebman conducted in the late 1960s among student activists and leftists indicate an acceptance of these rules of the political game.[65]

The National University is equally important because of its decided influence on Mexico's educational system. In the 1970s, it and the National Polytechnic Institute, also in Mexico City, captured 40 percent of the entire Mexican population enrolled in higher education.[66] Despite government efforts to decentralize, students continue flocking to the Federal District. Between 1970 and 1975, the student population at the preparatory and professional schools doubled, and in 1975-1976, the Federal District accounted for 36 percent of all college students.[67] One result of this concentration is that the National University has become the single largest employer of full-time researchers in Mexico. Of the 5,352 researchers in 1974, 17 percent were employed at UNAM.[68] Thus, the research and development potential of UNAM for the private sector and the state is tremendous because of the university's concentration in a single locale.

The National University has taken on added importance in higher education and in the intellectual community because of weaknesses in Mexico's private colleges. Private institutions in higher education do not account for large numbers of students. About 13 percent of Mexico's students are enrolled in private institutions, over half in four universities: the Technological Institute of Monterrey, the Autonomous University of Guadalajara, and the Iberoamerican and La Salle universities in Mexico City.[69]

The evidence is incomplete, but it seems clear that the private universities serve a different clientele from that served by the public universities.[70] Whereas the private sector supports the expansion of schools to train future managers and business leaders, most of whom are from upper- and middle-class families, the public sector supports universities supplying the lion's share of federal employees and intellectuals. If the curricula, the teachers, the social environment, and the students of these two sets of universities in Mexico are indeed different, and if they continue to differ, the division in higher education may contribute to differences among Mexico's leadership groups, especially between the entrepreneurs, on the one hand, and the intellectuals and politicians, on the other.

Because most large private universities have educated only a small minority of the leading intellectuals and an infinitesimal number of political leaders, the significance of the relationship between the National University (and secondarily, but increasingly important, the Colegio de México) and the state increases. Since these two institutions employ and educate the majority of Mexico's leading intellectuals, it is important to understand the government's control over them.

There are at least three avenues the government can follow to exert its influence over UNAM. One approach that directly affects the intellectual is government intervention in academic freedom. In many Latin American universities, academic freedom is nonexistent. But even in Mexico, where abuses at the National University in recent decades are rare or indirect, a subtle influence might well be exerted on the educator through the relationship between the state and the educational institution. Fernando Uricoechea believes that the teaching intellectual's awareness of the university's dependence on government funds subtly affects behavior.[71] Thus, the intellectual might be less willing to directly attack a government leader or agency in an outspoken fashion because of concern for his own position, for the institution, or for superiors. The individual's concern may be career advancement, and an individual who embarrasses superiors is not as likely to move quickly up the academic ladder.

As Daniel Levy suggests, there have been and are flagrant violations of academic freedom, but what is difficult to determine is the source of the oppression: student groups, individual professors and administrators, or someone in government. Levy has examined this question closely and has reached several conclusions about this mode of government influence. Although the expansion of the National University may have increased the government's desire for tighter control, at the same time, its very size has made it difficult for the government.[72] Infringements on academic freedom occur frequently in public universities in Mexico, often at the instigation of local or regional political leaders, but these incidents are more common at provincial institutions than at the National University itself. Ultimately, Levy's conclusion is that "academic freedom is generally respected even when it leads to direct criticism of the nature of the regime. Dissent is more institutionalized in the public university than anywhere else in Mexico. It is particularly significant that academic freedom transcends simple sanctuary privilege."[73]

The state can avoid direct mistreatment of individual freedom by dealing with administrative personnel, primarily the president or rector of the university. Government interference in the National University is invited by several conditions peculiar to this and other Latin American universities. As Larissa Lomnitz argues, the National University has two principal functions: academic performance, and politics. She suggests that the directors of schools and institutes not only are expected to plan and control teaching and research, but are "responsible for keeping a lid on conflict within the area of their administrative competence, so that the institution at large is not affected."[74] In recent years administrators have been appointed by the Governing Board, who must choose from a list of three candidates provided by the rector himself. Thus, both the rector and the board have substantial influence over the designation of influential administrators at the National University. But since the 1940s, there is no evidence that the government or the president has directly influenced the selection of a rector through the governing board. Rather, it would be fair to say that a rector would have a difficult time serving out his full term if the president of Mexico actively disliked him. Thus, as Levy concluded, the state's "power to depose UNAM's rector appears to exceed greatly its power to appoint its own choice."[75]

The most direct means the state has for influencing a public university, and the intellectuals who teach there, is control of the purse strings. In 1933, the state did use its funds to reduce the stature of the National University by suspending its annual subsidies and giving it an endowment so small that the university had to cut its budget by 75 percent, which ultimately caused the fall of Rector Luis Chico Goerne.[76] Four years later, the government and the university were reconciled, and the state tacitly agreed to the concept of academic freedom and resumed its annual subsidies, which continue to date.[77]

In a careful analysis of government subsidies to UNAM during subsequent decades—highly important, since it derives 95 percent of its income from the federal government—Levy found only one case of the government punishing the university by reducing or restricting the flow of funds: "There is only one clear statistical indication of government financial punishment: 1969 marks a decline from 1968 in the funds per student ratio."[78] During the period preceding 1969 the government did freeze funds to state universities and, simultaneous with its actions against UNAM, financially punished the National Polytechnic Institute more severely. The rector during 1969, Javier Barros Sierra, complained not only that the government restricted the funds to his and other provincial institutions in the aftermath of the 1968 student massacre, but that those funds came much more slowly.[79] Thus, with this notable exception, Levy could conclude that *"The Mexican government does not punish universities by cutting their funds.* Universities know this—and it provides them considerable security from blatant external control."[80]

The state has used its financial power on at least two other occasions to reduce the National University's influence on Mexico's higher education. During the 1930s, when relations between the university and the state were strained, the Secretariat of Public Education under Lázaro Cárdenas established the National Polytechnic Institute (IPN) in Mexico City. They intended to make it a direct rival of the National University, and although it has drained off a small number of students who have become government leaders, the IPN has never effectively competed with UNAM. Again, in the 1970s, after a period of strain between the state and the university, the government established and rapidly expanded a system of metropolitan universities in the Federal District. These institutions meet a clear need for Mexico City students, which the National University cannot meet, but some observers believe that they are also primarily designed to reduce UNAM's influence on higher education.[81]

The fact that the state has so rarely used direct financial and administrative pressure to control appointments to and curricula taught at the National University has important consequences for the intellectual community. Since most leading intellectuals have at some time been employed at the National University, and since many younger intellectuals are full-time employees of this institution, they are able to find relative financial security, employment stability, and protection for their ideological preferences within this academic community. Thus the National University is providing an opportunity and milieu previously unavailable to the Mexican intellectual.

The Colegio de México

Second in importance to the National University as a leading cultural institution is the Colegio de México, which wields an influence on intellectual life, and more recently on political life, disproportionate to its size and age. Founded in 1940 as a civil association, its membership included the federal government, the Bank of Mexico, the National University, the Fondo de Cultura Económica, and the Casa de España, which disappeared with the creation of the Colegio.[82] When founded, the Colegio depended directly on the president of Mexico for an annual subsidy of 200,000 pesos. It also received 50,000 pesos from the Bank of Mexico, and additional monies from the Fondo de Cultura Económica and UNAM.[83] Despite its image, and its legal standing as a private institution, it is a publicly funded institution that receives nearly as much federal support as the National University. In 1979, of its 180 million-peso budget, the federal government provided 88 percent, with additional support coming from such agencies as CONACYT (Consejo Nacional de Ciencia y Tecnología, the federal agency on science and technology), UNESCO, the Japan Foundation, and the Inter-American Development Bank.[84] In the early 1970s, the budget of the Colegio expanded rapidly, its importance symbolized by the new, ultramodern, and esthetically striking facility built for it on the outskirts of Mexico City.

The guiding light for the Colegio was Daniel Cosío Villegas, who served from 1957 to 1963 as rector. According to his biographer, Cosío Villegas saw the purpose of the Colegio as preparing intellectual leaders, educating future university professors, and stimulating and promoting research. Enrique Krauze suggests that the Colegio is a school of intellectuals, not professionals, and in purposely trying to create an intellectual elite, its function is different from that of the National University.[85] The students who attend the Colegio, more than their counterparts at the National University, are from middle- and upper-class families.[86] Its leadership has come from Mexico's most prominent intellectuals, either humanists or social scientists (Alfonso Reyes, 1939-1957, Daniel Cosío Villegas, 1957-1963, Silvio Zavala, 1963-1966, and Víctor Urquidi, 1966–present), all members of the National College. Its governing board includes intellectuals, former Colegio rectors, and influential government officials.

The relationship between the government and the Colegio is ambivalent. The Colegio has never become the center of student political activities, having been conceptualized along the lines of a North American graduate school, whose function is to use a variety of methodologies for serious academic research while remaining outside the realm of student and national political activities. Except for some serious labor problems in 1980 and 1983, the Colegio has never been characterized by the internal political disputes so prevalent at the National University. Thus, by design and practice, the Colegio does not attract the student who wishes to experience a political academic environment and therefore does not compete with the National University in this role.

The Colegio has produced alumni, and more often professors, who in the late 1970s and the 1980s pursued successful political careers. The implications of this changing pattern are threefold. First, the Colegio may increase its influence on policy through increased contact with government officials, thus providing one group within the intellectual community with easier access to government decision-making. Second, its increased contact with the government may be a mixed blessing, because as students perceive the Colegio as a channel to political power, even though it is still primarily a graduate school, the type of student attracted to it may change, thereby introducing characteristics not found at the Colegio long present in other public institutions. Since the Colegio is the only publicly funded institution in Mexico that follows the North American academic model, it provides a source of academic diversity not available elsewhere in public higher education. Third, if the Colegio begins to take on functions previously performed exclusively by the National and the public provincial universities, it could increase the competition between these two important types of cultural-educational institutions, the effects of which are difficult to predict.

The state does not appear to have had any influence over the selection of the Colegio's rectors. In fact, in his memoirs, Daniel Cosío Villegas makes it clear that he, with the permission of the board of directors, chose his successor for the rectorship.[87] The government's use of monies to control the Colegio is potentially more influential for this institution than for the National University. Unlike the latter institution, which receives a lump sum, the government allocates monies for specific activities within the Colegio, and therefore could exert greater pressure.[88] Again, the possibilities are present, but it appears that the government has never used this power to control academic policy.

Conclusions

Mexican intellectuals have been heavily dependent on the state for the cultural academies and educational institutions that provide them with the credentials and prestige important to successful careers. What is obvious from the analysis of leading academies and universities is the absence of the private sector or of other independent groups, and the overwhelming influence of the federal government. Furthermore, like so many other elements in the structure of intellectual life, these institutions are all centered in Mexico City, and thus they encourage the recruitment of the young, hopeful intellectual to, and the permanence of the mature intellectual in, a single geographic location.

Equally impressive is the diversity of the cultural institutions foremost in Mexico's intellectual life. Although the government has always taken the initiative in creating these institutions, or has responded to the request of an intellectual for such funds, it has not generally made an overt effort, at least since the 1940s, to control their policy or membership or the leadership and curriculum of the universities. Instead, one is struck by the absence of overt pressures on the part of the president or his representatives. On the other hand, in so many of these institutions, it is impossible to measure the subtle and indirect influence of the self-definition and attitude of the intellectual-public figure who has played such a dominant role in twentieth-century intellectual life.

As the cultural academies age, and as the university becomes more mature, a trend seems to be emerging in which nonpolitical intellectuals are increasing their influence in institutions like the National College and the National University. Interestingly, like the National College, the leadership of the National University has increasingly come from the scientists who have participated least in government activities and have rarely expressed strong social views.

The implications of the growing representation of the nonpolitical scientific intellectual in the leading cultural institutions are several. In tone and policy the may represent a narrowing group of Mexican intellectuals. As this narrowness becomes more pronounced, independent intellectuals will become increasingly isolated from the established cultural institutions. Thus, one effect may be further separation within the intellectual community between the scientific and humanistic or social-science intellectuals, and between the intellectuals following public versus private career choices. Simultaneously, however, such a separation may promote the development of new intellectual enterprises and organizations and thus contribute to the establishment of additional sources of intellectual support. On the other hand, if independent intellectuals are disproportionately excluded from the leadership of established academies and educational institutions, their views could become more critical of the state—of an "establishment intellectual group"—and could be ignored by those in power. The consequences of such a pattern developing, and its subsequent impact on political stability, are difficult to predict. But, as will be seen in the following chapter, the lack of communication or misunderstanding between the intellectual and the politician, and among intellectuals in general, encouraged by an environment created by the state, has already had and will continue to have major implications for issues confronting the intellectual and political communities in Mexico.

9. Media, Censorship, and Intellectual Life

The relationship between intellectuals and the state is multifaceted. The historical role of the intellectual, his background, education, and occupation, the nature of the political system, the social conditions of the masses, and the sophistication of the media determine the extent and style of interaction between the intellectual and the state. These conditions are found in all societies, but the characteristics they produce, reflecting their uniqueness in individual cultures, vary from one to another. Because media are essential to the vitality and expansion of intellectual activity, and because the state's attitude toward media reflects its perception of their importance to development of and support for intellectual life, an understanding of censorship is essential to analysis of the relationship between the intellectual and the state.

Each political system manipulates the media to achieve desired goals, and in turn is affected by groups that pressure the government to satisfy special interests. But the style and impact of this manipulation are determined to some extent by the characteristics of government decision-making, the mobilization of the population, and the attitude of the individual politician toward the media. Of these three, the informal relationships that govern Mexico's decision-making are most important. In the first place, as revealed in chapter 2, Mexican politics does not rely on a framework of established and interrelated institutions. Rather, it has developed a series of informal rules, well understood by the participants, for advancing careers and making decisions. Attempts to apply sophisticated social science models willy-nilly to Mexico usually fail because they only see the more obvious tip of what is the hidden iceberg of Mexican politics.

The president sets the tone and the style for decision-making in Mexico. As suggested earlier, scholars have argued about the restraints on the president's ability to wield political influence, but few scholars have suggested recently that he does not monopolize political power. Thus, loyalty to the president is essential to personal political advancement and to the production and implementation of a successful policy. This rule has been translated into a "way of doing things in Mexico" by subordinates' willingness to accept superiors' policy and personnel decisions, especially the president's. Therefore, innovation is not rewarded, but rather, efforts to keep the system well-balanced, in operation, and to keep superiors happy, become the overriding emphasis.[1]

To perpetuate Mexico's political system, its leadership believes in avoiding conflict, especially in the public arena. As the Purcells aptly note, avoidance of conflict explains the political system's preference for "behind-the-scenes decision-making limited to as few participants as possible," and for the "avoidance of public discussion of policy options."[2] The secretiveness of decision making and a lack of public discussion make information valuable—and crucial—to the formulation of policy.

Two related conditions in the Mexican system make information even more valuable. The highest officials, including the president himself, often lack access to significant information, whereas lower-level officials, acting on behalf of loyalties engendered by the political culture, withhold ideas and alternatives that they deem critical of current policies. Their behavior, carefully described by Evelyn Stevens, has led to a predicament for the president: "Like other powerful rulers in many historical periods and many parts of the world, modern Mexican presidents must fight vigorously to avoid becoming prisoners of their own advisors. If not, by the time the problem reaches the top, it has been shaped into a standardized product divested of any distinguishing characteristics which might cause the Ultimate Decision-Maker to hesitate in his applying the tried-and-true formula, and perhaps to search for alternatives."[3]

Media Impact

Ultimately, information, or those who have it, are important sources of political influence in Mexico. Astute politicians recognize the importance of having information, and they guard what they have jealously. The exchange of information, such as an agency study, is recognized as a legitimate favor worth bargaining for.[4] The politician's appreciation of the value of information, both to his agency and to his political career, is such that little of value is shared with the press. This stinginess generates a circular process in which the press feeds back news to the government that the government has already shared with it. In political systems like Mexico's, where the circulation of factual and significant information is minimal, the role of the "inside dopester" becomes more important than in societies in which such information is shared.[5] Furthermore, political gossip and rumors are encouraged, and their influence on both elites and the masses is enhanced by the absence of credible information sources.

Examples of the importance of rumor in Mexican society abound. One recent rumor with serious political implications concerned the possibility of a coup d'état by the army on November 19, 1976. According to Carlos Monsiváis, many people in Mexico City and the rest of the country believed or imagined that they believed in this possibility, so they did not raise rational responses to counteract these rumors. Moreover, the mass media did not put a stop to them.[6]

Political gossip is sought after, and hearsay substitutes for facts. Gossip is often transmitted in Mexico as an anecdote or joke, and political interpretations of policies or individuals are readily revealed in Mexican humor. Monsiváis notes that sayings like "La corrupción somos todos" or "La corrupción, S.A." were wordplays on mottoes of and the corruption in the Echeverría administration.[7]

The government's unwillingness to reveal noteworthy news items to the media illustrates, to some extent, how the press is "controlled." According to a former editor of the Mexico City English-language daily, *The News*, "While there is freedom of the press, there is not freedom of information. The government is not obliged to reveal anything."[8] Again, a circular process occurs because the government gives out very little information, and the press and other media sources demand little information from it. Since the press pressures politicians very little, they continue to keep whatever information they have to themselves.

Not only do high-level administrators protect their agencies' data so as to strengthen their position in interagency policy battles, but they also hoard career information that they value for outguessing competitors for highly sought-after offices; this explains to some extent why biographical data are scarce and contradictory.[9] According to one political informant, the only way a government official can obtain information in Mexico is through friendship, bribery, or by a superior's order. The consequence of the failure to share information is more harmful to efficiency in government planning than is extensive corruption.[10]

Politicians who hope to promote certain policies as well as their own careers use the media to publicize their efforts. The regular reader of Mexican newspapers and magazines soon comes to the realization that certain people make heavy use of specific periodicals.[11] Even though all politicians are aware of each other's manipulation of the media, there is a psychological effect on each reader because it is difficult to determine what is news versus what is propaganda in the guise of news. Thus, the media can be used to create an environment favorable to new policies and career advancement even among politicians, who cannot always determine whether that environment is officially condoned or not.

Access to information and the role of media are no less important to intellectuals in Mexico, but their importance takes on attributes different from their effects on politicians because of differences between the structure of intellectual life and that of the political system. The very definition of an intellectual makes mass media integral to intellectual life. Recalling my earlier definition, an intellectual is an individual who creates, evaluates, analyzes, or presents transcendental symbols, values, ideas, and interpretations on a regular basis to a broad audience. Without access to the media, the intellectual could not communicate his ideas to a broad audience, nor, it might be added, to other intellectuals.

Media, therefore, are essential to the livelihood, prestige, and recruitment of the intellectual. The writing of editorials for newspapers and essays for journals and magazines has more serious financial implications for the Mexican intellectual than for his North American counterpart because financial rewards from book publishing are unlikely. Lesley Byrd Simpson, a noted student of Mexican history, found this out in 1931, when he interviewed Mariano Azuela, one of Mexico's foremost twentieth-century novelists: " 'My friend,' he interrupted, peering at me quizzically, a glance half-pitying, half-deprecating, 'my friend, do you know how many copies of my books are sold here in Mexico? Naturally, you don't. Well, if the sale of any one of them should reach a thousand it would be a sensation. No. We Mexicans don't support our writers.' "[12] According to Sergio Galindo, a novelist interviewed by John Brushwood in 1973, it was not customary for Mexican authors to be paid for their books until 1959. As Brushwood suggests, the matter of financial compensation—or the lack of it—is a major consideration, often overlooked, in the history of Mexican literature.[13]

The media not only provide a source of livelihood for many Mexican intellectuals, they also are the primary means of exchanging intellectual views. Although some intellectuals claim they are uninfluenced by Mexican newspapers, or popular magazines, and others admit only to being influenced by their own journals, the majority can identify specific periodicals and the themes they emphasize.[14] Furthermore, a significant number of leaders in the political and mass-media elite read many of these same journals.[15] However, if reaching a broad audience is inherent in the definition of an intellectual, it is questionable whether journals play this role in the United States; it is even more questionable in Mexico, where financial limitations and circulation figures ensure a very small audience.

One of the peculiar creations of mass media in the United States is the intellectual celebrity. Lewis Coser describes this person as "a new type of intellectual on the American scene—he addresses a semieducated mass public that makes little claim to expert knowledge or refined taste, and that adheres to no commonly shared cultural standards."[16] Coser goes on to criticize this new phenomenon because, by short-circuiting the "arduous and complicated process through which other intellectuals attempt to gain recognition among qualified judges," and because intellectuals are not allowed time to mature their ideas, celebrity intellectuals repeat themselves and produce variations of essentially the same idea.[17] Coser correctly criticizes this type of intellectual for emphasizing what is new rather than what is valuable, but his criticisms ignore the inadequacies and biases of the regular process through which intellectuals are recruited and certified, a process that is elitist, arbitrary, and unrepresentative of social groups in Mexico and elsewhere.

It can be argued that the mass media provide channels to the intellectual outsider not provided by other intellectual institutions, and that, furthermore, the celebrity intellectual is subjected to much more open criticism, even if the source of that criticism is lesser minds. In Mexico this phenomenon is in an infant stage, and in fact, the clearest representative of it today is Octavio Paz. Paz, already certified by the intellectual community as one of Mexico's leading intellectuals, in the early 1980s received widespread exposure through the talk-show medium. Interestingly, some Mexican intellectuals believe he has demeaned his prestige and the quality of his ideas by using television.

The media play an equally important role in certifying and recruiting the intellectual. In the United States, intellectual circles with national prestige are generally tied to a specific journal, and its editorial board serves as an examining committee that admits a person to elite intellectual status.[18] According to one author writing about The *Washington Post*, those "people who agree with and conform to the wishes of their higher-ups, who have the same set of values, will find that this is helpful in their own career climb."[19] The same is true in Mexico, where at the apex of the board is the editor, who wields considerable influence on the career of the intellectual. Like the well-placed politician who controls an agency, the prominent editor influences the intellectual content of the magazine and chooses which writers write for it. The receptivity of the intellectual to the editor's guidelines may determine his career trajectory within that circle and journal or newspaper.

The impact of media on the general public and on other elites alters the importance of communication channels and their effects on intellectuals and politicians. Most observers believe that mass media in Mexico "are held in widespread disdain by the citizens at all levels of life."[20] Stevens asserts, for example, that nearly all of her informants made statements to the effect that the press was unreliable. One individual even stated, "If I read something in the paper, I must think to myself, 'Why am I being told this particular lie today?' "[21] Furthermore, because of the suspicion with which the average citizen regards communications from the mass media, rumors are stimulated as an alternate form of communication, and Mexicans find honest reporting difficult to discern. The political impact of the media is also determined by who follows this information. In Mexico as late as the early 1960s, less than a third of the people followed public affairs through mass-media channels.[22]

Characteristics of Mexican Media

Because mass media and information they communicate are critical to political promotions and decisions, to intellectual roles and recruitment, and to the public's knowledge about the conditions of society and the alternatives proposed for altering them, it is important to understand the characteristics of the various mass media in Mexico.

Newspapers

Three conditions are prominent in the Mexican newspaper scene. First, newspaper publishing is centralized geographically, in Mexico City. This trait, however, is typical of developing countries, which characteristically show a great disparity between the quantity and quality of urban and rural newspapers.[23] In 1970, thirty-two of the daily papers were published in the capital, accounting for 16 percent of all newspapers, a figure roughly comparable to the proportion of the population living there. However, those thirty-two papers published 4.5 million copies daily, or approximately 58 percent of the total.[24]

Centralization of newspapers in Mexico City has consequences for intellectual employment, since one of every ten intellectuals has made journalism his or her occupation. The focus of newspaper publishing in the capital is an additional attraction to the Mexican intellectual. Also, newspaper ownership, as in the United States, is controlled by a small number of chains. In 1973, eight chains controlled all 256 newspapers; four of them owned 60 percent of the newspapers.[25] And, competition is minimal in the provinces: only fifty-one cities have daily papers; twenty-two of those are served by only one daily.[26] On the other hand, competition is keen in the Federal District, especially if one considers that twelve hundred daily newspapers, special interest newspapers, and magazines are printed in Mexico City, 64 percent of the total for the entire country.[27] According to Robert Pierce, the competitiveness of the press in Mexico City contributes to low salaries, low advertising rates, and the lack of distinction between advertising and news.[28]

Ownership of major chains can and does affect editorial policy and therefore the freedom of intellectuals and opposition politicians to express their views. But it is difficult to determine who controls the chains. The reason for this, explains one scholar, is that a company stockholder may sign almost all his or her shares over to another person, a procedure that may be informal and not revealed in official records.[29] Some chains are controlled by prominent families, such as the Rómulo O'Farrill family, which has interests in other media, too. The O'Farrill family is also known to have important social ties with politicians.[30]

Generally, the government and individual politicians have developed approaches other than direct financial interest in order to influence press content. The most common form of individual influence is purchase of publicity. The buying of newspaper coverage takes a number of forms. The most innocuous is the weekly or monthly gratuity given to a reporter by private and public institutions on his beat. Known as the *iguala* among journalists, or as "public relations fees" by the givers, these payments are seen as a means of obtaining regular, permanent coverage of an organization. The perceptive reader of Mexican publications quickly notices, on the basis of excessive coverage, which agencies, private institutions, and individuals are subsidizing a writer's salary. Journalists themselves resist the termination of this practice because, for a big city reporter in the late 1970s, this additional income reached as much as $2,000 a month, accounting for half or more of a journalist's income. Individual reporters who attempt to "stay honest" are ostracized by their colleagues.[31] In government agencies, this practice has taken on a special quality, known as "to work the hook," which refers to releases hung in the reception rooms of government publicity offices to be picked up by the journalists.[32]

Of course, such opportunities are available to intellectual celebrities who would like greater prominence in the media, but I found no evidence of intellectuals using these channels to embellish their media image. Further, most individual intellectuals, unlike politicians, would not have adequate financial resources to take advantage of this publicity, even if they wanted to.

Government agencies and the private sector can also influence newspaper content by purchasing regular advertising space. Since advertising revenue is critical to a newspaper's financial success, it is important to know who is responsible for advertising in Mexico. It has been estimated that, in newspapers, the government accounts for roughly a fifth of all advertising space, ranging from official announcements to political propaganda.[33] Among the most important government advertisers are Aeroméxico, Lotería Nacional, and Nacional Financiera, S.A.[34] Although the remainder of the space is devoted to commercial advertisements, the ads themselves are usually handled by U.S.-owned ad agencies. Thus, the content of advertising in Mexico has a decidedly North American tone.

The government itself subsidizes newspapers through its control over the sale of newsprint. The agency responsible for this activity, PIPSA, buys and sells newsprint at a rate cheaper than can be obtained on the free market. Therefore, having PIPSA approval is financially beneficial to any newspaper. Furthermore, Pierce reports that PIPSA allocates newsprint to approved affiliates in excess of what they need, knowing that these companies will turn around and sell it at inflated prices to buyers who cannot obtain approval. According to his sources, such sales can account for up to

40 percent of a publication's revenues.[35] If one considers these indirect subsidies, the outright purchase of advertising space, and the supplements to the salaries of journalists, government influence is considerable, both on the content of newspapers as a vehicle for intellectual ideas, and on the employment of intellectual journalists.

Magazines

In the written media, magazines have had a considerable influence in Mexico. However, a definite bias—their foreign ownership and content— exists in those magazines having the highest circulation figures in Mexico. The leading magazines in Mexico in the 1970s were *Life en Español* (until it ceased publication), *Selecciones del Reader's Digest, Time,* and *Visión.* In the mid-1970s, the top magazine, *Reader's Digest,* was selling more than 400,000 copies monthly, and *Time,* the third-ranked, sold 23,000 weekly.[36]

In contrast, magazines with strong intellectual content, or a decidedly political orientation, have much smaller circulation figures. For example, *Vuelta,* Octavio Paz's journal, sells about six thousand copies, many to nonsubscribers.[37] The situation for intellectual journals described here is not confined to Mexico, since even in the United States not a single intellectual journal ranks in the top fifty circulating magazines, or has a circulation over one million.[38]

Many intellectuals and political leaders I interviewed attributed the small circulation figures to the narrow appeal of these magazines and to the size of special-interest audiences in Mexico. One interviewee described the evolution and results of this limitation: "I think each group has its own review—I do not think this is the best way to run a journal. I believe it is a consequence of our demographic development, which has been far ahead of our economic development. The result of this pattern for intellectuals is that there are very few opportunities available to them, and they have become protective of what opportunities they have."[39] This interpretation implies, therefore, that the process becomes cyclical, feeding on itself. Because each journal is financially marginal, it can only permit a small number of individuals to write for it, thereby limiting intellectual employment and its appeal. Such journals have been founded with the slimmest of financial resources, *Vuelta* being a case in point. Its start-up funds came from the raffle of a painting by Rufino Tamayo.[40] Therefore, the ability of small magazines to reach a wide audience in Mexico is limited.

They do, however, have some influence because of the quality of the audience they reach, and that influence is recognized by both intellectuals and politicians. For example, during the late 1950s, when many economists hoped to convince Mexico's leaders and key officials in the public and private sectors to join in the formation of the Latin American Free Trade Association, they used the media, especially the professional or academic journals read by Mexican economists, including *El Trimestre Económico* and *Comercio Exterior*.[41]

Historically, the little magazine has played an important role in other societies because, associated with small groups of innovative writers and artists, such journals spearheaded what Lewis Coser refers to as "the revolutionary attack on the received ideas of the age."[42] According to the students of Mexican intellectual life since the 1920s, this surely seems to be the case of literary magazines like *Contemporáneos* or political magazines like *Espectador*. Mexicans who are part of an older generation also believe that many of the magazines in the 1920s and 1930s were more open to a panorama of ideas, and several recall writing for such reviews. This may have been so, since cultural values and political orientations were unsettled and in great flux at a time when the presence of many charismatic personalities from the intellectual and political worlds often took precedence over written ideas.

Like newspaper editors, specialized-journal editors exert substantial control over content. Although their journals are financially marginal, they generally have the advantage of being independent, and therefore external economic influences are not as important in influencing content. Instead, because most journals adopt a fairly well-defined ideological position, the editor and his closest intellectual collaborators screen submissions so as to give preference to particular interpretations. The following view reveals how an intellectual, Luis Villoro, perceives group control over journals:

Yes, this is definitely the case with intellectual reviews in Mexico. It is a phenomenon of intellectual clientelism; each cultural group has a reduced number of readers and they are somewhat isolated from each other. But socially, wherever there is a major function, most of us are there and, in this sense, we know each other. This closed-group pattern has probably come about because of personalities, and political ideas. Each group has a somewhat different attitude toward political ideas, culture, and values. For example, *Nexos, Vuelta,* the new *Plural,* and the *Revista de la Universidad* are all different from each other.[43]

Comics and Cartoons

Whereas certain structural characteristics limit the influence of and intellectual accessibility to serious magazines in Mexico, such is not the case of a peculiar Mexican institution, the comic book. Not ordinarily appropriate to my subject, comic books deserve consideration in this analysis of the mass media because 90 percent of their clientele in Mexico is adult, because Mexico is the only country that supports daily comic magazines, and because the combined circulation of the comic magazines is greater than that of newspapers.[44] In fact, *Hispano Americano* reported that, as of 1980, 70 million photo novelettes and *historietas*, often illustrated in cartoon fashion, were published monthly in Mexico.[45]

Furthermore, according to one student of this phenomenon, a large proportion of comics are purchased by the middle class.[46] Additionally, some comic books, most notably Rius's, discuss political and social ideas.[47] However, intellectuals themselves have not taken up this medium to reach this large audience. This unused potential channel holds out opportunities to a future generation of writers.

Cartoons themselves are another form of media, most often appearing in newspapers and magazines. Unlike comics, intellectuals have used this medium. During the Revolution and the decades immediately following, there was little social criticism in the cartoon; essentially, they were political, focusing on individual leaders. Since the 1950s, however, the cartoon has become a vehicle for social ideas and for fighting traditional "customs, prejudices, and taboos. It is therefore fundamentally social, although the cartoonists clearly do not ignore political themes."[48] In the 1970s, there was a shift back, at least in the major Mexican newspapers, to the political cartoon, focusing on individual politicians, the political process, corruption in the party, and other similar issues. This change in direction may have been due to the effect of events of 1968 on the mentality of the cartoonist as well as of the intellectual.

Books

Books, in addition to newspapers and journals, form an essential part of the mass media in Mexico. Moreover, books are the single most important medium for intellectual communication. Unlike all other media, books have a certain aura attached to them, which transcends that of other media.[49] In structure, however, they have more in common with serious magazines than with newspapers.

The Mexican book industry has been slow to develop during the twentieth century. Primarily, this has been due to government competition. For example, under the revolutionary government of Venustiano Carranza, the National Printing Office was founded. It published not only state documents but many other works typically published by private firms in an industrialized nation.[50] As part of its education campaign, it began publishing its own textbooks in the 1920s, thereby making it difficult for commercial publishers to survive. Furthermore, the government did not protect the book industry, which suffers strong competition from the Spanish and Argentine publishers, as well as from the United States.[51]

More recently, the government has aided the industry through certain financial legislation, including reduced interest rates on loans to publishers, tax breaks for the purchase of paper and new machinery, tax credits for the hiring of new employees, and the elimination of consumer taxes on books. Furthermore, because of severe censorship, the Argentine publishing industry declined substantially in the 1970s, and many of its intellectuals and workers migrated to Mexico.[52] However, book publishing is concentrated in Mexico City, as are newspapers and cultural magazines; thus, publishers have been slow to extend their market to educated audiences in the provinces. Like Paris, which monopolizes book publishing in France, Mexico's capital continues to draw able writers and intellectuals to its fold, but this decreases the possibility for a decentralized publishing industry to emerge at the state level.[53]

As far back as the 1940s commercial publishers issued editions of 1,000 at a time, hardly a circulation designed to reach a broad audience, or of sufficient size to make a profit for the author or publisher. As Fernando Peñalosa suggests, Mexican publishers rarely risked publishing an unknown author, and often tried to publish books for which they would have to pay no royalties.[54] Between 1935 and 1956, the best-selling book in Mexico was José Vasconcelos's *Ulises criollo*: during those twenty-one years, it sold 34,000 copies. But in 1957, Luis Spota, Mexico's best-selling novelist, wrote *Casi el paraíso*, selling out 5,000 copies in the first week, a record for that time. After selling larger editions in the following years, Mexican publishers began to take a serious interest in Mexican writers, and Mexicans themselves began to read their own authors. A record edition for a first printing of a novel was Luis Spota's *El rostro del sueño*, printed in an edition of 120,000 in 1979.[55] Until then, the all-time record breaker was the autobiography of Irma Serrano, singer and mistress to President Díaz Ordaz, a crude but revealing book written in the style of a *National Enquirer* exposé. It sold 250,000 copies from late May to September 1978.[56] Obviously, *some* Mexican fiction and nonfiction is beginning to sell in large editions, but most nonfiction continues to sell less than 5,000. The consequence of limited sales for the intellectual is an inability to reach a large audience, even in the 1980s. Furthermore, as I suggested in chapter 6, the limited size of the publishing industry, traditionally an important employer of intellectuals, has provided few opportunities for Mexicans during most of this century.

The government itself is involved in the book industry. Most notable was its establishment of a government-financed publishing house, the Fondo de Cultura Económica, with the help of prominent intellectuals. A brief history of this firm, Mexico's most durable publishing house, illustrates some of the peculiarities of its publishing industry as a whole. Founded in 1934, the Fondo was established as a trust.[57] The first board of governors included Manuel Gómez Morín, leading intellectual and public figure from the 1920s; Adolfo Prieto, influential industrialist; Eduardo Villaseñor, later director general of the Bank of Mexico; Emigdio Martínez Adame, prominent party and public official; Gonzalo Robles, official of the Bank of Mexico; and Jesús Silva Herzog, intellectual and public official.[58] The trust structure was designed to provide the Fondo with economic security and independence, but funds from 1934 to 1946 came from a variety of private and government sources.[59] After 1947, the Secretariat of the Treasury began providing the Fondo with an annual contribution of one-half-million pesos.

Shortly after its founding, the Fondo benefited significantly from the influx of Spanish refugees, many of whom were prominent intellectuals who used their skills to improve the Fondo's organization and editorial process.[60] Although originally established to bring works in economics to a Mexican audience, under the leadership of Daniel Cosío Villegas (1934-1948) and his successors, the Fondo expanded its range of subjects and, according to Octavio Paz, promoted the revitalization of intellectual life in Mexico and Latin America.[61] From 1934 to 1979, it brought to light 2,992 books; 17 million copies were issued as first editions, and an equal number were new editions and reprintings. Of its top ten best-sellers, six have been by Mexican authors and intellectuals: Mariano Azuela, 590,000 copies of *The Underdogs* (1960); Juan Rulfo, 487,000 and 476,000 copies of *Pedro Páramo* (1955) and *Burning Lands* (1953), respectively; Octavio Paz, 288,000 copies of *The Labyrinth of Solitude* (1959); Jesús Silva Herzog, 235,000 copies of *A Brief History of the Mexican Revolution* (1960); and Carlos Fuentes, 175,000 copies of *The Death of Artemio Cruz* (1962). All of these were issued in inexpensive paperbacks and are used as texts in Mexican schools and universities.[62]

The growth of the Fondo has had mixed results for intellectuals. Although the government subsidized the intellectual community in much the same way it did higher education, its dominance over book publishing stunted private-sector growth. Thus, the long-run effects of this subsidy limited the number of intellectuals who were employed in this business, and indeed restricted access to this important channel of communication. Today, of course, this is not the case, since many strong competitors exist.

Yet the market for books, in general, is restricted in Mexico. The low numbers of persons with education sufficient to read a book of serious content, as well as the high price of a book, now comparable to prices in the United States, put their purchase out of the reach of most Mexicans. Education is also integrally tied to the expansion of the book industry. According to one expert, in fact, the sale of textbooks has been the most important development in the growth of book publishing in the United States.[63] Likewise, the expansion of secondary and university education will be a key to the growth of the publishing industry in Mexico, since one leading publisher estimates that three-fourths of his buyers are students and teachers.[64] Despite the growth in publishing, only about 6 percent of Mexico's population of 66 million in 1980 actually read and bought books.[65] Therefore, although books will continue to be the most prestigious and widely used vehicle for intellectual communication, the limited audience this medium reaches will continue to restrict the intellectual's ability to expand cultural and ideological influence.

Broadcasting

As in other countries, the media form that has the largest potential audience—because it does not depend on literacy—is broadcasting. The national government has clearly recognized that potential; therefore, it closely regulates and controls broadcasting, unlike written media.[66] The 1960 Radio and Television Law instructs the secretary of government to see that broadcasts do not violate rights of privacy, offend personal and moral dignity, or attack the rights of third parties.[67] To comply with provisions of the law, broadcasters must furnish copies of all scripts to the Office of Inspection and Intervention of the Secretariat of Communications, where inspectors, by spot-checking, compare the transcript with the actual broadcast. Discrepancies can subject broadcasters to license cancellation.[68]

Until recently, radio has not had any serious influence on channeling political and social views, since programming was devoid of social content. In 1973, however, as part of Mexico's "opening" of political participation, the government included provisions in the Federal Electoral Law that provided officially registered parties with ten minutes of television time and a larger amount of radio time for each fifteen-day period three months prior to national elections.[69] In 1978, the government liberalized its regulations to include four hours of free TV and radio time per month to all parties.[70] However, with the exception of campaign periods, radio continues to exclude serious commentary on public affairs.

Radio broadcasting began in Mexico in 1921. In 1923 the Ministry of War and Navy established the first station to broadcast concert music.[71] In only seven years, Mexico had 17 AM and FM stations; that number increased to over 750 in 1977, making Mexico sixth in the world in the number of transmitters. Furthermore, 1930 marked the beginning of the first full-time news department at a Mexican station, organized to report world news to radio listeners.[72] Ownership of radio receivers expanded at a rate comparable to the number of stations, and by 1962, nearly 90 percent of the homes in cities over fifty thousand had a radio.[73] By the mid-1970s, Mexicans were using more than seventeen million radios, or three for every ten persons.

The numerous radio stations have followed a pattern somewhat similar to that of newspapers. In the early 1970s more than 70 percent were controlled by nine groups. Over two-thirds of the radio stations are privately owned, and all are very much dependent on advertisements.[74] Again, advertising on the airwaves is dominated by foreign-controlled companies: in 1971, based on an analysis of station XEW in Mexico City, 84 percent of the products advertised were from firms owned or controlled by foreigners.[75]

Radio, because of strict government controls and centralization in the hands of a few private owners, has a tremendous but at present unused potential for intellectual use. These same controls, though, have made it unattractive as a source of employment for intellectuals. Although some programs are using intellectual contributions in music, they remain a minuscule part of all programming. The most significant consequence of radio at present is to steer intellectuals who want to express their views toward other media.

Equally stringent controls have governed television content, and government officials examine all films, series, and shows before they are aired. Television as a mass medium made its appearance in Mexico in the 1950s, and by the middle of that decade, at least fifty thousand persons had sets. Until 1968, television was dominated by a private group, Telesistema Mexicano, S.A., controlled by Rómulo O'Farrill, a major newspaper publisher; Miguel Alemán Velasco, son of President Alemán; and Emilio Azcárraga.[76] They lost their monopoly after 1968, but they still control 63 percent of the commercial stations. By 1977, an estimated 5.5 million sets were in operation in Mexico. The government operates its own station, Channel 13, and clearly demonstrated its interest in the medium by appointing former secretary general of the PRI, Enrique González Pedrero, as the director of its channel during the Echeverría administration. From 1976 to 1979, the direction of Channel 13 was in a constant state of flux because of the government's concern over its content; during those years five different individuals took over the management.[77]

Recently, some television talk shows have developed at least a semblance of seriousness, and the campaign law allows for a brief period of political advertising; but Mexican television, like radio, is generally devoid of serious content and is strongly influenced by North American programming. One student of Mexican media complained that it was probable that from Mexican television "the children of our country know the virtues of the 'marines,' the work of Walt Disney, the adopted ideas of Jefferson, and the actions of Superman better than Mexican history, the life of Benito Juárez, the political personality of Zapata, and the needs of our people."[78] In 1970, 36 percent of all programs aired in the Federal District were foreign, and most of those were from the United States.[79]

One of the reasons Mexican television has not been successful is that it attempts to imitate U.S. television, and its imitative practices are, at best, mediocre. But although Mexican intellectuals universally decry the quality of television, there have been some recent improvements. For example, Guillermo García Oropeza lauded the efforts of intellectuals Juan José Arreola and Octavio Paz to create a Mexican version of William Buckley's "Firing Line," even though it is lacking in level of analysis and freedom of expression. He also noted that several programs were using social satire and comedy in much the same way as does the cartoon, to get away with greater freedom of expression while making serious commentaries on society.[80]

Television, more than radio, is being used by a small number of intellectuals to communicate their views directly through interviews or through their creative works. Because of government controls, and limited commercial competition, television, like radio, remains a medium with tremendous potential, but serious investigative journalists or commentators have not yet found it to be an attractive working environment. If the efforts of Octavio Paz succeed in eliminating some of the prejudices of most Mexican intellectuals against this medium, even with stiff government controls, it could develop a larger audience for other goods produced by the intellectual community.

Films

The growth in both television and radio has been accompanied by an equally rapid growth in cinema viewing in Mexico. In 1975, the average person in Mexico saw four films a year, and Mexico, with nearly twenty-four hundred movie houses, ranked fifteenth in the world in number of theaters.[81] In the early 1930s, the Mexican government stimulated national film production by taxing foreign film imports. At the end of the decade, Mexico was producing over fifty films a year, and by the 1950s, over one hundred feature-length films annually.[82]

In spite of government subsidies, however, the industry has never become competitive with foreign imports. One reason, apparent even in the 1930s, is that Europe and the United States give the domestic industry stiff competition. For example, in 1937, of the 245 films shown in Mexico, only 33, or 13 percent, were Mexican-made, whereas the North Americans accounted for 139 films, or 57 percent of the total.[83] The influence of foreign films, especially those from Hollywood, has continued. Even by 1972, of the 431 films shown in the Federal District, only 80 were Mexican.[84] Instead of growing in strength, the Mexican film industry's influence over the Mexican viewer has remained static or declined.

In the 1970s, the Mexican film industry could be considered a state industry, since 90 percent of film financing was through the government film bank, and the government oversaw three production companies, five hundred theaters, and a film school.[85] Some intellectuals offer the government's control of financing as a cause for the decline in cinema quality. But one film director, analyzing the implications of this financing, suggested certain benefits when asked by an interviewer if state financing meant a compromise:

Curiously, no. The state offers more freedoms for the production of films than do private producers. Right now I'm thinking of at least three persons who, like me, have made films at Churubusco [government studios]. Neither the bank nor the studio tries to intervene with the script. As is natural, there is prior approval of the project, and there are cases in which, after reading a script, it's rejected. But this doesn't happen more in the state circle. This happens with producers, too. The good thing about Churubusco is that, when the script is given the go-ahead, the director is totally free.[86]

Although cinema viewing has long been the most frequent form of spectator entertainment in Mexico, films in Mexico are not noted for their dramatic content or social message. To some well-known writers, other government influences over the domestic industry, as well as mediocre film producers, have resulted in this state of affairs. According to producers themselves, additional reasons for mediocre films include the reduced market for intellectual films caused by the low-level literacy of the Mexican public, the decline of public interest in Mexican films, the lack of opportunity for new directors, the lack of up-to-date technical capabilities, the failure of producers to reinvest earnings in the film industry, and their inability to define their goals.[87] In the most comprehensive published account of Mexican films, which sets forth more than thirty-five categories for analysis, not one is devoted to films with political content.[88] There are infrequent exceptions, generally in the form of dramatic comedy, such as the recent hit *México, México, Rah, Rah, Rah,* where political and social satire is at its best.

Cinema has provided a mixed history of opportunities for writers, artists, and producers. Although original, creative, and imaginative films have been produced and screened in Mexico, especially in earlier eras, that has not been typical recently. Again, if private financing does become available and a diversity of sources exists, the potential for intellectual employment and expression is present, more than with television and radio. But for that to take place, the Mexican audience will have to be reeducated to accept films of higher intellectual quality.

Government Censorship

In Mexico, the intellectual and the politician both use mass media. But their accessibility to each of the media is determined by the legal restrictions placed on media content by the government, by the government's own control of certain media, by the government's perception of whom the media reach, and by various forms of censorship applied by the government, the private sector, and by intellectuals themselves. In terms of the number of people they reach, the Mexican mass media can be ranked in order of importance as radio, television, film, newspapers, comics, magazines, and books. Qualitative considerations can affect the order of this list, since film comes before newspapers and comics because, although more people each day read newspapers and comics than see films, a different audience, especially the illiterate, is exposed to films. Therefore, social and political messages in a film can reach and be understood by persons who cannot read newspapers and comics.

The size and the characteristics of the audience result in stringent government control over the three forms of mass media reaching the largest or the least-educated audience: radio, television, and film. The result is that the government itself takes advantage of these three forms, whereas critics of the regime and intellectuals must use written media. Not only government regulation determines media use by different groups, but political leaders frequently resort to censorship in written media, where liberty of expression is subject to interpretation.

Censorship in Mexico, and those responsible for it, affect the credibility of the media, their influence on decision making, and their use by intellectuals. To some extent, as Maxwell McCombs argues, the role a society assigns to media always reflects the basic assumptions that underlie that society. Historically, societies have taken two broad views toward freedom of expression: the authoritarian view, in which the state takes responsibility for making judgments about the content of the media; and the libertarian view, in which practitioners in the media take social responsibility for their communications.[89] In radio, television, and film, all recent media phenomena, Mexico has followed the authoritarian view; but in the case of written media, the government has vacillated between authoritarian and libertarian practices. The following discussion of censorship in Mexico will focus on written forms of expression, since, as explained earlier, this is the only mass media form open to intellectual views.

After the 1910 Revolution, during the brief period under Madero, periodicals and books were free from government control. But in 1916, the government introduced a ban on "malicious expressions calculated to excite hatred of the authorities, the army, the national guard, or the fundamental institutions of the country." According to Cole, this basic press law was not repealed until 1937.[90] In 1920, however, the government of President Obregón reintroduced a qualified version of freedom of expression. The press and other periodicals were permitted to reestablish a critical tradition, as long as they limited their remarks to the policies and behavior of individuals below the president himself. For example, José Vasconcelos, the minister of public education during this period, received a constant barrage of publicity, both critical and supportive of his programs. But in the view of Vasconcelos, when the president was implicated in a political scandal, no attempt was made to investigate his activities or accuse him of misconduct.[91]

According to Ernest Gruening, a well-known American journalist, press censorship was reintroduced in 1927.[92] Only official versions of the Cristero Rebellion, which occurred during this period, were reported in the press.[93] Furthermore, to limit Vasconcelos's influence in Mexico after his abortive campaign for the presidency in 1929, President Emilio Portes Gil ordered labor unions to boycott newspapers that published Vasconcelos's articles during his exile in Europe. Moreover, the conservative Catholic interpretation of what was happening to Mexico during the late 1920s and early 1930s, as expressed in foreign publications such as the book *Red Mexico*, was also prohibited.[94]

The most celebrated case of government censorship of freedom of expression during these years took place on January 31, 1931, when a leading revolutionary intellectual and lawyer, Luis Cabrera, made a speech in the National Library in which he amplified his ideas from an article published earlier in *Excélsior* entitled "The Balance of the Mexican Revolution." The radio transmission of his talk was deliberately interrupted; he was criticized by the president and other government officials; and, in spite of a writ of *amparo*, he was deported to Guatemala.[95] One courageous intellectual, Alberto Vázquez del Mercado, resigned as justice of the Supreme Court, protesting this obvious suppression of freedom of speech. Although his act has been pointed to as a principled defense of basic freedoms, it condemned Vázquez del Mercado to obscurity and to lack of access to public life until his death in 1980.[96]

When Miguel Alemán became president in 1946, the government passed a more stringent news law than had existed, giving the state the right to restrict or prohibit publication of photographs of people without their permission or of works considered contrary to the respect due private life, morals, and public peace.[97] This law, later repealed, not only serves as a reminder of what was possible during that era, but also demonstrates the extent to which censorship was accepted. An example of the attitude of President Alemán, or at the very least of his closest collaborators, occurred during 1947, when an article by Daniel Cosío Villegas, entitled "Crisis en México," was published by *Excélsior* without permission, after being pirated from *Cuadernos Americanos*. Cosío Villegas reportedly received a call from President Alemán's personal secretary telling him he had better "shut up" or everything about his personal life would be published in the press.[98]

The figure of the Mexican president continued beyond the reach of written criticism until 1968, when the harsh suppression of student strikes served as a catalyst for public expression critical of presidential policies. Since that time, it has become clear that presidents, while in office, generally are immune to press criticism, but they definitely become subject to it on leaving office.

Mexican writers and journalists have correctly perceived that freedom of expression wavers from one presidential administration to another. Their assessment is clearly reflected in two incidents regarding the deposed editor of *Excélsior*, Julio Scherer, in 1976. Seeking to publish a new magazine and wanting relief from the actions of Luis Echeverría and his collaborators in November 1976, Scherer sought out José López Portillo, the president-elect. López Portillo, only one month from taking office, promised to guarantee Scherer absolute liberty of expression, but only when he became president on December 1. Second, in the first year López Portillo was president, the press, which had previously ignored the plight of *Excélsior* and had even criticized Scherer, gave great fanfare and positive coverage to his receipt of a journalism award.[99] As Daniel Cosío Villegas suggests, and as some of these examples illustrate, political liberty in Mexico depends on the authenticity of the president's criticism, self-criticism, and dialog.[100]

In addition to the personal predilections of individual presidents, whose attitudes contribute to a lack of clarity surrounding the concept of freedom of expression in Mexico, geographic and social characteristics can also be significant. The geographic location and resulting audience impact of newspapers and magazines are important in determining the government's interest. For those writers who work for provincial periodicals, location is detrimental to freedom of expression and may subject them to abuses by local politicians who are not averse to using terrorism. An accusation of this happening on the state level was made as recently as 1980, when writer and journalist Margarita Michelena stated publicly that there was freedom of the press in the capital, but not in the states. She described how several articles written by Mauricio González de la Garza criticizing the candidacy of Emilio Martínez Manatou for governor of Tamaulipas were published in *Excélsior*, but were not republished in their entirety in *El Mañana*, the Nuevo Laredo paper. This censorship was traced to the press agent of the governor of Tamaulipas.[101]

Generally, the federal government shows little interest in regional publications that criticize it. Illustrative of this freedom in an influential publication is Erling Erlandson's claim that *Diario de Yucatán* was the most independent newspaper in Mexico during the 1960s, even though it sometimes criticized the president directly.[102] Although this and other publications were well known to the authorities, their treatment suggests that the federal government does not consider their influence worth restricting.

This is an important point because in Latin American countries where censorship is common, the most influential periodicals and writers are the least subject to harassment. Furthermore, a case can be made that writers having contacts with foreign authors also are in a stronger position because their allies in the foreign media can help them in the eyes of public opinion. For example, Alan Riding and Marlise Simmons helped the cause of Julio

Scherer García with supportive articles published abroad. On the other hand, the government sometimes sees the domestic press, when it attacks public policies, as serving the interests of transnational companies.[103] This somewhat paradoxical situation results from the government's hands-off policies with regard to well-connected intellectuals who are internationally known, such as President Echeverría's relations with Daniel Cosío Villegas, even as it realizes that it is the written media with national circulation that can bring it the most serious problems.[104]

Self-Censorship

Censorship in Mexico has followed two general patterns: censorship by the government and media self-censorship. Self-censorship results from intervention by the owner or editor, the author's fear of government reprisals, a bias in source material, and control by commercial advertisers. Self-censorship by editors or publishers has been strong in Mexico since the Revolution. Any Mexican publisher who has political ambitions must maintain good relations with the state. To do so he may ask his editors to change or remove material he believes offensive to the government;[105] or he may define the political boundaries within which his paper will stay. After his exile in the late 1920s, José Vasconcelos was told by the owner and editor of *El Universal* that he could write anything he wanted about the government, but he could not mention the name of former president Calles.[106] Moreover, no paper would publish his open telegram to President Emilio Portes Gil concerning the alleged assassination of one of Vasconcelos's supporters in Coahuila.[107]

Editors and publishers also exclude articles because they fear government intervention if they publish, even though they have no firm assurance that the government will intervene. This is an insidious form of censorship because it is inconsistent and unpredictable and depends strongly on what editors *believe* to be the government's definition of social responsibility. For example, in the recent past intellectual critics of the official regime had their names and their comments excluded by the press. Among them were José Vasconcelos in 1929, Julio Scherer in 1976, and José Luis Cuevas in 1977. The common denominator in each of these cases is that the media at that time considered their views to be unpopular with the political leaders of the moment. There is no evidence that the government itself censored the written media in any of these three cases. Political leaders who have left office recently have told me that they could not get their views published because they were considered too controversial. These politicians included two former cabinet officers and a senator.

The importance of self-censorship lies in its frequency, its presence in the freest of societies, and its unmeasurability. As Kadushin reports from his interviews with elite North American intellectuals, three said they were excluded from The *New York Times* and one from the *Saturday Review* because of views that were unpopular or too radical.[108] More recently, the *Washington Monthly* published an article by Suzannah Lessard critical of Ted Kennedy's treatment of women, which The *New Republic* had commissioned, but at the owner's instigation, refused to publish.[109] Cases in North America involving other forms of media have been well documented.

Even the most independent newspapers in Mexico are highly selective in what they print, and one wire service executive told Robert Pierce that *Excélsior*, under Scherer, often ducked investigations of actions against guerrillas.[110] Furthermore, cartoonists, who have traditionally had the most freedom in newspapers, also feel certain restraints. As Abel Quezada, one of Mexico's foremost cartoonists, admitted to me, "Even though I have considerable freedom, I am aware of the general policies of the newspapers I write for and I try to be discreet in not abusing those guidelines in such a way as to harm the paper."[111]

Book publishing also includes this practice, as I can attest to. As the author of a directory of Mexican political leaders, I received an offer from a government press for a Spanish-language edition, which I accepted. While working on a second edition of the book, I approached a different government publisher and asked whether they would be interested in the new edition. The editor glanced through the book and quickly replied that, since I might have left some people out while including others, it was too delicate for a publisher in their position to handle. Nevertheless, unknown to this editor was the fact that the original book had already been accepted for publication by another government publisher. All of this clearly indicates that each publisher has unique criteria to apply to similar situations, and the basis for establishing those criteria is vague.

Publisher's fears can, of course, be real, especially if they are dependent on government funds. The major precedent for this concern stems from the firing of Orfila Reynal, the editor of the Fondo de Cultura Económica, after he published Oscar Lewis's *Children of Sánchez* in 1965.[112] Whether real or imagined, fear of the government is the cause of self-censorship, and it is important to remember that writers must express themselves in an environment that results in vagueness, contradictions, and superficiality in written formats.[113] Too many observers are quick to claim that freedom of expression is alive and well in Mexico, and that censorship is self-imposed, without considering the causes of that self-imposed censorship.

Those who control the written media in Mexico have their own biases, intellectual journals not excluded. The practice of omitting the names of particular individuals or their ideas has been described by one prominent Mexican poet:

Yes, these intellectual journals are very much closed. If you belong to one group, you cannot exchange ideas in another group's journal. I could give you the names of fifty persons who would never appear in *Vuelta* or in *Excélsior* articles. An excellent recent example was the reporting on Carlos Chávez's funeral. Octavio Paz gave the main oration and his name was not even mentioned in the *Excélsior* articles. When I give a lecture at the Museum of Modern Art, *Excélsior* announces the title of my talk, the time and place, and leaves out my name. We have a name for this in Mexico, *ninguneo*, a word that refers to the policy of never mentioning someone's name in the history of literature or art.[114]

Last, self-censorship occurs because ownership is centralized and control is exerted by a small number of chains, and because of the owners' concern for the attitudes of their advertisers. Advertisers can exert tremendous pressure on all Mexican media, since there is no question that they are vital to the media's financial survival. The effectiveness of an advertising boycott can be seen in the 1972 case involving *Excélsior*, brought against that newspaper by the private sector because of the paper's liberal, moderately critical editorial position. This boycott pushed *Excélsior* from first place in ad copy to fourth in just three months. *Excélsior* survived because President Echeverría ordered public-sector enterprises to cover the commercial void.[115] However, being saved by the government is a mixed blessing because it places the paper in a difficult situation by compromising its editorial independence.

Government Censorship Techniques

Self-censorship in magazines, intellectual reviews, and newspapers has restricted intellectual expression in Mexico, whether the source has been the publisher, editor, or advertiser. The government itself, however, has been guilty of censorship during this same period and has developed numerous techniques, variations of which can be found in Mexico today, for the manipulation of publishers through organized groups or their representatives. The use of these groups takes two forms: the internal persuasive approach; and the external approach, which relies on violence. Gruening describes a classic case of the first technique, used during President Calles's administration and told to Gruening by its perpetrator, the head of the linotype union and a leader of the Regional Workers Federation of Mexico (Confederación Regional Obrera Mexicana, CROM):

"Comrade, this is a pretty bad article. I think we should cooperate with the government by not letting it appear."

He read the article and said: "It is pretty strong, I really had not noticed it."

"It is agreed then that it will not appear," I said.

He protested that he had nothing to put in its place, that as the editor-in-chief had gone home he had no authority to hold it out, and finally convinced of his bad faith, I said to him: "This article will not appear and if it does, there will be no paper tomorrow."

I then had several proofs pulled and called the head make-up man, the head stereotyper, and the head pressman and said to each respectively: "You will not make up this article, you will not stereotype it, and you will not print it. And if you do you will be punished, and there will be no paper tomorrow."

They agreed.

The next day I got a very vicious letter from Señor Miguel Lanz Duret (the owner and editor) threatening me with court action. I took the letter and the article down to President Calles. When he read the article, he colored and when I told him what I had done, he said "Very good."[116]

The same union provided additional examples of controlling publications through the use of force. On September 7, 1922, armed workers from CROM took over *El Universal* under the pretext of collective bargaining, when, in fact, they wanted to control the paper to prevent it from criticizing the union. When the owner asked the government for relief, he received a promise of assistance from President Obregón.[117] That assistance never came. This case has certain similarities to the celebrated removal of Julio Scherer as editor of *Excélsior* in 1976. In that case, the government organized a group of peasants to occupy, forcefully and illegally, some property owned by the *Excélsior* cooperative in Mexico City, real estate that the paper hoped to develop to increase its financial resources. Using this occupation as a pretext, government agents manipulated the cooperative members to vote the editorial and management staff out of office.

Thus, although not using force to take over the control of *Excélsior* workers directly, the government used it to provide an incident, with intervention in the internal affairs of the cooperative the means for achieving control. The intent was the same in both cases, but the government in 1976 was more concerned with the impression it made and with providing an image of legality. The deposed leader of *Excélsior* sought relief from the president both before and after their departure and, like the owner of *El Universal*, they were assured of help, which never came.[118] In cases like this, government agencies in Mexico sometimes seem to conveniently forget to enforce the law.

The government also promotes subtle forms of censorship through its financial largesse. Financially, it can support the media and individuals it favors while withholding assistance from those who are unacceptable. This has taken the form of direct subsidies to certain newspapers. One scholar claims that *El Universal* is reported to have received a subsidy of some twenty-four thousand dollars monthly.[119] The government can, however, choose the less obvious method of providing loans through Nacional Financiera for the purchase or improvement of buildings and equipment. "Newspapers with official subsidies find that with politically acceptable behavior on their part loan repayments are left uncalled for over an indefinite period. Once official hostility is sufficiently aroused, however, typically the government lending agency calls in (or threatens to call in) for immediate repayment of a newspaper's by then long overdue note."[120] Another method is to tie up financial assets in some legal case, a threat made to Scherer after he was ousted. A further technique is for the government to purchase the controlling stock of a major chain, something that occurred in 1972 when the government-owned Mexican Industrial Credit Society took over the García Valseca chain of thirty-seven daily newspapers. This technique was further modified by direct governmental intervention, when President Luis Echeverría, in February 1976, became a major shareholder of the Mexican Editorial Organization by purchasing *El Universal* and buying back from the government the controlling interest in the García Valseca chain. One of Echeverría's closest collaborators, Fausto Zapata, became publisher of that chain.[121]

Government efforts to favor certain social and political views may take the form of subsidizing the work of individuals. Initially, the government's encouragement of mural art in 1922, through the efforts of José Vasconcelos, promoted art as a profession, with no strings attached. Later, when the murals were criticized by the media and defaced by students, the original contracts were terminated, and only one artist, Diego Rivera, was recommissioned.[122] Interestingly, Rivera himself claimed to have suffered government censorship at the hands of his former friend Carlos Chávez and his assistant, Fernando Gamboa, after the government removed a contracted painting because of the subject matter.[123] Mural art, had it continued to expand and develop, might well have joined other mass media as a form unique to Mexico.

The arbitrariness of the government when it is confronted with an individual who does not conform to its definition of what an artist or intellectual should contribute was reflected in the experience of Carlos Chávez as director of the Mexican Symphony Orchestra. Because of his modernistic tendencies, he was told at the beginning of his fifteenth symphony season that funds were no longer available.[124] Similarly, the government suppressed freedom of speech and press by imprisoning Eduardo Pallares, after removing him from his professorship at the National School of Law. President Calles even exiled Pallares on one occasion. Such personal persecution is an often-used technique against political figures who are out of favor or who are opposed to the government. James Wilkie provides several examples in the case of General Almazán, all of which span a number of years and administrations.[125]

Contrarily, the government can offer rewards to those it favors, and these can take the form of gifts, bribes, employment, or psychological recognition. Vicente Leñero describes a generous gift of wines and preserves Julio Scherer received from the then minister of interior, Mario Moya Palencia, for Christmas 1974. He also describes how one well-known television interviewer and commentator, who attacked *Excélsior* when it came under pressure from the government, was given the national prize for journalism.[126] The latter technique may be seen as a refinement of the government's highly successful approach to political opposition, that of divide and conquer, by co-opting groups by means of political and economic rewards to their leaders.

Another effective technique the goverment has made use of, effective because it has relatively unlimited resources and because its "intellectual authorship" is difficult to trace, is that of buying adverse articles and pamphlets designed to smear and discredit a leader or intellectual. Mario Guerra Leal, who often did this for a living, unabashedly describes numerous cases in his memoirs. He asserts that he was paid 100,000 pesos to write articles against union leader Demetrio Vallejo during the 1959 railroad strike, on orders from President Adolfo López Mateos through General Agustín Olachea, then secretary of national defense.[127]

In a more recent case involving an intellectual, Daniel Cosío Villegas was the subject of an Echeverría administration campaign to discredit him for his criticism of the president. The government used the pens of other figures, including politicians and intellectuals, as well as subsidizing the publication of fifty thousand copies of a libelous pamphlet entitled *Dany, el sobrino del Tío Sam* (*Danny, the Nephew of Uncle Sam*), filled with lies about Cosío's career and writings.[128] Political leaders, then, inadvertently or intentionally, use their resources to promote disunity among intellectual critics and political opponents, those groups for whom complete freedom of expression is most essential.

The government has used other financial techniques as well. Like the Internal Revenue Service's harassment of individuals disliked by the Nixon administration, Jorge Ayala Blanco has suggested that there are cases of severe tax quotas being applied to enterprises unfriendly to the government.[129] This has been documented by one former government official, Alberto J. Pani, who states that, without abusing his legal position as secretary of the treasury, he ordered tax inspections of two businesses advertising in *El Globo*, a newspaper he considered to have libeled him. Other businesses that feared inspection abstained from advertising, and the paper stopped criticizing Pani.[130]

Government advertising can put equally intense pressure on publishers, either by increasing copy in publications that have government approval, or by reducing or withdrawing it altogether in publications the government disapproves of. Since government advertising accounted for 20 to 30 percent of all ad copy in the 1960s and 1970s, those decisions are significant. For example, in January 1976, Channel 13, the government station, canceled its contract with *Excélsior*, further contributing to *Excélsior* management's financial difficulties.[131] For a short period of time, from 1975 to 1977, probably in recognition of the pressure the government could exert over the media through advertising, a central agency was established to funnel all payments for government advertising or propaganda. For unexplained reasons, the agency was allowed to expire.[132]

The most well-known control government has over the print media is over the sale of newsprint (institutionalized in PIPSA). In addition to newsprint sales, the government controls imports of printing and broadcasting equipment and parts, and through tax rates and rebates, it supervises the domestic manufacture of these items in Mexico.[133] It is important to understand that PIPSA's control over newsprint does not prevent a publisher from buying imported paper, which is available on the black market; rather, it subsidizes favored publishers by providing them with paper at a price 80 percent lower than the cost of imported paper. Publishers support the continuation of PIPSA, even though they are wary of its possible abuses, because their costs would soar without its subsidies.[134] Furthermore, a cutoff of paper by PIPSA means that on short notice firms can only buy inferior quality paper, since the best paper must be imported.

It has been asserted that, before 1964, no newspaper's newsprint supply was suspended by PIPSA, but there have been cases of partial suspension.[135] In June 1962, *Política*, a left-wing magazine, did not receive newsprint deliveries for two weeks. This effectively prevented nationwide circulation of an issue attacking President Kennedy before his visit to Mexico. On the other hand, during the same year the government allowed an issue accusing President López Mateos of serving Yankee imperialism to be published without reprisal. In 1967, however, it stopped newsprint allocations to *Política* permanently. The government also forced *Por Qué*, another magazine critical of official corruption, to buy newsprint on the open market. In 1969, one issue of *Orden*, a right-wing publication, was delayed for five days before newsprint supplies were resumed.[136] Most recently, Julio Scherer, in founding *Proceso* after his ouster from *Excélsior*, could not get the director of PIPSA to give him paper. *Proceso* was forced to buy it on the black market.

When pressed, the government will prevent certain forms of media from being produced, or it will censor them in part. In the film industry, the government has frequently banned or deleted scenes in U.S. movies that they deem offensive to Mexicans. "In 1938, the year of the oil nationalization, Mexican censors removed reference to the War of 1847 from paramount's *Wells Fargo*, deleted shots showing Mexicans as bandits in MGM's *The Girl of the Golden West*, and banned Columbia Pictures' *Lawless Rider* because it showed a Mexican being kicked and ridiculed."[137] Of the films banned during 1939 and 1940, eleven were forbidden for religious comments, three for political material, and seven for degrading references to Mexican history or culture. Again, unions played a role in the censorship process, oftentimes making their own decisions about showing a film. The Mexican Federation of Labor refused to show the Italian film *Scipio, L'Africano* because of its pro-Italian imperialism and the North American film *Ninotchka* because it apparently ridiculed communism.[138] In 1952, Twentieth-Century Fox's *Viva Zapata*, with Marlon Brando, was banned from Mexico for gravely altering the historic truth.[139] And in 1965, while in Mexico, I saw a version of *Giant* in which all of the scenes depicting Texas prejudice against Mexican-Americans were deleted, thus making the movie practically unintelligible.

In radio, as in the film industry, the government has clearer legal control and has less need to use other forms of censorship, since control is implicit. Alisky has concluded that, since 1934, not one broadcasting license has been revoked outright, though several owners were officially pressured into selling to new owners.[140] Furthermore, attempts by individuals or groups to broadcast views unacceptable to the government have resulted in orders to cancel or suspend individual broadcasts under penalty of losing an operator's license.[141] There also have been complaints that the government has not complied with its own equal-time campaign laws. José Angel Conchello charged that he received only five minutes of television time each day for his gubernatorial campaign, in contrast to the fifteen minutes given to the PRI candidate in Nuevo León.[142]

Threats or even "friendly" suggestions by individual government leaders have been directed in equal force to publishers. Personal pressures against Julio Scherer, well before the government intervention in 1976, have been well documented by Vicente Leñero. They range from President Díaz Ordaz's accusing Scherer of treason in Los Pinos in 1968, to President Echeverría's having his phone tapped and using the information gained from the tap to forestall Scherer's efforts to take his case of government censorship to the international media.[143] President Díaz Ordaz also sent a letter to Daniel Cosío Villegas criticizing his newspaper articles on the government's suppression of the 1968 student demonstration.[144]

When financial pressures, internal intervention, partial restraints, and selective censorship are insufficient, the government has been known to resort to violence. On the local and state levels this has resulted in the assassination of newspaper editors and journalists.[145] During the 1950s, regional boss Gonzalo Santos used armed men to force advertisers to boycott the important San Luis Potosí daily *El Heraldo*.[146] On the national level, physical abuse and direct threats of bodily harm have been used, most notably in shutting down *Por Qué*. According to two authors, *Por Qué*'s staff was detained for two weeks at an army torture center and was beaten and threatened with death if it resumed publication. The editor, Mario Menéndez Rodríguez, who was put into Lecumberri prison in 1970 and then fled into exile to Cuba from 1971 to 1980, was granted amnesty by the government in 1980.[147]

Violent reprisals appear to be few. What is significant, though, is not their number but the environment they create. Some North American observers of the Mexican media cite the low number of such incidents as a confirmation of freedom of expression, without duly recognizing the impact of the range of government activities that promote self-censorship as a protection against real or imagined fears.

Conclusions

The interrelationship of the media, censorship, and the structure of intellectual life is complex but significant. The structure and quality of the media in Mexico deeply affect the interaction between the state and the intellectual community. Several conclusions about this interrelationship are worth summarizing. In Mexico, the quality and credibility of a particular medium improves as its audience declines. Correspondingly, censorship, legal or illegal, adversely affects the quality and credibility of these media, and is stronger the larger and more uneducated the audience.

The politician's perception of the expansion of political participation in Mexico may well have affected the evolution of this pattern. It has been asserted that, even when Mexico's politically active population was quite small, during the nineteenth century, newspapers supporting Benito Juárez, although few in number, were a factor in the overthrow and execution of the French puppet, Maximilian, in 1867.[148] Books, which have the smallest circulation but are read by the most well-educated audience, have been the least censored, as the works of Irma Serrano, Vicente Leñero, and Carlos Loret de Mola testify. They are left untouched because politicians themselves believe the audience to be sufficiently well-educated, cultured, and sophisticated to distinguish fact from inflammatory material and to react judiciously and responsibly to dissenting ideas. Politicians consistently have stated to me that they do not resist the expansion of political participation per se, but they do care that the people to whom this privilege is given be educated to use it in a mature way.[149]

Politicians' fears about the misuse of the media derive from a mental image that differs from intellectuals' in two ways. First, the intellectual and the politician have a different notion of what is socially responsible media use. The divergent perceptions of these two groups are universal; it appears, however, that the gap separating them is somewhat greater in Mexico than in the United States. It is unlikely in any society that the two groups' perceptions will ever coincide, but they might be brought closer together. There is a resistance in Mexico, according to Octavio Paz, to accepting "anything like intellectual criticism and dissidence. A difference in opinion instantly and unconsciously becomes a personal quarrel."[150]

The distinct views of the politician and the intellectual arise because of differences in background (although my explorations suggest that for some their backgrounds are somewhat similar), and more important, because of differences in education and career experience. Their differing image of social responsibility is made more complex because politicians view intellectuals as forming two groups: those who are independent of politics, and those who have actively participated in the state.[151] This difference also suggests the importance of career determinants on the outlooks of the politician and the intellectual, on their definition of what an intellectual is, and on their view of social responsibility.

Representative of the differing attitudes of politicians and intellectuals is their view of the Mexican president. A myth evolved in Mexico after the 1920s, with a short relapse under Cárdenas, that the president, while he is in office, is untouchable in the media. To politicians, the stature of the president mirrors the stature of the state. When Julio Scherer began his efforts to publish *Proceso*, Javier Alejo, the minister of government properties, told him the following: "With the publication of this weekly, you intend to alter order and assume a frontal posture against President Echeverría. The government cannot permit this. In situations like this, the security of the state depends on the public credibility of the president of the republic. To attack the president is to attack the state."[152]

Politicians, therefore, have confused the legitimacy of the individual who holds the office with the office itself, further implying that the stability of the president determines the stability of the regime. Regardless of the confusion, they believe this principle, and it is fair to say that it has grown into a tenet of political elitelore in Mexico. This myth has been so strongly adhered to that it has become part of Mexican folklore; that is, those outside of political life also believe in it and for the most part adhere to it. Víctor Alba describes a peculiar popular feature of the presidential image:

This characteristic [image of political figures] is seen primarily in the unique treatment of the President of the Republic, in what is written, drawn, and spoken about him. The jokes that pass from mouth to mouth about the president are legion, and are not generally adapted from foreign jokes, as they are frequently in other countries; they are newly invented stories and excellent verbal cartoons, usually portraits of the first magistrate as the public sees him. They are frequently facetious, not rarely coarse, and almost always devastating, but they refer to the man and not to his office. On the other hand, sarcasm about the president never appears in the press.[153]

Politicians have put themselves in a straightjacket by their unwillingness to listen to complaints in the media if they are couched in terms of the president.

The expansion of the media in Mexico has further affected the structure of intellectual life. The limited size of the well-educated, well-read audience makes an intellectual's survival, using those media in which he can most freely express himself, difficult. Therefore the most creative, provocative, and critical ideas of Mexico's intellectual elite receive the least exposure and the smallest economic rewards. This "intellectual sector" of the mass media produces a fierce level of competition among publishers, editors, and intellectual writers. Their competitiveness has further fractured the intellectual community into producing magazines that have only a limited appeal, even among the educated elite. Because intellectuals are writing for each other in Mexico, and because their ideas do not receive wide attention in the press, they not only seldom write for a mass audience, but, equally important, they often lack contact with and sensitivity to the masses, especially the rural population. Their social isolation causes intellectuals to focus on cosmopolitan problems, urban questions, and issues of political freedom, all of which are of only marginal importance to the illiterate and poor and, perhaps, to the future well-being of Mexico.

In addition to the structural patterns that lead to fissures in the intellectual community, censorship, too, produces a divisive environment. Although the press can be counted on to scream loudly if a local journalist or newspaper is suppressed, when the government moves forcefully and internally against a competitor, as in the case of *Excélsior* in 1976, few papers come to its defense. Either because of a short-run interest in benefiting from the financial woes of a suffering colleague, or because of fear of government reprisals themselves, isolation of one group from one another further fractures intellectual unity. Personalities and ideological orientations have exacerbated these differences, but the gatekeepers of the media, in denying other intellectuals and writers access to their publications, have contributed to the continuation of these divisions and the perpetuation of intellectual disunity.

Most important, politicians and intellectuals are communicating on different wavelengths. The inhibitions in expression brought on by the unpredictability of government censorship, and the lack of credibility engendered among many media forms in Mexico, encourage intellectuals to ignore what may be truthful in the media, particularly in newspapers, and to rely not only on their own media sources, but moreover, on sources outside of Mexico. In reverse, of course, government officials read the popular mass media and the writings of intellectuals who participate in the state, ignoring those who are independent, or at least convincing themselves to disbelieve what the independents have to say. Thus, the exchange of information takes place in an artificial environment created by a media lacking in credibility.

The impact of the media on the general public and on opposition groups is also important. Some Mexicans have demonstrated a willingness to talk about politics, but of those who discuss politics (about a third of all Mexicans in the 1960s), only half felt relatively free to talk about it with anyone.[154] Furthermore, compared with other nationalities, Mexicans discussed politics even though they were uninformed. One study has suggested that, although many Mexicans follow politics, half of the Mexicans interviewed could not correctly name a political leader or a government department.[155] In part, the structure of the media is responsible for their lack of information.

Those Mexicans who become politically active are further affected by the restrictions of freedom of expression that limit communication with one another and with the government. Evelyn Stevens aptly describes why this is so in her case studies of several protest movements: "During a crucial final state of a protest movement, communication among the members is disrupted and individuals, cut off from the real world, are forced to fall back on symbols provided by the mass media."[156] Since the media withhold certain information, the symbols are distorted, and opposition groups, just like politicians and intellectuals, are operating in an unreal environment.

Last, because the media in Mexico are inhibited, neither intellectuals nor politicians are receiving adequate information about their society, the impact of programs, or the reactions of important groups to their social conditions. The scarcity of information does little to improve the adequacy of decision making within the state, nor does it contribute to the accuracy of intellectual thought. Both groups require dependable sources of information, politicians to cope with increasing social and economic problems facing Mexico, intellectuals to provide realistic alternatives to and constructive criticisms of government policies. The patterns of media development, the presence of government and self-censorship, and their interaction with the characteristics of the Mexican political system and intellectual life magnify the obstacles to a meaningful exchange of views and accurate information in Mexico.

10. Serving the State

The previous analysis, whether focusing on the careers of intellectuals and politicians, on the structure of cultural institutions and academies, on intellectual circles and mentors, or on the relationship between the government and the media, identifies many elements important to the relationship between the intellectual and the Mexican state. The historical experiences of this relationship since 1920 are important, but it is more significant to understand the present relationship between the intellectual and the politician, how it has changed from the previous periods, and what has contributed to recent changes. Furthermore, it is worthwhile to examine the reasons why numerous Mexican intellectuals have served the state, the extent of their influence, both from their point of view and that of the politicians, and the likelihood of their future influence.

The Consequences of 1968

There is no doubt that the most important single event affecting intellectual-government relationships in the last twenty years is the government-ordered massacre of student demonstrators at Tlatelolco, in Mexico City in 1968. In one sense, if one looks at the intellectual and the state's relationship only as a division between intellectuals who have remained independent of the state and those who have not, little change took place from 1920 to 1968. Luis Villoro argues that, since 1920,

those who want to be independent do not have the political organizations to join to express their independent views. Therefore, what has happened in Mexico is that intellectuals have fled to the universities, which have become ghettolike structures for those not in agreement with the state. Still, these organizations receive their funds from the state. Another aspect of this ghetto life is the publications that provide intellectuals with a forum for their ideas. But these, too, are indirectly controlled by the state through its control over newsprint and ads. In 1968 almost all intellectuals reacted against the position of the state, but these reactions came from small political organizations and the universities, which did not have much political influence.[1]

Intellectuals did not have much influence on the state in the aftermath of 1968, which is important as an illustration of their lack of political clout. But the events themselves and the intellectual's reaction to them did indeed affect the relationship and the state's desire to reestablish the traditional pattern. Among the most important consequences for intellectuals were the following: the student massacre broke the link between future intellectuals (then students) and the state, a tie that is crucial if the intellectual is the link between the state and the intelligentsia; it reflected the deterioration of the optimistic image many educated Mexicans had about Mexico's development and precipitated a revision in certain governmental structures; it encouraged the development of intellectual groups that believe that only with the creation of large groups or political organizations can intellectuals have a real chance of influencing governmental policy in Mexico, and that an intellectual's personal work has a very limited audience and influence; it encouraged intellectuals to take the lead in criticizing the government and defending the students, thereby making intellectuals more open about their ideas and promoting a more realistic posture in the expression of their views; it discouraged the view that Mexican intellectuals could be the source of a new model for their country's development; it decreased the control of the state over public universities, especially the National University, thus increasing the university's isolation from the state while decreasing the influence of its intellectuals; it made the middle class more aware of intellectual opinion and the state more concerned with public opinion; it destroyed the myth that the culture of the state is dominant; it established a pre- and post-1968 culture in Mexico; and it demonstrated the existence and crystallized Mexicans' awareness of the plurality in their society, the disequilibrium of many points of view, and it offered young people many new ideas and directions.[2]

These short- and long-term effects of 1968 continue to affect the relationship between the intellectual and the state. The most striking initiative in this pattern was the attempt by the Echeverría and López Portillo administrations to co-opt intellectuals. Although Echeverría tried to increase communication between politicians and intellectuals, currently a sort of neutrality exists between the two groups, but there is still a strong resistance to serving in government. Many intellectuals did allow themselves to be co-opted, whether for prestige or economic security, or on the firm belief that they could influence the direction of government policy.

Another consequence of the government effort to co-opt intellectuals was its encouragement of a small number of intellectuals to become more radical and to associate themselves with new political organizations opposed to the state. The 1968 episode, although widening the gap between the intellectual and the state, present since the 1940s, paradoxically forced a reconciliation between intellectuals and politicians. In other words, the unanimity of intellectual opinion in condemning the government in 1968 and the consequences of the subsequent rupture forced the state to take the initiative in seeking intellectual participation, after having neglected them since the 1950s.[3]

In assessing the present situation in Mexico, most intellectuals, although recognizing the efforts of the two administrations since 1970 to compensate for the alienation of the intellectual after 1968, agree that the government and the intellectual are not reconciled. There are several reasons for the government's inability to recapture the affiliation of many intellectuals. One explanation, offered by Abel Quezada, is that the post-1968 situation is more complex. Instead of the differences between the masses and the government, characteristic of the pre-1968 era, the government is part of a triangle involving differences among the masses, the government, and intellectuals.[4] Furthermore, 1968 forced many intellectuals "into the university to oppose the state, even with the existence of the tradition of doing something within the government, the attraction of power, prestige and money."[5] By granting them haven, in what Arturo Warman earlier termed "intellectual ghettos," the government encouraged intellectual independence at the price of noncooperation.

After liberating political prisoners, cultivating intellectuals, increasing the university budget, allowing the university true autonomy, and tolerating substantial criticism in the press, Echeverría once again confused the intellectual's relationship to the state by intervening in *Excélsior*. This intervention in press freedom increased the suspicion of the outspoken intellectual toward the government, although López Portillo counteracted his predecessor's intervention by encouraging an environment of press freedom. The only reason the government's support of an internal takeover in *Excélsior* has not been more important is that the motives were unclear, and were those of a president rather than of the government.

The images of the president and the government are intertwined and confused, but there has been substantial publicity about the *Excélsior* affair among educated Mexicans so as to distinguish between the two in this event, not the case in 1968. Thus, although Octavio Paz's possible explanations for President Echeverría's interest in controlling *Excélsior*—that the president was power crazy, bad-tempered, or vindictive in wanting to punish *Excélsior* for its criticism of his administration, although internal problems already existed within the *Excélsior* cooperative; that the president was interested in developing his own chain of newspapers, using front men to purchase them for him so that he could use the media, behind the throne, to promote his power; and last, that he hoped to be the leader of the independent Left in Mexico, making them a force, like the CTM (Confederación de Trabajadores de México, Federation of Mexican Labor) and the important industrialist groups, with which the government would have to contend[6]—are plausible and interesting, the affair itself has had less influence on intellectuals than the events of 1968 because fewer parties were involved in the abuse of power.

The structural consequences of the 1968 affair on the relationship between the intellectual and the state are several. Because the number of intellectuals in the university has increased, and because government financial support for the university has expanded, the state has encouraged public awareness of the value of university education and expertise. Again, by recruiting intellectuals the government symbolically stresses their role, and the role of the institution certifying them. This emphasis is likely to increase the competition among political groups that wish to exploit the university and, consequently, the university's products.

A further consequence of government efforts is that the state has moved away from crude or obvious means of co-optation to subtler methods. By financing institutions that support the activities of intellectuals, the state has created a buffer organization, thereby allowing the intellectual to save face while still being supported by the state. The state is now incorporating intellectuals into institutions removed from the government bureaucracy itself, but it is helping to create and sustain the image of autonomy in these same institutions. There are certain short-run benefits of creating a myth of autonomy among these institutions, but if done over long periods, as in the case of the National College, or the National University, the myth becomes a reality, one that the state itself can no longer afford to shatter. To do so would produce effects that it might not be able to control.

Finally, 1968 had a number of important psychological consequences for the individual Mexican intellectual. The most important was forcing many intellectuals into reexamining their present or future relationship to the state: I noted previously that Octavio Paz illustrated this turnabout in the Mexican intellectual's attitude with his resignation as ambassador to India. In an interview, Paz described his personal involvement in the events, which led to his belief that he could no longer represent the Mexican government:

I received a telegram from the secretary of foreign relations asking all ambassadors to give a report on the student activities in their respective countries and how the government, in my case, India, was dealing with student unrest. I sent a very long official letter to the secretary of foreign relations (Antonio Carrillo Flores) telling him the following: I asked him to read the previous reports which I had sent regularly as part of my ambassadorial responsibilities; I suggested to him that he would find out by reading those reports that the Indian government always resolved their difficulties with students through political means, not through the use of force; last, I said I would like to write a personal analysis of this problem in Mexico, not as ambassador to India but as a Mexican citizen, which I proceeded to do. I tried to explain what I thought were the reasons for student unrest, and to suggest that the students had some valid demands. I suggested that the communications between the government and the students was lacking because the channels had been monopolized by other groups. The problems stemmed from the rebellion present among many youths of this generation, from the terrible overcrowding of students at the universities, and third and most important, from the lack of communication. I did not agree with all of their demands, but I argued that peaceful means should be used.

I then received a wire from the foreign secretary, congratulating me on my letter and saying that the president was reading it with great interest. After that, the army abandoned the National University, and I was temporarily happy to think that perhaps they were following the policy I had recommended. Of course, a few days later they reversed themselves and the massacre occurred.[7]

Paz felt a very deep and personal frustration in not being able to influence government policy, especially as a member of a government implementing a policy contrary to his own values.

The self-examination of individual motives and a questioning attitude toward the integration of the intellectual and the state may not be a permanent consequence of the 1968 affair. The break that occurred after 1968 between many intellectuals and the state has become part of the mythology of the relationship between intellectuals and the state. But as Lewis Feuer suggests, a process of demystification always occurs after new ideologies come to the forefront, and a younger generation of intellectuals will likely redefine its role and consequently its relationship to the state.[8] Yet their redefinition may be a long time coming, since intellectual disciples are very much influenced by the model of their mentors. If the majority of the present generation subscribes to the view that intellectuals should be independent of the state, most will pass on that view, in spite of demystification, to the next generation.

Patterns of Intellectual Relationships to the State

Several possible patterns characterize the relationship between intellectuals and the state in Mexico and elsewhere. In Mexico, whether their influence is direct or indirect, intellectuals generally see three broad types of intellectual as prevailing: the independent intellectual, an individual uncompromised by the state or any single group, whose ideas are influential and considered by various institutions and individuals; the compromised intellectual, who represents the ideological interests of a political party or group; and the official intellectual, who works for the state and is prepared to contribute his energies to the government, regardless of administration or orientation. It is clear from Kadushin's study that North American intellectuals are characterized by the same divisions. The important difference, however, is that the separation between the political leader and the intellectual in North America is much more extreme than in Mexico. Mexican intellectuals in much larger numbers use direct channels of influence, since nearly half have been in a position to have made or affected decisions themselves within the government bureaucracy. Additionally, other intellectuals, who have never held political office, have had widespread contact with Mexican public figures.

As I suggested earlier, however, the Mexican pattern is in flux as younger intellectuals increasingly choose to follow the model found among their North American colleagues. Among Mexicans there is not always a rational explanation for their movement away from or toward the state; rather, it is often an emotional commitment that stems from self-definition of intellectual roles, tradition, and disciple modeling. What Thomas Kuhn found to be the cause of scientific revolutions can also be used to explain the changing directions in the relationship between intellectuals and the state. Mexican intellectuals believe in certain values that determine their relationship to the state not because of any overwhelming evidence for one position versus the other, but because they want to believe their choice is correct.[9]

Why Intellectuals Have Served the State

With the relationship between the intellectual and the state in limbo, why has the Mexican intellectual been so willing to serve the state? Historically, Mexico has a tradition of intellectual participation in government affairs, since independence, at the time of the reform in the nineteenth century, and prior to the Revolution. In nineteenth-century Mexico, to be an intellectual and a politician was almost indistinguishable: to be an intellectual was to be a politician. Perhaps no better example of this exists than Octavio Paz's grandfather Irineo, who mixed politics, including important public offices, with writing and publishing throughout his career. An attitude of government patronizing the intellectual developed from a tradition of active participation, a condition accepted by both politicians and intellectuals.[10]

An Intellectual's View

Other than historical precedent, intellectuals themselves commonly give economic reasons as an explanation for serving the state. I have suggested throughout this book that Mexico's economic situation has affected many structural aspects of intellectual life and, indeed, the intellectual's self-definition. For example, Abel Quezada, actually one of the few to be able to make a living from his intellectual work, has noted that, "in Mexico, there are very few means for an intellectual to make a living. It is almost impossible to survive on the basis of his own intellectual work, since books sell so little. It is a physical necessity to choose public office because it is the shortest and easiest route to live. The result is that many intellectuals have become government servants."[11]

Many observers believe that the Mexican intellectual has not willingly associated with the state, but has done so because no viable choices exist. John P. Harrison argues that "the only reasonably sure way to advance both their ideas and their personal well-being has been through politics. There is no connotation of 'second choice' in this process, for the Latin American usually regards the highest expression of his intellectual efforts to be their effect on national and continental politics."[12] Still other intellectuals would go further than Quezada and, using the rationale provided by Harrison, argue that practically every intellectual is related to the power structure in one way or another.

Mexico is not unique, and the trend of intellectuals serving the state is true of other developing countries outside of Latin America, such as India, and in European countries with a similar heritage, such as France. A recent description of this relationship in France concluded that "the state is the employer of first and last resort here, and there are actually very few Paris intellectuals who do not work, directly or indirectly, for the government."[13] Thus, it is important to remember that, although economic conditions perpetuate this relationship and, indeed, in part have been a historical cause of intellectual employment in government, economic factors became intermixed with the acceptable tradition, even desire, to serve the state, so much so that this pattern prevails even in modern France. Many politicians also agree that economic conditions have been largely responsible for the intellectual's relationship to the Mexican state. This is a natural view for them to hold, since many public figures themselves expressed similar reasons for choosing careers in the public sector.

A third reason intellectuals give for serving the state is a moral commitment to improving their society. As a mentor to many younger generations of intellectuals, José Vasconcelos set the tone for this commitment, like many others of his generation. As his biographer suggests, "On the one hand, he felt it his duty to resist the 'triumph of the wicked, the imbeciles,' in Mexican politics, to oppose corruption and tyranny in his country. On the other, he clearly felt from an early age that it was his duty to work for better living, working, and cultural conditions for the Mexican."[14]

This moral commitment has been so strong among the older intellectual generations that it has led them to support the state, even when opposed to the government, in some rather astounding situations. An excellent illustration is revealed in an anecdote about Manuel Gómez Morín, founder and president of the opposition National Action party and leading intellectual figure of the 1920s and 1930s:

Antonio Bermúdez [then director of Pemex] called Manuel Gómez Morín in 1954 on the day the devaluation [of the peso] was announced in the press. He asked him for his help, explaining that only the president, one close adviser, and the secretary of the treasury knew of the decision in advance. Gómez Morín explained that he would help Bermúdez because it would help Mexico and Mexicans.[15]

Beyond a moral commitment, which may ask other, more selfish, motives for serving the state, intellectuals and politicians have identified perhaps the most important reason, one that goes beyond the economic alternatives available to the intellectual and is likely to influence his choice in the foreseeable future. Intellectuals and politicians believe that since 1920 the state is the only organization providing resources accessible to the intellectual who wishes to influence society. An intellectual prominent in the 1920s, and especially noteworthy because he himself was isolated from public affairs from 1929 until his death in 1980, expressed this view: "Those who criticize the government while in office have a moral obligation to leave their positions. . . . But you can accomplish little unless you are a part of the government. This is the reason why practically all important intellectuals in Mexico have had a governmental position."[16]

A Politician's View

Public figures firmly believe that the intellectual's contribution in state agencies is the most important justification for their past and future involvement. Many put their contribution into a social perspective. Pedro Daniel Martínez García, who as a physician made a lifelong commitment to the public-health sector, eventually serving as assistant secretary of health, concisely states this view: "Outside of the government there are no other alternatives in which an intellectual could have as transcendental an influence. From a social point of view, only in government could a person have this type of influence. There are two types of intellectuals, those divorced from social life, and those who try to serve mankind. To me, the first type is really not an intellectual."[17]

But intellectuals, whether they have been in public life or have remained outside it, would not be able to make this type of contribution without retaining personal contacts with political leaders. Not only is such contact crucial to exchanging views necessary for understanding what is going on inside and outside of the system, but, equally important, the intellectual requires access to information, data on which to base some of these opinions. In a system as closed as Mexico's, anyone on the margin of public life will be unable to obtain these data. As José Juan de Olloqui argues, "You are considered an outsider unless you are a public servant your entire life."[18] Therefore, although the intellectual may choose not to serve directly in a public post, he or she, unlike the North American intellectual, often will maintain close ties to public figures because it is the sole means of access to crucial sources of information.

The last, but least frequently mentioned, reason intellectuals serve the state is self-aggrandizement, or personal power. Paz argues, in agreement with Glen Dealy, that "the obsession of the Mexican intellectual for power, is understandable. In our scale of values, power comes before wealth and, naturally, before knowledge."[19] Although Paz stated this publicly, in writing, only one intellectual willingly admitted orally that the intellectual's lust for power was an important factor. His statement reflects the strength of this belief:

The explanation, I think, is power. Intellectuals sell out so easily because like other Mexicans they are after power. People really have to have balls to resist the importance of the position, all of the trappings of power. It is sheer ambition. And although most intellectuals are not real machos, which might make this explanation less valid, maybe it is a way of demonstrating their influence, their power to the society as a whole.[20]

From a Mexican point of view, one of the consequences of focusing the search for power in government is the lower value Mexican intellectuals place on independence from the state. Although leftist intellectuals would be less inclined to participate in the state, because the climate would be less conducive to their involvement, their ideological commitment to changing the government's structure is such that they become politically active in the opposition. Overall, Mexican leftists participate more actively in politics, as distinct from serving the government, than their conservative counterparts.[21] One of the dangers of the intellectual's concern with power and prestige is the risk of destroying the traditional "ideal of intellectual detachment and the disinterested search for truth."[22] In Mexico, however, this pattern is unlikely to occur, since the present direction is *away* from serving the state, whatever the reason.

Consequences of Serving the State

Assuming that intellectuals do serve the state, as do so many in Mexico, what are the important consequences of their collaboration? Many intellectuals and observers believe the most subjective but important consequence to be the loss of intellectual detachment as an honest critic. Although one might be able to retain an intellectual honesty, it is difficult to survive in Mexican politics, or in any organization, without being a team player. Thus, although you may not agree with a policy, in Mexico, and in most governments, you must publicly support a policy once the government commits itself to its implementation. Because most observers perceive Mexican politics to be characterized by substantial rhetoric, the intellectual has had a hard time being an honest critic in government. Intellectuals, however, are not in agreement about their ability to remain intellectually honest and serve the state at the same time. An influential intellectual-public man argued, "I believe that you are honest whether you are in government or outside of government. If you are dishonest, you will be in either situation. Serving the government does not compromise your intellectual honesty if you have some."[23]

Mexican politicians recognize the difficulty of placing independent intellectuals in a high-level, policymaking post, however much they would like to co-opt them for other reasons. For example, underlying Krauze's analysis of Daniel Cosío Villegas's desire to obtain a cabinet post is the explanation that it was unlikely that he would have been chosen, not because of his intellectual ability, but because his brusque and independent manner would quickly have thrust him into hot water in Mexican politics. Intellectuals who have served the state in a cabinet-level position, such as Narciso Bassols and Manuel Gómez Morín, have retained their influence among certain groups of intellectuals, but it would be fair to say that their appeal is not as broad as it was early in their careers. They often have a strong ideological following, but independent intellectuals tend to write off their influence. However, intellectuals can serve the state and retain or recover their prestige, if they abandon their government careers. This is illustrated by the resignation of Octavio Paz as ambassador to India. Paz recovered his leadership in the intellectual community, but he can never return to government service without losing that moral position.

Another important consequence of serving the state is that many intellectuals begin to lose their identity as intellectuals, or become insensitive to the concerns of their former colleagues. It is only natural that intellectuals be influenced by the environment and the colleagues they work with, especially if they continue to remain in government. Of course, the intellectual who has an unpleasant experience in government service might abandon such a career and, instead of becoming sympathetic to the perspectives and problems of the public figure, become more critical of that person's failures. Unknowingly, intellectuals with government experience may also be influenced in their outlook on society as a whole as they unconsciously respond to problems differently from their independent colleagues.[24] Other than resigning, intellectuals who play a decision-making role can follow three alternatives: they can accommodate their own values to those of government; they can try to alter the prevailing values; or they can function as technical advisers without imposing their own values on government.[25]

More important than the effects on the intellectual of serving the state are the consequences intellectuals produce by serving the state. Do intellectuals have a serious impact on public figures and their policies? If not, why not, and is their influence increasing or declining? The difficulty in answering these questions lies in the near impossibility of measuring an intellectual's influence on personal ideas or his impact on policy or culture. Our best indicator of intellectual influence is how they and politicians respond to the question of whether intellectuals have had some influence. My numerous interviews with leading intellectuals and public figures suggest two clear consensuses about Mexican intellectuals: they have had a significant impact on Mexican society as a whole, that is, on the transformation of Mexican culture; and individual intellectuals are responsible for the personal formation of political leaders.

One of the areas in which intellectuals see their influence expanding is in public opinion, if we confine public opinion to opinions held by the well-educated middle classes. The intellectual has created a climate of opinion among this group of Mexicans, and although they are few in number, the number of persons who really count in Mexico, who themselves have influence on others, is also small. Following this idea, an intellectual with a perspective from the 1920s through 1980 argues that intellectuals have had sufficient influence in recent years to prevent the state from going in certain directions, but never enough importance to have complete control.[26] Thus, the power of Mexican intellectuals is negative, like a veto, and they can bring it to bear, or are willing to bring it to bear, only infrequently.

This is not to say that the intellectual has not had a positive influence on public figures, since Mexican political leaders readily admit that certain individuals, either personally as teachers, or through their writings and actions, have influenced their attitudes and behavior as individuals and public servants. In their choices of individual intellectuals, public figures most often seem to be influenced by those who were their professors, or those with whom they had personal contact. Their preference for intellectuals with whom they had some personal contact also explains why they often choose intellectuals who have followed public careers. Intellectuals, on the other hand, especially if they have not been active politically, are less impressed by their colleagues' personal qualities than by the individual's work. And yet, although intellectuals may be influenced more indirectly and abstractly by the work of others, they too include intellectual influences stemming from personal contact, usually from a mentor or teacher in their discipline.

What is most significant about the intellectual's influence on public figures is that it often comes from intellectuals who have not had a similar impact on their colleagues. The division between whom Mexican politicians consult or listen to, and whom intellectuals themselves choose, is not nearly as wide as the gap between North American politicians and intellectuals. A reason is that in the past Mexico's intellectual and political leaders were brought together by their family backgrounds, their socioeconomic position, their residence in Mexico City, and their education in the same universities. The geographic size of the political and intellectual community made this homogenization and overlap possible.

As Mexican society has become more complex, as urban centers have expanded, and as education becomes more diversified, there has been a gradual decline in the parallel experiences of the two groups. This can even be seen in their actual choices of intellectual influences. Intellectuals and politicians do not disagree on their older choices, men like Manuel Gómez Morín, José Vasconcelos, Vicente Lombardo Toledano, Luis Cabrera—all of whom combined intellectual activity with politics—rather, they disagree in their choices of younger intellectuals. This phenomenon seems natural, for as their experiences broaden, so do their contacts and influences, and therefore, the list of those most influential with regard to their ideas. It is unlikely, however, that the Mexican intellectual and the politician will ever become as separated as their North American counterparts because, although two different sets of intellectuals may increasingly influence them, unlike North American intellectuals, few Mexican intellectuals are without access to politicians. More recently, many younger Mexican intellectuals have chosen not to use those channels for influencing policy or developing their own careers.

The influence of intellectuals on the state goes beyond the personal influence on individual public figures. Intellectuals since the 1920s have determined or influenced the outcome of government policy. When asked to identify concrete examples of their influence on government policy, intellectuals and public figures often give examples of Luis Cabrera's authorship of the 1915 Agrarian Law, which affected subsequent agrarian legislation, and José Vasconcelos's impact on education. From the 1920s another frequently mentioned example includes Manuel Gómez Morín's impact on banking legislation, and in the following decade Vicente Lombardo Toledano's influence on the labor movements and Eduardo Suárez's influence on finance. In the 1940s and 1950s, Jaime Torres Bodet has been singled out for his sytem of prefabricated schools and his literacy campaign, Gustavo Baz for his contributions to public health, and Ramón Beteta for his economic theories. More recently, many respondents use the example of Jesús Reyes Heroles and the political reforms in the López Portillo administration; and in Echeverría's administration, Grindle suggests that intellectual scholars provided the theoretical underpinnings for government policy concerning rural development.[27]

Concrete evidence of intellectual influence on public policy exists for every administration since 1920, yet, in spite of these many individual examples, the influence has been exceptional rather than typical. The intellectual's influence is infrequent because it is often undiscernible. Leopoldo Zea suggests that intellectuals have been significant in the transformation of Mexico in the twentieth century, but that their role is "difficult to see or express because it is hard to measure the influence of writings or ideas and to determine their impact over the long run."[28] Not only are the results of abstract ideas difficult to identify, but many intellectuals may not hold visible positions although they actually influence the direction of government programs.

Society's attitude toward intellectual participation also masks the influence of intellectuals. Since 1968, when the government tried to co-opt intellectuals, it has created more publicity about the contributions such individuals might make. By promoting intellectual cooperation, the state has increased the visibility of certain intellectuals, and the popularity of their works, whether they have resisted co-optation, as in the case of Octavio Paz and Daniel Cosío Villegas, or acquiesced to it, as has Carlos Fuentes. This publicity creates the false impression that intellectuals are much more involved in public life than in the 1950s or 1960s, when really the extent of their involvement has not changed.

Even if we assume that the intellectual's influence is greater than it seems, there are a number of reasons why Mexican intellectuals and public figures believe their impact has generally been minimal. One of the most important theoretical explanations for their lack of influence in many cultures is the intellectual's style. Many intellectuals are maverick personalities and may be arrogant or self-centered. These qualities do not lend themselves to success as administrators, in Mexico or elsewhere. For example, José Vasconcelos's uncompromising attitude, his arrogance toward those who were uneducated, his deprecation of other intellectuals, all of these personality characteristics led one intellectual to conclude that it was doubtful that Vasconcelos could have effectively guided Mexico had he been allowed to capture the presidency in 1929.[29]

But intellectuals whose personalities make them good candidates for public office are still likely to have difficulties putting their ideas into practice. The intellectual finds it difficult to act within the boundaries demanded by a real situation and by the political arena. The shift from theorizing to pragmatism requires that an individual use his intellectual powers in a different way.[30] In doing so, however, he often moves out of the realm of an intellectual role, into that of an expert or technician. In other words, instead of evaluating the merits of a policy, or its moral implications, the intellectual focuses on making the policy work.[31] Once the intellectual follows this path, whether temporarily or for a long period, he is playing another role, one more compatible with the state. The technicians, in the minds of most intellectuals, are much more influential than intellectuals.

To many intellectuals, the movement toward the specialist is part of the general movement toward the bureaucratization of political power since the 1940s, when Alemán introduced the professional politician or administrator. Rather than increase the influence of intellectuals, Alemán expanded the influence of the intelligentsia, thereby depreciating the long-run, direct influence of intellectuals in government. Alemán also introduced a long-run trend that produced another tension in Mexican public life, that between the technician and the politician. The establishment administrator has replaced the militant, ideologically oriented politician. Thus the specialist who now has the formal credentials that were once the domain of the intellectual is superseding the intellectual and the militant politician.

Their elitist concerns lessen the influence of intellectuals in public life. For the same reason that much of their work finds only a limited audience among the masses, so too are they unattractive to politicians. An ability to appeal to the masses is a vehicle through which the intellectual could influence the government, because the Mexican state is aware of individuals who can manipulate public opinion or organize the unorganized masses. Many public figures argue that intellectuals is the 1920s and 1930s spoke about issues that most uneducated Mexicans could identify with because those issues applied to them personally. Others attribute the intellectual's declining influence in Mexico to the poor quality of education and the evolution of a mass society that no longer values the authority of an intellectual class. One older intellectual expressed this view: "Many intellectuals today lack a public reputation, fame, and this affects their ability to influence the government and others around them as we did in my generation. . . . In my era, everyone knew all the first-rate intellectuals. There are members of the National College whom most people do not know."[32]

The expansion of the political bureaucracy and the growth in the size of the state in some ways have reduced the opportunities for the intellectual to affect government policy. This interpretation suggests that structures have much more influence than individuals and that, when those structures were rebuilt in the 1920s, intellectuals were often the authors of the new organizations. Today, the intellectual is incorporated into an already-existing organization rather than creating a new one. Intellectuals, therefore, are more influential in societies that are structurally underdeveloped, and whose physical size is rather small. But even if Mexico's bureaucracy were not so large and complex, intellectuals would be hampered in their efforts to influence policy because they are too individualistic. Ignacio Chávez pondered the effects of this on intellectuals:

Each person seems to be working his own area; people participate in their special activities in a quiet fashion. We lack the discussion of ideas outside of our individual areas. We are collective in the sense that, because of our specialization we need the help of others in carrying out our special projects, but in the other sense of sharing, we have become egotists concentrating on our own individual interests instead of the collective interests of Mexico and the world as a whole. In this sense, the lack of collectivism is the sin of our age.[33]

Finally, intellectuals have found it difficult to influence government decisions because of the general attitude of the Mexican state toward criticism and dissent. I analyzed the many implications of this ambience for the structure of intellectual life in the previous chapter, but in the context of serving the state, it is again worthwhile to summarize its importance. Paz has spoken most vociferously and articulately about this problem in Mexico. He clearly states that intellectuals and politicians cannot tolerate dissent, and they thus create "a desert in public life, and in cultural life too. There are no dialogues in Mexico—only monologues."[34] Intellectual critics often adapt their views to those of leading intellectuals, and the ordinary critic's lack of incisive interpretations makes it difficult for him to explain Mexican culture.[35] Furthermore, intellectual discussions, instead of focusing on the issues, take on emotional overtones and often deal with personalities rather than content.[36]

The lack of an effective dialog between intellectuals and politicians, and among intellectuals themselves produces a tension that encourages the suspicion both groups have of each other. The feeling of being ignored encourages intellectuals to take out their frustration on politicians and other groups, whom they consider to be "inferior" and lacking in appreciation for the intellectual. It also makes them less willing to raise a criticism before government officials because of their own disrespect for politicians, or because of their feeling of neglect.

Numerous twists and turns have characterized the path of intellectual relationships to the Mexican state in this century. Although many characteristics in this relationship are found in the United States and elsewhere in Latin America and the developing world, other features are unique to Mexico, products of its culture and political system. The contributions that intellectuals can make to the Mexican state are subject to numerous influences stemming from the self-views of intellectuals and politicians, their backgrounds, and their roles in society. The influence of the Mexican intellectual could well be crucial to the future of his society, but paradoxical forces are at work today that alternately increase and decrease the intellectual's impact.

11. Conclusions

The preceding pages describe and analyze a wide range of patterns for intellectual life in twentieth-century Mexico, but one central focus runs throughout: the relationship between the intellectual and the state. This relationship has guided my study because it is crucial to understanding the role intellectuals play in any culture, historically or in the present, and because, in developing countries, the extent to which intellectuals are uninvolved in state activities has widespread consequences for the social, political, and economic development of those societies. Mexico is no exception.

From my analysis, six major themes concerning the intellectual and the state emerge: (1) present economic and political conditions in Mexico are favorable to an increasingly prominent role for intellectuals; (2) Mexican intellectuals do not share a homogeneous view about who they are and what role they should play; (3) various background characteristics and experiences are instrumental in encouraging intellectual diversity and in producing new trends among intellectual leaders; (4) recruitment into intellectual leadership positions has followed patterns similar to those found among Mexican politicians, but is undergoing a significant change; (5) the quality of the media and the nature of censorship affect communication among intellectuals and between intellectuals and politicians; and (6) any influence of the intellectual on public policy has been the exception rather than the rule.

The potential role for the Mexican intellectual is likely to expand because of important structural changes taking place within the political and economic system. Perhaps most important, in terms of the intellectual's relationship to the state, is the initiation of political reforms. Regardless of the degree to which these reforms have been implemented, since the mid-1970s they have produced a new political milieu. As the state helps to legitimize increased political opposition, various groups, including new political parties, are increasing their autonomy. Their independent behavior, whether it takes the form of an opposition party or a labor-union movement, provides organizations that intellectuals can lead. As these groups formulate or reformulate their ideologies, they borrow from past intellectual contributions and promote the growth of fresh ideas. Intellectuals who attach themselves to these movements, whether, ideologically or concretely, are likely to have a greater influence on society and on political leaders than if they remained isolated, directing their work toward an audience of their peers.

Even if most intellectuals were to decide to avoid political activism, the state has set in motion forces producing social and economic changes. Social groups, primarily the middle class, are searching for a statement of values to help them confront and understand these changes. Issues like pollution, nuclear energy, family planning, illegal migration and immigration, inflation, distribution of income, urbanization, public transportation, and housing, most of which can be found in any industrial society, are affecting a widening audience in Mexico. The position of the intellectual, as both a socializer and a synthesizer of mass views, has expanded. The dynamic nature of these changes has encouraged growth in the knowledge industry. The expansion of the Mexican media, especially radio, television, newspapers, and magazines, has been phenomenal. As a high-growth industry, the media provide economic opportunities to intellectuals who would have had to look elsewhere for employment just two decades ago.

As communications become more important in Mexico, groups competing for control over economic resources, both public and private, recognize the value of using communications for their own ends. Thus, intellectuals find their skills in increased demand from groups inside or outside the state. However, they may find themselves in a paradoxical situation: they have the skills necessary to use these opportunities, but they may not be able to use them, because the increased recognition of the importance of communications has encouraged the state to produce its own technocrats, intelligentsia who are experts in the manipulation of mass media. These individuals, lacking in imagination and creativity compared to the intellectual, concentrate on method. And it may well be that method is far more effective than content in swaying Mexico's masses.

The emphasis on the expert within the communications field is not an isolated phenomenon. As I argued in chapter 2, the trend in Mexican political leadership definitely favors the technocrat, whose education, experience, and values give him the orientation and skills to solve problems with technical expertise, not political manipulation. Mexicans have only recently recognized the influx of technocrats—the most important issue to emerge within the PRI in the 1982 presidential campaign was the replacement of the traditional politician with the technocrat. Despite denials to the contrary, Mexican politicians are increasingly being produced in the technocratic mode, distinct from the old-style politicians who earned their steps up the career ladder through elective political posts, union positions, party offices, and mass-oriented political skills.

The consequences of the rise of the political technocrat for the Mexican intellectual are twofold. The technocrat's presence reduces the state's demand for the intellectual's skills. On the other hand, however, a real conflict exists within the political leadership between the traditional politician and the political technocrat, one that the intellectual might solve. By replacing many political generalists with technical specialists, the state has produced a conflict between the two groups over who should be in control, thereby creating a demand for an individual who can bridge the gap between the old and the new. The intellectual, having an advanced education comparable to the technocrat, also has the breadth of interests and training of a generalist.

The growth of the knowledge industry and the manipulation of the media have other important consequences, for both the Mexican state and the intellectual community. The state's perception of the media affects its attitude toward controlling communications. Censorship by the state, implied or real, has had a significant effect on the relationship between the intellectual and the state. The state can be instrumental in creating an environment conducive to the free exchange of ideas, or it can encourage the suspicions of each set of leaders toward the other. The analysis in chapters 2 and 9 suggests that the politician and the intellectual have different views of what is socially responsible communication. The unwillingness of the politician to listen to the independent intellectual, who expresses criticism by describing the weaknesses of important decision-makers or the president himself, discourages a constructive exchange. Furthermore, those who wish to use the media labor under a cloud of insecurity, since the president himself is most responsible for determing the tone surrounding freedom of press and speech during any six-year term.

Censorship, as I have shown, is not solely the product of the state. Intellectuals themselves have perpetrated much of the censorship taking place in Mexico. To some extent, the state must take responsibility even here, for, although it is not directly involved in making the decisions, the state's inconsistency produces self-censorship on the part of editors and publishers who are unsure about what is acceptable or unacceptable. In addition, censorship takes place unrelated to what the government's reaction to the material might be: individuals purposely exclude material because they dislike its author. Mexican intellectuals are divided into numerous groups or circles, generally surrounding an important publication, and that publication is closed to the ideas of most intellectuals who are not members of their group. Although some overlapping among groups takes place, and intellectuals exist who are unaffiliated with any group, the intellectual circle is the dominant pattern.

Government censorship and intellectual self-censorship exacerbate the distrust between Mexican intellectuals and politicians and among intellectuals themselves. The most significant consequence of this is that few political decision-makers receive an objective view of what the educated public believes about contemporary problems and their possible solutions. Moreover, intellectuals themselves are not exchanging freely the views essential to their own growth and an awareness of the changes taking place in their society. The lack of open exchange polarizes them and focuses their disputes on small, personal issues essentially inconsequential to the main issues confronting Mexican society. Their inability to speak with a united voice on any single issue lessens their influence on politicians.

Certain structural biases, brought out in previous chapters, suggest that the Mexican intellectual reaches a very limited audience. Intellectual life is clearly centered in Mexico City. Other major cities, such as Guadalajara, offer no real competition. Intellectuals, even more than politicians, have flocked to the capital, where they find the institutions to support their careers, the colleagues to serve as mentors or disciples, the academies to give them prestige, and the politicians to provide to those who wish it a role in public life. That most Mexican intellectuals since the Revolution have come from middle- and upper-class urban families, and have spent nearly all their adult lives living in Mexico City, gives them a perspective oriented toward urban, middle-class issues. Because of the general level of education, and the size of the audience that can understand and is interested in intellectual interpretations, the typical Mexican intellectual is reaching only a small portion of the Mexican people, generally limited to urban, highly educated, middle-class individuals who live in Mexico City. The biases inherent in the structures and attitudes of cultural life that encourage the centralization of intellectual activity in Mexico City distort the concerns of the intellectual even as they determine which intellectuals are heard.

Among the consequences of this distortion, two are worth summarizing here, especially because their implications go beyond Mexico. Mexico has already undergone one revolution in the twentieth century, and even though it was a major social upheaval, many of the expected social and structural changes did not occur. The role of intellectuals in that violent phase of Mexico's history has not been well studied, but those few examinations that do exist suggest that intellectual precursors of this movement did not come from Mexico City, but rather, like the popular masses themselves, from the provinces. Since the 1920s, the structure of intellectual life, through centralization in Mexico City, has encouraged those who have intellectual prestige to ignore their few peers who remain in the provinces and has drawn the provincial intellectual to Mexico City and socialized him into its norm, ignorant of and uninterested in provincial issues. By ignoring this provincial group, the state has repeated an error it made in the prerevolutionary period.

The second consequence of the centralization of Mexican life is international. I have argued that this pattern is universal to many developing countries, whether in Africa, Asia, the Middle East, or Latin America. The efforts of the North American scholarly and diplomatic community to ascertain the currents of thought in a developing society, through the published views of its intellectual community, are undertaken with a biased sample, the intellectuals, who are certified by their peers in Mexico City and who have, in many cases, been prominent as a result of their experiences abroad, in Europe and the United States.

This bias tends to be a self-prepetuating phenomenon because the more attention the North American community pays to an individual, in the form of guest lectures or the translation or showing of his works abroad, the more attention that individual receives within his own society. Because one central community certifies intellectuals, and because there is the influence of outside certifiers—in this case, North American scholars—our own decision makers and information gatherers, whether in the country or in Washington, receive a distorted image of Mexican society and what is happening politically and socially, especially in the provinces.

The centralization of intellectual life in Mexico City explains, in part, why the recruitment of the intellectual, at least in the past, has followed a pattern similar to that of the politician. The educational institutions attracting the Mexican politician were located, for the most part, in Mexico City. The same was true for intellectuals. In the years following the Revolution, intellectuals and politicians found mentors among their professors at these public institutions. In many cases the mentors for both groups were prominent intellectual-politicians, men known for their ideas and public careers. But as the media industry grows, and opportunities in the private sector and in higher education expand, mentors are increasingly being found among editors and publishers, who form the basis for intellectual circles, rather than among professors.

The mentor's role extends beyond getting a disciple certified and accepted into the intellectual community. The mentor actually determines, to a great extent, the role the intellectual will play. As I suggested in chapter 6, Mexican intellectuals follow three prototypes in their career choices: a government career, one of extended public service in the bureaucracy; a quasi-government career, in a government-funded institution such as a public university, but lacking direct government control; and an independent career, in which a person is self-employed as a professional, is independently wealthy, or employed full-time in a knowledge industry. The prototypes most commonly followed earlier in this century were in governmental or quasi-governmental careers because, in part, the mentors doing the recruiting had followed similar patterns. But in recent years more mentors are following the independent model, the future consequence of which is that their disciples are likely to follow a similar pattern.

It is ironic that the state is assisting a trend toward the more independent intellectual through those cultural academies and institutions that provide the most prestige and financial support to the intellectual. My examination of the most important of these institutions demonstrates that the state almost completely dominates the financial resources that sustain them. Thus, the private sector in Mexico has done little to develop independent groups of intellectuals, either through research monies or cultural institutions. Interestingly, the type of intellectual who receives membership in the most prominent academies, such as the National College, is increasingly nonpolitical. Scientists, especially, are well represented. Intellectuals who have not taken a strong stand on important social and economic issues facing the typical Mexican, and who do not, by their subject matter, reach a very large audience, are unrepresentative of all intellectuals. As literary intellectuals and humanists become more and more ignored, their frustration may increase and their isolation may further divide the intellectual community. Furthermore, the independent intellectual is moving farther away from the state.

The separation of intellectuals into several factions, as encouraged by the admission of only certain types of intellectuals to the leading academies, is furthered even more strongly by the state's support of higher education. Most of the Mexican resources devoted to research and development are funneled through the National University. Increasingly, intellectuals are finding *full-time* employment at the National University or the Colegio de México. Although funded almost entirely by the government, these institutions have not shown any evidence of state control. The state, itself, therefore, is giving the intellectual an alternative to serving it: a career in higher education. Although since the 1920s most intellectuals taught, almost none made their living from this occupation, since so few full-time positions were available.

The separation of intellectuals into several broad groups, encouraged by various actions of the state, has taken place gradually. Equally important as a source of intellectual diversity are a number of background characteristics. One significant finding is that residence, place of education, and family ties are instrumental in bringing together intellectuals and politicians. Again, centralization in Mexico City has played a role in expanding this contact, and in an earlier period state capitals functioned similarly. The evidence presented shows that sizeable numbers of intellectuals in the postrevolutionary era were related to or had close family ties to prominent politicians. Even though the Mexican Revolution brought about a renovation in political leadership, intellectuals did not lose their ties to politicians. In some cases family ties persisted, or merely jumped a generation, as illustrated by José López Portillo's family. In other cases, education at the same institution made up for the intellectual's lack of family ties with a new working-class generation of political leaders.

Although structural conditions have worked to bring some intellectuals into greater social contact with politicians, equally important conditions have worked to separate other intellectuals from politicians. One of the causes for intellectuals separating themselves into two groups stems from differences in the family background and educational experiences of intellectuals and politicians. Among the findings presented in the tables is the fact that most intellectuals, unlike politicians, have always come from middle- and upper-class families. The continuity among intellectuals from the pre- to the postrevolutionary generation seems much greater than for politicians. The intellectual who was associated with the Porfiriato, if only ideologically, was not excluded in the same way as the politician. Because of their upper socioeconomic situation, many intellectuals had access to or were sent to a different type of school. Those who received private educations, secular or religious, often developed views that differed from those of political leaders. Moreover, as was shown in the case of the preparatory school they attended (table 9), the social contact established as a result of similar school experiences with politicians substantially increased their choice of a public career. On the other hand, of intellectuals who did not attend the state institutions most frequently attended by future political leaders, most would follow careers independent of the government.

As intellectuals reached college, not only was their choice of institution important to whether or not they followed a public or independent career, but as I demonstrated earlier, the professional degree they chose affected their susceptibility to public or nongovernment careers. What is most important about the educational data, however, is that the degree choices of intellectuals today differ from those of thirty or forty years ago, and these differences are translated into intellectual roles. The most remarkable increase has taken place among leading intellectuals who have followed literary careers after majoring in the liberal arts rather than law, medicine, or engineering, choices more common to their predecessors. Again, as with the shift taking place in intellectual mentors, the choice of professional discipline and its effect on role definition will determine the patterns of the generation of intellectuals who will reach their prime at the turn of the century. The trend is pronounced among young intellectuals who are following liberal-arts degrees and literary and humanistic vocations.

The intellectual's choice of a college major affects his relationship to the Mexican state, and to politicians, in that it widens the separation between the two intellectual groups. In the third and fourth chapters I established that intellectuals do not share a homogeneous view of who they are and the role they should play. On the central issue of whether it is their function to serve the state, intellectuals split down the middle. About half the intellectual community argues that, for many reasons, some of which are historical, the Mexican intellectual has served and should serve the state. The other half suggests that this is no longer necessary, and that their very strength is their independence. Moreover, politicians express a view substantially different from that of many intellectuals.

As I argued previously, this division in intellectuals' self-concept is not just semantic; it has serious consequences for Mexican intellectual life and for the relationship between intellectuals and politicians. The most important single event contributing to the crystallization of this separation between intellectuals and the state, something built up to gradually since 1920 as alternative opportunities grew and as the influence of North American intellectual models became more pronounced in Mexico, was the government repression of students in 1968. Although the student massacre at Tlatelolco might not seem to have any bearing on the structure of intellectual life, it was decisive. By their own admission, and that of politicians, this action brought to the forefront the long-simmering relationship of the intellectual to the state, raising the issue in blunt terms as to whether the intellectual, by serving the state, was only legitimizing the state's activities, both harmful and beneficial to society.

The consequences for intellectuals of the issues raised by the events of 1968 were many, as suggested in the previous chapter, but the overall outcome has been definite. The number of intellectuals choosing to remain independent of the state has increased since 1968, and important independent mentors have emerged since then to serve as models. Although intellectuals do not all agree on the issue of separating themselves from public careers, the present trend favors the independent.

The fact that intellectuals are so sharply divided on serving or remaining independent of the state directly affects their relationship to politicians. Politicians, as I have shown, favor the group that argues that intellectuals should serve the state. This is only natural. Persons who devote their lives to a public career, whatever the reason, are bound by their own values to be attracted to this side of the intellectual argument. But as a result, Mexican politicians who listen to the opinions of intellectuals, and most do, are listening to one group and ignoring the other. Not surprisingly, they listen to intellectuals who themselves have served the state. Thus the division among Mexican intellectuals has produced a situation in which a large number of them have little or no impact on those in a position to solve Mexico's problems.

Because intellectuals, like politicians, listen to those who share similar values, the division between Mexican intellectuals and politicians is further exaggerated. The group of intellectuals who are independent—the group increasing in size and influence among the younger generations—is socialized by older intellectuals who have *not* served the state. Thus, they are most influenced by intellectuals who have the least impact on politicians. This situation will only worsen in the near future, as the independent group becomes larger. Furthermore, by closing themselves off from their peers who serve the state, young intellectuals block communications that might expand their perspectives. Therefore, just as self-censorship within the intellectual community impedes communication, so do sharply defined role definitions separate intellectuals and impede the circulation of ideas.

The trend in the relationship between the state and the intellectual will follow the North American model, even though it is foreign to the historical model in Mexico. Yet the pattern is likely to become more entrenched. As it does, the probability for conflict between the intellectual and the politician will increase because these structural patterns have separated intellectuals and politicians while the state has moved purposely or inadvertently to increase the autonomy of nonintellectual groups. The overall political environment, therefore, is also more conflictual. The division within the intellectual community and between the intellectual and the politician can only enhance this condition.

Although the Mexican intellectual's influence on public policy, whether direct or indirect, is impossible to measure, both politicians and intellectuals believe it has existed. In the previous chapter I concluded, however, that their impact seems to have been an exceptional rather than a typical occurrence. I would further argue that it was much more definite in the 1920s and 1930s, partly because circumstances made the skills intellectuals had to offer much more useful. The situation has changed. Whereas some observers might argue that the problems facing Mexico today are no less serious than they were following the Revolution, the politician has acquired the skills, in the technocrat, that the intellectual supplied in an earlier era. In this respect, then, the political technician has displaced the intellectual, making it less likely that the intellectual will hold decision-making positions in the government.

The one modifying circumstance, which might help to overcome the various patterns leading the intellectual away from the state, is the state's own desire to reincorporate the intellectual into public life to legitimate its activities. The events of 1968 did increase the schism between the state and intellectual, but the state has devoted substantial resources to recapturing the intellectual support it lost. Although most of these resources went into institutions, such as the universities, thereby increasing intellectual autonomy, efforts were made to recruit intellectuals to posts in the diplomatic corps, cultural agencies, and even, in some cases, the cabinet. Of course, increased efforts by the state to force its marriage, however shaky, to intellectuals, can backfire and increase the intransigence of the intellectuals. But when given the opportunity to manage large resources and apply them to a problem about which they are concerned, few intellectuals can resist.

Although the state will probably persist in its pattern of recruiting the intellectual, I doubt whether intellectual cooperation will show a substantial increase in the next decade. What is more likely, and what intellectuals believe themselves, is that they, through association with or leadership of other groups, will have an indirect impact on public policy. Thus, as the number of autonomous groups in Mexico increases and they voice their differences through the electoral process, or through other means, the opportunities for intellectuals to have an influence also increases. Those intellectuals who refuse to become politically involved, inside or outside of the government, will never have this type of influence.

Finally, many of the characteristics so influential in intellectual life in Mexico can be found elsewhere in the developing world. Among the more important conditions that might well encourage patterns similar to those found in Mexico are the concentration of intellectual and political leadership in one location, the dominance of one or two educational institutions, the size of the audience for intellectual goods, the influence of North American culture on the certification process of the intellectual, the lack of economic opportunities for the intellectual, the division of intellectuals into competing groups, the role of the state as an employer of intellectuals, and the concentration of the media in the capital. The influence these conditions exert on intellectual life, and on the relationship between intellectuals and the state, is affected not only by the peculiarities of each culture, but by the pace of development and the number of years since national independence. Regardless of these variations, I believe that many of the hypotheses and speculations suggested by conclusions drawn from the Mexican case will help us explore the role intellectuals play elsewhere in the developing world and their impact on solving problems common to all societies.

Notes

1: Introduction

1. There have been numerous studies of certain eras in American intellectual life, or of certain literary circles in the twentieth century. But the only study of twentieth-century American intellectuals that analyzes their structure and their background in depth, as distinct from their ideas, is that of Charles Kadushin, *American Intellectual Elite* (Boston: Little, Brown, 1974).

2. See the recent collection edited by B. Bruce-Briggs, *The New Class?* (New Brunswick, N.J.: Transaction Books, 1979).

3. Kadushin, *American Intellectual Elite*, p. 335.

4. The first serious effort to examine revolutionary and postrevolutionary generations for coherent patterns appears in the recent work of Luis González, *Los artífices del cardenismo*, Historia de la revolución mexicana, 1934-1940, no. 14 (Mexico City: Colegio de México, 1979), p. 97ff; and Enrique Krauze's *Caudillos culturales en la revolución mexicana* (Mexico City: Siglo XXI, 1976).

5. See, for example, Lewis A. Coser, "The Differing Roles of Intellectuals in Contemporary France, England and America" (Paper presented at the Symposium on Sociology of the Intellectual, Buenos Aires, 3-5 July 1967).

2: Politics, the State, and Intellectuals

1. For the evolution of these views, see Robert E. Scott, *Mexican Government in Transition*, 2d ed. (Urbana: University of Illinois Press, 1964); Frank Brandenburg, *Making of Modern Mexico* (Englewood Cliffs, N.J.: Prentice-Hall, 1964); Martin C. Needler, "The Political Development of Mexico," *American Political Science Review* 55 (June 1961): 308-312; and idem, *Politics and Society in Mexico* (Albuquerque: University of New Mexico Press, 1971); Leon Padgett, *The Mexican Political System*, 2d ed. (Boston: Houghton Mifflin, 1976); Kenneth F. Johnson, *Mexican Democracy: A Critical View*, rev. (New York: Praeger, 1978); Susan Purcell, "Decision-Making in an Authoritarian Regime: Theoretical Implications from a Mexican Case Study," *World Politics* 26 (October 1973):28-54; John H. Coatsworth, "Los orígenes del autoritarismo moderno en México," *Foro Internacional* 16 (October-December 1975): 205-232; José Luis Reyna and Richard S. Weinert, eds., *Authoritarianism in Mexico* (New York: ISHI, 1977); and Peter H. Smith, *Labyrinths of Power: Political Recruitment in Twentieth-Century Mexico* (Princeton: Princeton University Press, 1979).

2. Daniel Cosío Villegas, *La sucesión presidencial* (Mexico City: Joaquín Mortiz, 1975), p. 18.

3. Johnson, *Mexican Democracy*, p. 231.

4. Aurora Loyo Brambila and Ricardo Pozas Horcasitas, "Notes on the Mechanisms of Control Exercised by the Mexican State over the Organized Sector of the Working Class, A Case Study: The Political Crisis of 1958" (Paper presented to the Center for Inter-American Relations, April 1975).

5. For evidence of these beliefs, see my *La formación de un político: La socialización de los funcionarios públicos en México post-revolucionario* (Mexico City: Fondo de Cultura Económica, 1981), and "The Elitelore of Mexico's Revolutionary Family," *Journal of Latin American Lore* 4, no. 2 (1978):149-182.

6. Kevin J. Middlebrook, "Political Change in Mexico," in *Mexico-United States Relations*, ed. Susan K. Purcell (New York: Academy of Political Science, 1981), p. 58ff.

7. Ibid., p. 15.

8. Carlos Pereyra has advanced this interpretation in "Estado y sociedad," in *México, hoy*, ed. Pablo González Casanova and Enrique Florescano (Mexico City: Siglo XXI, 1979), pp. 304-305.

9. I am indebted to Edward J. Williams for suggesting this interpretation to me.

10. Kevin Middlebrook, "Political Change and Political Reform in Mexico (Paper presented at the Ninth National Latin American Studies Association Meeting, Bloomington, Indiana, October 1980), p. 19.

11. Glen Dealy, *The Public Man: An Interpretation of Latin American and Other Catholic Countries* (Amherst: University of Massachusetts Press, 1977), p. 8.

12. Ibid., p. 12.

13. Larissa Lomnitz, "Horizontal and Vertical Relations and the Social Structure of Urban Mexico" (Unpublished, 1980), p. 47.

14. These changes have been well illustrated by the political career of the former governor of Yucatán, Carlos Loret de Mola, *Confesiones de un gobernador* (Mexico City: Grijalbo, 1978).

15. Edmundo González Llaca, "El presidencialismo o la personalización del poder," *Revista Mexicana de Ciencia Política* 21 (April-June 1975):36-37.

16. See Merilee Grindle, "Patrons and Clients in the Bureaucracy: Career Networks in Mexico," *Latin American Research Review* 12, no. 1 (1977):49, for some examples.

17. Octavio Paz, *The Labyrinth of Solitude: Life and Thought in Mexico* (New York: Grove Press, 1961), p. 158.

18. David Schers, "The Popular Sector of the Mexican *PRI*" (Ph.D. diss., University of New Mexico, 1972), p. 39.

19. See the comment by the former majority leader of the Senate, Manuel Moreno Sánchez, *Mexico: 1968-72* (Austin: University of Texas, Institute of Latin American Studies, 1973), p. 8.

20. Evelyn P. Stevens, *Protest and Response in Mexico* (Cambridge, Mass.: MIT Press, 1974), p. 25.

21. Vicente Leñero, *Los periodistas* (Mexico City: Joaquín Mortiz, 1978), p. 82. A verbatim example can be found in a discussion between Miguel Alemán and Daniel Cosío Villegas in Miguel Alemán, *Miguel Alemán contesta* (Austin: University of Texas, Institute of Latin American Studies, 1975).

22. This can be seen repeatedly in the conversations between the politicians and journalists in Vicente Leñero's *Los periodistas* and in Daniel Cosío Villegas's *Memorias* (Mexico City: Joaquín Mortiz, 1976).

23. Roderic A. Camp, "Mexico's Presidential Pre-Candidates, Changes and Portents for the Future," *Polity* 16 (Summer 1984):588-605.

24. Roderic A. Camp, *Mexico's Leaders: Their Education and Recruitment* (Tucson: University of Arizona Press, 1980).

25. C. Wright Mills, *The Power Elite* (New York: Oxford University Press, 1959), p. 282.

26. This is how I shall use the term "decision maker" or "policymaker." See Mostafa Rejai, "Toward the Comparative Study of Political Decision-Makers," *Comparative Political Studies* 2 (October 1969):351.

27. For evidence of intra-agency rivalries, see Guy Benveniste, *Bureaucracy and National Planning: A Sociological Case Study in Mexico* (New York: Praeger, 1970), p. 57.

28. Van Whiting, Jr., in his "Political and Institutional Aspects of Technology Transfer in Mexico (Unpublished, 1980), p. 46, has demonstrated this phenomenon in the case of business firms.

29. Martin H. Greenberg, *Bureaucracy and Development: A Mexican Case Study* (Lexington, Mass.: D. C. Heath, 1970), p. 57; and for some actual examples of independence in decision making by a cabinet secretary, see Jaime Torres Bodet, a poet and intellectual turned bureaucrat, *Equinoccio* (Mexico City: Porrúa, 1974), pp. 260-262.

30. Eduardo Suárez, *Comentarios y recuerdos 1926-1946* (Mexico City: Porrúa, 1977), p. 107.

31. For the most insightful look at how this takes place, see Loret de Mola's *Confesiones de un gobernador*, p. 92.

32. Benveniste, *Bureaucracy and National Planning*, p. 60.

33. See Susan Purcell's statement that "personal 'connections' become an important factor in distributive decisions" (*The Mexican Profit-Sharing Decision: Politics in an Authoritarian Regime* [Berkeley & Los Angeles: University of California Press, 1975], p. 41).

34. Luis Garrido, *El tiempo de mi vida: Memorias* (Mexico City: Porrúa, 1974), p. 239. For other specific examples, see Eduardo Villaseñor, *Memorias-Testimonio* (Mexico City: Fondo de Cultura Económica, 1974), p.141; and Jacinto B. Treviño, *Memorias* (Mexico City: Orion, 1961), pp. 201-202.

35. Antonio Carrillo Flores, "Introduction," in Suárez, *Comentarios*, p. xli.

36. Richard Fagen and William Tuohy, *Politics and Privilege in a Mexican City* (Stanford: Stanford University Press, 1972), p. 27.

37. Luis León responding to Pindaro Urióstegui Miranda, *Testimonios del proceso revolucionario de México* (Mexico City: Argrin, 1970), p. 541).

38. Suárez, *Comentarios*, pp. xxxi, 100-101.

39. See my "Un intelectual en la política mexicana: Agustín Yáñez," *Relaciones* 2 (Summer 1981):137-162.

40. For examples of who was responsible for each office held by a public figure spanning the entire period from 1910 to the present, see Alberto Bremauntz, *Setenta años de mi vida* (Mexico City: Ediciones Jurídicas Sociales, 1968), pp. 65, 79; and

Enrique Beltrán, *Medio siglo de recuerdos de un biólogo mexicano* (Mexico City: SMHN, 1977), p. 19. The best written evidence of a career spanning the 1930s through the 1970s can be found in Victor Manuel Villaseñor's frank and detailed memoirs, *Memorias de un hombre de izquierda*, 2 vols. (Mexico City: Grijalbo, 1976).

41. For examples from the 1950s, see the statement by Carlos Ramírez Ladewig that President Adolfo Ruiz Cortines selected him as a federal deputy, and that the president imposed his choice as their leader in the chamber (*Proceso* [5 February 1977], p. 8).

42. On the basis of data in the *MPBP*, of the more than three hundred governors in Mexico since 1935, only five, or 2 percent, have been among my group of leading intellectuals: Francisco Martínez de la Vega, governor of San Luis Potosí, 1959-1961; Agustín Yáñez, governor of Jalisco, 1953-1958; Gustavo Baz, governor of Mexico, 1957-1963; and Isidro Fabela, also governor of Mexico, 1942-1945; Enrique González Pedrero, governor of Tabasco, 1983- .

43. For the most thorough description and analysis of gubernatorial decisions over time, see Roger C. Anderson's "The Functional Role of the Governors and their States in the Political Development of Mexico, 1940-64" (Ph.D. diss., University of Wisconsin, 1971).

44. A small but steady number of Catholic intellectuals inside and outside the church appear among prominent intellectuals since the 1920s. In Mexico, the philosophical rather than the institutional legacy of the church may be more important.

45. Since the Revolution, the lack of a secular conservative party probably explains why the military finds itself without political and intellectual allies. This relationship, which is so common to the military in other Latin American countries, deserves much closer examination in Mexico.

46. Several authors believe that both in 1968 and during the regime of Luis Echeverría, the army may have been on the verge of reasserting itself in Mexican politics, or, at least, the president considered this a strong possibility. For 1968, see Johnson, *Mexican Democracy*, p. 106; for the early 1970s, see Judith A. Hellman, *Mexico in Crisis* (New York: Holmes and Meier, 1978), p. 166.

47. The only exception to this, which essentially was a negotiated arrangement, took place in 1976, when the leader of the Popular Socialist party became the official PRI candidate for senator from Oaxaca.

48. Stevens, *Protest and Response in Mexico*, p. 66.

49. See Dale Story, "Entrepreneurs and the State in Mexico: Examining the Authoritarian Thesis," Technical Papers series, no. 30 (Austin: University of Texas, Institute of Latin American Studies, 1980).

50. John Womack, Jr., "The Spoils of the Mexican Revolution," *Foreign Affairs* 48 (July 1970):681.

51. For the view that business is interested in its own political party, see Carlos Arriola, "Los empresarios tras el estado," *Nexos*, no. 14 (February 1979), pp. 3-4; and for their changing views on economic policy, see E. V. K. FitzGerald, "Mexico, A New Direction in Economic Policy?" *Bank of London and South American Review* 12 (October 1978):535.

52. Luis Villoro, *Signos políticos* (Mexico City: Grijalbo, 1974), p. 92.

53. Larissa Lomnitz, "Horizontal and Vertical Relations," p. 29.

54. Larissa Lomnitz and Marisol Pérez-Lizaur, "The History of an Urban Upper-Class Family in Mexico," *Journal of the Family History* (Winter 1978), p. 407.

55. See my *Mexico's Leaders*, p. 203.

56. For example, among the younger generation of intellectuals, Gabriel Zaid, poet and essayist, and Enrique Krauze, historian, both received their degrees in engineering before engaging in further study, and both manage and live from their own businesses (personal interview with Enrique Krauze, Mexico City, 28 August 1978, and Pella, Iowa, 20 October 1980).

57. Edward J. Williams, *The Rebirth of the Mexican Petroleum Industry* (Lexington, Mass.: D. C. Heath, 1979), p. 97ff.

58. Personal interview with José Rogelio Alvarez, Mexico City, 18 July 1978.

59. Raymond Aron, *The Opium of the Intellectuals* (New York: Doubleday, 1957), p. 205.

60. Many writers believe that ideology, worldwide, has become "the primary instrument of the modern secular intellectual classes in their bid to be considered generally important." For this view, see Talcott Parsons, " 'The Intellectual': A Special Role Category," in *On Intellectuals: Theoretical Studies, Case Studies*, ed. Philip Rieff (Garden City, N.Y.: Doubleday, 1969), p. 24.

61. Robert D. Putnam argues that one of the reasons is their sensitivity to "discrepancies between distant ideals and contemporary realities" (*The Comparative Study of Political Elites* [Englewood Cliffs, N.J.: Prentice-Hall, 1976], p. 194).

62. Jeane Kirkpatrick, "Politics and the New Class," in *The New Class?* ed. B. Bruce-Briggs (New Brunswick, N.J.: Transaction Books, 1979), p. 37.

63. Zbigniew Brzezinski, "America in the Technetronic Age," *Encounter* 30 (January 1968):16,18.

64. Ibid., p. 18. Alvin Gouldner expresses this same sentiment in his statement that intellectuals are a cultured bourgeoisie whose capital is knowledge ("Prologue to a Theory of Revolutionary Intellectuals," *Telos*, no. 26 [Winter 1975-1976], p. 6).

65. See Norman Birnbaum, "Problem of a Knowledge Elite," *Massachusetts Review* 12 (Summer 1971):622.

66. Fritz Machlup, *Production and Distribution of Knowledge in the United States* (Princeton, N.J.: Princeton University Press, 1962), p. 374.

67. Lewis A. Coser, *Men of Ideas: A Sociologist's View* (New York: Free Press, 1965), pp. 6, 44.

68. Patricia Holt, "Publishing in Mexico, Its Time Has Come," *Publishers' Weekly* 207, no. 16 (25 April 1980):34.

69. Seymour Martin Lipset, "The New Class and the Professoriate," *Society* 16 (January-February 1979):36.

70. Roderic A. Camp, "Los intelectuales y la política en el México postrevolu-cionario, el caso de los profesores," in Instituto Mexicano de Cultura, *Sociología de la paz y de la guerra* (Mexico City, 1979), pp. 523-552.

71. See the arguments of F. A. Hayek, "The Intellectuals and Socialism," in *The Intellectuals, A Controversial Portrait*, ed. George B. De Huszar (Glencoe, Ill.: Free Press, 1960), p. 373; Alvin Gouldner, *The Dialectic of Ideology and Technology* (New York: Seabury Press, 1976), p. 191; Heinz Eulau, *Technology*

and Civility: The Skill Revolution in Politics (Stanford, Cal.: Hoover Institution, 1977), p. 70.

72. Seymour Martin Lipset and Richard Dobson, "The Intellectual as Critic and Rebel," *Daedalus* 101 (Summer 1972):175.

73. Ibid., citing Leszek Kolakowski, p. 137.

74. Milton Gordon, "Social Class and the American Intellectuals," *A.A.U.P. Bulletin* 40 (1955):522.

75. Thomas P. Neill, "The Social Function of the Intellectual," *Thought* 32 (June 1957):208.

3: The Mexican Intellectual

1. Roberto Michels, "The Intellectuals," *Encyclopedia of Social Sciences* (1936), p. 118.

2. Robert K. Merton, "Role of the Intellectual in Public Bureaucracy," in *Social Theory and Social Structure*, ed. Robert K. Merton (New York: Free Press, 1968), p. 263.

3. Alvin Gouldner, "Prologue to a Theory of Revolutionary Intellectuals," *Telos*, no. 26 (Winter 1975-1976), p. 6.

4. Kenneth Tynan, "Foreword," in Lenny Bruce, *How to Talk Dirty and Influence People, An Autobiography* (Chicago: Playboy Press, 1967), p. ix.

5. Karl Deutsch, "Comments on 'American Intellectuals: Their Politics and Status,'" *Daedalus* 88 (Summer 1959):489.

6. Max Beloff, *The Intellectual in Politics and Other Essays* (London: Weidenfield and Nicolson, 1970), p. 9.

7. Arthur M. Schlesinger, Jr., "El intelectual y la sociedad nortamericana," in *Los intelectuales y el poder*, ed. Gabriel Careaga (Mexico City: Sepsetentas, 1972), p. 80.

8. Lewis A. Coser, *Men of Ideas: A Sociologist's View* (New York: Free Press, 1965), p. x.

9. Thomas P. Neill, "The Social Function of the Intellectual," *Thought* 32 (June 1957):201.

10. Michael Novak, "Power of the New Class," *US News and World Report* 88 (25 February 1980):70.

11. Lewis S. Feuer, "What Is an Intellectual?" in *The Intelligentsia and the Intellectuals*, ed. Alexander Gella (Beverly Hills, Cal.: Sage Studies in International Sociology, 1976), p. 51.

12. I have taken the liberty of adapting this concept from Johan Galtung's "Development and Intellectual Styles, Some Notes on the Case of the Lawyers" (Paper presented at the International Conference on Comparative Social Research in Developing Countries, Buenos Aires, 9-15 September 1964), p. 5.

13. Marcus Cunliffe, "The Intellectuals: Part II, The United States," *Encounter* (England) 4 (May 1955):23.

14. Roderic A. Camp, "An Image of Mexican Intellectuals, Some Preliminary Observations," *Mexican Studies/Estudios Mexicanos* (in press).

15. Charles Kadushin, *American Intellectual Elite* (Boston: Little, Brown, 1974), p. 7.

16. Edward Shils, "Intellectuals," *International Encyclopedia of the Social*

Sciences (1968), p. 399.

17. Bennet M. Berger, "Sociology and the Intellectuals: An Analysis of a Stereotype," *Antioch Review* 17 (1957):282.

18. Gouldner, "Prologue to a Theory of Revolutionary Intellectuals," p. 16.

19. Coser, *Men of Ideas*, p. x.

20. Paul A. Baran, "The Commitment of the Intellectual," *Monthly Review* 13 (May 1961):17.

21. Lewis S. Feuer, *Marx and the Intellectuals* (New York: Doubleday, 1969), p. 11.

22. Daniel Bell, "The New Class: A Muddled Concept," *Society* 16 (January-February 1979):19.

23. Antonio Gramsci, *The Modern Prince and Other Writings* (New York: International Publishers, 1957), p. 120.

24. For example, see Juan Marsal, who summarizes five definitions of intellectuals, "Los ensayistas socio-políticos de Argentina y México (aportes para el estudio de sus roles, su ideología y su acción política)," Working paper, Instituto Torcuato di Tella (Buenos Aires, September 1969), p. 7.

25. Antonio Marimón, "Los intelectuales, impugnadores del poder," *Uno Más Uno, Sábado* (supplement), 12 August 1978, p. 11, in an interview with Masao Yamaguchi, a Japanese scholar; Juan F. Marsal, "Los intelectuales latinoamericanos y el cambio social," *Desarrollo Económico* 6 (July-December 1966):299.

26. Charles Kadushin, *American Intellectual Elite*, p. 8.

27. B. Bruce-Briggs, *The New Class?* (New Brunswick, N.J.:Transaction Books, 1979), p. 192.

28. Camp, "Image of Mexican Intellectuals."

29. Personal interview with Ignacio Chávez, Mexico City, 13 June 1978.

30. Personal interview with Alejandro Gómez Arias, Mexico City, 31 May 1978.

31. Personal interview with José Rogelio Alvarez, Mexico City, 18 June 1978; and with Enrique Florescano, Mexico City, 27 June 1978; Daniel Olmedo, Mexico City, 25 July 1978; and Ricardo Guerra, Mexico City, 26 May 1978.

32. Personal interview with Miguel Palacios Macedo, Mexico City, 12 July 1978.

33. Personal interview with Pedro Ramírez Vázquez, Mexico City, 19 July 1978.

34. Personal interview, Mexico City, 20 August 1978. Of course, many intellectuals expressed a view similar to Villoro's.

35. Personal interview with Ignacio Arriola Haro, Guadalajara, 28 July 1980.

36. Personal interview with Daniel Cosío Villegas, Mexico City, 30 June 1975.

37. Personal interview with Leopoldo Zea, Mexico City, 25 July 1978.

38. Personal interview, Mexico City, 29 May 1978.

39. Personal interview with José Rogelio Alvarez, Mexico City, 18 June 1978.

40. See Enrique Krauze, "Daniel Cosío Villegas, el empresario cultural," *Plural* 5, no. 55 (April 1976):7-17; and idem, *Daniel Cosío Villegas: Una biografía intelectual* (Mexico City: Joaquín Mortiz, 1980).

41. Octavio Paz, *The Labyrinth of Solitude: Life and Thought in Mexico* (New York: Grove Press, 1961), pp. 151-152.

42. Personal interview with Octavio Paz, Mexico City, 29 June 1978. Also see his interview with Julio Scherer García, "Entrevista con Octavio Paz," *Proceso*, no.

58 (12 December 1978), p. 8.

43. Personal interview with José Joaquín Blanco, Mexico City, 1 August 1978.

44. Personal interview with Salvador Elizondo, Mexico City, 4 August 1978.

45. Personal interview with Víctor Manuel Villaseñor, 22 May 1978.

46. For the purposes of this study, "some government service" is defined as havng held two or more government offices or having worked in the public sector for five or more years.

47. Personal interview with Antonio Armendáriz, Mexico City, 24 May 1978.

48. These phrases were used by Fernando Zertuche Muñoz, subsecretary of labor during the de la Madrid administration, and by Mariano Azuela, Jr. (personal interviews, Mexico City, 26 July 1978, and 31 May 1978).

49. Personal interview with Andrés Serra Rojas, Mexico City, 8 June 1978.

50. Personal interview with José Juan de Olloqui, former assistant secretary of foreign relations, Mexico City, 12 July 1978.

51. These data are taken from the intellectual activities engaged in by those individuals listed in table 4.

52. Personal interview, Mexico City, 23 May 1978.

53. Personal interview with Rosa Luz Alegría, Mexico City, 7 August 1978.

54. Camp, "Intellectuals: Agents of Change in Mexico," *Journal of Inter-American Studies and World Affairs* 23 (August 1981):8.

55. Ibid., pp. 9-10.

4: The Function of the Mexican Intellectual

1. Fernando Uricoechea, *Intelectuales y desarrollo en América Latina* (Buenos Aires: Centro Editor de América Latina, 1969), p. 16.

2. Lewis A. Coser, *Men of Ideas: A Sociologist's View* (New York: Free Press, 1965), p. 38.

3. For example, 66 percent of the most influential officeholders during Lázaro Cárdenas's administration (1935 to 1940) had college degrees. See my *Mexico's Leaders: Their Education and Recruitment* (Tucson: University of Arizona Press, 1980), p. 70ff, for evidence of this and other educational trends. Middle- or upper-class backgrounds in the Cárdenas administration accounted for 48 percent of his collaborators, a figure that increased in each succeeding administration. These figures are from the 1980 *MPBP*.

4. For budgetary evidence of this decline, see James W. Wilkie, *The Mexican Revolution: Federal Expenditure and Social Change since 1910* (Berkeley & Los Angeles: University of California Press, 1970), p. 85. As for population growth rates, although illiteracy declined from 77 percent in 1910 to 38 percent in 1960, the numbers show a different result. Of the 15 million persons in Mexico in 1910, 11.5 million were illiterate. Of the 66 million in 1977, 35 percent, or 23 million, were illiterate. For statistical data on these trends, see James W. Wilkie and Peter Reich, eds., *Statistical Abstract of Latin America*, Vol. 20 (Los Angeles: UCLA Latin America Center Publications, University of California, 1980), pp. 121-142.

5. Fred P. Ellison, "The Writer," in *Continuity and Change in Latin America*, ed. John J. Johnson (Stanford, Cal.: Stanford University Press, 1964), p. 84.

6. Gabriel Zaid, *El progreso improductivo* (Mexico City: Siglo XXI, 1979), p. 265.

7. Charles Kadushin, *American Intellectual Elite* (Boston: Little, Brown, 1974), p. 348.

8. George Lichtheim, "The Role of the Intellectual," *Commentary* 29 (1960):296.

9. For evidence of this in Mexico, see my "The Influence of European and North American Ideas on Students at Mexico's National School of Law," *New Scholar* 8 (1982):289-307.

10. Of the 332 intellectuals about whom I have information, 221, or two-thirds, have actually lived abroad for one or more years, which clearly suggests the direct exposure of intellectuals to foreign influences. For scientists alone, this figure is 56 percent. Of the 221 intellectuals who lived abroad, 141 (64 percent) lived in the United States; of the scientists, 89 percent lived in the United States. The influence of North America on Mexican science was recognized as early as the 1940s by one of Mexico's most renowned scientists, Manuel Sandoval Vallarta, himself a graduate of MIT and a Guggenheim fellow to Berlin.

11. Larissa Lomnitz provides evidence of this: "The Challenge of Peripherality: Science and Organization in a Mexican Research Institute" (Unpublished, 1980); and idem, "Organizational Structure of a Mexican Research Institute" (Unpublished, 1980).

12. In 1965, 80 percent of the books read in Spanish in Mexico were imported. Furthermore, if one examines the best-sellers by discipline in the forty-five-year history of Mexico's major press, the Fondo de Cultura Económica, of the top ten authors in economics, sociology, and history, there were no Mexicans. See its *Libro conmemorativo del 45 aniversario del Fondo de Cultura Económica* (Mexico City, 1980), p. 114ff.

13. A recent example of this surfaced in an interview with the painter José Luis Cuevas, who told a journalist that he was proposed as a candidate for the National Prize in Art by several individuals prominent in Mexican cultural circles, but that "some hidden elements intervened" to prevent his name from being considered (*Hispano Americano* [1 December 1980], p. 12).

14. Tamayo lived in New York for eighteen years and Paris for ten. Many artists ostracized him because his painting was largely abstract and devoid of any ideological content. At present, he is Mexico's most famous living painter.

15. Camp, "An Image of Mexican Intellectuals, Some Preliminary Observations," *Mexican Studies/Estudios Mexicanos* (in press).

16. Ibid.

17. See "Mexico's El Colegio: From Refugee to Respected Graduate Institution," *The Chronicle of Higher Education*, 16 June 1980, p. 14.

18. Enrique Krauze, "The Intellectual as Cultural Entrepreneur, the Case of Daniel Cosío Villegas" (Paper presented at the International Symposium on Intellectuals as Agents of Change in Mexico and Latin America, Central College, Pella, Iowa, 19-20 October 1980).

19. Vicente Leñero, *Los periodistas* (Mexico City: Joaquín Mortiz, 1978), p. 85.

20. Raúl Cardiel Reyes, senior professor among those teaching at the School of Political and Social Sciences at the National University in 1978, told me that he could not publish a book review in the *Revista Mexicana de Ciencias Políticas*, the

official publication of his school, because his views were not Marxist (personal interview, Mexico City, 2 June 1978).

21. Cinna Lomnitz, "Science and Social Change in Latin America" (Paper presented at the International Symposium on Intellectuals as Agents of Change in Mexico and Latin America, Central College, Pella, Iowa, 19-20 October 1980).

22. Melvin Seeman, "The Intellectual and the Language of Minorities," *American Journal of Sociology* 64 (July 1958):35.

23. Coser, *Men of Ideas*, p. 3.

24. Ellison, "The Writer," p. 38.

25. John P. Harrison, "The Role of the Intellectual in Fomenting Change: The University," in *Explosive Forces in Latin America*, ed. J. J. Te Paske and S. Nettleton (Columbus: Ohio State University Press, 1964), p. 27.

26. John Rutherford, *Mexican Society during the Revolution* (Oxford: Clarendon Press, 1971), p. 81.

27. Daniel Cosío Villegas, who some might consider to have tried and failed as a politician, reportedly told John P. Harrison that "every intellectual in Latin America is a failed politician."

28. Glen Dealy, *"The Public Man: An Interpretation of Latin American and Other Catholic Countries* (Amherst: University of Massachusetts Press, 1977), pp. 10-12.

29. Thomas P. Neill, "The Social Function of the Intellectual," *Thought* 32 (June 1957):208.

30. Lewis S. Feuer, "What Is an Intellectual?" in *The Intelligentsia and the Intellectuals*, ed. Alexander Gella (Beverly Hills, Cal.: Sage Studies in International Sociology, 1976), p. 56.

31. For nationalistic values in education, see Josefina Vázquez de Knauth, "La educación socialista de los años treinta," *Historia Mexicana* 18 (January-March 1969):408-423, and idem, *Nacionalismo y educación en Mexico* (Mexico City: Colegio de México, 1970), p. 151ff; and Mary Kay Vaughan, "History Textbooks in Mexico in the 1920s," Council on International Studies, State University of New York at Buffalo, Special Studies no. 53, 1974.

32. Henry C. Schmidt, *The Roots of Lo Mexicano: Self and Society in Mexican Thought, 1900-1934* (College Station: Texas A & M Press, 1978), p. 28.

33. John Friedmann, "Intellectuals in Developing Societies," *Kyklos* 13 (1960):520.

34. Kadushin, *American Intellectual Elite*, p. 341.

35. Lewis S. Feuer, *Ideology and the Ideologists* (New York: Harper & Row, 1975), p. 5; and Juan F. Marsal and Margery J. Arent, "Right-wing Intelligentsia in Argentina: An Analysis of its Ideology and Political Activity," *Social Research* 37 (Autumn 1970):466.

36. Juan F. Marsal, "The Latin American Intellectuals and the Problem of Change" (Paper presented at the Sixth World Congress of Sociology, 4-11 September 1966, Evian, France), p. 9.

37. Friedmann, "Intellectuals in Developing Societies," p. 534.

38. Uriocoechea, *Intelectuales y desarrollo en América Latina*, p. 78.

39. Germán Arciniegas, "Intellectuals in the Politics of Latin America," in *Constructive Change in Latin America*, ed. Cole Blasier (Pittsburgh: University of

Pittsburgh Press, 1968), p. 162.

40. Gabriel Careaga, *Los intelectuales y la política en México* (Mexico City: Extemporáneos, 1971), p. 10.

41. Edward Shils, "Intellectuals in the Political Development of the New States," in Shils, *The Intellectuals and the Powers and Other Essays* (Chicago: University of Chicago Press, 1972), p. 387.

42. Harry J. Benda, "Non-Western Intelligentsias as Political Elites," *Australian Journal of Politics and History* 6 (November 1960):208.

43. James W. Wilkie and Edna Monzón de Wilkie, eds., *Elitelore as a New Field of Inquiry* (Los Angeles: UCLA Graduate School of Management, 1979), p. x.

44. This is well illustrated in the resignations from *Política* of a group of prominent intellectuals in the mid-1960s. See Ermilo Abreu Gómez, " 'Política' y la política de los intelectuales," *Política* 5, no. 104 (15 August 1964):26.

45. Alvin Gouldner, "Prologue to a Theory of Revolutionary Intellectuals," *Telos*, no. 26 (Winter 1975-1976), p. 8.

46. For example, Fernando Benítez, a well-known anthropologist, essayist, and journalist, organized an experimental *ejido*. Prominent Mexican intellectuals who have written on agrarian problems include Jesús Silva Herzog, Ramón Beteta, Arturo Warman, and Fernando González Roa.

47. This alliance between the intellectual and the working classes was a definite goal of the precursor movement led by Enrique and Ricardo Flores Magón before the Mexican Revolution of 1910.

48. This is the goal, for example, of historian Luis Villoro, who is actively involved in encouraging political participation of workers through his membership in the Mexican Labor party (personal interview with me, Mexico City, 20 August 1978).

49. See Harry J. Benda, "Non-Western Intelligentsias as Political Elites," p. 209.

50. Charles Kadushin, *American Intellectual Elite*, p. 5.

51. Ibid., p. 299.

52. Stanley R. Ross, "La protesta de los intelectuales ante México y su Revolución," *Historia Mexicana* 26, no. 3 (January-March, 1977):430. For more on the social mission of the intellectual, see François Bourricaud, "Adventures of Ariel," *Daedalus* 101 (Summer 1972):113.

53. Germán Arciniegas, "Intellectuals in the Politics of Latin America," p. 162.

54. Ibid., p. 164.

55. Enrique Krauze, *Daniel Cosío Villegas: Una biografía intelectual* (Mexico City: Joaquín Mortiz, 1980), p. 232. Interestingly, intellectuals, rather than aiding Francisco Madero, the first popularly elected president in Mexico in the twentieth century, "indulged in carping criticism" of his regime. See Charles C. Cumberland, *Mexican Revolution: Genesis under Madero* (Austin: University of Texas Press, 1974), p. 257.

56. Personal interview with Enrique Florescano, Mexico City, 27 June 1978.

57. Personal interview with Octavio Paz, Mexico City, 29 June 1978.

58. Pablo González Casanova, "Las alternativas de la democracia," in *México, hoy*, ed. Pablo González Casanova and Enrique Florescano (Mexico City: Siglo XXI, 1979), p. 369.

59. Personal interview with Ignacio Arriola Haro, Guadalajara, 28 July 1980; and with Leopoldo Zea, Mexico City, 25 July 1978.

60. Octavio Paz, *Labyrinth of Solitude: Life and Thought in Mexico* (New York: Grove Press, 1961), p. 159.

61. Paz obviously placed his intellectual independence above his public career, although his decision should be seen in the light of his holding a government position that, unlike most positions, has security (career foreign service). However, the failure of other intellectuals to demonstrate their displeasure by some symbolic form of protest, if indeed they agreed with the widespread condemnation of the government in the press and in middle-class circles in general, is notable. The individuals in that administration with intellectual credentials included Jesús Reyes Heroles, director of the Mexican Petroleum Company; Antonio Carrillo Flores, secretary of foreign relations; Gabino Fraga, assistant secretary of foreign relations; Eduardo Suárez, ambassador to the United Kingdom; Silvio Zavala, ambassador to France; Rodolfo Usigli, ambassador to the Low Countries; and Agustín Yáñez, secretary of public education, all of whom completed their terms in office without any public statement.

62. According to what Paz told me, this is the first time he has revealed this incident publicly (personal interview, Mexico City, 4 July 1978).

63. Personal interview with Fernando Benítez, Mexico City, 30 June 1978; Lucio Mendieta y Núñez expressed a similar view, Mexico City, 17 May 1978.

64. Personal interview with Jesús Puente Leyva, Mexico City, 15 August 1978.

65. Ibid.

66. Personal interview with Antonio Martínez Báez. Leopoldo Solís also concurred in his interpretation (personal interview, Mexico City, 25 May 1978).

67. Personal interview with Manuel Hinojosa Ortiz, Mexico City, 19 July 1978.

68. Personal interview with Antonio Carrillo Flores, Mexico City, 12 June 1978.

5: Family Background and Education

1. Peter H. Smith, *Labyrinths of Power: Political Recruitment in Twentieth-Century Mexico* (Princeton: Princeton University Press, 1979), p. 70.

2. Roderic A. Camp, "A Reexamination of Political Leadership and Allocation of Federal Revenues in Mexico, 1934-1973," *Journal of Developing Areas* 10 (January 1976):199.

3. Roderic A. Camp, *Mexican Political Biographies, 1935-1975* (Tucson: University of Arizona Press, 1976), p. 314.

4. Legally, the 1944 Law of Professions prohibits anyone not born in Mexico from holding administrative positions in government agencies.

5. His father, Rafael Fuentes Boettiger, joined the Foreign Service in 1925, and in 1932 became secretary to Alfonso Reyes, a leading intellectual and Mexico's ambassador to Brazil. The senior Fuentes later reached ambassadorial rank, serving in various posts in Panama, Belgium, Italy, and Portugal. See Daniel de Guzmán, *Carlos Fuentes* (New York: Twayne, 1972); *International Who's Who, 1979-80*, p. 411; *Current Biography*, October 1972, p. 10.

6. This statement is well illustrated for Mexico by the career of José Gaos, who came to the capital in 1938, cofounded the Colegio de México, and taught at the National University, the Women's University of Mexico, and Mexico City College. According to Patricia Fagen, after "attracting a small group of Mexican students to

his seminars at the Casa [Colegio de México], he founded what he called the Grupo Hiperión. Through this group, young Mexican scholars, including Leopoldo Zea, Octavio Paz, and Luis González, were encouraged to use existentialist German and Spanish Ortegian thought as a basis for examining the essence of Mexican identity" (*Exiles and Citizens: Spanish Republicans in Mexico* [Austin: University of Texas Press, 1973], pp. 64-65).

7. Fagen, *Exiles and Citizens,* pp. 66, 76. Jaime García Terrés, prominent poet and director of the Fondo de Cultura Económica, considered their importance to be of the greatest magnitude to Mexico. According to him, "Many of the things that exist today in the cultural world would not exist without the Spaniards" (personal interview, Mexico City, 9 August 1978).

8. See my "Un intelectual en la política mexicana: Agustín Yáñez," *Relaciones* 2 (Summer 1981):137-162.

9. Smith, *Labyrinths of Power,* p. 6.

10. E. Bradford Burns, *The Poverty of Progress: Latin America in the Nineteenth Century* (Berkeley & Los Angeles: University of California Press, 1980), p. 38.

11. Charles Kadushin, *American Intellectual Elite* (Boston: Little, Brown, 1974), pp. 23-34.

12. Guy Benusan, "Review of Claes Geijerstam, *Popular Music in Mexico,"* *Latin American Research Review* 15, no. 1 (1980):263.

13. Lewis A. Coser, "The Differing Roles of Intellectuals in Contemporary France, England and America" (Paper presented at the Symposium on Sociology of the Intellectual, Buenos Aires, 3-5 July 1967), p. 5; and Jane Kramer, "A Reporter in Europe," The *New Yorker,* 30 June 1980, p. 42.

14. Coser, "The Differing Roles of Intellectuals," p. 6.

15. Based on an examination of the two papers for July 1980. Typical is the 21 July 1980 issue, in which *Excélsior* devoted 6.5 pages of a 62-page paper to cultural topics, whereas *El Occidental,* in a 52-page edition, devoted only one-fourth page.

16. Personal interview with Manuel Rodríguez Lapuente, Guadalajara, 22 July 1980.

17. Personal interview with Ignacio Arriola Haro, director of theater at the University of Guadalajara, 28 July 1980.

18. Only nine galleries, defined very broadly, appeared in the 1980 telephone book for Guadalajara, with a population of three million, and there is not much to most of those listed. A theater company does not exist in Guadalajara, nor are there any state institutions comparable to the government-sponsored National College in Mexico City, which recognizes and supports intellectuals in their creative activities (personal interview with Carmen Castañeda, director of the Casa de Cultura, Guadalajara, 2 July 1980, and with Manuel Rodríguez Lapuente, 22 July 1980).

19. Personal interview with Guillermo García Oropeza, Guadalajara, 10 July 1980.

20. Personal interview with Juan López, Guadalajara, 14 July 1980.

21. Carlos Landeros, "En Madrid con las dos Elenas," *Siempre,* 6 August 1980, p. 70.

22. Orlando Fals Borda, "The Negation of Sociology and its Promise: Perspectives of Social Science in Latin America Today," *Latin American Research Review* 15, no. 1 (1980):163.

23. Lewis Coser believes that the decentralization of American intellectuals, in contrast with the centralization of English intellectuals in London, is more conducive to creative unrest and the emergence of "truly distinctive intellectual departures than the bland establishmentarianism of its British counterpart" ("The Differing Roles of Intellectuals," p. 10).

24. Roderic A. Camp, *Mexico's Leaders: Their Education and Recruitment* (Tucson: University of Arizona Press, 1980), p. 145.

25. Coser, "The Differing Roles of Intellectuals," p. 6.

26. Enrique Krauze, "The Intellectual as Cultural Entrepreneur, the Case of Daniel Cosío Villegas" (Paper presented at the International Symposium on Intellectuals as Agents of Change in Mexico and Latin America, Central College, Pella, Iowa, 19-20 October 1980), p. 8.

27. Nelson Polsby, *Community Power and Political Theory* (New Haven: Yale University Press, 1974), p. 106.

28. Smith, *Labyrinths of Power*, pp. 13-14.

29. Roderic A. Camp, *La formación de un gobernante: La socialización de los líderes políticos en México post-revolucionario* (Mexico City: Fondo de Cultura Económica, 1981), p. 47ff.

30. Coser, "The Differing Roles of Intellectuals," p. 7; Stuart Samuels, "English Intellectuals and Politics in the 1930s," in *On Intellectuals: Theoretical Case Studies*, ed. Philip Rieff (New York: Doubleday, 1969), p. 215; and Raymond Aron, *The Opium of the Intellectuals* (New York: Doubleday, 1957), p. 213.

31. Theda Skocpol, *States and Social Revolutions* (Cambridge: At the University Press, 1979), p. 165.

32. Aron, *The Opium of the Intellectuals,* p. 210.

33. Rosalio Wences Reza, *El movimiento estudiantil y los problemas nacionales* (Mexico City: Nuestro Tiempo, 1971), pp. 124-125.

34. Camp, *La formación de un gobernante,* chap. 2.

35. James D. Cockcroft, *Intellectual Precursors of the Mexican Revolution, 1900-1913,* Latin American Monographs, no. 14 (Austin: University of Texas Press, 1968), pp. 87-88.

36. Charles Kadushin, *American Intellectual Elite* (Boston: Little, Brown, 1974), p. 26. For further evidence of this, see Frank Bonilla's study of a group of intellectuals during the 1960s, "Un Babbit renuente," in *Los intelectuales políticos*, ed. Juan F. Marsal (Buenos Aires: Ediciones Nueva Visión, 1971), p. 299, in which he found that 94 percent of his sample of Mexican intellectuals came from middle- and upper-class families.

37. In a recent study of scientists, Larissa Lomnitz found that 83 percent were from middle-class or well-to-do families ("Organizational Structure of a Mexican Research Institute [Unpublished, 1980], p. 16).

38. Personal interview with Arturo Warman, Mexico City, 22 August 1978.

39. Personal letter to me from Martha Robles, Mexico City, 4 June 1978. For additional biographical information about her career, see *Excélsior*, 3 February 1980, p. 14B, and Jesús Silva Herzog, *Biografías de amigos* (Mexico City: Cuadernos Americanos, 1980), pp. 338-340.

40. In all of my data concerning relatives, I have included only the following as kinship ties: sanguinal kin (uncles and aunts, parents, grandparents, children); and

fictive kin (spouses, brothers-in-law, sisters-in-law, sons-in-law, and daughters-in-law). The family background interviews referred to in this sentence were confined only to parents and grandparents.

41. I obtained the information for the Sierra family from numerous biographical sources and from personal letters from Santiago X. Sierra, 25 October 1974; and a personal interview with Cristina Barros de Stivalet, Mexico City, 3 August 1978.

42. I obtained information for the Azuela family from numerous biographical sources and a personal interview with Mariano Azuela, Jr., Mexico City, 31 May 1978; a personal letter from Salvador Azuela, Mexico City, 14 July 1974; and a personal interview with Salvador Azuela, Mexico City, 26 June 1975.

43. Smith, *Labyrinths of Power*, p. 79.

44. Carl Leiden and Karl M. Schmitt, *The Politics of Violence: Revolution in the Modern World* (Englewood Cliffs, N.J.: Prentice-Hall, 1968), p. 135.

45. Mark Wasserman, in his examination of the regional groups in the northern state of Chihuahua, concluded that "while the Revolution, most assuredly, spawned new political and economic elites, these elites often had close family ties to the old Porfirian elite" ("Patterns of Family Alliances in the Mexican Revolution: The Case of Chihuahua" [Paper presented to the Annual Meeting of the American Historical Association, Washington, D.C., 1980], p. 2).

46. Personal interview with Víctor Manuel Villaseñor, Mexico City, 22 May 1978; Víctor Manuel Villaseñor, *Memorias de un hombre de izquierda*, 2 vols. (Mexico City: Grijalbo, 1976).

47. Jesús Silva Herzog, *El pensamiento económico, social y político de México, 1810-1964* (Mexico City: Instituto Mexicano de Investigaciones Económicas, 1967), p. 624.

48. Other Mexican intellectuals who were prominent after 1920 and whose parents or grandparents were supporters of Juárez or Lerdo include Antonio Díaz Soto y Gama, Víctor Manuel Villaseñor, Alberto Vázquez del Mercado, José Vasconcelos, and José C. Valadez.

49. Enrique Krauze, *Caudillos culturales en la revolución mexicana* (Mexico City: Siglo XXI, 1976), p. 97; and idem, *Historia de la revolución mexicana, 1924-1928, la reconstrucción económica* (Mexico City: Colegio de México, 1977), p. 295.

50. David Burg, "Observations on Soviet University Students," in *The Russian Intelligentsia*, ed. Richard Pipes (New York: Columbia University Press, 1961), p. 80.

51. C. Wright Mills, *The Power Elite* (New York: Oxford University Press, 1959), p. 10.

52. For the purposes of these data, only those who were brothers-sisters, mothers-fathers, sons-daughters, uncles-aunts, nephews-nieces, or grandfathers-grandmothers were considered to be "related." Anthony Leeds found these kinship linkages to be most common in his study in Brazil: "Brazilian Careers and Social Structure," *American Anthropologist* 66 (December 1964):1331.

53. Camp, *Mexico's Leaders*, p. 70ff.

54. Ibid., p. 96.

55. Ibid., p. 54.

56. Alberto J. Pani, *Apuntes autobiográficos*, vol. 1 (Mexico City: Librería Manuel Porrúa, 1951), p. 33.

57. For example, Gildardo Magaña, precursor of the 1910 Revolution, a

Zapatista, governor of Michoacán from 1936 to 1939 and precandidate for president of Mexico in 1939, studied at the Colegio de Jacona Seminary in Zamora, Michoacán.

58. Roderic A. Camp, "University Environment and Socialization: The Case of Mexican Politicians," *History of Education Quarterly* 20 (Fall 1980):313-335. In separate interviews, both Agustín Yáñez, who attended a seminary, and Martín Luis Guzmán made definite references to this educational-environmental influence (personal interview with Agustín Yáñez, Mexico City, 22 August 1978, and with Martín Luis Guzmán, Mexico City, 21 October 1976).

59. None of the prominent musicians or artists in my sample held high-level political offices, although many earned their living by holding positions in government-supported agencies. Artists were very involved politically, especially during the first three decades of this century, but interestingly, when so involved, their activities universally were confined to opposition movements or out groups, generally of the political Left. Although artists in many societies, in temperament and behavior, seem to be antiestablishment, the explanation for this distinct political pattern in Mexico may in part be their early education in an institution separate from that of other intellectual and political leaders. As a distinctive subgroup, artists need further investigation and comparisons with other groups.

60. Kadushin, *American Intellectual Elite*, p. 20.

61. Clarence H. Haring, "The University in Latin American Life and Culture," in *Responsible Freedom in the Americas*, ed. Angel del Río (New York: Doubleday, 1955), p. 119.

6: Career Patterns

1. Charles Kadushin, *American Intellectual Elite* (Boston: Little, Brown, 1974), p. 5.

2. William S. Ackroyd, "Civil-Military Relations in Mexico: A Study of Mexican Military Perceptions and Behavior" (Paper presented at the Rocky Mountain States Conference on Latin American Studies, Las Cruces, New Mexico, 1980).

3. Lyle N. McAlister, *The Military in Latin American Socio-political Evolution: Four Case Studies* (Washington, D.C.: Center for Research in Social Systems, 1970); and Roderic A. Camp, *Mexico's Leaders: Their Education and Recruitment* (Tucson: University of Arizona Press, 1980).

4. Camp, *Mexico's Leaders*, p. 77ff.

5. Personal interview with Manuel Becerra Acosta, Mexico City, 26 July 1978.

6. Beatriz Reyes Nevares, *The Mexican Cinema: Interviews with Thirteen Directors* (Albuquerque: University of New Mexico Press, 1976), p. 91.

7. Frederick Turner, *The Dynamic of Mexican Nationalism* (Chapel Hill: University of North Carolina Press, 1968), p. 281.

8. Interview with singers Anthar and Margarita Ponce in Roberto E. Ponce, "La música es también una actitud política," *Excélsior*, 8 June 1978, p. 1B.

9. David López Alonso, *Manuel M. Ponce* (Mexico City: Ediciones Botas, 1971), pp. 6-10. Ponce's great-nephew, Antonio Ponce, is a prominent nuclear physicist: see *Uno Más Uno*, 14 July 1980, p. 1.

10. Juan F. Marsal, "Los ensayistas socio-políticos de Argentina y México (aportes para el estudio de sus roles, su ideología y su acción política)," Working paper, Instituto Torcuato di Tella (Buenos Aires, September 1969), p. 10.

11. Personal interview with Father Daniel Olmedo, Mexico City, 25 July 1978.

12. Larissa Lomnitz, "Organizational Structure of a Mexican Research Institute" (Unpublished, 1980), p. 6.

13. Talcott Parsons, "The 'Intellectual': A Special Role Category," in *On Intellectuals: Theoretical Case Studies*, ed. Philip Rieff (New York: Doubleday, 1969), p. 16.

14. Bernardo A. Houssay, "Academic Freedom and Scientific Research in Latin America," in *Responsible Freedom in the Americas*, ed. Angel del Río (New York: Doubleday, 1955), p. 149.

15. Patricia Holt, "Publishing in Mexico, Its Time Has Come," *Publishers' Weekly* 207, no. 16 (25 April 1980):43-44.

16. Charles Davy, citing C. P. Snow in *Towards a Third Culture* (London: Faber & Faber, 1961), pp. 11-12.

17. Larissa Lomnitz, "Anthropology and Development in Latin America" (Paper presented at the Tenth International Congress of Anthropological and Ethnological Sciences, Ranchi, India, December 1978), p. 13.

18. See, for example, tables 2, 3, and 4.

19. Kadushin, *American Intellectual Elite*, p. 21.

20. Personal interview with Arturo Warman, Mexico City, 22 August 1978.

21. Larissa Lomnitz, "Organizational Structure of a Mexican Research Institute," p. 18. In another study, of biomedical scientists, Larissa Lomnitz and Jacqueline Fortes found that most of them received their graduate training abroad, in the United States: "Socialization of Scientists: The Ideal Model" (Unpublished, 1980), p. 4.

22. Cinna Lomnitz, "Science and Social Change in Latin America" (Paper presented at the International Symposium on Intellectuals as Agents of Change in Mexico and Latin America, Central College, Pella, Iowa, 19-20 October 1980), p. 10.

23. Kadushin, *American Intellectual Elite*, p. 20.

24. Marsal, "Los ensayistas socio-políticos de Argentina y México," p. 11.

25. Kadushin, *American Intellectual Elite*, p. 36.

26. Clarence Haring, "The University in Latin American Life and Culture," in *Responsible Freedom in the Americas*, ed. Angel del Río (New York: Doubleday, 1955), p. 122.

27. The most successful politician who has taught at the Colegio is Porfirio Muñoz Ledo, who began his teaching career there in 1964. He held cabinet posts in both the Echeverría and López Portillo administrations.

28. Roderic A. Camp, *La formación de un gobernante: La socialización de los líderes políticos en México post-revolucionario* (Mexico City: Fondo de Cultura Económica, 1981).

29. Roderic A. Camp, *Mexico's Leaders*, table 7-3, p. 171.

30. Ibid., table 7-6, p. 176.

31. Kadushin, *American Intellectual Elite*, pp. 20, 33.

32. Enrique Krauze, *Daniel Cosío Villegas: Una biografía intelectual* (Mexico City: Joaquín Mortiz, 1980), p. 280.

33. Personal interview with Carmen Castañeda, Guadalajara, 2 July 1980.

34. Kadushin, *American Intellectual Elite*, p. 340.

35. John Brushwood, "The Creative Writer in the Mexican Intellectual Community" (Paper presented at the International Symposium on Intellectuals as Agents of Change in Mexico and Latin America, Central College, Pella, Iowa, 19-20 October 1980), p. 4.

36. For example, both Jaime Torres Bodet and Agustín Yáñez used their positions in public life to support intellectual publications and projects of other writers. For illustrations from Torres Bodet's life, see his multivolume memoirs, especially *Equinoccio* (Mexico City: Porrúa, 1974). For Yáñez, see my "An Intellectual in Mexican Politics: The Case of Agustín Yáñez," *Relaciones* 2 (Summer 1981):137-162.

37. Ronald Christ, "Talk with Vargas Llosa," *New York Times Book Review*, 9 April 1978, p. 32.

38. Germán Arciniegas, "Intellectuals in the Politics of Latin America," in *Constructive Change in Latin America*, ed. Cole Blasier (Pittsburgh: University of Pittsburgh Press, 1968), p. 165.

39. Personal interview with Pedro Ramírez Vázquez, Mexico City, 19 July 1978.

40. Donald L. Herman, *The Comintern in Mexico* (Washington, D.C.: Public Affairs Press, 1974), p. 71.

41. Alistair Hennessy, "Artists, Intellectuals and Revolution: Recent Books on Mexico," *Journal of Latin American Studies* 3 (May 1971):71.

42. Jorge Alberto Manrique, "El proceso de las artes, 1910-1970," in *Historia General de México*, 1976, Vol. 4 (Mexico City: Colegio de México), p. 293.

43. Hennessy, "Artists, Intellectuals and Revolution," p. 73; and Mary Kay Vaughan, "Education and Class Struggle in the Mexican Revolution," *Latin American Perspectives* 2 (Summer 1975):24.

44. Personal interview with Octavio Paz, Mexico City, 29 June 1978.

45. Personal interview with Abel Quezada, Mexico City, 4 August 1978.

46. Virginia B. Derr, "The Rise of a Middle-Class Tradition in Mexican Art," *Journal of Inter-American Studies* 3 (July 1961):393; Octavio Paz, *The Other Mexico, Critique of the Pyramid* (New York: Grove Press, 1972), p. 49.

47. Derr, "Middle-Class Tradition," p. 396.

48. Letter from Mathias Goeritz to Thomas Messer, in Thomas Messer, *The Emergent Decade: Latin American Painters and Painting in the 1960s* (Ithaca, N.Y.: Cornell University Press, 1966), pp. 147, 159.

49. Manrique, "El proceso de las artes," p. 293.

50. Personal interview with Juan O'Gorman, Mexico City, 6 June 1978.

51. James D. Cockcroft, *Intellectual Precursors of the Mexican Revolution, 1900-1913*, Latin American Monographs, no. 14 (Austin: University of Texas Press, 1968), p. 57.

52. Data are from the *MIBP*, specifically, 29 percent in government, 20 percent in writing and poetry, 17 percent in journalism, 15 percent in education, and 14 percent in art.

53. The decline has been gradual but clear. Of the 151 intellectuals born before 1900, 60 percent had public careers; of the 114 born between 1900 and 1919, 56 percent had similar careers; and of the 66 born after 1920, only 27 percent had such careers.

54. Edward Shils, *The Intellectual between Tradition and Modernity: The Indian Situation* (The Hague: Mouton, 1961), p. 33.

55. For background on his earlier years, see Orlando S. Suárez, *Inventario del muralismo mexicano* (Mexico City: UNAM, 1972), pp. 49-58.

56. Roderic A. Camp, "Un intelectual en la política mexicana: Agustín Yáñez," *Relaciones* 2 (Summer 1981):137-162.

57. Personal interviews with Ignacio Chávez, Mexico City, 15 August 1974, 13 June 1978.

7: Intellectual Mentors and Circles

1. Robert D. Putnam, *The Comparative Study of Political Elites* (Englewood Cliffs, N.J.: Prentice-Hall, 1976), p. 46ff.

2. Charles Kadushin, *American Intellectual Elite* (Boston: Little, Brown, 1974), p. 25.

3. Lewis A. Coser, "The Differing Roles of Intellectuals in Contemporary France, England and America," (Paper presented at the Symposium on Sociology of the Intellectual, Buenos Aires, 3-5 July 1967).

4. Kadushin, *American Intellectual Elite*, p. 52.

5. Henry C. Schmidt, *The Roots of Lo Mexicano: Self and Society in Mexican Thought , 1900-1934* (College Station: Texas A & M Press, 1978), p. 140.

6. Roderic A. Camp, *Mexico's Leaders: Their Education and Recruitment* (Tucson: University of Arizona Press, 1980), p. 7ff; and Peter H. Smith, *Labyrinths of Power: Political Recruitment in Twentieth-Century Mexico* (Princeton: Princeton University Press, 1979).

7. For example, see Edmund Morris's excellent biography *The Rise of Theodore Roosevelt* (New York: Ballantine, 1979), p. 104ff, for the importance of Harvard in this respect.

8. Coser, "The Differing Roles of Intellectuals," p. 7.

9. Personal interviews with José Rogelio Alvarez, Mexico City, 18 July 1978; Pedro Ramírez Vázquez, Mexico City, 19 July 1978; Jesús Reyes Heroles, Mexico City, 18 July 1978; and Jaime García Terrés, Mexico City, 9 August 1978.

10. Bernardo A. Houssay, "Academic Freedom and Scientific Research in Latin America," in *Responsible Freedom in the Americas*, ed. Angel del Río (New York: Doubleday, 1955), p. 150.

11. Larissa Lomnitz, "Organizational Structure of a Mexican Research Institute" (Unpublished, 1980), p. 35.

12. Personal interview with architect Pedro Ramírez Vázquez, Mexico City, 19 July 1978.

13. Coser, "The Differing Roles of Intellectuals," p. 8.

14. Joseph Nocera, "Making it at *The Washington Post*," *Washington Monthly*, January 1979, p. 20.

15. Kadushin, *American Intellectual Elite*, p. 55.

16. *Excélsior*, 16 November 1979, p. 1.

17. Kadushin, *American Intellectual Elite*, p. 25.

18. Richard G. King, *The Provincial Universities of Mexico: An Analysis of Growth and Development* (New York: Praeger, 1971), p. 64.

19. Larissa Lomnitz, "Conflict and Mediation in a Latin American University," *Journal of Inter-American Studies and World Affairs* 19 (August 1977):323.

20. Camp, *Mexico's Leaders*, p. 18ff.

21. Larissa Lomnitz, "Organizational Structure of a Mexican Research Institute," p. 25.

22. Ibid., p. 23.

23. Ibid., p. 27.

24. See my *La formación de un gobernante: La socialización de los líderes políticos en México post-revolucionario* (Mexico City: Fondo de Cultura Económica, 1981).

25. Charles N. Myers, *Education and National Development in Mexico* (Princeton: Princeton University Press, 1965), p. 104.

26. Martin H. Greenberg, *Bureaucracy and Development: A Mexican Case Study* (Lexington, Mass.: D. C. Heath, 1970), p. 100.

27. E. Wight Bakke, "Students on the March: The Cases of Mexico and Colombia," *Sociology of Education* 37 (Spring 1964):203.

28. See Jaime Torres Bodet, "Tiempo de arena," in *Obras Escogidas* (Mexico City: Fondo de Cultura Económica, 1961), pp. 191-386.

29. Personal interviews with Luis Villoro, Mexico City, 20 August 1978; and Cristina Barros de Stivalet, 3 August 1978.

30. Roderic A. Camp, "Un intelectual en la política mexicana: Agustín Yáñez," *Relaciones* 2 (Summer 1981):137-162.

31. Personal letters to me from José Rogelio Alvarez, Mexico City, September 1980; from Emmanuel Palacios, Mexico City, September 1980; and from Raúl Cardiel Reyes, Mexico City, 9 September 1980.

32. José Vasconcelos never taught formally at the National University, although he was called the "Teacher of Youth." This explains why none of his disciples were students and were instead recruited through his academic posts or from his journals. See Schmidt, *The Roots of Lo Mexicano*, p. 122; Richard B. Phillips, "José Vasconcelos and the Mexican Revolution of 1910" (Ph.D. diss., Stanford University, 1953), p. 189; and José Joaquín Blanco, *Se llamaba Vasconcelos* (Mexico City: Fondo de Cultura Económica, 1977), p. 132.

33. Kadushin, *American Intellectual Elite,* p. 63.

34. Ibid., pp. 51, 57.

35. Personal interview with Alfonso Pulido Islas, Mexico City, 18 August 1978.

36. Based on an analysis of those contributors who wrote ten or more essays for *Cuadernos Americanos* from 1942 through 1971.

37. Based on an analysis of those contributors with five or more articles and reviews in *Historia Mexicana* from 1951 through 1971.

38. Personal interview with philosopher Ricardo Guerra, Mexico City, 26 May 1978.

39. Personal interview with Martha Robles, Mexico City, 27 June 1978.

40. Personal interview with Jaime García Terrés, Mexico City, 9 August 1978.

41. Irving Howe, "The New York Intellectuals: A Chronicle and a Critique," *Commentary* 4 (October 1968):30.

42. Ibid., p. 29.

43. Coser, "The Differing Roles of Intellectuals," p. 3.

44. Kadushin, *American Intellectual Elite,* p. 9.

45. Shifra Goldman, *Contemporary Mexican Painting in a Time of Change* (Austin: University of Texas Press, 1981), pp. 64-65.

46. Personal interview with Arturo Warman, Mexico City, 22 August 1978.

47. Selden Rodman, *Mexican Journal* (Carbondale: Southern Illinois University Press, 1958), p. 194.

48. Personal interview with Alberto Vázquez del Mercado, Mexico City, 19 May 1978.

49. Personal interview with Ricardo Guerra, Mexico City, 26 May 1978.

50. Charles A. Hale, "The Científicos as Constitutionalists: Mexico's Great Debate of 1893" (Paper presented at the Latin American Studies Association Meeting, Bloomington, Indiana, 18 October 1980).

51. Blanco, *Se llamaba Vasconcelos*, p. 133.

52. Ibid., p. 57.

53. Larissa Lomnitz, "Organizational Structure of a Mexican Research Institute," p. 35.

54. Ibid., pp. 36-37.

55. Robert Peterson, "Psychological Assumptions Regarding Mexican Elite-Non-Elite Motivation and Behavior: A Critique of North American Scholarly Perceptions and Analyses" (Paper presented at the Fourteenth Annual Meeting of the Southwestern Council on Latin American Studies, Arlington, Texas, 5-7 March 1981).

56. This might be symbolized in Vicente Leñero's label of Julio Scherer García as "the Vatican of our church." See his *Los periodistas* (Mexico City: Joaquín Mortiz, 1978), p. 287.

57. Personal interviews with Arturo Warman, Mexico City, 22 August 1978, and Salvador Elizondo, Mexico City, 4 August 1978.

58. Personal interview with José Joaquín Blanco, Mexico City, 1 August 1978.

59. Personal interview with Guillermo García Oropeza, Guadalajara, 10 July 1980.

60. Personal interview with Rosa Luz Alegría, Mexico City, 7 August 1978.

61. Personal interview with Jaime García Terrés, Mexico City, 9 August 1978.

62. José Vasconcelos, *El desastre* (Mexico City: Jus, 1968), p. 11.

63. *Excélsior*, 27 January 1980, p. 15B.

64. Rodman, *Mexican Journal*, p. 100.

65. Personal interview with Lucio Mendieta y Núñez, Mexico City, 17 May 1978.

66. Personal interview with Agustín Yáñez, Mexico City, 22 August 1978.

67. Kadushin, *American Intellectual Elite*, p. 57.

68. Personal interview with Edmundo O'Gorman, Mexico City, 8 August 1978.

69. As the long-time director of the Center of Mexican Writers, Rulfo does have considerable influence by certifying young writers and aiding them financially with fellowships from this important institution. But he has not personally had disciples or a group.

70. Larissa Lomnitz, "Organizational Structure of a Mexican Research Institute," p. 36.

71. Luis Leal, "Octavio Paz y la novela mexicana," *Revista Interamericana de Bibliografía* 29, nos. 3-4 (1979):310.

72. *Hispano Americano*, 27 February 1978, p. 10.

73. Coser, "The Differing Roles of Intellectuals," p. 4.

74. María Rosa Uría-Santos, "El Ateneo de la Juventud: Su influencia en la vida intelectual de Mexico" (Ph.D. diss., University of Florida, 1965), p. 106.

75. Ibid.

76. Carlos Monsiváis, "Notas sobre la cultura mexicana en el siglo XX," in *Historia general de México* (Mexico City: Colegio de México, 1976), pp. 322-323; and José Vasconcelos, *Ulises criollo* (Mexico City: Editorial Jus, 1978), p. 242.

77. Monsiváis, "Notas sobre la cultura mexicana," p. 324.

78. Phillips, "José Vasconcelos," p. 51; personal interview with Mario de la Cueva, Mexico City, August 9, 1978; Blanco, *Se llamaba Vasconcelos*, p. 42; Gabriel Careaga, *Los intelectuales y la política en México* (Mexico City: Extemporáneos, 1971), p. 49.

79. Enrique Krauze, *Caudillos culturales en la revolución mexicana* (Mexico City: Siglo XXI, 1976).

80. Monsiváis, "Notas sobre la cultura mexicana," p. 364ff; Merlin H. Forster, "The 'Contemporáneos,' 1915-1932: A Study in Twentieth-Century Mexican Letters" (Ph.D. diss., University of Illinois, 1960), pp. 5, 28.

81. Monsiváis, "Notas sobre la cultura mexicana," p. 363.

82. Patricia Fagen, *Exiles and Citizens: Spanish Republicans in Mexico* (Austin: University of Texas Press, 1973), p. 66.

83. Personal interviews with José Rogelio Alvarez, Mexico City, 18 July 1978; Jaime García Terrés, Mexico City, 9 August 1978; and José Joaquín Blanco, Mexico City, 1 August 1978.

84. Personal interview with Hiperión member Ricardo Guerra, Mexico City, 26 May 1978.

85. Personal interview with Hiperión member Luis Villoro, Mexico City, 20 August 1978; also see Monsiváis, "Notas sobre la cultura mexicana," p. 400.

86. Personal interview with José Rogelio Alvarez, Mexico City, 18 July 1978.

87. Careaga, *Los intelectuales,* p. 89.

88. Ibid., pp. 70-71; personal interview with Fernando Zertuche Muñoz, 26 July 1978.

89. Personal interview with Arturo Warman, Mexico City, 22 August 1978.

90. *Política* 1, no. 1 (1 May 1960).

91. Ermilo Abreu Gómez, " 'Política' y la política de los intelectuales," *Política* 5, no. 104 (15 August 1964):26; Carlo Coccioli, "Mexico's Wobbling Left," *Atlas World Press Review*, 9 (February 1965):113.

92. Careaga, *Los intelectuales,* p. 81.

93. Daniel James, "Rumbles on the Mexican Left: The Myth of Lázaro Cárdenas," *New Leader* 44 (30 October 1961):18.

94. Personal interview with Octavio Paz, Mexico City, 4 July 1978.

95. Stanley R. Ross, "La protesta de los intelectuales ante México y su Revolución," *Historia Mexicana* 26, no. 3 (January-March 1977):430.

96. Personal interview with Octavio Paz, Mexico City, 4 July 1978.

97. *Nexos*, no. 1 (January 1978), p. 2.

8: Cultural Academies and Institutions

1. Edward Shils, "Intellectuals, Tradition and the Traditions of Intellectuals: Some Preliminary Considerations," *Daedalus* 101, no. 2 (Summer 1972):25.

2. Personal interview with Enrique Krauze, Mexico City, 28 August 1978.

3. Personal interview with Rosa Luz Alegría, Mexico City, 7 August 1978.

4. Enrique Krauze, *Daniel Cosío Villegas: Una biografía intelectual* (Mexico City: Joaquín Mortiz, 1980).

5. Personal interview with José Rogelio Alvarez, Mexico City, 18 July 1978.

6. Personal interview with Jaime García Terrés, Mexico City, 9 August 1978.

7. "Incremento a la lectura," *Hispano Americano*, 14 July 1980, p. 11.

8. Howard P. Cline, "Librarians and Libraries in the Americas," in *Responsible Freedom in the Americas*, ed. Angel del Río (New York: Doubleday, 1955), p. 324.

9. Personal interviews with José Joaquín Blanco, Mexico City, 1 August 1978, and José Rogelio Alvarez, Mexico City, 18 July 1978.

10. Julián Marías, "The Situation of the Intelligentsia in Spain Today," in *The Russian Intelligentsia*, ed. Richard Pipes (New York: Columbia University Press, 1961), p. 187.

11. Charles Kadushin, *American Intellectual Elite* (Boston: Little, Brown, 1974), p. 340.

12. Krauze, *Daniel Cosío Villegas*, p. 182.

13. Seymour Martin Lipset, "The New Class and the Professoriate," *Society* 16 (January-February 1979):36.

14. Personal interview with José Rogelio Alvarez, Mexico City, 18 July 1978.

15. *Excélsior* 19 August 1980, p. 2B; *Enciclopedia de México*, Vol. 2, p. 453.

16. Heriberto García Rivas, *Historia de la literatura mexicana*, Vol. 4 (Mexico City: Librería de Manuel Porrúa, 1974), p. 594.

17. Edward Shils, *The Intellectual between Tradition and Modernity: The Indian Situation* (The Hague: Mouton, 1961), p. 37.

18. Angela M. Delli Sante, "The Private Sector Business Organizations and International Influence: A Case Study of Mexico," in *Capitalism and the State in U.S.-Latin American Relations*, ed. Richard R. Fagen (Stanford, Cal.: Stanford University Press, 1979), p. 348.

19. Personal interview with José Rogelio Alvarez, Mexico City, 18 July 1978.

20. *Hispano Americano*, 10 September 1979, p. 49.

21. El Colegio Nacional, *Memorias* 1 (1946):8.

22. Personal interview with Alejandro Gómez Arias, Mexico City, 31 May 1978.

23. El Colegio Nacional, *Memorias* 1 (1946):134.

24. For more information about the backgrounds of foreign service leaders, see James D. Cochrane, "Mexico's Secretaries of Foreign Relations, 1935-1974: Career Characteristics," *SELA* 24, no. 4 (March 1981):1-10.

25. *Enciclopedia de México*, Vol. 11, pp. 375-376.

26. Academia de Artes, *Curricula vitárum de los académicos de número* (Mexico City: Academia de Artes, 1977), p. 5.

27. Academia Mexicana de Historia, *Memorias* 1, no. 4 (October-December 1942); vol. 24 (January-February 1965).

28. Ibid. 1, no. 1 (January-March 1942); vol. 9, no. 1 (January-March 1950); vol. 22, no. 3 (July-September 1963); vol. 29, no. 1 (January-March 1970); and Juan B. Iguíniz, "La fundación de la Academia Mexicana de la Historia," *Memorias* 25, no.3 (July-September 1966):315-328.

29. *Enciclopedia de México*, Vol. 10, p. 425.

30. *Proceso*, 15 December 1980, p. 49.

31. Hugh H. Smyth, "Nigerian Elite: Role of Education," *Sociology and Social*

Research 45 (October 1960):71.

32. Kadushin, *American Intellectual Elite*, pp. 15, 339-340.

33. Norman Birnbaum, "Problem of a Knowledge Elite," *Massachusetts Review* 12 (Summer 1971):620-621.

34. Daniel Levy, "El gobierno de las universidades en México," *Foro International* 19, no. 4 (1979):576-599.

35. *Hispano Americano*, 5 May 1980, p. 12.

36. John Britton, "Urban Education and Social Change in the Mexican Revolution, 1931-40," *Journal of Latin American Studies* 5 (November 1973):243.

37. Edward Shils, "Intellectuals, Public Opinion, and Economic Development," *World Politics* 10 (January 1958):247.

38. Seymour Martin Lipset, and David Riesman, *Education and Politics at Harvard* (New York: McGraw-Hill, 1975), p. 8.

39. Francisco Miró Quesada, "The University South and North: The University and Society," *Americas* 12 (December 1960):3.

40. Everett Ladd and Seymour Martin Lipset, *The Divided Academy: Professors and Politics* (New York: W. W. Norton, 1976), p. 46.

41. A. H. Halsey and Martin Trow, *The British Academics* (Cambridge: Harvard University Press, 1971), p. 403.

42. Ladd and Lipset, *The Divided Academy*, p. 26.

43. Ibid., pp. 77-78.

44. Ibid., p. 76.

45. Alvin W. Gouldner, *The Dialectic of Ideology and Technology* (New York: Seabury Press, 1976), p. 188; also see Ladd and Lipset, *The Divided Academy*, p. 73, for additional evidence.

46. Juan F. Marsal, "Los ensayistas socio-políticos de Argentina y México (aportes para el estudio de sus roles, su ideología y su acción política)," Working paper, Instituto Torcuato di Tella, Buenos Aires, September 1969.

47. Personal interview with Arturo Warman, Mexico City, 10 August 1978.

48. See Johan Galtung, "Development and Intellectual Styles: Some Notes on the Case of the Lawyer" (Paper presented at the International Conference on Comparative Social Research in Developing Countries, Buenos Aires, 9-15 September 1964), p. 7.

49. Ernesto Schiefelbein and M. C. Grossi, "Differences between the United States and Latin American Premises about Education and Work," in Council on Higher Education in the American Republics, *Education and Work: A Symposium* (New York: Institute of International Education, 1979), p. 18.

50. Michael E. Burke, "The University of Mexico and the Revolution, 1910-1940," *The Americas* 34 (October 1977):260.

51. Britton, "Urban Education and Social Change," p. 236; and Daniel C. Levy, "Comparative Perspectives on Academic Governance in Mexico" (Working paper, Yale Higher Education Research Group, July 1977), p. 3.

52. David Barkin, "Education and Class Structure: The Dynamics of Social Control in Mexico," *Politics and Society* 5, no. 2 (1975):187.

53. Ladd and Lipset, *The Divided Academy*, pp. 88-89; and Roderic A. Camp, *Mexico's Leaders: Their Education and Recruitment* (Tucson: University of Arizona Press, 1980), p. 170ff.

54. Barkin, "Education and Class Structure," pp. 187, 189.

55. Harold Perkin, "British Society and Higher Education" (Working paper, Yale Higher Education Research Group, October 1977), p. 26.

56. Larissa Lomnitz, "The Latin American University: Breeding Ground of the New State Elites" (Paper presented at the American Association of Anthropological Sciences, Houston, Texas, 3-6 January 1979), p. 3.

57. Personal interview Andrés Serra Rojas, Mexico City, 8 June 1978.

58. T. S. Eliot, "The Man of Letters and the Future of Europe," in *The Intellectuals: A Controversial Portrait*, ed. George B. De Huszar (Glencoe, Ill.: Free Press, 1960), p. 259.

59. Personal interview with Ignacio Arriola Haro, Guadalajara, 28 July 1980.

60. Glen Dealy, *The Public Man: An Interpretation of Latin American and Other Catholic Countries* (Amherst: University of Massachusetts Press, 1977), p. 28.

61. Larissa Lomnitz, "Latin American University," p. 5; and Juan Hernández Luna, "Sobre la fundación de la Universidad Nacional: Antonio Caso vs. Agustín Aragón," *Historia Mexicana* 16, no. 3 (January-March 1967):368.

62. Henry C. Schmidt, *The Roots of Lo Mexicano: Self and Society in Mexican Thought, 1900-1934* (College Station: Texas A & M University Press, 1978), p. 73.

63. Roderic A. Camp, *La formación de un gobernante: La socialización de los líderes políticos en México post-revolucionario* (Mexico City: Fondo de Cultura Económica, 1981).

64. Larissa Lomnitz, "Latin American University," p. 8.

65. Arthur Liebman, Kenneth Walker, and Myron Glazer, *Latin American University Students: A Six Nation Study* (Cambridge: Harvard University Press, 1972), pp. 178, 184.

66. Levy, "Comparative Perspectives," p. 6.

67. *Hispano Americano*, 5 May 1980, p. 12.

68. Van R. Whiting, Jr., "Political and Institutional Aspects of Technology Transfer in Mexico" (Unpublished, 1980), p. 53.

69. Levy, "Comparative Perspectives," p. 7.

70. Francisco Ortiz Pinchetti, "El Grupo Monterrey crea sus propias fábricas de hombres," *Proceso*, 23 June 1980, pp. 10, 12. In Monterrey, where privately supported schools are expanding more rapidly than anywhere else in Mexico, representatives of the major industrial groups control boards of education. Typical of one type of private school is the University of Monterrey, whose students come from the following socioeconomic background: 53 percent from parents who are industrialists; 24 percent from white-collar workers; 22 percent from self-employed workers; and 2 percent from blue-collar parents. The tuition is substantial, but only 14 percent receive scholarships.

71. Fernando Uricoechea, *Intelectuales y desarrollo en América Latina* (Buenos Aires: Centro Editor de América Latina, 1969), pp. 17-18.

72. Levy, "Comparative Perspectives," pp. 27, 35.

73. Daniel Levy, *University and Government in Mexico: Autonomy in an Authoritarian Regime* (New York: Praeger, 1979), p. 97.

74. Larissa Lomnitz, "The Exercise of Power in a Latin American University,"

(Paper presented at the Symposium on the Exercise of Power in Complex Organizations, Burg Wartenstein, 19-27 July 1980), p. 27.

75. Levy, "Comparative Perspectives," p. 13. For more details about the relationship between the rector and the president of Mexico, see Jesús Silva Herzog, *Una historia de la Universidad de México y sus problemas* (Mexico City: Siglo XXI, 1974), p. 96.

76. Victoria Lerner, *La educación socialista* (Mexico City: Colegio de México, 1979), p. 49.

77. Burke, "University of Mexico," p. 270.

78. Levy, *University and Government in Mexico*, p. 132.

79. Javier Barros Sierra and Gastón García Cantú, *1968* (Mexico City: Siglo XXI, 1976), p. 99.

80. Levy, "Limits on Government Financial Control of the University: Mexico" (Working paper, Yale Higher Education Research Group, December 1977), p. 7.

81. Yoram Shapira, "Mexico, the Impact of the 1968 Student Protest on Echeverría's Reformism," *Journal of Inter-American Studies and World Affairs* 19 (November 1977):568.

82. Colegio de México, *El Colegio de México* (Mexico City,1976), p. 5.

83. Krauze, *Daniel Cosío Villegas*, pp. 98, 100.

84. Fernando Ortega Pizarro, "El Colegio de México," *Proceso*, 22 July 1980, p. 24.

85. Krauze, *Daniel Cosío Villegas*, pp. 101, 214.

86. "Mexico's El Colegio: From Refugee to Respected Graduate Institution," *The Chronicle of Higher Education*, 16 June 1980, p. 14.

87. Daniel Cosío Villegas, *Memorias* (Mexico City: Joaquín Mortiz, 1976), pp. 254-255.

88. Personal interview with Arturo Warman, Mexico City, 10 August 1978.

9: Media, Censorship, and Intellectual Life

1. Richard Fagen and William Tuohy, *Politics and Privilege in a Mexican City* (Stanford, Cal.: Stanford University Press, 1972), p. 27.

2. Susan K. Purcell and John Purcell, "State and Society in Mexico," *World Politics* 32 (January 1980):7.

3. Evelyn P. Stevens, *Protest and Response in Mexico* (Cambridge, Mass.: MIT Press, 1974), p. 283.

4. I have witnessed such exchanges, wherein future favors are promised during telephone conversations between government officials.

5. Stevens, *Protest and Response in Mexico*, p. 26.

6. Carlos Monsiváis, "La ofensiva ideológica de la derecha," in *México, hoy*, ed. Pablo González Casanova and Enrique Florescano (Mexico City: Siglo XXI, 1979), p. 321.

7. Ibid., p. 322.

8. Albert L. Hester and Richard R. Cole, eds., *Mass Communication in Mexico* (Brookings, S.D.: Association for Education in Journalism, 1975), p. 39.

9. This accounts for the surprising popularity of my own reference work *Mexican Political Biographies, 1935-1975* in Mexico. Many of the politicians I

interviewed had acquired a copy of this book, and several explained to me that they made useful gifts to friends.

10. Van Whiting, Jr., "Political and Institutional Aspects of Technology Transfer in Mexico" (Unpublished, 1980), p. 47.

11. For example, there was rarely an issue of *Tiempo* that did not have a captioned photograph of Miguel Alemán performing some task as director of the National Tourism Council, something not regularly covered in other media sources.

12. Mariano Azuela, *Two Novels of Mexico* (Berkeley & Los Angeles: University of California Press, 1965), p. xxi.

13. John Brushwood, "Literary Periods in Twentieth-Century Mexico: The Transformation of Reality," in *Contemporary Mexico*, ed. James W. Wilkie et al. (Los Angeles: UCLA Latin American Center, 1976), p. 679.

14. The same reaction was true of politicians. See my "University Environment and Socialization: The Case of Mexican Politicians," *History of Education Quarterly* 20 (Fall 1980):313-335.

15. Roderic A. Camp, "The Elitelore of Mexico's Revolutionary Family," *Journal of Latin American Lore* 4, no. 2 (1978):149-182.

16. Lewis A. Coser, "The Intellectual as Celebrity,"*Dissent* 20 (Winter 1973):46.

17. Ibid., pp. 46-47, 49.

18. Charles Kadushin, *American Intellectual Elite* (Boston: Little, Brown, 1974), p. 8.

19. Joseph Nocera, "Making it at *The Washington Post*," *Washington Monthly*, January 1979, p. 20.

20. Robert N. Pierce, *Keeping the Flame: Media and Government in Latin America* (New York: Hastings House, 1979), p. 97.

21. Stevens, *Protest and Response in Mexico*, p. 32.

22. Gabriel Almond and Sidney Verba, *The Civic Culture: Political Attitudes and Democracy in Five Nations* (Princeton: Princeton University Press, 1963), p. 56; although in Mexico City, among the urban poor, Wayne Cornelius found these figures to be about double. See his *Politics and the Migrant Poor in Mexico City* (Stanford, Cal.: Stanford University Press, 1975), p. 82.

23. Lloyd E. Sommerlad, *The Press in Developing Countries* (Sydney: Sydney University Press, 1966), p. 2.

24. Cámara Nacional de la Industria Editorial, *Informe del Sr. Fernando Rodríguez Díaz* (Mexico City, 1969), p. 17.

25. Richard Cole, "The Mass Media of Mexico: Ownership and Control" (Ph.D. diss., University of Minnesota, 1972), p. 105.

26. Marvin Alisky, "Growth of Newspapers in Mexico's Provinces,"*Journalism Quarterly* 37 (Winter 1960):79.

27. Regina Jiménez de Ottalengo, "El periódico mexicano, su situación social y sus fuentes de información," *Revista Mexicana de Sociología* 36, no. 4 (1974):778.

28. Pierce, *Keeping the Flame*, p. 105.

29. Cole, "Mass Media of Mexico," p. 155.

30. *Excélsior*, 12 July 1980, p. 2B.

31. Carlo Coccioli, "Mexico's Wobbling Left," *Atlas World Press Review* 9 (February 1965):114.

32. Stevens, *Protest and Response in Mexico*, p. 42.

33. Pierce, *Keeping the Flame*, p. 106.

34. Cole, "The Mexican Press System: Aspects of Growth, Control and Censorship," *Gazette* 21, no. 2 (1975):69.

35. Pierce, *Keeping the Flame*, p. 109.

36. Víctor Bernal Sahagún, *Anatomía de la publicidad* (Mexico City: Nuestro Tiempo, 1974), p. 161.

37. Personal interview with Enrique Krauze, managing editor, *Vuelta*, Mexico City, 28 August 1978.

38. See Ray E. Hiebert et al., *Mass Media: An Introduction to Modern Communications* (New York: David McKay, 1974), p. 227.

39. Personal interview with Rosa Luz Alegría, the first woman in Mexico's history to reach a cabinet post, Mexico City, 7 August 1978.

40. Vicente Leñero, *Los periodistas* (Mexico City: Joaquín Mortiz, 1978), p. 303.

41. Roderic A. Camp, *The Role of Economists in Policy-making: A Comparative Case Study of Mexico and the United States* (Tucson: University of Arizona Press, 1977).

42. Lewis A. Coser, *Men of Ideas: A Sociologist's View* (New York: Free Press, 1965), p. 9.

43. Personal interview with Luis Villoro, Mexico City, 20 August 1978.

44. Fernando Peñalosa, *The Mexican Book Industry* (New York: Scarecrow Press, 1957), p. 39.

45. "Incremento a la lectura," *Hispano Americano*, 14 July 1980, pp. 11-12.

46. Harold Hinds, Jr., "Literatura popular: Kalimán," *Hispamérica* 6, no. 18 (1977):31-32.

47. Pierce, *Keeping the Flame*, p. 102. Political cartoons have generally provided the harshest political and social criticism published in Mexico, even before the Revolution of 1910.

48. Víctor Alba, "The Mexican Revolution and the Cartoon," *Comparative Studies in Society and History* 9 (January 1967):130-131.

49. Hiebert, *Mass Media*, p. 203.

50. Antonio Acevedo Escobedo, *Entre prensas anda el jugo* (Mexico City: Seminario de Cultura Económica, 1967), pp. 111-112.

51. Peñalosa, *Mexican Book Industry*, pp. 25, 27.

52. Patricia Holt, "Publishing in Mexico, Its Time Has Come," *Publishers' Weekly* 207, no. 16 (25 April 1980):34.

53. Lewis A. Coser, "The Differing Roles of Intellectuals in Contemporary France, England and America" (Paper presented at the Symposium on Sociology of the Intellectual, Buenos Aires, July 1967), p. 5.

54. See Alda Reboredo, "El criterio para escoger un nuevo libro y publicarlo en *Joaquín Mortiz*, es humanístico dice Diez-Canedo," *Uno Más Uno*, 9 July 1980, p. 16.

55. *Excélsior*, 30 March 1979, p. 7.

56. Jacobo Morett, "Con tinta negra," *Teleguía*, 27 July 1978, p. 87.

57. Enrique Krauze, *Daniel Cosío Villegas: Una biografía intelectual* (Mexico City: Joaquín Mortiz, 1980), p. 78.

58. Enrique Krauze, "Daniel Cosío Villegas, el empresario cultural," *Plural* 5, no. 55 (April 1976):9. Over the years, the Fondo's board of governors shows the interrelationship between the cultural and political leadership in Mexican intellectual life (Fondo de Cultura Económica, *Libro conmemorativo del 45 aniversario del Fondo de Cultura Económica* [Mexico City, 1980], pp. 8, 12-13.

59. Krauze, *Daniel Cosío Villegas*, p. 118.

60. Susan Elizabeth Russell, "The Fondo de Cultura Económica: A Mexican Publishing House" (Ph.D. diss., University of Texas, Austin, 1971), p. 6.

61. Octavio Paz, *The Labyrinth of Solitude: Life and Thought in Mexico* (New York: Grove Press, 1961), p. 162.

62. Fondo de Cultura Económica, *Libro conmemorativo*, pp. 113, 124ff.

63. Hiebert, *Mass Media*, p. 196.

64. Reboredo, "El criterio," p. 16.

65. Holt, "Publishing in Mexico," p. 34.

66. Dennis T. Lowry, "Broadcasting's Expanding Social Role in Mexico," *Journalism Quarterly* 46 (Summer 1969):333.

67. Moisés Ochoa Campos, *Reseña histórica de periodismo mexicano* (Mexico City: Porrúa, 1968), p. 165.

68. Stevens, *Protest and Response in Mexico*, pp. 56-57.

69. Ibid., p. 54.

70. Marvin Alisky, "Governmental Mechanisms of Mass Media Control in Mexico" (Paper presented at the Southeast Council on Latin American Studies, Tampa, Florida, April 1979), p. 14.

71. Marvin Alisky, "Radio's Role in Mexico: A First-Hand Survey," *Journalism Quarterly* 31 (Winter 1954):67.

72. Marvin Alisky, "Early Mexican Broadcasting," *Hispanic American Historical Review* 34 (November 1954):520.

73. Arthur S. Banks, ed., *Political Handbook of the World: 1979* (New York: McGraw-Hill, 1979), p. 302.

74. Claes Geijerstam, *Popular Music in Mexico* (Albuquerque: University of New Mexico Press, 1976), p. 110.

75. Bernal Sahagún, *Anatomía de la publicidad*, p. 117.

76. Jorge Alberto Lozoya, "La TV estatal en México: Notas sobre un intento," in *La vida política en México (1970-73)* (Mexico City: Colegio de México, 1974), p. 167.

77. Fátima Fernández Christlieb, "El derecho a la información y los medios de difusión masiva," in *México, hoy*, ed. Pablo González Casanova and Enrique Florescano (Mexico City: Siglo XXI, 1979), p. 345.

78. José González Pedrero, "La responsabilidad social de los medios de comunicación de masas," in *Los medios de comunicación de masas en México* (Mexico City: UNAM, 1969), p. 75.

79. Regina Jiménez de Ottalengo and Georgina Paulín de Siade, "La comunicación colectiva en México y la dependencia," *Revista Mexicana de Sociología* 34 (1972):604.

80. Personal interview with Guillermo García Oropeza, Guadalajara, 10 July 1980.

81. George T. Kurian, *The Book of World Rankings*, pp. 353-354.

82. Frederick Turner, *The Dynamic of Mexican Nationalism* (Chapel Hill: University of North Carolina Press, 1968), pp. 299-300.

83. Alfonso Pulido Islas, *La industria cinematográfica de México* (Mexico City: Talleres Gráficos de la Nación, 1939), pp. 66-67, 83.

84. Bernal Sahagún, *Anatomía de la publicidad*, p. 162.

85. Pierce, *Keeping the Flame*, p. 111.

86. Beatriz Reyes Nevares, *The Mexican Cinema: Interviews with Thirteen Directors* (Albuquerque: University of New Mexico Press, 1976), p. 168.

87. Reyes Nevares, *The Mexican Cinema*, pp. 4, 28, 38, 106, 144.

88. Jorge Ayala Blanco, *La aventura del cine mexicano* (Mexico City: Ediciones Era, 1968).

89. Maxwell E. McCombs and Lee B. Becker, *Using Mass Communication Theory* (New York: Prentice-Hall, 1979), p. 102.

90. Cole, "Mexican Press System," p. 67.

91. José Vasconcelos, *El desastre* (Mexico City: Jus, 1968), p. 181.

92. Ernest Gruening, *Mexico and Its Heritage* (New York: D. Appleton-Century, 1928), p. 664.

93. Jean Meyer et al., *Historia de la revolución mexicana, 1924-1928: Estado y sociedad con Calles* (Mexico City: Colegio de México, 1977), p. 105.

94. José Vasconcelos, *El proconsulado* (Mexico City: Jus, 1978), pp. 17, 89.

95. Manuel Mesa Andraca, "Ha muerto Alberto Vázquez del Mercado, un guerrerense ejemplar," *Siempre*, 6 August 1980, p. 62.

96. Personal interview, Mexico City, 19 May 1978.

97. Cole, "Mass Media of Mexico," p. 45.

98. As told to me by an intellectual who was a personal friend of Daniel Cosío Villegas.

99. Leñero, *Los periodistas*, pp. 310, 342.

100. Krauze, *Daniel Cosío Villegas*, p. 261.

101. Margarita Michelena, "Qué pasa allí?, sucesiones y secesiones," *Excélsior*, 8 July 1980, p. 7A.

102. Erling H. Erlandson, "The Press in Mexico: Past, Present, and Future," *Journalism Quarterly* 41 (Spring 1964), p. 235.

103. Leñero, *Los periodistas*, pp. 265, 302.

104. See Daniel Cosío Villegas, *Memorias* (Mexico City: Joaquín Mortiz, 1976), p. 293ff.

105. David Ronfeldt and William S. Tuohy, "Political Control and the Recruitment of Middle-Level Elites in Mexico: An Example from Agrarian Politics," *Western Political Quarterly* 22, no. 2 (June 1969):368.

106. Vasconcelos, *El desastre*, p. 243.

107. Vasconcelos, *El proconsulado*, p. 171.

108. Kadushin, *American Intellectual Elite*, p. 56.

109. Suzannah Lessard, "Kennedy's Woman Problem, Women's Kennedy Problem," *Washington Monthly*, December 1979, p. 10.

110. Pierce, *Keeping the Flame*, pp. 104-105.

111. Personal interview with Abel Quezada, Mexico City, 4 August 1978.

112. Manuel Durán, "The Beleaguered Latin American Intellectual: A Success Story," *Ventures* 7 (Fall 1967):60.

> 113. Robert Bruce Underwood, "A Survey of Contemporary Newspapers of Mexico" (Ph.D. diss., University of Missouri, 1965), p. 118.

114. Personal interview with a prominent Mexican poet and author, Mexico City, 4 August 1978.

115. Philip Russell, *Mexico in Transition* (Austin, Tex.: Colorado River Press, 1977), p. 141.

116. Gruening, *Mexico and Its Heritage*, p. 374.

117. Ibid., pp. 356-357.

118. Leñero, *Los periodistas*, p. 156.

119. Underwood, "A Survey of Contemporary Newspapers," p. 352.

120. Ronfeldt and Touhy, "Political Control and Recruitment," p. 367.

121. Alisky, "Governmental Mechanisms," pp. 8, 11.

122. George Biddle, *An American Artist's Story* (Boston: Little, Brown, 1939), pp. 264-265; and Jean Charlot, *The Mexican Mural Renaissance, 1920-25* (New Haven: Yale University Press, 1963), pp. 291-293.

123. Diego Rivera, *My Art, My Life* (New York: Harcourt, Brace, 1960), pp. 274-275.

124. Betty Kirk, *Covering the Mexican Front* (Norman: University of Oklahoma Press, 1942), pp. 154-155.

125. James W. Wilkie, "El complejo militar-industrial en México durante la década de 1930: Diálogo con el general Juan Andreu Almazán," *Revista Mexicana de Ciencia Política* 20 (July-September 1974):63ff.

126. Leñero, *Los periodistas,* pp. 77, 127.

127. Mario Guerra Leal, *La grilla* (Mexico City: Diana, 1978), pp. 34, 138-139.

128. Cosío Villegas, *Memorias*, p. 284.

129. Ayala Blanco, *La aventura del cine mexicano*, p. 133.

130. Alberto J. Pani, *Apuntes autobiográficos*, Vol. 2 (Mexico City: Librería Manuel Porrúa, 1951), pp. 15-16.

131. Leñero, *Los periodistas*, pp. 120-121, 304.

132. Pierce, *Keeping the Flame*, pp. 106-107.

133. Alisky, "Governmental Mechanisms," p. 2.

134. Cole, "The Mass Media of Mexico," p. 71.

135. Erlandson, "The Press in Mexico," p. 235.

136. Alisky, "Governmental Mechanisms," pp. 7-8.

137. Turner, *The Dynamic of Mexican Nationalism*, p. 299.

138. John Eugene Harley, *World-Wide Influence of the Cinema: A Study of Official Censorship and the International Cultural Aspects of Motion Pictures* (Los Angeles: University of Southern California Press, 1940), pp. 163-167. Harley includes numerous additional examples.

139. Tomme Clark Call, *Mexican Venture* (New York: Oxford University Press, 1953), p. 203.

140. Alisky, "Governmental Mechanisms," p. 13.

141. Pablo G. Macías, *Octubre sangriento en Morelia* (Morelia: Acasim, 1968), p. 92, 307.

142. *Excélsior*, 28 March 1979, p. 15.

143. Leñero, *Los periodistas*, pp. 74, 90, 119-120, 264.

144. Cosío Villegas, *Memorias*, pp. 261-262. Of course, American presidents have done this. The difference, however, lies in the influence the Mexican president exerts over the political system and the media.

145. *New York Times*, 10 April 1947, p. 5; *Excélsior*, 11 November 1979, p. 4; *Hispano Americano*, 21 July 1980, pp. 41-42.

146. Carlos Loret de Mola, *Los caciques* (Mexico City: Grijalbo, 1979), pp. 26-27.

147. Arturo Martínez Náteras, "Bienvenido, Mario," *Excélsior*, 3 July 1980, p. 7A.

148. Alfonso Argudín, "Mexican Press Is Attaining Influence and Stability," *Journalism Quarterly* 24 (June 1947):138.

149. Roderic A. Camp, "The Elitelore of Mexico's Revolutionary Family," *Journal of Latin American Lore* 4, no. 2 (1978):177-179.

150. Paz, *The Other Mexico*, p. 30.

151. Roderic A. Camp, "Intellectuals, Agents of Change in Mexico?" *Journal of Inter-American Studies and World Affairs* 23 (August 1981):297-320.

152. Leñero, *Los periodistas*, p. 293.

153. Alba, "The Mexican Revolution and the Cartoon," p. 131.

154. Almond and Verba, *The Civic Culture*, pp. 58-59, 61.

155. Ibid., pp. 58-59.

156. Stevens, *Protest and Response*, p. 288.

10: Serving the State

1. Personal interview with Luis Villoro, Mexico City, 20 August 1978.

2. Personal interviews with numerous intellectuals, Mexico City, 1978.

3. Octavio Paz, "The Philanthropic Ogre," *NCCLA Boletín* 12, no. 2 (December 1980):15.

4. Personal interview with Abel Quezada, Mexico City, 4 August 1978.

5. Personal interview with Enrique Krauze, Mexico City, 28 August 1978.

6. Personal interview with Octavio Paz, Mexico City, 4 July 1978.

7. Ibid. Paz indicated that he had never made this information public prior to our interview.

8. Lewis S. Feuer, *Ideology and the Ideologists* (New York: Harper & Row, 1975), p. 72.

9. Thomas Kuhn, *The Structure of Scientific Revolutions* (Chicago: University of Chicago Press, 1962).

10. John P. Harrison, "The Role of the Intellectual in Fomenting Change: The University," in *Explosive Forces in Latin America*, ed. J. J. Te Paske and S. Nettleton (Columbus: Ohio State University Press, 1964), pp. 29-30.

11. Personal interview with Abel Quezada, Mexico City, 4 August 1978.

12. Harrison, "Role of the Intellectual," p. 30.

13. Jane Kramer, "A Reporter in Europe," *New Yorker,* 30 June 1980, p. 50.

14. John H. Haddox, *Vasconcelos of Mexico* (Austin: University of Texas Press, 1967), pp. 7-8.

15. Personal interview with Father Daniel Olmedo, Mexico City, 25 July 1978.

16. Personal interview with Alberto Vázquez del Mercado, Mexico City, 19 May 1978.

17. Personal interview with Pedro Daniel Martínez, Mexico City, 26 July 1978. Similar views were expressed in personal interviews with Alfonso Pulido Islas, Mexico City, 18 August 1978; and with Fernando Zertuche Muñoz, Mexico City, 26 July 1978.

18. Personal interview with José Juan de Olloqui, Mexico City, 12 July 1978.

19. Julio Scherer García, "Entrevista con Octavio Paz," *Proceso*, no. 57 (5 December 1977), p. 8.

20. Personal interview with Guillermo García Oropeza, Guadalajara, 10 July 1980.

21. Juan F. Marsal, "Los ensayistas socio-políticos de Argentina y México (aportes para el estudio de sus roles, su ideología y su acción política)," Working paper, Instituto Torcuato di Tella, Buenos Aires, September 1969, pp. 19, 20.

22. Zbigniew Brzezinski, "America in the Technetronic Age," *Encounter* 30 (January 1968):22.

23. Personal interview with Jesús Reyes Heroles, Mexico City, 18 July 1978.

24. S. N. Eisenstadt, "Intellectuals and Tradition," *Daedalus* 101 (Spring 1972):9.

25. Robert K. Merton, "Role of the Intellectual in Public Bureaucracy," in *Social Theory and Social Structure*, ed. Robert K. Merton (New York: Free Press, 1968), p. 273.

26. Personal interview with Miguel Palacios Macedo, Mexico City, 12 July 1978.

27. Merilee S. Grindle, "Policy Change in an Authoritarian Regime under Echeverría," *Journal of Inter-American Studies and World Affairs* 19 (November 1977):548.

28. Personal interview with Leopoldo Zea, Mexico City, 25 July 1978.

29. Germán Arciniegas, "Intellectuals in the Politics of Latin America," in *Constructive Change in Latin America*, ed. Cole Blasier (Pittsburgh: University of Pittsburgh Press, 1968), p. 167.

30. Max Beloff, *The Intellectual in Politics and Other Essays* (London: Weidenfield & Nicolson, 1970), p. 10.

31. John Brademas, "The Role of the Intellectual in Politics—An American View," *Texas Quarterly* 8 (Winter 1965):23.

32. Personal interview with Ignacio Chávez, Mexico City, 13 June 1978.

33. Ibid.

34. Selden Rodman, *Mexican Journal* (Carbondale: Southern Illinois University Press, 1958, p. 203.

35. Jorge Aguilar Mora, *La divina pareja* (Mexico City: ERA, 1978), p. 18.

36. John A. Crow, *Mexico Today* (New York: Harper & Row, 1957), p. 304.

Bibliographic Essay

The subject of intellectuals, as implied in the Introduction, has received considerable attention in some respects, but very little in others. Its coverage in the scholarly literature is broad, but superficial and spotty. Documentary research for this book covered more than seventeen hundred sources, which, for reasons of space, cannot be fully listed. I cite most sources used in the endnotes. The purpose of this essay, however, is to present the most important sources from a theoretical to a concrete, and a universal to a specific, focus, to facilitate further research on the structure of intellectual life.

Any introduction to the subject of contemporary intellectuals would find the work of four scholars essential. The first of these contributors is Lewis A. Coser, who, writing from a sociologist's point of view, has contributed the best single comparative study of the structure of intellectual life. Oddly, it is not easily accessible. Entitled "The Differing Roles of Intellectuals in Contemporary France, England and America," it is an unpublished paper presented at the Symposium on Sociology of the Intellectual, Buenos Aires, 3-5 July 1967. This lengthy essay, one of many excellent presentations made at this conference, is available (as are all other presentations from the conference) from Washington University, St. Louis. Coser's standard work on the subject is his earlier book, *Men of Ideas: A Sociologist's View* (New York: Free Press, 1965). He also has made a unique contribution to a recent phenomenon among industrialized countries by defining an intellectual in "The Intellectual as Celebrity," *Dissent* 20 (Winter 1973):46-56.

Recently, however, the author who tried most to tackle the importance of intellectuals as a "class" or social group, including them as part of a much larger educated population, was the late Alvin Gouldner. Gouldner, who approached this task from a Marxist point of view, provides the most comprehensive analytical framework from which to interpret the development of intellectuals as a class and their impact on society. Originally, his goal was to produce a trilogy, the first of which is *The Dialectic of Ideology and Technology* (New York: Seabury Press, 1976), which lays the groundwork for the environmental influences technology has on intellectual roles. His second volume, the provocative *The Future of Intellectuals and the Rise of the New Class* (New York: Seabury Press, 1979), looks more closely at the interplay of many elements in intellectual life. This work formed the basis of his 1977 NEH Seminar on Revolutionary Intellectuals, in which I was a fortunate participant, and therefore, I may have been more informally influenced by his ideas as formulated then, rather than by the later, formal product. Finally, an excellent introduction to his thoughts is found in his "Prologue to a Theory of Revolutionary Intellectuals," *Telos*, no. 26 (Winter 1975-1976), pp. 3-36.

A third major contributor to the study of intellectuals is Charles Kadushin. As I suggested at the beginning of the book, any study of intellectuals must examine Kadushin's contributions, for, unlike most other authors, he is a pioneer in the use of collective biography, empirical surveys, and interviews. Thus, his study of North American intellectuals, although covering a brief period and, by definition, a selective group, has a useful empirical foundation. For an initial exploration of his methodology, see "Power, Influence, and Social Circles: A New Methodology for Studying Opinion Makers," *American Sociology Review* 33 (October 1968):685-699. For his more specific analysis and justification of a definition for intellectuals, see "Who Are the Elite Intellectuals?" *The Public Interest* 29 (Fall 1972):109-127. His major work, of course, and the only recent study of a single country that many aspects of the structure of intellectual life, from which many theoretical and empirical comparisons may be drawn, is *American Intellectual Elite* (Boston: Little, Brown, 1974).

Chronologically, the first significant contribution toward an analysis of the structure of intellectual life is that by Edward A. Shils. His work is particularly important because initially his interpretations were based on field research in India in the 1950s, a country that shares with most developing societies many social and economic similarities that have an impact on the relationship between the intellectual and the state. Fortunately for scholars, most of Shils's essays have been collected in *The Intellectuals and the Powers and Other Essays* (Chicago: University of Chicago Press, 1972). For concrete examples from India, although during a period in India's development different from contemporary Mexico, see *The Intellectual between Tradition and Modernity: The Indian Situation* (The Hague: Mouton, 1961). For an excellent starting place, his "Intellectuals," *International Encyclopedia of the Social Sciences* 7 (1968):399-415, is now a classic piece. Shils's most recent article, which confronts some of the more contemporary issues, is "Intellectuals, Tradition and the Traditions of Intellectuals: Some Preliminary Considerations," *Daedulus* 101, no. 2 (Summer 1972):21-34.

Coser, Gouldner, Kadushin, and Shils have each made significant theoretical contributions to an analysis of intellectual life. In addition, however, other authors, in articles or collected essays, have identified many problems in the definition of intellectuals and their role. These contributions were crucial in formulating my own definitions and in developing the ideas in chapters three and four. Not all can be named here, but a selection deserve brief mention. One of the few theoretical contributions on the subject of defining an intellectual from a non-Western, and therefore generally a Third World, perspective, is that by Harry J. Benda, "Non-Western Intelligentsias as Political Elites," *Australian Journal of Politics and History* 6 (November 1960):205-218. A North American interpretation with many applications to the Latin American and Mexican situations is offered by Norman Birnbaum, "Problem of a Knowledge Elite," *Massachusetts Review* 12 (Summer 1971):620-636. The best series of essays to pose the question (raised also by Alvin Gouldner) of intellectuals as part of a "new class," is presented in the essays collected by B. Bruce-Briggs, *The New Class?* (New Brunswick, N.J.: Transaction

Books, 1979). But for a provocative, far-seeing view of how technology might transform intellectuals and the educated elite in general, the reader should consult Zbigniew Brzezinski, "America in the Technetronic Age," *Encounter* 30 (January 1968):16-26. A different comparative view, from a socialist perspective, but as valuable as Shils's work on India and Benda's on the non-Western world, is the collection edited by L. G. Churchward, *The Soviet Intelligentsia: An Essay on the Social Structure and Roles of Soviet Intellectuals during the 1960's* (London: Routledge & Kegan Paul, 1973).

Two early theoretical views of intellectual roles, again from a North American perspective, can be found in Marcus Cunliffe, "The Intellectuals: Part II, The United States," *Encounter* 4 (May 1955):23-33; and Merle Curti, "Intellectuals and Other People," *American Historical Review* 60 (January 1955):259-282. One of the best single articles on the problems of defining an intellectual is that by Lewis S. Feuer: "What Is an Intellectual?" in *The Intelligentsia and the Intellectuals*, edited by Alexander Gella (Beverly Hills, Cal.: Sage Studies in International Sociology, 1976), pp. 47-58. Feuer has taken more than a passing interest in the subject, having written other articles and books focusing on intellectual ideas and the importance of Marxism.

The other North American educator and intellectual, who like Feuer has contributed more than one essay to the subject of intellectuals, is Seymour Martin Lipset. His most insightful ideas on the role of intellectuals can be found in "American Intellectuals: Their Politics and Status," *Daedalus* 88 (Summer 1959):460-498; (with Asoke Basu) "The Roles of the Intellectual and Political Roles," in *The Intelligentsia and the Intellectuals*, edited by Alexander Gella, pages 111-150; and "The Intellectual as Critic and Rebel: With Special Reference to the United States and the Soviet Union," *Daedalus* 101, no. 3 (Summer 1972):138-198, coauthored with Richard B. Dobson. This last is one of the few available articles comparing two countries. Intellectuals in the Soviet Union have received considerable attention from intellectuals themselves and, although extending beyond the definition of intellectuals used in this book, Richard Pipes's *The Russian Intelligentsia* (New York: Columbia University Press, 1961) provides many useful insights. Another edited volume that collects some of the better interpretations of intellectual roles is Philip Rieff, *On Intellectuals: Theoretical Studies, Case Studies* (Garden City, N.Y.: Doubleday, 1969).

A primary focus of my book has been the relationship between the state and the intellectual. For some specific suggestions on this topic, see Paul H. Nitze's "Role of the Learned Man in Government," *Review of Politics* 20 (July 1958):275-288, in which he comments on difficulties intellectuals encounter in public service.

Other North American authors, who have not had a primary interest in intellectuals, have, on the other hand, written significant works forecasting trends in the technology of intellectuals' cultural products and the importance of widespread, advanced education on society as a whole. These works are essential to understanding the impact of the intellectual within a changing environment that not only affects North America and other industrialized nations, but the Third World, too. I found the most useful of these books to be Heinz Eulau's *Technology and Civility: The Skill Revolution in Politics* (Stanford, Cal.: Hoover Institution, 1977); Fritz Machlup, *Production and Distributiom of Knowledge in the United*

States (Princeton: Princeton University Press, 1962); and Gary S. Becker, *Human Capital: A Theoretical and Empirical Analysis with Special Refrence to New York* (New York: National Bureau of Economic Research, 1975).

When the focus in the literature on intellectuals moves away from a universal or North American model to Latin America and Mexico, the quality, and especially the quantity, of works drops sharply. The work on Latin America in general that does exist has been done by Latin Americans. The exception to this is an article by John P. Harrison, which suggests the role of the intellectual in the Latin American university environment: "The Role of the Intellectual in Fomenting Change: The University," in *Explosive Forces in Latin America*, edited by J. J. Te Paske and S. Nettleton (Columbus: Ohio State University Press, 1964), pages 27-42. But the major work to date on Latin American intellectuals was completed in the late 1960s by Juan Marsal and collected in his *El intelectual latinoamericano* (Buenos Aires: Instituto Torcuato di Tella, 1970).

Marsal deserves a notable place in the literature on Latin American intellectuals. He was the first author to attempt any empirical studies in this region, and the only author to make comparisons between two countries. His work appears in several forms and has, in part, been translated into English. The most pertinent of his work are "Los ensayistas socio-políticos de Argentina y México (aportes para el estudio de sus roles, su ideología y su acción política)," Working paper, Instituto Torcuato di Tella, Buenos Aires, September 1969; *Los intelectuales políticos* (Buenos Aires: Ediciones Nueva Visión, 1971); and his excellent comparative survey, coauthored with Margery J. Arent, entitled   "Right-wing Intelligentsia in Argentina: An Analysis of its Ideology and Political Activity," *Social Research* 37 (Autumn 1970), pages 447-481.

Except for Marsal's, the work on Mexico is more plentiful and of better quality than that available on Latin America in general. My own preliminary work appeared in "Los intelectuales y la política en el México postrevolucionario, el caso de los profesores," in Instituto Mexicano de Cultura, *Sociologia de la paz y de la guerra* (Mexico City, 1979), pages 523-552; "An Intellectual in Mexican Politics: The Case of Agustín Yáñez," *Relaciones* (Summer 1981), pages 137-162, which explores several models the intellectual in politics can follow; "Intellectuals: Agents of Change in Mexico?" *Journal of Inter-American Studies and World Affairs* 23 (August 1981), pages 297-320; and "Censure, Media et vie intellectuelle," *Etudes Mexicaines* 5 (1982):29-57. But the Mexican who first took up the subject of intellectuals, if not always with much methodological rigor, is Gabriel Careaga. Careaga's two books are useful starting places for the subject of Mexican intellectuals: *Los intelectuales y la política en México* (Mexico City: Extemporáneos), and *Los intelectuales y el poder* (Mexico City: Sepsetentas, 1972).

Jean Meyer has also interested the French in this subject, and they have begun to publish a series of works. The most helpful is the Centre Regional de Publications de Toulouse, *Intellectuels et état au mexique au XX sièle* (Paris: Editions de CNRS, 1979). A serious comment on Mexican intellectuals by an intellectual was made some time ago by Daniel Cosío Villegas, "Politics and Mexican Intellectuals," *Texas Quarterly* 8 (Winter 1965):38-48. But the best work by a Mexican is that of Enrique Krauze, who has used an intellectual's and historian's eye to describe an important Mexican generation in his *Caudillos culturales en la revolución mexicana* (Mexico City: Siglo XXI, 1976), and the life of an intellectual in a hot and cold relationship with the state, in *Daniel Cosío Villegas: Una biografía intelectual* (Mexico City: Joaquín Mortiz, 1980). Similarly, the North American historian Henry C. Schmidt has done this for another generation in his *The Roots of Lo Mexicano: Self and Society in Mexican Thought, 1900-1934* (College Station: Texas A & M University Press, 1978), as well as in several recent articles. Another, more specific, historical view has been suggested by Stanley Ross's "La protesta de los intelectuales ante México y su Revolución," *Historia Mexicana* 26, no. 3 (January-March 1977):396-437. Although using traditional cultural focus, Carlos Monsiváis provides a useful survey of trends taking place in Mexican intellectual life in his "Notas sobre la cultura mexicana en el siglo XX," *Historia general de México* (Mexico City: Colegio de México, 1976), pages 303-476.

The most institutionalized aspects of Mexican intellectual life have received little attention in the literature. There are essentially no books or articles on cultural institutions and academies other than in-house histories. The exception occurs in analyses of Mexican higher education, notably the National University. None of the best works deal specifically with the role of the intellectual in the university, but they touch on many issues affecting the working enviroment of the intellectual and, indirectly, his relationship with the state. For a historical understanding of the relationship between the National University and the state, the best book is that by Donald Mabry, *The Mexican University-State Conflict: UNAM Students, 1910-1971* (College Station: Texas A & M University Press, 1982). From a theoretical angle, and a work that looks at public universities in general, Daniel Levy's *University and Government in Mexico: Autonomy in an Authoritarian Regime* (New York: Praeger, 1980) contains much that explains the intellectual's attitude toward the state. Levy has continued his interest in this subject and will be publishing a study, the first, on private universities in Mexico and Latin America.

For understanding career development, recruitment patterns, and especially the direction that scientists are following inside the academic community, the best source is the work of Larissa Lomnitz, who, in addition to many unpublished papers cited in this book, has written "Conflict and Mediation in a Latin American University," *Journal of Inter-American Studies and World Affairs* 19 (August 1977):315-338.

The other peripheral area in the literature on Mexico related to intellectual life is mass communications. The North American pioneer in this field is Marvin Alisky, whose many articles on radio and the news media are cited frequently in chapter 9. Another contributor to this field is Richard R. Cole, whose dissertation is entitled "The Mass Media of Mexico: Ownership and Control," University of Minnesota, 1972. The Mexicans, however, have done more work on developing theoretical interpretations concerning the patterns of public-private ownership and control over media resources. The most important contributions are by Regina Jiménez de Ottalengo, "El periódico mexicano, su situación social y sus fuentes de información," *Revista Mexicana de Sociología* 36, no. 4 (1974):767-806; and her "La comunicación colectiva en México y la dependencia," *Revista Mexicana de Sociología* 34, nos. 3-4 (1972):595-610, coauthored with Georgina Paulin de Siade. One of the more creative articles on the importance of the Mexican communications milieu is that on rumor by Soledad Loaeza, "La política del rumor: Mexico, noviembre-diciembre de 1976," in Centro de Estudios Internacionales, *Las crises en el sistema político mexicano* (Mexico City: Colegio de México, 1977), pages 121-150. Finally, Evelyn P. Stevens also provides an overview of the relationship between the government and various groups, and the impact of communications on that relationship, in *Protest and Response in Mexico* (Cambridge, Mass.: MIT Press, 1974), and "Legality and Extra-legality in Mexico," *Journal of Inter-American Studies and World Affairs* 12 (January 1970):62-75.

There needs to be greater interest in this subject, and attempts at comparative theorizing and empirical case studies, and even intellectual biographies. Many scholars were attracted, at least temporarily, by the topic of intellectuals and the state as the subject for the VI Conference of Mexican-United States Historians, in Chicago in 1981. The proceedings of that conference contain many useful papers and were edited by Charles A. Hale, Josefina Vázquez de Knauth, and myself. They will be published as *Intellectuals and the State in Mexico* (Los Angeles: Latin American Center, UCLA, 1984).

Index